SRA Open Court Reading

Kindergarten   Book A

School

Program Authors

Marilyn Jager Adams
Carl Bereiter
Iva Carruthers
Robbie Case
Jan Hirshberg
Anne McKeough
Michael Pressley
Marsha Roit
Marlene Scardamalia
Gerald H. Treadway, Jr.

A Division of The McGraw-Hill Companies

Columbus, Ohio

Acknowledgements

Atheneum Books for Young Readers, Simon & Schuster Children's Publishing Division: **WHAT WILL MOMMY DO WHEN I'M AT SCHOOL? by Delores Johnson.** This edition is reprinted by arrangement with Atheneum Books for Young Readers, Simon & Schuster Children's Publishing Division. **Copyright © 1990, by Delores Johnson. All rights reserved.**

Chronicle Books: BOOMER GOES TO SCHOOL by Constance W. McGeorge, illustrations by Mary Whyte. Text copyright © 1996 by Constance W. McGeorge. Illustrations copyright © 1996 by Mary Whyte. Reprinted with permission of Chronicle Books.

Simon & Schuster Books for Young Readers, an imprint of Simon & Schuster Children's Publishing Division: "I Brought a Worm" by Kalli Dakos. Reprinted with the permission of Simon & Schuster Books for Young Readers, an imprint of Simon & Schuster Children's Publishing Division from IF YOU'RE NOT HERE, PLEASE RAISE YOUR HAND by Kalli Dakos. Copyright © 1990 Kalli Dakos.

Orchard Books: **ANNABELLE SWIFT KINDERGARTNER by Amy Schwartz. Copyright ©1988 by Amy Schwartz. Reprinted by permission of the publisher Orchard Books, New York.**

Greenwillow Books, a division of William Morrow & Company, Inc.: "An Anteater" (one verse) and "Saucy Little Ocelot" (one verse) from THE SHERIFF OF ROTTENSHOT by Jack Prelutsky. Text copyright © 1982 by Jack Prelutsky. By permission of Greenwillow Books, a division of William Morrow & Company, Inc..

"I'd Walk Halfway to Your House" from HALFWAY TO YOUR HOUSE by Charlotte Pomerantz. Text copyright © 1993 by Charlotte Pomerantz. By permission of Greenwillow Books, a division of William Morrow & Company, Inc..

Harcourt Brace & Company: "Gazelle" from **THE LLAMA WHO HAD NO PAJAMA: 100 FAVORITE POEMS,** copyright © 1973 by Mary Ann Hoberman, reprinted by permission of Harcourt Brace & Company.

HarperCollins Publishers: "DUCKS IN THE RAIN" from CRICKETY CRICKET! THE BEST LOVED POEMS OF JAMES S. TIPPETT by JAMES TIPPETT. COPYRIGHT 1933, COPYRIGHT RENEWED © 1973 BY MARTHA K. TIPPETT. Used by permission of HarperCollins Publishers.

Henry Holt and Company, Inc.: "KEEPSAKES" FROM IS SOMEWHERE ALWAYS FAR AWAY, © 1993 by Allan D. Jacobs. Reprinted by permission of Henry Holt and Company, Inc.

Little, Brown and Company: "Eletelephony" from TIRRA LIRRA: RHYMES OLD AND NEW by Laura Richards. Copyright © 1932 by Laura E. Richards; copyright © renewed1960 by Hamilton Richards. By permission of Little, Brown and Company.

Lothrop, Lee & Shepard Books, a division of William Morrow & Company, Inc.: "Busy Busy Busy" from WHAT TO DO WHEN A BUG CLIMBS IN YOUR MOUTH by Rick Walton. Text copyright © 1995 by Rick Walton. By permission of Lothrop, Lee & Shepard Books, a division of William Morrow & Company, Inc..

Gina Maccoby Literary Agency: "It's Fun to be a Fire Dog" (two verses) from A FINE FAT PIG by Mary Ann Hoberman. Reprinted by permission of Gina Maccoby Literary Agency. Copyright © 1991 by Mary Ann Hoberman.

Meadowbrook Press: "Jack was Nimble" (two verses) and "Row, Row, Row Your Boat" (one verse) from THE NEW ADVENTURES OF MOTHER GOOSE: GENTLE RHYMES FOR HAPPY TIMES by Bruce Lansky. Copyright © 1993. Reprinted with permission of Meadowbrook Press.

Millbrook Press: "Norman Says Nelly is Noisy" (two verses) from MICHAEL ROSEN'S ABC by Michael Rosen. Copyright © 1996. Reprinted with permission of Millbrook Press.

G.P. Putnam's Sons, a division of Penguin Putnam Inc.: "Lizard Longing," from I'M GONNA TELL MAMA I WANT AN IGUANA by Tony Johnston. Copyright © 1990 by Tony Johnston. Used by permission of G.P. Putnam's Sons, a division of Penguin Putnam Inc.

Marian Reiner: "Crusty Corn Bread" from YOU BE GOOD & I'LL BE NIGHT by Eve Merriam. Copyright © 1988 by Eve Merriam. Reprinted by permission of Marian Reiner. "Molly's Glasses" from A POEM FOR A PICKLE by Eve Merriam. Copyright © 1989 by Eve Merriam. Reprinted by permission of Marian Reiner.

HarperCollins*PublishersLtd.*: "Maxie and the Taxi" and "Popping Popcorn" from THE ICE CREAM STORE by Dennis Lee. Published by HarperCollins*PublishersLtd.* Copyright ©1991 by Dennis Lee.

Elizabeth Hauser: "Sleeping Outdoors" from RHYMES ABOUT US by Marchette Chute. Published 1974 by E.P. Dutton. Copyright 1974 by Marchette Chute. Reprinted by permission of Elizabeth Hauser.

SRA/McGraw-Hill

A Division of The **McGraw·Hill** *Companies*

Send all inquiries to:
SRA/McGraw-Hill
8787 Orion Place
Columbus, OH 43240-4027

Printed in the United States of America.

ISBN 0-02-830901-4

3 4 5 6 7 8 9 WEB 04 03 02 01 00

Table *of* Contents

UNIT

1 School

Introducing

SRA Open Court Reading

Reading in the 21ˢᵗ Century

"Research shows that whether or not kids read adequately at the end of grade one is not just a powerful predictor of how well they'll read later, but also of general school achievement."

—SRA/Open Court Reading
Author, Marilyn Jager Adams

About 30% of school-age children have serious reading problems. Children do not outgrow these difficulties. Studies indicate that 74% of the children who are poor readers at the end of third grade will be poor readers in the ninth grade. Adults who cannot read well cannot succeed in today's environment. This is why national and state initiatives are mandating that all children will demonstrate that they can read by the end of third grade.

Reading by 3ʳᵈ Grade Is Not Good Enough

Research in reading has shown that effective classroom instruction in the early grades by well-prepared teachers is the most powerful method for preventing reading and learning problems. Further, the most effective instruction for early reading involves a combination of explicit instruction in word recognition skills and reading comprehension strategies with opportunities to apply and practice these skills in literature.

SRA/Open Court Reading is the only reading program with a history of preparing teachers with the understanding and tools they need to provide the right balance of literature and skills. When provided with this balance, all children can learn to read, become fluent in reading, comprehend what they read, and benefit from reading. It is the only program that is and has been based on a generation of intense empirical research that identifies the factors that lead to success in early reading…with proven results.

This approach to beginning reading instruction has been successful in many thousands of classrooms for more than three decades. Since the first publication of the program in the early 1960s, the approach has recognized that if children are to learn to read with fluency and comprehension, they need explicit, systematic skills instruction *and* rich experiences with authentic literature.

In *SRA/Open Court Reading*, explicit phonics and comprehension skills instruction is *balanced* with extensive reading of both decodable texts and quality literature. In addition to explicit skills, from the very beginning, children experience a wide variety of literary forms and genres in a program that emphasizes reading, writing, and learning.

The Goal: Reading in the 1ˢᵗ Grade

For *SRA/Open Court Reading*, the goal of having all students reading by the end of third grade is not good enough. This program is designed to ensure that by the end of the first half of first grade, all students have the tools they need to begin reading authentic literature on grade level. In addition, from kindergarten through Level 6, the program emphasizes fluency, comprehension, writing, research, and inquiry with the goal of developing students who are truly lifelong learners and readers.

Reading gives children the power to learn and invites them to explore a world of information that is real and useful. Reading also opens the door for students to explore a world of stories, both real and fantasy.

Learning to read empowers children.

This program is designed to ensure that by the end of the first half of Grade 1, all students have the tools they need to begin reading authentic literature on grade level.

Principles

Research Based Teaching

SRA/Open Court Reading's approach to initial reading instruction relies on the explicit teaching of sounds, on the blending of sounds into words, and on the leverage of using this knowledge for reading and writing. From the beginning *SRA/Open Court Reading* also develops explicit instruction and modeling of comprehension strategies and skills.

The *SRA/Open Court Reading **Teacher's Edition*** provides valuable information about *how, when,* and *why* to use proven effective strategies throughout the program. In addition to information at point of use in the actual lessons, the following issues, as well as others, are addressed specifically with complete instructions in the **Program Appendix** section in the back of each *Teacher's Edition:*

The Foundations for Reading

- Reading aloud
- Print awareness
- Phonemic awareness through oral blending and segmentation
- Alphabetic principle
- Explicit systematic phonics and blending
- Fluency using decodable books for initial reading experience
- Comprehension strategies and skills
- Spelling
- Writing

The Goals of Reading

- Authentic literary experiences
- Learning through themes
- Inquiry and research

High Expectations and Support for All Students

SRA/Open Court Reading comes from a long tradition of respecting the intelligence of children and teachers. The program offers the best in reading instruction and expects the best. By making no assumptions about prior knowledge, *SRA/Open Court Reading* ensures that no children fall through the cracks. Phonemic awareness, print awareness, and an understanding of the alphabetic principle are not taken for granted. The program includes:

- Solid foundation for building instruction in decoding, fluency, and comprehension skills.
- Plenty of repetition for students who need help.
- Relevant and efficient practice.
- Daily **Independent Work Time** so that teachers have a chance to focus on specific needs and deficits of individuals. Diverse and individual needs are met by varying the time and intensity of instruction.
- A variety of proven learning experiences that provide for differing language proficiencies and abilities.
- The expectation that all children will be reading on level by the middle of first grade.
- The expectation that children can produce works of genuine research that seeks answers to real questions or solutions to real problems.

Phonemic Awareness
Print Awareness
Explicit Systematic Phonics

Before children can learn the sound/spelling relationships that constitute written language, they need to understand how individual sounds, or phonemes, work together to create spoken language. This awareness of how the system works—*phonemic awareness*—is the first piece of the foundation children need in order to go on to the next step—assigning written symbols to these sounds.

Written English is not perfectly regular, but a more or less predictable association exists between the sounds of the spoken language and the letters in the written language. This *alphabetic principle* that translates spoken sounds into written language permits us to represent thousands of words with just a few symbols. Learning these sound-symbol relationships enables children to decode most of the words in the English language instead of learning each word individually.

Research shows that phonics instruction has to be systematic if it is to work. It cannot start somewhere in the middle or be random or haphazard in approach.

SRA/Open Court Reading does not assume that students can distinguish individual sounds or already know the spellings of these sounds. *SRA/Open Court Reading:*

- Systematically teaches letter knowledge and phonemic awareness in kindergarten.
- Introduces sound/spellings systematically in Level 1.
- Offers direct instruction in blending all of the sounds in words.
- Builds fluency, the key to comprehension through the use of decodable books.
- Connects spelling to phonics through **Dictation and Spelling** activities.

The goal of all of the instruction in phonemic awareness and phonics is to provide children with the tools they need to read with *fluency*. Phonics skills enable children to get beyond the distractions and mechanics of decoding words to focus on the goal of reading—*comprehension.*

> ## Laying the Foundation

Fluency

Students need to remain mindful of the ultimate goal of phonics instruction: real reading and writing.

Since the best way to practice reading is to read, *SRA/Open Court Reading* provides a wealth of reading materials at each step along the way. Even after they have learned only a few sounds, there are real books for students to read. These ***Decodable Books*** (Levels K–3) are carefully crafted so that students practice the skills they are learning with connected text and therefore gain confidence in their reading abilities. When all the sound/spellings have been learned, the students continue to develop fluency through authentic reading and writing.

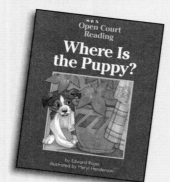

Authentic Literary Experiences

Throughout the program, students participate daily in reading, writing, discussing, researching, and thinking about authentic, high-quality literature in ***Big Books*** (Levels K and 1) and ***Student Anthologies*** (Levels 1–6). Beginning in Kindergarten and continuing through Level 6, students experience a range of text genres, including different forms of fiction and nonfiction. There are also multiple opportunities for writing, allowing students to understand the uses of writing even as they are learning to write. These experiences help to reinforce students' understanding of the structure and conventions of written language.

Building on the Foundation

Integrated Instruction

Learning units are tied to important concepts that call on students to make connections across all areas of the curriculum and to acquire knowledge that can be used beyond a single lesson. Each unit is organized so that a reading selection adds more information or a different perspective to the students' knowledge of a concept. Throughout all units, the focus is on learning *how* to learn through inquiry and research.

Reading, writing, discussion, research, and exploration activities are integrated through lessons that evolve sequentially, becoming increasingly complex and demanding. Through individual, collaborative learning groups, and whole-class activities, students are encouraged to bring their own experiences to the learning situation and, through exploration, to gain deeper understandings. The student's responsibilities are to learn more, and to help classmates discover more about the unit concepts.

Every lesson throughout the program emphasizes the combination of reading skills, comprehension, and learning so that children acquire the tools they need to read and then learn from what they read. The three parts of every ***Teacher's Edition*** lesson provide the lesson plan to teach all of the dimensions of reading.

① Preparing to Read

The first part of every lesson includes the skills of reading, including introduction to sounds and letters, vocabulary, print awareness, and word knowledge.

② Reading and Responding

The second part of every lesson emphasizes comprehension skills and strategies as students read the lesson selection. This part concludes by exploring how the selection adds a perspective to the unit theme.

③ Integrating the Curriculum

The third section of each lesson engages students in the writing process and develops vital language arts skills. **Across the Curriculum** activities extend the selection to other curriculum areas.

Meaningful Comprehension
Inquiry and Research

Throughout the program, students are encouraged to construct meaning by interacting with and responding to outstanding literature. They read widely, write frequently, and listen and speak effectively. The focus is always on building knowledge and deeper understanding. The intent of instruction is to engage students in the kinds of activities that will prepare them for the reading, thinking, and problem solving typical of real-world situations. To participate productively in that world, graduates must know how to go about gaining information, to evaluate it critically, and to adapt it for differing purposes. They must be equipped to deal with a variety of fields, including some that do not even exist today, and to understand and participate in scientific reasoning and problem solving.

Reaching the Goal

Every grade level has specific goals to ensure that children are developing strong, effective reading skills and comprehension.

Kindergarten

The kindergarten level of *SRA/Open Court Reading* has drawn the best available information from research and effective practice to provide maximum flexibility in providing all students with a solid, successful introduction to literacy. The kindergarten program:

- Introduces children to the alphabet and how it works.
- Teaches phonemic awareness.
- Connects sounds with letters.
- Exposes children to how the sounds of the language work together.
- Develops print and book awareness.
- Provides early reading experiences at which children can be successful.
- Helps children focus on the importance of learning and the joy it can bring.
- Explores concepts in science, social studies, literature, and the arts.
- Teaches thinking through story making and participative listening.

Level 1

It is no exaggeration to say that how well children learn to read in first grade profoundly affects how well they do throughout their school years—and their lives. Children who quickly develop the skills necessary to read with fluency and comprehension gain access to all the world's knowledge. They acquire the power to educate themselves and to expand their range of thought and reflection. Level 1 accomplishes the following goals:

- Strengthens the solid foundation in phonemic awareness.
- Introduces children to sound/spelling associations in a systematic manner.
- Teaches the sounds and letters early, intensely, and quickly.
- Launches students into real literature as quickly as possible so that they do not lose sight of the purpose and goal of learning the skills.
- Develops reading fluency.
- Allows students to gain fluency in writing, enabling them to use it as a tool of inquiry as well as communication.
- Gives children responsibility for their own work, their own mental development, and their own paths of inquiry as soon as possible.

Levels 2–6

In Levels 2–6, children continue developing reading fluency, which leads to greater comprehension and enjoyment of reading and the ability to use reading skills and strategies for inquiry and research. Levels 2–6:

- Review the phonetic word knowledge and skill foundation that is developed in Levels K and 1 and provide intervention for students as needed.

- Build fluency in reading.
- Emphasize the presentation of instruction in meaning-based learning units, each of which revolves around compelling concepts from across the curriculum.
- Include many opportunities to read texts that will build comprehension in order to prepare students for the kinds of reading they will encounter in content-area textbooks and in nonacademic texts.
- Lead students to pursue personal and collaborative inquiry through study and research, to identify and access the information they need and to communicate their findings to their classmates.
- Develop writing skills to communicate knowledge.

To thrive in the twenty-first century, students will have to learn how to think about what they read, to put together information from many sources, to communicate effectively in writing and with speech, and to give sustained effort to thinking and problem solving. Becoming this kind of reader, writer, and learner can be a reality for all students. The teacher and student materials of *SRA/Open Court Reading* all focus on developing self-directed, highly motivated students who take primary responsibility for their own learning.

SRA/Open Court Reading is a comprehensive reading, writing, and learning program that:

- Develops confident and fluent readers through print and phonemic awareness activities and explicit, systematic phonics instruction.
- Engages students in constructing meaning through the teaching and application of comprehension skills and strategies and meaningful discussions.
- Incorporates writing as a form of learning and personal communication.
- Creates a classroom environment in which students explore, discuss, and research ideas.
- Develops research and study skills that give students the tools to become independent, self-directed learners.

What does all this mean to teachers, the most important people in students' educational lives? It means that they need to have a thorough understanding of the processes they are teaching so that at each step, they can help their young apprentices thoroughly master the skills they need.

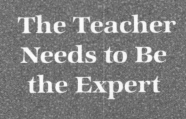

Children who are thoroughly prepared in kindergarten excel in first grade. Those who sufficiently strengthen their knowledge and skills in first grade shine in second grade. Children who spend second grade honing these skills soar in third grade. In order for this to happen, teachers need the appropriate knowledge and skills to help each and every student build on his or her natural abilities.

SRA/Open Court Reading, gives *you*, the expert, the proven tools and information you need to help your students be the best they can be. If teachers are accountable, this is what they are accountable for.

What Is Reading?

"Skillful reading is not one skill. It is a whole complex system of skills and knowledge. Within this system, the knowledge and activities involved in visually recognizing individual printed words are useless in and of themselves. They are valuable and, in a strong sense, possible only as they are guided and received by complementary knowledge and activities of language comprehension. On the other hand, unless the processes involved in individual word recognition operate properly, nothing else in the system can either."

—SRA/Open Court Reading
Author, Marilyn Jager Adams

Reading is defined differently for different ages. Parents take pictures of infants who are holding books looking at pictures and call that "reading." For preschoolers reading may indicate that children can recognize signs and logos or are able to recite the alphabet. Many young children memorize the text of books after repeated readings by parents and that is counted as reading for that age.

All of these events are delightful in young children and announce their interest in and excitement about reading. The same events in older children or adults are signs of reading disability.

Real reading includes:

- Understanding of how phonemes (speech sounds) are connected to print.
- Ability to decode unfamiliar words.
- Ability to read with fluency.
- Knowledge of sufficient background information and vocabulary to foster reading comprehension.
- Ability to use comprehension skills and strategies to get meaning from text.

Many children get by reading poorly in the early grades. It is fourth grade that has been identified as a pivotal year for most readers. In fourth grade much more emphasis is placed on informational reading, and teachers provide much less reading skill instruction. Students are expected to have made the transformation from learning to read to reading to learn. Several states are now mandating that children demonstrate their ability to read at the end of third grade so that they are prepared for this shift in emphasis.

Reading comprehension is an extremely complex behavior. Skillful readers have the ability to recognize letter/sound correspondences automatically, and they interpret sentence structure immediately as they read. The most profound reading problems come from difficulties in recognizing and decoding words and identifying the meanings of individual words. Fluency is also problematic. If a reader does not recognize words quickly enough, the meaning is lost. Even skillful decoders often have difficulty comprehending what has been read. Reading is not the ability to simply decode but also to read with fluency and comprehend text.

Skills in decoding and fluency are necessary but not sufficient to make children successful readers. Comprehension strategies and skills must also be taught in order for students to have the tools they need to understand what they decode.

Reading Instruction in *SRA/Open Court Reading*

In *SRA/Open Court Reading*, reading is a developmental process. Comprehension strategies and skills and writing are emphasized from the very beginning of Level K, even before children can read. At Levels K and 1, decoding skills are developed and combined with **Predecodable** and **Decodable Books** and authentic literary experiences. After Level 1, once decoding skills are in place, emphasis gradually shifts to developing reading fluency and comprehension. In the upper levels reading instruction emphasizes reading to learn, to write, and to gain deeper understanding.

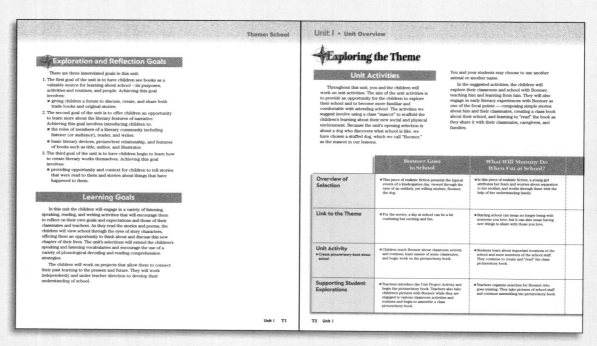

Reading Aloud

"It is not just reading to children that makes the difference, it is enjoying the books with them and reflecting on their form and content. It is developing and supporting the children's curiosity about text and the meanings it conveys....And it is showing the children that we value and enjoy reading and we hope that they will too."

—SRA/Open Court Reading
Author, Marilyn Jager Adams

Reading aloud is simply reading out loud to someone else. Teachers, parents, grandparents, and older siblings commonly read aloud to children who may or may not be able to read on their own. It is also a valuable learning technique.

Research has shown that children who are read to by teachers or parents or other adults are more likely than those who do not have this experience to develop the skills they need to read successfully on their own. Reading aloud serves multiple purposes for both readers and nonreaders as it:

- Provokes children's curiosity about text.
- Conveys an awareness that text has meaning.
- Offers both teachers and children the opportunity to model critical reading strategies such as clarifying, predicting, and summarizing—the strategies that children will need in order to become successful readers.
- Demonstrates the various reasons for reading text (for example, to find out about the world around them, to learn useful new information and new skills, or simply for pleasure).
- Exposes children to the "language of literature" which is more complex than the language they ordinarily use and hear.
- Enables good readers a chance to model their own interest in and enjoyment of reading.
- Provides an opportunity to teach the problem-solving strategies that good readers employ.
- Introduces children to a variety of literature.
- Develops vocabulary.
- Builds knowledge.
- Fosters important reading behaviors.
- Provides a natural avenue for discussion.

The importance of reading aloud to children cannot be overemphasized. Reading aloud provides an opportunity to communicate the active nature of reading. As children observe you interacting with the text, expressing your own enthusiasm, and modeling your thinking aloud, they perceive these as valid responses and begin to respond to text in similar ways. They become active listeners and later, when they begin reading on their own, they will begin engaging in the same behaviors.

Reading Aloud in *SRA/Open Court Reading*

Read-Aloud selections in the *Teacher's Editions* are directly related to the unit theme. Suggestions in the *Teacher's Edition* for stopping to think aloud and to stimulate discussion are included to help teachers focus **Read Aloud** sessions.

Reading aloud is an integral part of the Levels K and 1 lessons. Suggestions for materials that could be read aloud are provided in the *Teacher's Editions* for Levels 2–6.

✓ Reading aloud
  Print awareness
  Phonemic awareness through oral blending and segmentation
  Alphabetic principle
  Explicit systematic phonics and blending
  Fluency using decodable books for initial reading experience
  Comprehension strategies and skills
  Learning through themes
  Authentic literary experiences
  Spelling
  Writing
  Inquiry and research

References

Adams, M. J. (1990) *Beginning to Read: Thinking and Learning about Print.* Cambridge, MA: M.I.T. Press.

Anderson, R. et al. (1984) *Becoming a Nation of Readers: The Report on the Commission on Reading.* Washington DC: The National Institute of Education, U.S. Department of Education.

Sulzby, E. and Teale, W. (1991) Emergent literacy. In R. Barr, M. L. Kamile, P. B. Mosenthal, and P. D. Pearson (eds.)

Handbook of Reading Research (pp.727–758). NY: Longmann.

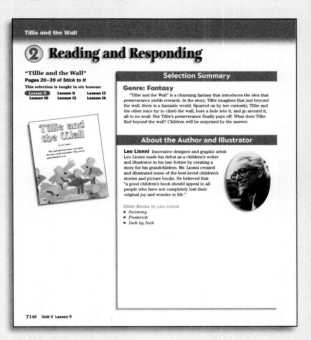

Print Awareness

✓ **Reading aloud**

✓ **Print awareness**

Phonemic awareness through oral blending and segmentation

Alphabetic principle

Explicit systematic phonics and blending

Fluency using decodable books for initial reading experience

Comprehension strategies and skills

Learning through themes

Authentic literary experiences

Spelling

Writing

Inquiry and research

"Print awareness is found to predict future reading achievement and to be strongly correlated with other, more traditional measures of reading readiness and achievement. More than that, analyses of the interdependencies among measures of reading readiness and achievement indicate that basic knowledge about print generally precedes and appears to serve as the very foundation on which orthographic and phonological skills are built."

—*SRA/Open Court Reading*
Author, Marilyn Jager Adams

Print awareness involves an understanding of the forms, functions, and uses of print. Print awareness is a learner's growing recognition of conventions and characteristics of written language. For early readers this includes such features as the recognition that reading is from left to right, that print corresponds to speech, that white spaces mark boundaries between words, that books progress from front to back, and so on. A child's level of print awareness has been shown to be a key predictor of his or her future reading achievement. Basic knowledge about print precedes and appears to serve as the foundation for the understanding of the written language.

Reading books to children helps engage students in unlocking the selections' messages at the same time it develops print awareness. In school, shared big book reading experiences invite children to participate in good reading behaviors. The teacher models what a good reader does: remarking on the illustrations and the title, wondering about the content and what might happen, making predictions, and commenting on events. The teacher points to each word as it is read, thus demonstrating that text proceeds from left to right and from top to bottom and helping advance the idea that words are individually spoken and written units. Enjoying the illustrations and connecting them to the text help students learn to explore books for enjoyment and information.

The shared reading experiences offered with *Big Books* (Levels K and 1) invite children to participate in reading behaviors and reading strategies of expert readers: responding to illustrations, thinking about content, predicting what might happen, and making connections between ideas in the story and events in their own lives.

Print Awareness in *SRA/Open Court Reading*

Children using *SRA/Open Court Reading* are given many opportunities, through varied uses of *Big Books,* to become familiar and comfortable with the conventions of print and books. The use of *Big Books* also introduces children to the reading behaviors they will need long before they actually read on their own. In Kindergarten, *Pre-Decodable Books* also help establish print awareness.

Strategies for developing print awareness appear throughout the *Teacher's Edition* in the **Reading and Responding** section of appropriate lessons. These strategies are tools for directing the students' attention to words, letters, and illustrations. They can be used with reading materials from any subject area in addition to the *SRA/Open Court Reading* **Big Books.**

In Kindergarten and Level 1, lessons are centered on the reading of particular **Big Books** that help develop print awareness. By the second half of Level 1, students should have a strong foundation in print awareness but print awareness strategies appear as reteaching and intervention strategies throughout Levels 2-6 for those students who do not have this foundation.

References

Adams, M. J. (1990) *Beginning to Read: Thinking and Learning about Print.* Cambridge, MA: M.I.T. Press.

Clay, M. M. (1979) *What Did I Write? Beginning Writing Behavior.* Portsmouth, NH: Heinemann Educational Books.

Sulzby, E. and Teale, W. (1991) Emergent Literacy. In R. Barr, M. L. Kamile, P. B. Mosenthal, and P. D. Pearson (eds), *Handbook of Reading Research* (pp. 727-758). NY: Longmann.

Phonemic Awareness

"A lack of appreciation of phonemic awareness is found to be the single most prevalent cause of reading disability. And it's not easy. It does not come naturally from teaching children letter sound correspondences, from engaging them in reading, or from giving them spelling drill."

**—SRA/Open Court Reading
Author, Marilyn Jager Adams**

Phonemic awareness is the awareness of the sounds that make up spoken words. While speaking and understanding the English language do not require a conscious reflection on its sounds, reading and writing do. In English, letters represent sounds, or phonemes. In order to learn the correspondences between letters and sounds, a child must have some understanding of the notion that words are made up of phonemes. Poorly developed phonemic awareness is the leading cause of reading failure.

The ability to distinguish individual sounds within words is an essential prerequisite to associating sounds with letters. The students need a strong phonemic awareness in order for phonics instruction to be successful. Frequently, children who have difficulties with phonics do so because they have not developed the prerequisite phonemic awareness. Until children develop an awareness of the component parts of words, they have no tools with which to decode words or put letters together to form words. The basic purpose of providing structured practice in phonemic awareness is to help children hear and understand the sounds from which words are made.

Once children begin reading and writing, this experience with manipulating sounds will help them use what they know about sounds and letters to sound out and spell unfamiliar words. As children progress through different phonemic awareness activities, they will become proficient at listening for and reproducing the sounds they hear.

Oral Blending and Segmentation

Two basic formats are used for teaching phonemic awareness—*oral blending* and *segmentation*. Oral blending helps children understand that words contain component parts—syllables and single sounds—and that these parts can be put together to make words. Segmentation and oral blending complement each other: Oral blending encourages the students to combine sounds to make words. Segmentation, conversely, requires them to isolate sounds from words.

Phonemic Awareness in *SRA/Open Court Reading*

Phonemic awareness activities found primarily at Levels K and 1 provide children with easy practice in discriminating the sounds that make up words. These are brief, teacher-directed exercises that involve some form of word play: words are taken apart in various ways and put back together. With the support of a puppet, children delight in manipulating the sounds of language and playing language games. The activities are carefully sequenced. At the beginning of each series of exercises, the students are given a great deal of support. As students progress, the support is gradually removed, and the exercises become more challenging. From these playful activities, children derive serious knowledge about language. As children gain awareness of how sounds combine to make words, they will be ready to progress to phonics and reading.

Phonemic awareness background information appears in the **Teacher's Editions** in Levels 2-6 for reteaching and intervention for those students who have not yet fully developed phonemic awareness.

References

Adams, M. J. (1990) *Beginning to Read: Learning about Print.* Cambridge, MA: M.I.T. Press.

Honig, B. (1996) *How Shall We Teach Our Children to Read?* Thousand Oaks, CA: Corwin Press.

Yopp, H. (1992) Developing phonemic awareness in young children. *The Reading Teacher*, 45, 696-703.

- ✓ Reading aloud
- ✓ Print awareness
- ✓ Phonemic awareness through oral blending and segmentation
- Alphabetic principle
- Explicit systematic phonics and blending
- Fluency using decodable books for initial reading experience
- Comprehension strategies and skills
- Learning through themes
- Authentic literary experiences
- Spelling
- Writing
- Inquiry and research

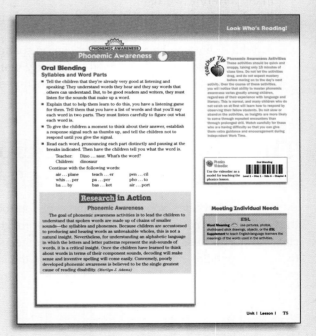

Alphabetic Principle: How the Alphabet Works

"In order for children to learn how to read, they have got to break the code. And by teaching them about how the sound structure of their language works, you're only making it that much easier for them to break the code."

—SRA/Open Court Reading
Author, Jan Hirshberg

The *alphabetic principle* is simply that there is a fairly predictable association between sounds and the letters that represent them. An understanding of the alphabetic principle extends children's phonemic awareness, that words are made up of sounds to include the notion of how those sounds relate to letters and writing.

The English language has 43 common sounds. Those sounds are represented by 26 letters alone or in some combination. The letters and sounds work together in a systematic way to connect spoken language to written words. Before learning the relationships between sounds and letters, children must learn that such a relationship exists. Like phonemic awareness, for many children the alphabetic principle is not intuitive. To become proficient readers, children must understand the alphabetic principle, that letters represent the sounds of the language.

Key concepts that children need to understand about the alphabetic principle are that

- A limited number of letters combine in different ways to make many different words.
- Words are composed of sounds, and letters represent those sounds.
- Anything that can be pronounced can be spelled.
- Letters and sounds can be used to identify words.
- Meaning can be obtained by using letters and sounds to figure out words.

The Alphabetic Principle
SRA/Open Court Reading

How the Alphabet Works lessons in Level K introduce children to the relationships between sounds and letters through collaborative classroom activities. The activities present a limited set of letters and their corresponding sounds and focus solely on the *concept* of the relationship. With this information and a carefully structured set of activities, children begin to explore and understand the alphabetic principle in a straightforward and thorough manner. This lays the foundation for explicit systematic phonics instruction. Naturally, keeping children focused on the idea that they are learning about sounds and letters so they can read these books themselves makes the lessons more relevant for children.

The alphabetic principle is reinforced throughout kindergarten as well as in first grade. By the end of Level 1, most students should have established an understanding of the alphabetic principle. Strategies appear throughout the **Teacher's Editions** in all levels for reteaching and intervention for those students who have not yet fully developed an understanding of the alphabetic principle.

References

Beck, I. L. and Juel C. (1995). The role of decoding in learning to read. *American Educator*, 19, 8.

Ehri, L. C. (1994) Development of the ability to read words. In R. Rudell and H. Singer (eds.), *Theoretical Models and Process of Reading, 4th Edition.* (pp. 323-358) Newark, DE: International Reading Association.

Honig, B. (1996) *How Shall We Teach Our Children to Read?* Thousand Oaks, CA: Corwin Press.

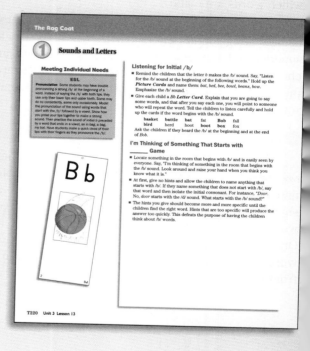

- ✓ Reading aloud
- ✓ Print awareness
- ✓ Phonemic awareness through oral blending and segmentation
- ✓ Alphabetic principle

Explicit systematic phonics and blending

Fluency using decodable books for initial reading experience

Comprehension strategies and skills

Learning through themes

Authentic literary experiences

Spelling

Writing

Inquiry and research

Explicit Systematic Phonics Instruction

"When children are taught about phonics, then phonemic awareness is also increased so the two sort of help one another. Children can learn about phonemic awareness without necessarily having to attach it to spellings, but phonics helps them to see these direct attachments to spellings. Even children who come to school reading can benefit from learning about phonics and the sound system because it can help them with their writing and their spelling."

—SRA/Open Court Reading
Author, Jan Hirshberg

Phonics is a way to teach decoding and spelling that stresses sound/symbol relationships. Explicit systematic phonics is a system of teaching that systematically introduces the spelling of each sound to students, teaches blending directly, and follows up with ***Decodable Books*** (Levels K–3) for practice so that the reason for learning the sound symbol relationships is reinforced. ***Decodable Books*** include words comprised of sounds and spellings that have been taught.

Phonics in *SRA/Open Court Reading*

In *SRA/Open Court Reading,* children learn to relate sounds to letters through a careful series of lessons in the ***Teacher's Edition*** that incorporates the use of 43 ***Sound/Spelling Cards*** (Levels 1–6). Each card contains the capital and small letter, and a picture that shows the sound being produced. In Level K the purpose of the ***Alphabet/Sound Cards*** is to remind children of the sounds of the English language and their letter correspondences. The name of the picture on each card contains the target sound at the beginning of the word for the consonants, and in the middle for the short-vowel sounds. In addition, the picture associates a sound with an action. This action-sound association is introduced through a short, interactive poem found in the ***Teacher's Edition*** in which the pictured object or character "makes" the sound of the letter. These cards are a resource for children to use to remember sound-letter associations for both reading and spelling.

The ***Decodable Books*** are used for reading aloud and for class discussion. Repeated reading fosters fluency.

Beginning in kindergarten, children learn the sounds and letters of the alphabet plus the five short vowels. This knowledge forms the foundation for first grade, when children learn the 43 common sounds of the language and the letters or combinations of letters (spellings) that represent those sounds. Second grade begins with a review of these sounds and spellings. Phonetic principles are reviewed throughout each subsequent grade level of the program as reteaching and intervention strategies.

References

Adams, M. J., Treiman, R., and Pressley, M. Reading, writing, and literacy. I. Sigel and A. Renninger (eds.), *Handbook of Child Psychology, Volume 4, Child Psychology and Practice.* New York: John Wiley and Sons.

Anderson, R. et al. (1984) *Becoming a Nation of Readers: The Report of the Commission on Reading.* Washington DC: The National Institute of Education, U.S. Department of Education.

Treiman, R. (1993) *Beginning to Spell.* New York: Oxford University Press.

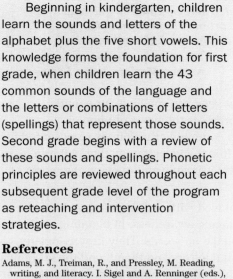

- ✓ Reading aloud
- ✓ Print awareness
- ✓ Phonemic awareness through oral blending and segmentation
- ✓ Alphabetic principle
- ✓ Explicit systematic phonics and blending
- Fluency using decodable books for initial reading experience
- Comprehension strategies and skills
- Learning through themes
- Authentic literary experiences
- Spelling
- Writing
- Inquiry and research

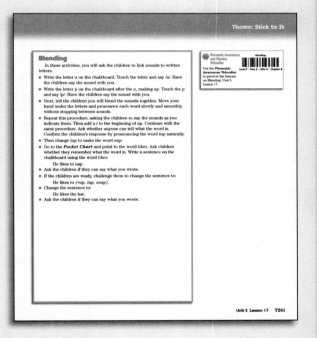

Blending

"Deep and thorough knowledge of letters, spelling patterns, and words, and of the phonological translations of all three, are of inescapable importance to both skillful reading and its acquisition. By extension, instruction designed to develop children's sensitivity to spellings and their relations to pronunciations should be of paramount importance in the development of reading skills."

—*SRA/Open Court Reading*
Author, Marilyn Jager Adams

Blending—learning to put separate spellings for sounds together smoothly to read words—is the heart of phonics instruction. Blending involves combining the sounds represented by letters to pronounce a word. It is the key strategy that children learn in order to apply the alphabetic principle and open up the world of written text.

Blending is not to be confused with *oral blending*, which is a strategy used to develop phonemic awareness. In blending students are looking at *spellings* that make up words. They first associate individual sounds with print and letters and then blend those sounds into recognizable words. In short, they actually read the words. Oral blending involves just listening and combining *sounds* to make words.

The purpose of blending is to teach children a strategy for figuring out unfamiliar words. Learning the sounds and their spellings is only the first step in learning to read and write. The second step is learning to blend the sounds into words. Initially, children blend sound by sound, then word by word. By blending words sound by sound, children learn the blending process, which allows them to work out for themselves the words they meet in their reading. Blending words into sentences is the logical extension of blending words. Blending words into sentences helps children move from word fluency to sentence fluency, and the procedure varies greatly from early to later sentences as children's skills develop.

The goal of blending instruction is to have children reading words and stopping to blend only those that are problematic. Ultimately children will sound and blend only those words that they cannot read. Eventually, the blending process will become quick and comfortable for them.

Blending in SRA/Open Court Reading

In *SRA/Open Court Reading* Levels 1 and 2, blending is a daily routine developed in the first part of the lessons in the **Teacher's Edition.** Children learn to blend sounds and spellings to read words. As the teacher writes the spelling for each sound in a word, students say the sound, relying on the associations fixed by the **Sound/Spelling Cards.** Then they will blend the sounds together into a word. To be sure that they recognize the word in the string of sounds that they have put together, they use the word in a sentence. The connection between the blended words and the word meaning is constantly reinforced, so that students recognize that the sounds they have blended are indeed the word they know from spoken language.

✓ Reading aloud
✓ Print awareness
✓ Phonemic awareness through oral blending and segmentation
✓ Alphabetic principle
✓ Explicit systematic phonics and blending

Fluency using decodable books for initial reading experience

Comprehension strategies and skills

Learning through themes

Authentic literary experiences

Spelling

Writing

Inquiry and research

Students use the blending strategy when they read **Decodable Books** and other materials. Initially, children use this strategy for many of the words they read. In time, high-utility words are automatically recognized and the blending strategy is used only for unfamiliar words. The systematic introduction of sounds and spellings coupled with blending develops independent readers in first grade. By second grade, most students may not need to blend words sound by sound and can begin by blending words using the whole-word procedure. Blending is reinforced in reteaching and intervention strategies in Levels 3–6.

References

Adams, M. J. (1990) *Beginning to Read: Thinking and Learning about Print*, Cambridge, MA: M.I.T. Press.

Beck, I. L. and Juel, C. (1995) The role of decoding in learning to read. *American Educator*, 19, 8.

Ehri, L. C. (1992) Reconceptualizing the development of sight word reading and its relationship to recoding. In P. B. Gough. L. C. Ehri, and R. Treiman (eds.). *Reading Acquisition* (pp. 107-144). Hillsdale, NJ: Earlbaum Associates.

Fluency

"The single greatest flaw of reading programs is that they don't give children enough to read and what they do give them gets too hard too fast. The more children read the better they'll read. We want to move them to the point where they like to read but that only happens when they feel that they can read."

**—SRA/Open Court Reading
Author, Marilyn Jager Adams**

Decoding is the process of analyzing graphic symbols to determine their intended meaning. To learn to read, a child must learn the code in which something is written in order to decode the written message. *Reading fluency* is the freedom from word-identification problems that hinders reading comprehension.

Gaining reading fluency automatically allows children to use their time and energy to comprehend the whole text rather than using up all their energy in simple word-by-word decoding. Becoming fluent is essential to comprehension. Without fluency there is no comprehension.

The best way for children to gain fluency is to practice reading—even when they have a limited knowledge of sounds and spellings. Practice reading is most effective when the material is decodable with sounds and spellings students already know and sight words they have learned.

Truly decodable books are those in which more than 60% of the words in the book either:

- Contain only sound/spellings that have been explicitly taught.
- Are high-frequency words that have been taught.
- Are nondecodable (irregular) words that have been explicitly taught.

Even high-frequency words such as *and* are considered nondecodable until each and every sound/symbol relationship has been explicitly taught.

Decodable books help children who have learned only a limited number of sounds and spellings practice reading. Most importantly, they help students grasp the idea that learning to use sound/spelling correspondences and a blending strategy unlocks the world of written language.

Applying their growing knowledge of words and phonic elements, children can read these simple, engaging stories themselves and thereby experience early success with reading. As children read and reread these materials, they gain crucial practice in reading and develop fluency, which is the gateway to comprehension.

Fluency in *SRA/Open Court Reading*

✓ Reading aloud
✓ Print awareness
✓ Phonemic awareness through oral blending and segmentation
✓ Alphabetic principle
✓ Explicit systematic phonics and blending
✓ Fluency using decodable books for initial reading experience

Comprehension strategies and skills

Learning through themes

Authentic literary experiences

Spelling

Writing

Inquiry and research

The **Decodable Books** in Levels K–3 of *SRA/Open Court Reading* are designed to help students review and reinforce their expanding knowledge of sound/spelling correspondences. Lessons for use with these books are included in the **Teacher's Edition.** These short, easy stories help students experience success with reading from virtually the beginning of first grade. Each story supports instruction in new phonic elements and incorporates elements and words that have been learned earlier.

Very simple questions are included in the **Teacher's Edition** to check both understanding and attention to words. Since the primary focus for these books is decoding the words and gaining fluency, rather than intensive work on comprehension, the application of strategies is simplified and de-emphasized. Naturally, though, children should understand what they are reading and should feel free to discuss anything in the story that interests them.

The **Decodable Books** are simple, colorfully illustrated stories available to be read again and again. They are also available in consumable and blackline forms that children can decorate and take home to share with their families.

At Level 1, **Decodable Books** help children build fluency and confidence as they apply their growing knowledge of phonics. In Levels 2 and 3, the **Decodable Books** provide further practice and continue to build fluency.

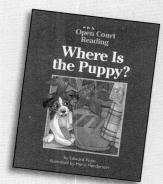

As students acquire fluency, they comprehend better because they are free to concentrate on meaning instead of focusing their attention on decoding words.

References

Adams, M. J. (1990) *Beginning to Read: Thinking and Learning about Print.* Cambridge, MA: M.I.T. Press.

Anderson, R. et al. (1984) *Becoming a Nation of Readers: The Report of the Commission on Reading.* Washington D.C.: The National Institute of Education, U.S. Department of Education.

Honig, B. (1996) *How Shall We Teach Our Children to Read?* Thousand Oaks, CA: Corwin Press.

Comprehension Strategies and Skills

"The active construction of meaning is what reading is all about. The focus has shifted away from teaching isolated skills and asking comprehension questions to teaching the comprehension process itself."

—*SRA/Open Court Reading*
Author, **Michael Pressley**

The primary aim of reading is comprehension. Experienced readers generally understand most of what they read, but just as importantly, they recognize when they do not understand, and they have at their command an assortment of comprehension strategies for monitoring and furthering their understanding.

Research has shown that students don't develop comprehension skills and strategies on their own. These strategies need to be taught and modeled before students begin to use them effectively. These strategies include the following.

Set Reading Goals

Good readers usually know what they want from a text. They:

- **Activate prior knowledge,** considering what they already know about the subject.
- **Browse the text** to get an idea of what to expect from a text.
- **Consider the purpose of reading,** whether it is reading for pleasure or to learn something specific.

Use Comprehension Strategies to Respond to Text

Good readers continually respond to the text they are reading and self check to make sure they're understanding. They

- **Ask questions** about what they are reading to monitor comprehension.
- **Clarify** the meanings of words, phrases, and longer pieces of text. They stop when they don't understand and clarify by rereading, using context, or asking someone else.
- **Make connections** between what they read and what they already know.
- **Make predictions** about what they are reading and then *confirm* or revise those predictions as they read.
- **Summarize** periodically to check their understanding.
- **Visualize,** or picture, what is happening in the text to comprehend descriptions, complex activities, or processes.

Develop Comprehension Skills

Good readers know that they are wasting their time if they don't understand what the author is saying. Good readers have learned to

- Consider the **author's point of view.**
- Understand the **author's purpose.**
- Comprehend **cause-and-effect** relationships.

- **Compare and contrast** items and events.
- **Draw conclusions** from what is read.
- Distinguish **fact from opinion.**
- Identify **main ideas and details.**
- **Make inferences** that help them understand what they are reading.
- Distinguish **reality from fantasy.**
- Understand **sequence** of events.

Comprehension Strategies and Skills in *SRA/Open Court Reading*

SRA/Open Court Reading is based on the belief that students learn best when they are actively involved in constructing meaning. Instruction builds and supports the development of critical metacognitive strategies through teacher modeling and by demonstrating behaviors and strategies used by expert readers. The second part of every lesson, **Reading and Responding,** focuses on modeling comprehension strategies while reading **Big Book** and **Anthology** selections. Critical comprehension skills such as *classifying* and *sequencing* help students organize information, while skills such as *inferring* and *drawing conclusions* help students develop a deeper understanding of the author's meaning.

After the teacher models each strategy, gradually the responsibility for using strategies shifts to the students.

References

Anderson, V. and Roit, M. L. (1992) Implementing collaborative reading instruction for delayed readers in grades 6–10. *Elementary School Journal*, 92, 511–554.

Brown, A. L. et al. (1983) Learning, remembering and understanding. In J. H. Flavell and E. M. Markman (eds.) *Handbook of Child Psychology, Volume 3, Cognitive Development* (pp. 77–166). NY: John Wiley.

Pressley, M. and Woloshyn, V. (1995) *Cognitive Strategy Instruction That Really Improves Children's Academic Performance.* Cambridge, MA: Brookline Books.

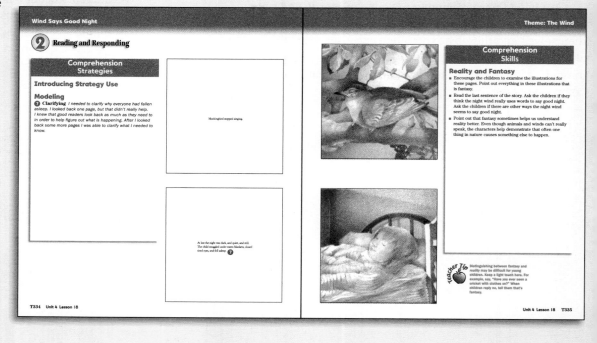

Themes

"If schools are going to change in any direction that's relevant to the future, it has to be in helping students work toward deeper knowledge."

—SRA/Open Court Reading
Author, Carl Bereiter

There are many ways of organizing collections of literature—by genre, by author, by time period, by geographic area of author or subject matter. Each of these organizational methods has its strengths and is appropriate depending on the desired outcome of the reading.

A theme is another way of organizing literature. Themes are often considered to be topics, such as *animals* or *holidays*, around which literature, subject matter, or art projects are loosely organized. In traditional English literature instruction, themes are familiar as the central or dominating idea in a literary work. In this sense, a theme such as *humans versus nature* is made concrete through the people or action of a work of fiction. Subject areas organize content around themes as well. In the area of science, for example, *patterns of change* and *systems and interactions* are considered themes.

For the purposes of *SRA/Open Court Reading*, a *theme* is a carefully chosen *universal* concept or idea that gives the reader a point of reference from which to think, discuss, and learn.

Themes in *SRA/Open Court Reading*

There are two types of themes in *SRA/Open Court Reading* around which the unit literature is organized. One type of theme is based on *universal topics of interest* such as *Friendship, Perseverance,* and *Courage.* The literature in these units is organized to help students expand their perspectives in familiar areas. As they explore and discuss the unit concepts related to each topic, students are involved in activities that extend their experiences and offer opportunities for reflection.

Other units are organized around *research themes.* In these units, literature has been selected to provide students with a very solid base of information upon which they can base their own inquiry and research. These units delving into such areas as *Fossils* or *Our Country and Its People* invite students to become true researchers by choosing definite areas of interest to research and explore further.

Each unit contains a variety of selections presented as ***Big Books*** and stories in the ***Student Anthologies*** that are sequenced in a way that enables students to progressively deepen their insights. Each selection adds more information or a different perspective to a student's growing body of knowledge. The selections reflect various types of writing, including fiction and nonfiction, all building on the unit theme.

The driving force behind the selection of literature for each unit was its ability to deepen or elaborate upon the theme. Therefore, the *Courage* unit at Level 4 does not just contain a group of stories loosely related to courage. Each selection adds a different insight into what courage is and how different people respond and cope with life challenges that call for courage.

The unit on the *Civil War* at Level 5 broadens students' understanding of what it was like to live through such a period by presenting the war through the eyes of youngsters and adults, soldiers and civilians, and slaves. Through both fiction and nonfiction, students see one event through the perspective of widely varying individuals. From these differing accounts and perspectives, students deepen their understanding of the period, the event, and the people who lived through it.

Themes are the major organizing principle of the literature in *SRA/Open Court Reading* from Levels K–6. The end of the second part of each lesson's selection, **Reading and Responding,** engages students in **Exploring the Theme.** Teaching strategies and suggestions are included in the ***Teacher's Edition*** in Levels K–6.

References

Brown, A. and Campione, J. (1990) Communities of learning and thinking, or a context by any other name. *Human Development,* 21, 108-125.

Spiro, R. J. et al. (1987) Knowledge acquisition for application: Cognitive flexibility and transfer in complex content domains. In B. K. Britton and S. M. Blynn (eds.), *Executive Control Processes in Reading.* Hillsdale, NJ: Earlbaum.

Willis, S. (1992) Interdisciplinary Learning. *ASCD Curriculum Update,* November, 1-8.

- ✓ Reading aloud
- ✓ Print awareness
- ✓ Phonemic awareness through oral blending and segmentation
- ✓ Alphabetic principle
- ✓ Explicit systematic phonics and blending
- ✓ Fluency using decodable books for initial reading experience
- ✓ Comprehension strategies and skills
- ✓ Learning through themes
- Authentic literary experiences
- Spelling
- Writing
- Inquiry and research

Unit 4 • Unit Overview   Theme: The Wind

Exploring the Theme

Introduction

Wind is something we often take for granted. Children, too, are likely to take the wind for granted. They may have seen tornadoes and hurricanes on the television, or even experienced the terror that these natural phenomena elicit more directly. But they are unlikely to connect these gale force winds to the more moderate winds that they experience daily.

Once they start to think about the wind, however, children are likely to begin to ask some very basic questions: What is the wind? What makes the wind blow? Where does the wind come from? The purpose of this unit is not to present children with pre-formed answers to these questions, or to convey some fixed body of scientific knowledge. Rather, it is to have them pose questions and discuss possible answers with each other—then go to other sources for additional information, doing their own hands-on inquiry, and present the results in a picture-book format.

In effect, this unit continues the process that was begun in Unit 2, Shadows. Although most of the children are too young to read informational prose on their own, they will not be too young to understand it when it is read to them. They will not be too young to look at and discuss pictures. They will not be too young to understand that one of the major joys of reading is acquiring new information, especially information of relevance to questions of their choosing. Finally, they are not too young to learn what is involved in creating a new information resource for others, and thus participating in a broader community of learners.

Exploration and Inquiry Goals

There are three goals in the present unit.
1. Learning more about the wind through books, pictures, discussion, and active experimentation.
2. Learning more about informational prose, and its difference from narrative.
3. Learning more about informational writing and illustration, and their relationship to the inquiry process.

Learning Goals

Within each of the general objectives just mentioned, a number of more specific learning goals are pursued. Throughout this unit children will:

- draw on background knowledge, reading, and discussions to formulate specific questions about wind and move towards answering them.
- listen to and read a variety of genres to understand and explore how wind is created.
- learn more about wind through guided and independent discussions and hands-on experimentation.
- use prior knowledge to anticipate the content of selections about wind and to interpret them.
- draw inferences about wind from discussions, experiments, and books.
- distinguish expository (informational) texts from narratives in terms of content focus.
- identify structural features of informational prose, including main point supporting evidence, and examples.
- generate relevant ideas for informational writing by using prewriting techniques such as listing key thoughts.
- identify questions and researchable topics that are relevant and of personal interest.
- use multiple sources, including print, experts, and experimentation, to locate information that addresses these questions.

T1 Unit 4   Unit 4 T1

Literature

"The notion of bringing students up to fine literature, to history, to sociology, to astronomy instead of bringing the content down to them is critical both to the program and to the spirit students can develop. It's a real "I can do it" spirit, and indeed they can."

—SRA/Open Court Reading
Author, Marlene Scardamalia

Literature is defined as "writing that is regarded as having permanent worth through the very nature of its excellence." Whether the piece of literature is a finely turned short story, a riveting mystery, a moving essay, or a masterful piece of informational writing, literature is defined by its excellence.

Literature is often organized by *genre*, a term used to designate the types or categories of forms of literature. Traditional genres include kinds of literature such as tragedy, comedy, or poetry. Today genre would include novel, short story, essay, drama, mystery, realistic fiction, fantasy, fable, or even television play and informational article.

Classic or great works of literature are those which by common consent have achieved a recognized position in literary history for their superior qualities.

Literature in *SRA/Open Court Reading*

The literature selections in *SRA/Open Court Reading* as well as the approach to teaching the selections represent a long-standing commitment to teachers who are, in turn, committed to teaching children to be competent, independent learners through reading, writing, speaking, and listening. What better way for children to learn to read and grow as readers than through reading and listening to literature that has the stamp of approval of generations of readers?

One of the founding principles of *SRA/Open Court Reading* is that children need to read fine literature. Through fine literature—of every genre—they would and could learn from the best thinkers of every age. They would learn the beauty of the language. They would learn the beauty of an idea. They would and could learn the importance of clarity of thought and word.

Through each level of *SRA/Open Court Reading,* students are given a sampling of fine traditional literature that has withstood the test of time along with contemporary pieces that will someday join the ranks of the classics.

Since the literature pieces form the center core of the instruction, abundant care is taken to present the students with fine, thought-provoking models that they can follow in their own writing and that they can use as springboards for their thinking, researching, and knowledge building. Students learn from classic and contemporary children's fiction authors such as Don Freeman, Eve Bunting, Patricia Maclachlan, Lloyd Alexander, Lucille Clifton, and Patricia Polacco as well as a growing number of fine writers of nonfiction for children— Milton Meltzer, Barbara Bash, and Ethan Herberman.

Each selection in *SRA/Open Court Reading* from Levels K–6 was chosen specifically because it added a new dimension of thought to the concept of a unit and because it was the best possible example of how different forms of literature can all express a particular theme. These two criteria—deepening of the concept and quality of the literature—formed the basis for all selections found in the program.

Through fine writing, fine minds can be developed.

- ✓ Reading aloud
- ✓ Print awareness
- ✓ Phonemic awareness through oral blending and segmentation
- ✓ Alphabetic principle
- ✓ Explicit systematic phonics and blending
- ✓ Fluency using decodable books for initial reading experience
- ✓ Comprehension strategies and skills
- ✓ Learning through themes
- ✓ Authentic literary experiences

Spelling

Writing

Inquiry and research

References

Brown, A. and Campione, J. (1990) *Communities of learning and thinking, or a context by any other name.* Human Development, 21, 108-125.

International Reading Association. (1997) *More Teachers' Favorite Books for Kids: Teachers' Choices 1994-1996.* Newark, DE: International Reading Association.

Meltzer, Milton. (1994) *Non-Fiction for the Classroom: Milton Meltzer on Writing, History, and Social Responsibility.* Newark, DE: International Reading Association.

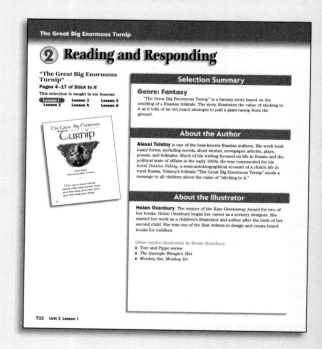

Dictation and Spelling

"One of the best ways to improve skill and fluency in decoding (figuring out written words by sounding them out) is encoding (putting spoken words into writing, or spelling)."

—SRA/Open Court Reading
Author, Jan Hirshberg

Reading and writing work hand in hand in teaching children how to read. By teaching students to recognize the spellings of the different speech sounds of the language, they learn to read. By teaching them to *listen* to the sounds of the language and assign the appropriate symbols to those sounds, we teach them to write. Reading and writing—these are the goals of all literacy instruction.

Dictation simply means listening carefully as a word or sentence is pronounced and then writing the words. The purpose of dictation is to teach children to write out words based on the sounds and spellings they have already learned. In order to write the words correctly, students must first hear the individual sounds, associate those sounds with specific spelling patterns, and then produce the written symbol that represents the sounds. These constitute a very complex series of ability and skills.

These first steps in spelling instruction give students a vast advantage over spelling instruction that is based solely on memorization. The students learn quickly that there is no need to memorize most words that they need to spell—they can sound them out to themselves and write the spellings for the sounds they hear. This understanding alone gives students a level of comfort with spelling that cannot be achieved otherwise.

By using dictation as a teaching device rather than an assessment device, students learn the importance of listening carefully without the pressures associated with "testing." Daily dictation sessions enable students to make the connection between *decoding* (reading) and *encoding* (writing) so that they can see and understand the cumulative effects of all that they learn.

Benefits of Sound, Whole Word, and Sentence Dictation

- Increases students' familiarity with sound/spelling correspondences.
- Helps children develop a spelling strategy and integrate reading and writing.
- Introduces proofreading, a critical skill that children will use whenever they write.
- Gives students additional practice in using the conventions of writing, such as capitalization and end punctuation.
- Develops writing fluency as students apply the strategy of reflecting on the sounds they hear to writing unfamiliar words.

Dictation and Spelling in *SRA/Open Court Reading*

Dictation plays an integral part in the students' efforts to learn to read and write in *SRA/Open Court Reading*. From the very first introduction to phonics instruction and decoding, students reinforce their knowledge of sound/symbol relationships through dictation. Initially, they use **Letter Cards** (Levels K and 1) to build words. Soon, they begin writing words the teacher dictates. These activities give students practice writing words based on the sounds and spellings they have learned. After the teacher dictates a word, students identify the individual sounds and spellings in order to write the word. Dictation also includes the writing of sentences, which gives students additional practice using the conventions of writing, such as capitalization and punctuation. Students are at all times aware of the connection between what they hear and what they write.

Throughout the instruction and review of sounds and spellings in Level 1 and through the phonics review lessons in Levels 2 and 3, students are always given the opportunity to exhibit through dictation the sound/spelling knowledge they are acquiring or reviewing.

References

Adams, M. J. (1990) *Beginning to Read: Thinking and Learning about Print.* Cambridge, MA: M.I.T. Press.

Honig, B. (1996) *How Shall We Teach Our Children to Read?* Thousand Oaks, CA: Corwin Press.

Treiman, R. (1993) *Beginning to Spell.* NY: Oxford University Press.

- ✓ Reading aloud
- ✓ Print awareness
- ✓ Phonemic awareness through oral blending and segmentation
- ✓ Alphabetic principle
- ✓ Explicit systematic phonics and blending
- ✓ Fluency using decodable books for initial reading experience
- ✓ Comprehension strategies and skills
- ✓ Learning through themes
- ✓ Authentic literary experiences
- ✓ Spelling
-   Writing
-   Inquiry and research

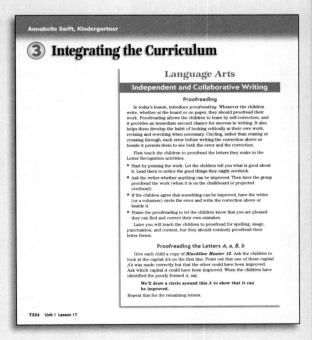

Writing

"Our role as teachers of young writers is to coach, encourage, and help children move toward conventional writing."

—*SRA/Open Court Reading*
Author, Marsha Roit

Professional writers go through a process that has implications for students learning to write. Many good writers begin by making notes of writing ideas in journals. They read writing produced by other writers and learn from it. They write for a particular purpose and with a particular audience in mind. They revise their writing until they are satisfied that it achieves its purpose. Often, as they revise, they rethink their original ideas and change their goals for a piece of writing. They may even begin again. They edit their writing to correct errors in spelling, punctuation, and grammar. They seek the advice of editors or other writers. Finally, they publish their work to share it with the audience for whom it is intended.

Writing is a recursive process as authors move back and forth through writing activities, from drafting to revising and back to drafting, to create their final pieces. It is a process of thinking, experimenting, and evaluating.

Children learn to write more effectively if they experience the writing process. Writing is a way of learning. When students work through the phases of the writing process, they gain important insights that promote deeper thinking and reasoning. This is especially true when writing has a clear purpose and is shared with others who respond to it constructively.

The writing process introduces students to the problem-solving and reasoning activities that writers engage in as they form ideas and, finally, communicate them through print. Systematically progressing through the process of prewriting, drafting, revising, proofreading, and sometimes publishing helps students clarify both their thinking and their writing so they can communicate effectively.

An environment with an emphasis on writing provides a multifaceted context for the development of higher-order thinking. Students learn to plan, which allows them to work out ideas in their heads; to set goals, which promotes interest and the ability to monitor progress; and to revise content, which engages them in the reworking and rethinking activities that elevate writing from a craft to a tool for discovery.

Writing in *SRA/Open Court Reading*

In *SRA/Open Court Reading,* writing provides students with a way to explore ideas that interest them and a way to share what they learn with others. Beginning in Level K, children develop their understanding of the writing process through shared writing activities. Opportunities for independent writing are provided as well. Group and individual writing activities conducted in Level 1 lay the foundation for Levels 2-6, when students use writing as a tool for building and sharing knowledge.

In *SRA/Open Court Reading,* critical writing conventions—spelling, punctuation, and grammar—are taught in the natural context of writing and emphasized as aids to communication. Activities like **Sentence Lifting** (Levels 2–6), a proofreading technique, use actual sentences from students' own written works as a vehicle for learning and applying writing skills and for developing proofreading skills.

Writing Seminar (Levels K–6) gives all students—from the most accomplished to the novice—an audience for their writing and a forum for discussing the stages of the writing process with others. As students' writing abilities increase, the kinds of writing they do become more varied, demanding, and challenging.

Throughout the program, from Levels K–6, students write daily. They learn to revise and to ask their peers for feedback. Students are given guidelines for presenting their work and for critiquing the work of their classmates. As students progress, they are expected to write to inform their peers of the research and exploration they are engaged in. Students become comfortable with the idea of revision and review. They learn to ask pertinent questions that help the writer sharpen a piece of writing and become clear and precise in the presentation of his or her ideas.

All of these writing skills work together to help the students become precise, clear thinkers who are capable of presenting their views in a manner that is informative, entertaining, and appropriate to the task and to the audience.

References

Bereiter, C. and Scardamalia, M. (1987) *The Psychology of Written Composition.* Hillsdale, NJ: Lawrence Erlbaum Associates.

Lucas. J. (1993) Teaching writing. *ASCD Curriculum Update,* January, 1-8.

Pressley, M. and Woloshyn, V. (1995) *Cognitive Strategy Instruction That Really Improves Children's Academic Performance.* Cambridge, MA: Brookline Books.

Roit, Marsha. (1992) *Creating a Community of Writers.* Peru, IL: Open Court Publishing Co.

- ✓ Reading aloud
- ✓ Print awareness
- ✓ Phonemic awareness through oral blending and segmentation
- ✓ Alphabetic principle
- ✓ Explicit systematic phonics and blending
- ✓ Fluency using decodable books for initial reading experience
- ✓ Comprehension strategies and skills
- ✓ Learning through themes
- ✓ Authentic literary experiences
- ✓ Spelling
- ✓ Writing
-   Inquiry and research

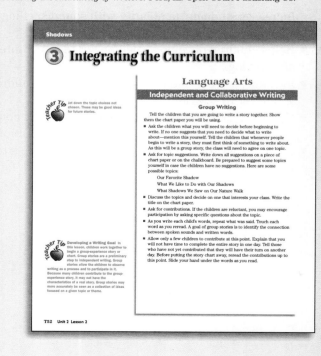

Inquiry, Research, and Exploration

"Expertise is acquired through deep and ever-increasing knowledge of a particular subject."

—SRA/Open Court Reading
Author, Carl Bereiter

As they become more fluent readers and writers, students find out that reading and writing give them power: the power to take control of their learning.

Although at times the purpose of reading is the simple pleasure of a good story or a wonderful poem, most adults and all school children spend more time reading to learn specific knowledge than they do reading for pleasure. Students need to be able to read and integrate into their knowledge system such diverse areas of study as American history and biology.

Adult readers research information on topics ranging from tax laws to lawn mower repair and maintenance. The ability to read to find out what you need or want to find out is one of the prime objectives of education.

Helping students learn how to do this—how to research and explore any area in which they are interested or for some reason need to know—is an aspect of education that is often neglected until high school or even college. By that time, it is very hard for many to break away from the simple read-and-report methods of research and exploration most students devise.

True research is a never-ending recursive cycle in which the researcher actively questions, develops ideas, or conjectures about why something is the way it is, and then pursues the answers. The answers for a researcher may never come. What does come is more questions. Developing the questions, pursuing the answers, developing conjectures, revising ideas, and setting off on new avenues of research and exploration are the stuff of which strong, deep knowledge and expertise are made.

Typically research involves the following steps.

- Decide on a problem or question to research.
- Formulate an idea or conjecture about the research problem.
- Identify needs and make plans.
- Reevaluate the problem or question based on what we have learned so far and the feedback we have received.
- Revise the idea or conjecture.
- Identify new needs and make new plans.
- Informally and formally present findings.
- Develop new questions.

Inquiry, Research, and Exploration in *SRA/Open Court Reading*

Inquiry, research, and exploration form the heart of *SRA/Open Court Reading*. In order to encourage students to understand how reading can enhance their lives and help them to become mature,

educated adults, they are asked in each unit to use what they are learning in the unit as the basis for further exploration and research. The unit selections are the base for their explorations.

In *SRA/Open Court Reading*, students model the behavior of expert learners and researchers. Opportunities for students, individually and in groups, to explore, to write about, and to discuss key concepts in a specific area lead to improved critical thinking and reading skills. Students become independent, intentional, self-directed learners.

The idea of research is introduced as early as Kindergarten. Procedures for collaborative research are formalized further in first grade. Beginning in second grade and continuing through sixth grade, students are led, working individually or collaboratively, to pursue problems that interest them in the same manner that an adult would conduct research.

Students use the **Anthology** selections as a knowledge base for further exploration. They read to learn, then share what they learn with each other.

Because each student contributes to the research in a unique way, all students feel the sense of purpose and accomplishment achieved through collaborative research.

References

Brown, A. and Campione, J. (1990) Communities of learning and thinking, or a context by any other name. *Human Development*, 21, 109-125.

Heckman, P. E., et. al. (1994) Planting seeds: Understanding through investigation. *Educational Leadership*, February, 36-39.

Schack, G. D. (1993) Involving students in authentic research. *Educational Leadership*, April, 29-31.

- ✓ Reading aloud
- ✓ Print awareness
- ✓ Phonemic awareness through oral blending and segmentation
- ✓ Alphabetic principle
- ✓ Explicit systematic phonics and blending
- ✓ Fluency using decodable books for initial reading experience
- ✓ Comprehension strategies and skills
- ✓ Learning through themes
- ✓ Authentic literary experiences
- ✓ Spelling
- ✓ Writing
- ✓ Inquiry and research

Teaching Techniques

"We really see a lot of agreement that people want students working on longer-term projects, thinking in depth about things, working collaboratively, and taking responsibility for their own learning. I think that's true of parents, teachers, and administrators."

**—SRA/Open Court Reading
Author, Joe Campione**

Deciding how you and your students will interact most effectively, how you will best help all of your students learn, how your students can interact with each other to optimize their learning—these are the decisions and considerations all teachers take into account when they decide which teaching techniques will work best. The different techniques include:

- **Whole-Class Instruction.** The understanding that all students in a classroom—the stars as well as those who are faltering—will benefit from the presentation, discussion, and review of all of the subject matter covered is the basis for whole-class instruction. By making whole-class presentations, the student who is struggling gets the benefit of the initial instruction and the discussion and then benefits from the reteaching and reinforcement. He or she is not left out and expected to do and learn less than his or her classmates.

- **Collaborative Learning.** Collaborative learning can take place in whole-class or small-group situations. Collaboration is the process of working with others on classroom instruction as well as on projects. Collaboration occurs in discussions, in research, and in presenting and reviewing another's work.

- **Small-Group Instruction.** Small-group instruction is useful for collaborative research and study, and it is also appropriate for reteaching. Students can strengthen their knowledge and skills and can work with the teacher or their peers to gain the skills and knowledge that they need. In addition, small groups and individuals who are excelling can benefit from the extra encouragement and affirmation that working in small groups or meeting individually with the teacher can afford.

- **Individual Instruction.** Individual instruction provides an opportunity to address the specific needs of a student. It may be listening to him or her read aloud, discussing a piece of writing, answering and asking questions, or providing specific, focused instruction or help with the particular needs of one student.

Teaching Techniques in SRA/Open Court Reading

Different teaching techniques have been woven into *SRA/Open Court Reading* to provide for the most effective instruction.

Whole-Class Instruction. In *SRA/Open Court Reading* rather than breaking the class into "ability groups," the initial instruction is presented to all children. Some will understand it right away, some will understand it as a result of the discussions that take place about the subject, and some won't understand at all. It is only after students have been presented with the material that those who don't understand are singled out for extra help and encouragement.

Collaborative Learning. Discussion plays an integral part in *SRA/Open Court Reading* in whole-class or small-group situations, as students learn to express their opinions, defend their positions, and explain their thoughts. They discover that by working together, they all learn much more than they would have learned individually. Discussion also offers English Language Learners the nonthreatening environment needed for expressing opinions and verifying understandings.

From Level K through Level 6, whole-class discussions of reading selections provide opportunities for students to think, predict, and draw connections between the selection they are reading, other selections, and of their own experiences.

Small-Group and Individual Instruction. Once problem areas are identified, small groups or individuals can be given the extra help they need. **Independent Work Time,** built into every day's lesson plan, is the opportune time to administer this extra help. **Independent Work Time** is the regular, established time each day in which students work individually or in small groups, with or without the teacher. Once students become used to **Independent Work Time** and take responsibility for their time and work, the teacher is free to meet individually with students.

References

Aronson, E. (1978) *The Jigsaw Classroom*. Beverly Hills, CA: Sage.

Brown, A. and Campione, J. (1990) Communities of learning and thinking, or a context by any other name. *Human Development*, 21, 108-125.

Willis, S. (1992) Cooperative Learning Shows Staying Power. *ASCD Update*, 34, 1-2.

- ✓ Reading aloud
- ✓ Print awareness
- ✓ Phonemic awareness through oral blending and segmentation
- ✓ Alphabetic principle
- ✓ Explicit systematic phonics and blending
- ✓ Fluency using decodable books for initial reading experience
- ✓ Comprehension strategies and skills
- ✓ Learning through themes
- ✓ Authentic literary experiences
- ✓ Spelling
- ✓ Writing
- ✓ Inquiry and research

Technology

At one time, the biggest advance in technology applicable to schools was the invention of the ballpoint pen. The disappearance of inkwells made everyone's life easier and more efficient. Today, the advances in technology and the possible effects these advances may have on schools, teaching, and children is almost mind-boggling. What is technology? How good is it? What can it do for my students and me? When will there be time to learn how to use it all?

Basically, *technology* is applying science to needs. Technology that is applicable to the classroom runs the gamut from overhead projectors to powerful computers. Videocassette players, videodisc players, filmstrip machines, printers, and copiers fall somewhere in between.

Much of this is a boon to the classroom. Movies are now easily accessed and can be shown on television screens—movie projectors are no longer needed. Overhead projectors allow for visual organizers that can be tailored for particular classes. And then there is the computer. There is no doubt that the computer can and does enhance the teaching and learning that goes on in a classroom, but the flood of materials—especially those called educational materials—is overwhelming.

The essential questions to ask about any piece of technology are What can I accomplish with this that I couldn't do without it? and What are the costs and benefits to my students and me?

Technology in *SRA/Open Court Reading*

In *SRA/Open Court Reading*, technology serves very specific purposes. These are

To help expand the students' knowledge of the concepts being presented.

Listening Library Audiotapes of the selections presented in the program are available to enhance student experience of the selections as well as to help any students who may be having difficulty reading a selection. In addition to stories, students will delight in the silly, alliterative stories that help them remember the sounds represented on the **Sound/Spelling Cards.** Each consonant and short vowel is introduced by an engaging character that is the personification of the sound.

To give students multidimensional avenues of review and practice.

Phonics instruction is augmented with an audiocassette of interactive stories to help students hear the sounds they are studying. Along with the audiocassette, students have the opportunity to review and practice their growing phonics skills and increasing fluency by using the **Phonics CD-ROM** (Levels K–3) or accessing these lessons through the **SRA Web Site (www.SRA-4kids.com).** These activities offer students an opportunity to interact with animated **Sound/Spelling Cards** as well as review their reading of **Decodable Books** with interactive versions of the stories.

To allow students to learn about information gathering and communication and to use available technology to the best advantage.

Research is an integral part of the *SRA/Open Court Reading* program. Students using the program have access through the **SRA Web Site** to **Internet** sites specifically chosen for their relevance to the concepts the students are working with. Students are able, through the site, to communicate with other students around the country who are using *SRA/Open Court Reading* and can thus extend and deepen their knowledge and insights into the concepts. In addition, the **Research CD-ROM** (Levels 1–6) can help them organize their research and keep track of what they are learning.

To help the teacher develop the techniques that have been proven effective in teaching children to become strong, competent readers.

Video presentations on videodisc of lessons in Kindergarten through Level 3, help teachers new to *SRA/Open Court Reading* quickly learn the methods and routines found effective in presenting the phonics skills and helping the children become strong, competent readers. These lesson presentations—keyed to specific lessons and lesson parts—can be accessed through a simple swipe of a videodisc barcode. Teachers who do not have access to a videodisc player can view the same material with VCR equipment.

In addition, **Program Videos** are available for training and informational purposes. This video series will give you a full overview of the program, its philosophy, its authors, and very helpful hints and tips on achieving the best results with your class.

To help the teacher manage the lessons and materials.

The **Lesson Planner CD-ROM** can help you manage your teaching schedule, the materials you need to use, and the scores the students attain. You can rearrange your week, make note of what needs to be done on a given day, and print your updated schedules as needed.

- ✓ Reading aloud
- ✓ Print awareness
- ✓ Phonemic awareness through oral blending and segmentation
- ✓ Alphabetic principle
- ✓ Explicit systematic phonics and blending
- ✓ Fluency using decodable books for initial reading experience
- ✓ Comprehension strategies and skills
- ✓ Learning through themes
- ✓ Authentic literary experiences
- ✓ Spelling
- ✓ Writing
- ✓ Inquiry and research

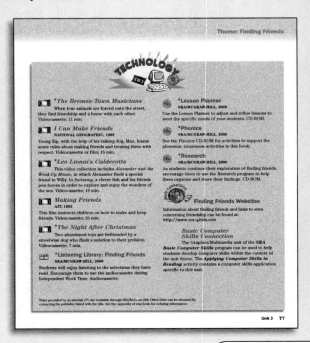

Assessment

True assessment is a tool for learning rather than a mere measure of achievement.

—*SRA/Open Court Reading*
Author, Joe Campione

The goal of true assessment is to provide information for instruction. It helps determine what students know and how to change the instruction to help students learn what they need to know.

Assessment in any form is most valuable when it leads to changes in classroom instruction. Assessment tasks should reflect classroom practices and the abilities students are expected to acquire. When the results of assessment suggest that students are having a difficult time mastering a skill, the teacher should implement alternate instructional strategies and materials.

Informal teacher observations, structured assessments, and on-demand reading and writing evaluations, provide a comprehensive picture of student growth and progress and avoids the more limited view of performance that results from basing assessment on just one or two measures.

The teacher's professional judgment is the keystone of the evaluation process. The teacher is the person who knows the student best, and teacher observations are the single most important source of information about student growth and potential.

Assessment in *SRA/Open Court Reading*

The assessment components of *SRA/Open Court Reading* reflect the balanced nature of the series itself. The following are principles that guided the development of the assessment components.

- **Ease of use for the teacher.** The assessments are easily administered and scored, feature the same language that is used in the instructional components of the series, and correspond to the sequence of instruction in the series. The assessments are typically short enough to prevent fatigue from affecting student performance yet long enough to provide a dependable measure of student skills and abilities. Assessments are distributed throughout the units of a given grade level so teachers have an opportunity to engage in "continuous assessment," diminishing the likelihood that a student will fall behind without the teacher being aware of it and having an opportunity to intervene.

- **Assessment of critical skills.** The skills that are featured prominently in the series—the skills that are critical to the reading process—are the focus of assessment. These same skills are typically included on standardized tests and in state standards, so the assessments will help teachers respond to the accountability system under which they work.

- **Variety in assessment.** In order to gather evidence of student performance from a range of sources, in addition to the formal and informal assessments described above, *SRA/Open Court Reading* includes

  - **Pre- and Post-tests. Pre-** and **Post-tests** at each grade level (There is no Pretest for Kindergarten) that can be used to guide instruction or for accountability purposes.

- **Unit Tests.** These cover the concepts that were introduced in each unit and give the teacher an opportunity to observe how well students have mastered a range of skills and how they can apply what they have learned in an independent reading situation.

- **Comprehension Assessment.** Selections in the **Anthology** serve as the basis for a comprehension assessment that includes multiple choice, short answer, and extended answer items.

- **Self-Assessment.** The students are continually involved in the process of self-assessment, especially as they meet in **Writing Seminar,** present their findings to their peers and complete the informal end-of-unit wrap-up pages in the **Inquiry Journal** (Levels 2–6).

- **Portfolio Assessment.** The **Inquiry Journal,** an ongoing, cumulative record of the students' explorations and research activities, provides a clear picture of their growth. Throughout the program all student writing is an opportunity for portfolio assessment.

- **Family Evaluation.** A variety of resources promote family involvement and provide the opportunity for home evaluation of a student's progress. Convenient blackline masters of letters, written in English as well as Spanish, explain to families what the students are learning in class. These letters, along with being informative, contain activities that children and their families can complete together.

✓ Reading aloud
✓ Print awareness
✓ Phonemic awareness through oral blending and segmentation
✓ Alphabetic principle
✓ Explicit systematic phonics and blending
✓ Fluency using decodable books for initial reading experience
✓ Comprehension strategies and skills
✓ Learning through themes
✓ Authentic literary experiences
✓ Spelling
✓ Writing
✓ Inquiry and research

References

Hansen, J. (1992) Students' evaluations bring reading and writing together. *The Reading Teacher*, 46, 100-105.

Paris, S. G. et. al. (1992) A framework for authentic literacy assessment. *The Reading Teacher*, 46, 88-98.

Winograd, P. et. al. (1991) Improving the assessment of literacy. *The Reading Teacher*, 45, 108-116.

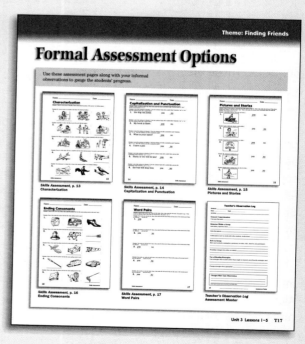

Open Court Reading
Program Authors

Well credentialed leaders in their fields of specialization, Open Court's authors are at the forefront of educational research. They are experts on how children learn to read and learn to learn. The instructional components of *SRA/Open Court Reading* provide teachers and students all the advantages that the very best in educational research has to offer to the field of reading instruction.

Marilyn Jager Adams

is a Senior Scientist in the Psychology Department at Bolt Beranek and Newman, Inc., a research and development laboratory in Cambridge, Massachusetts. She has been a Senior Research Scientist at Brown University and has been affiliated with the Center for the Study of Reading at the University of Illinois since 1975. She is the author of *Beginning to Read: Thinking and Learning About Print* (MIT Press, 1990), written on behalf of the U.S. Secretary of Education as mandated by Congress. The book, the most comprehensive study of beginning reading undertaken to date, examines instructional practices from a historical perspective and critiques them in terms of theoretical and empirical research in education, psychology, and linguistics.

Carl Bereiter

is Professor at the Centre for Applied Cognitive Science at the Ontario Institute for Studies in Education in Toronto. Both he and Open Court author Ann Brown are members of the National Academy of Education. He has co-authored many curriculum projects including SRA/Open Court's reading and mathematics programs. He is the co-author with Marlene Scardamalia of *The Psychology of Written Composition* (1987) *and Surpassing Ourselves: The Nature and Implications of Expertise* (1993) and has published extensively on the nature of teaching and learning.

Ann Brown

is Professor in Math, Science, and Technology in the Graduate School of Education at the University of California at Berkeley. She is Past President of the American Educational Research Association (AERA) and served on the congressional panel to monitor National Assessment of Educational Progress (NAEP) state-by-state assessments. She has received many honors and awards in both the United States and England for her contributions to educational research. At present, Dr. Brown and her husband, Joe Campione, are focusing their classroom research on students as researchers and teachers, a significant aspect of their study of distributed expertise in the classroom.

Joe Campione

is Professor in the School of Education at the University of California at Berkeley. He has long been known for his work in cognitive development, transfer of learning, individual differences, and assessment. He is working with Ann Brown to discover ways to restructure grade-school learning environments to take advantage of distributed expertise in the classroom and to use interactive learning to promote scientific literacy within communities of learners.

Iva Carruthers

is President of Nexus Unlimited, Inc., a human resources development and computer services consulting firm; and Ed Tech, a computer software development company. Formerly Chairperson and Professor of the Sociology Department at Northeastern Illinois University, Dr. Carruthers has also been an elementary school teacher, a high school counselor, and a research-historian. In addition to developing software for teaching African-American history and interdisciplinary subjects, she has produced study guides on African-American and African history used by students to prepare for appearances on the televised academic quiz show, "Know Your Heritage," which she coproduces. She travels worldwide as a consultant and lecturer in both educational technology and matters of multicultural inclusion.

Robbie Case

is Professor of Education at Stanford University and Director of the Laidlaw-Centre at the Institute of Child Study, University of Toronto. He received his Ph.D. from the Ontario Institute for Studies in Education. For the past twenty-five years he has conducted research on the relationship between children's learning and their cognitive development during the elementary school years. His books and scholarly articles on that topic have been translated into many languages.

Jan Hirshberg

holds an Ed.D. in Reading, Language, and Learning Disabilities from Harvard University. She has taught in elementary school classrooms and has also served as a school district reading consultant. At Harvard she was a teaching fellow, research assistant, instructor, and lecturer at the Graduate School of Education. Her reading specialties are in linguistics and early literacy. Her work has focused on how children learn to read and write and the logistics of teaching reading and writing in the early elementary grades. She is an author of the kindergarten and grade 1 levels of Open Court's 1989 reading and writing program as well as *Collections for Young Scholars*, Open Court's 1995 reading, writing, and learning program.

Anne McKeough

is an Associate Professor in the Department of Educational Psychology at the University of Calgary. She holds a Ph.D. in Cognitive Science from the Ontario

Institute for Studies in Education, University of Toronto, and has received a number of research awards and grants. She is coeditor of two volumes, *Toward the Practice of Theory Based Instruction: Current Cognitive Theories and Their Educational Promise* (1991) *and Teaching for Transfer: Fostering Generalization in Learning* (1995), and has authored a number of book chapters and articles advocating the benefits of a continued and reflective partnership between teaching practices and child development. Her current research focuses on the cognitive development and developmentally based instruction.

Michael Pressley

is the Director of Masters of Education Program and Programs in Teaching and Leadership, and Professor of Psychology at the University of Notre Dame. Dr. Pressley's wide-ranging research interests have included a mixture of experimental psychology and ethnographic projects. He does both basic laboratory research on cognition and learning and applied work in educational settings. Memory development and reading comprehension strategies have received much of his attention. He is the North American editor of *Applied Cognitive Psychology* and coeditor of the *Journal of Reading Behavior*. He is coeditor of *Promoting Academic Competence and Literacy in School* (1992) and co-author of *Cognitive Strategy Instruction that Really Improves Children's Academic Performance* (1995).

Marsha Roit

a national consultant on reading, holds a Ph.D. from Harvard University where her studies focused on reading and language

development. She spends considerable time in classrooms working with children to develop and demonstrate reading and writing activities and training teachers and administrators. Her work has been published in a variety of education journals, including *Exceptional Children, Journal of Learning Disabilities*, and *The Elementary School Journal*. She has presented her work at national and international conferences.

Marlene Scardamalia

is Professor and Head of the Centre for Applied Cognitive Science at the Ontario Institute for Studies in Education, Toronto. She is a member of editorial and review boards for scholarly journals in areas encompassing research, theory, and application of written communication; learning and instructional sciences; and educational computing. Her published work has focused on developmental and instructional psychology. Dr. Scardamalia is presently engaged in studies of textbased and knowledge-based questioning by children, computer technology for collaborative processes, and collaborative knowledge-building environments for tomorrow's schools.

Gerald H. Treadway, Jr.

is a Professor in the College of Education at San Diego State University. He is responsible for teaching Literacy Training, Bilingual Methods, and

Reading Comprehension, Diagnosis, and Assessment. He has been involved with California's Curriculum Development and Supplemental Materials Commission, the California Reading and Literature Project, and the Center for the Improvement of Reading Instruction. He was also chief consultant for Reading Programs in the Dallas Independent School District. He is a frequent speaker at the International Reading Association conference, as well as the California Reading Association conferences.

Open Court Reading
Teacher Reviewers

Raquel Alcocer   Grade: 2
Lozano Special Emphasis
Corpus Christi, TX

Janice Baggett   Grade: 4
Canopy Oaks Elm
Tallahassee, FL

Martha Berreda   Grade: 3
Los Fresnos ISD
Los Fresnos, TX

Stacey Brazzel   Grade: 1
Pasadena ISD
Houston, TX

Roberta Carter   Grade: 6
Arlington ISD
Arlington, TX

Shirley Castoldi   Grade: 5
Canopy Oaks Elm
Tallahassee, FL

Cindy Coffland   Grade: K
Rulon M Ellis Elm
Chubbock, ID

Mary Coppage   Grade: K
Garden Grove Elm
Garden Grove, FL

Ann Danford   Grade: 2
Canopy Oaks Elm
Tallahassee, FL

Emmy Daniel   Grade: 1
S Shores Elm
Decatur, IL

Linda English   Grade: 3
Pope Elm
Arlington, TX

Pam Everett   Grade: 3
Vern Patrick Elm
Redmond, OR

Bobbette Finch   Grade: 4
Indian Hills Elm
Pocatello, ID

Anne Fowler   Grade: K
Smith Elm
Raleigh, NC

Twyla Jo French   Grade: 5
New Highland Elm
Elizabethtown, KY

Eva Garcia   Grade: K
WB Travis Elm
Corpus Christi, TX

Mandy Garcia-Lopez   Grade: 2
Abraham Lincoln Elm
Pomona, CA

Melissa Garza   Grade: 2
WB Travis Elm
Corpus Christi, TX

Theresa Gore   Grade: 3
Canopy Oaks Elm
Tallahassee, FL

Lupe Guel   Grade: 3
WB Travis Elm
Corpus Christi, TX

Kristen Guyon   Grade: 3
Edahow Elm
Pocatello, ID

Nancy Hanssen   Grade: K
Highland Ranch Elm
San Diego, CA

Maxine Haywood   Grade: 5
WB Travis Elm
Corpus Christi, TX

Jennifer Heath   Grade: 4
Kelso Elm
Inglewood, CA

Angela Holt   Grade: 2
Stephen C. Foster Elm
Indianapolis, IN

Laura Joanos   Grade: 1
Canopy Oaks Elm
Tallahassee, FL

Linda Kehe   Grade: 1
Tualatin Elm
Tualatin, OR

Nancy Kotkosky   Grade: 6
State Street Elm
South Gate, CA

Helen Lee   Grade: 1
George R Stuart Elm
Cleveland, TN

Millie Lively   Grade: 1
Monclam Elm
Princeton, WV

Mary Massey   Grade: K
Schallert Elm
Alice, TX

Pauline McClendon   Grade: 4
Odem ISD
Odem, TX

Pauline McClendon   Grade: 2
Odem ISD
Odem, TX

Anne McKee   Grade: 2
Tualatin Elm.
Tualatin, OR

Lannie McNeese   Grade: 1
WB Travis Elm
Corpus Christi, TX

Maxine McPherson   Grade: 6
Canopy Oaks Elm
Tallahassee, FL

Patricia Morwood   Grade: 2
Marva Collins Prep
Cincinnati, OH

Kristi Mullinix   Grade: 5
S Shores Elm
Decatur, IL

Margaret Parker   Grade: 5
Hovart Elm
Los Angeles, CA

Merilee Patrick   Grade: 4
Vern Patrick Elm
Redmond, OR

Rosa Pope   Grade: 3
Camella Elm
Whittier, CA

Laura Powell   Grade: 5
Heflen Elm
Houston, TX

Mary Quintal   Grade: 1
Hanna Ranch Elm
Hercules, CA

Alice Rabagos   Grade: 4
WB Travis Elm
Corpus Christi, TX

Chequetta Roberts   Grade: 1
PS 241
Brooklyn, NY

Brenda Scheer   Grade: 6
Tendoy Elm
Pocatello, ID

Ruth Ann Schum   Grade: 2
S Shores Elm
Decatur, IL

Ana Silva   Grade: ESL2
Ysleta ISD
El Paso, TX

Homero Silva   Grade: ESL3
Ysleta ISD
El Paso, TX

Cherry Mae Smith   Grade: 2
Heyburn Elm
Heyburn, ID

Kathryn Sprinkle   Grade: 1
Benito-Martinez Elm
El Paso, TX

Suzanne Stidom   Grade: 3
Mary Moore Elm
Arlington, TX

Thelma Strong   Grade: 6
Walsh Elm
Chicago, IL

Maryanne Tinker   Grade: 1
Robert Lee Frost Elm
Indianapolis, IN

Marsha Van Huss   Grade: 1
John F Kennedy Elm
Kingsport, TN

Teresa Vargas   Grade: 1
Heyburn Elm
Heyburn, ID

Lorraine Villareal   Grade: 1
Los Fresnos ISD
Los Fresnos, TX

Bev Wilker   Grade: 5
Tyhee Elm
Pocatello, ID

Getting Started

Preparing to Use
SRA Open Court Reading

This section provides an overview of classroom management issues and introductory activities that explain the function of the **SRA/Open Court Reading** program elements and how to use them.

Organizing Your Classroom

Phonemic Awareness and Phonics Instruction

In the ***SRA/Open Court Reading*** program, early reading instruction does not assume that students already have the ability to consciously attend to, discriminate, and manipulate the sounds of words—phonemic awareness or knowledge of the alphabetic principle. Although speaking and understanding the English language do not require a conscious understanding of or ability in either of these, reading and writing do. Instruction involves the systematic, explicit teaching of the relationship of individual sounds to spoken language, sound/spellings, the blending of sounds into words, and the application of this knowledge to reading and writing.

Alphabet/Sound Cards

The purpose of the **Alphabet/Sound Cards** is to remind the children of the sounds of the English language and their letter correspondences.

The **Alphabet/Sound Cards** are numbered and should be displayed in order. Place them in a prominent place in the classroom so that all students can see them and use them for reference. As you proceed through the instruction, you and your students will need to point out specific cards. Therefore, the cards should be placed low enough to make this possible but high enough for all students to have an unobstructed view of them. The **Alphabet/Sound Cards** should remain on display for the entire school year. They are an invaluable tool for the students in both their reading and writing.

Reading

For students to become more than competent decoders, they must become strategic readers. That is, they must learn how to think about what they read and to use specific reading strategies and behaviors. Teachers help students become strategic readers by modeling the key reading strategies used by expert readers and by providing them with multiple opportunities to read fine literature. First-rate reading selections illustrate for students the best possible use of language and stimulates them to think about, write about, and discuss important ideas and concepts.

Oral Reading

Research has shown that children who are read to are more likely to develop the skills they need to read successfully on their own. Reading aloud serves multiple purposes. It provokes children's curiosity about text, conveys to them an awareness that text has meaning, and demonstrates to them the various reasons for reading text—to find something out, for pleasure, to learn something useful. Listening to authentic text exposes children to the "language of literature" which is more complex than the language they ordinarily use and hear.

Just as you read to the students, encourage them to "read" to you. At first this may mean simply pointing at pictures and telling picture stories. As they become more aware of text and how it works, they will start recognizing words they see often. Have the students "read" to each other from books of their choice, the small versions of the Big Books, or from the Predecodable books.

Predecodables

The Predecodables are rebus stories designed to introduce students to the high utility sight words they need to recognize quickly and effortlessly. Words such as *the*, *as*, *an*, *and*, and *but* constitute many of the words the students see in print in the books they are using in the classroom as well as any books they may have at home. Being able to recognize these quickly and effortlessly frees the students to concentrate on the story or, as they actually begin to read, the words in the story that carry meaning.

Have the students read and reread these little books. They can read them to you, to each other, and to their families. The more they read them, the more quickly they will master these sight words.

You may want to make a chart for students to keep track of their reading of the Predecodables.

	First Reading	Second Reading	Third Reading	Fourth Reading	Fifth Reading
Predecodable 1 Title	X	X	X		
Predecodable 2 Title	X	X			

Reading Center

Provide as many books as possible for your classroom Reading Center. During the course of the year the students will be asked to share information on specific subjects. Prepare your classroom ahead of time by bringing in books on the concepts or themes the students will be studying. You may choose to order the **Classroom Library** that accompanies the program or you may decide to provide your own library. In either case, you should encourage students to bring in books that they have enjoyed and want to share with their classmates.

Word Wall

Create and maintain a high-frequency word Word Wall in your classroom. The students will be introduced to many new sight words. They will see these in their Predecodable books as well as in the Big Books. Most of these words are very familiar to the students since they hear them every day. They need to start recognizing these words in print.

You may want to start by asking the children if there are any words they can read. Print on index cards the words the students offer. Start your word wall with these words. As you introduce Predecodable books and as you work with the Big Books, encourage the students to point out words that they recognize. As they do this, print the words on index cards and place them on the Word Wall. Encourage the students to spend extra time each day reading the words on the Word Wall to each other. Students will be thrilled as they see their Word Wall growing and growing throughout the year.

Listening Center

Each selection in the Big Books is recorded on audiotape for use in your classroom. As you read each selection, encourage students to listen to the recording during Independent Work Time. Provide one or two tape recorders that work both with and without earphones. In this way, individual students may listen to selections without disturbing the rest of the class. You will also be able to play the tapes for the whole class if you choose.

You should also encourage students to record their own stories, then share these stories with their classmates.

Discussion

Discussion is an integral part of learning. Through discussion, students are exposed to different points of view and reactions to text. Also, it is through discussion that students learn to express their thoughts and opinions coherently as well as to respect the ideas and opinions of others.

Listening and responding to each other's ideas and questions is fundamental to learning. Throughout the program students are expected to listen and respond to each other—during Writing Seminar, collaborative activities, exploration of the unit concepts—not just in a discussion about a story.

Talk to the students about what a discussion is and what is expected of participants during a discussion. Students must listen to what others are saying and respond to what is being said. Students should:

- not interrupt.
- raise their hands when they want to say something.
- ask questions of each other.
- not talk while others are speaking.
- take turns.
- respond directly to each other's questions or ideas rather than going off on a different or unrelated thought or tangent.

Handing Off

Through a process called handing off, students learn to take the primary responsibility for holding and controlling discussions. Handing off simply means that each student who responds in a discussion is responsible for drawing another student into the discussion.

This is a skill students will build on throughout their experience with the *SRA/Open Court Reading* program. You can start the process with your Kindergarten children by having the students get used to calling on one other classmate as they complete a response. For example, if the students are discussing their favorite stories, as one student completes his or her response, he or she can point to another student and say, "Tell us about your favorite story, Jan."

In order for discussions and handing off to work effectively, a seating arrangement that allows students to see one another is important just as in a real conversation or discussion. A circle or a semi-circle is effective.

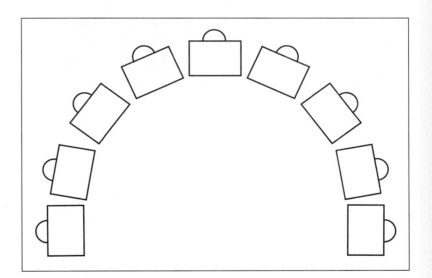

Writing

Reading and writing are interwoven processes, and each helps build and strengthen the other. Throughout the year, students do a tremendous amount of writing, both independently and collaboratively. They write for an array of purposes and audiences. Extended writing includes stories and various nonfiction pieces such as research reports, biographies, persuasive papers, and letters. In addition, they write daily in the form of note taking, making lists, labeling pictures, and making journal entries.

To assure success in writing, the students will need:

- **A Writing Journal**
  Each student should provide his or her own Writing Journal. This journal can be writing paper stapled together with construction paper; however, a spiral notebook with sections will work also.

- **A Writing Portfolio**
  An artist's portfolio contains pieces that the artist considers the best of his or her work. Help students to develop a similar portfolio of their writing. From time to time, hold conferences with individual students so that they can show you the work they have put in their portfolios and explain what they particularly like about the pieces they have chosen to keep.

You should keep your own portfolio for each student in which you place samples of written work that show the student's progress throughout the year.

- **A Writing-in-Progress Folder**
  Students should be encouraged continually to revise and edit their writing. Each student should have a folder in which they keep this writing-in-progress. Any pocket folder will work for this purpose; however, you may choose to order the **Writing Folders** that accompany the ***SRA/Open Court Reading*** program. In addition to pockets to hold student writing, these folders contain a list of proofreading marks and tips for revising that students will find useful.

Writing Center

The Writing Center should contain materials students can use to write and illustrate their work such as pencils, crayons, pens, white paper, colored paper, old magazines they can cut up, scissors, and staplers.

Writing Seminar

Seminar is a time when two or three students will share their work with the class and then their classmates will have time to give feedback. Seminar participants must listen carefully and politely, just as they do during discussion and handing off. When the author is finished reading, the other students should say something positive about what the author wrote. They can tell what they liked and why, how the author's story made them feel good, and what the author's story reminded them of. You may need to model this in the beginning by telling what you liked about the story and why.

At first, students will be sharing drawings that they have done to show stories. As the year progresses, they will write simple captions. The purpose of seminar is to help students see that they can get valuable help with their writing from their peers. It also is an invaluable tool for teaching the students how to give constructive, positive feedback.

Inquiry, Reflection, and Exploration

In *SRA/Open Court Reading*, lessons are integrated through extensive reading, writing, and discussion. In turn, the lessons are organized into learning units, with each selection in a unit adding more information or a different perspective to the students' growing knowledge of a theme or concept.

The program contains two kinds of units. **Reflection** units allow students to expand their perspectives on universal themes such as kindness, courage, perseverance, and friendship by relating what they read to their own experiences. **Inquiry** units involve students in the research process, giving them the tools they need to discover and learn on their own and as part of a collaborative group. Inquiry activities provide students with a systematic structure for exploration that is driven by their own interests and conjectures.

Both Reflection and Inquiry units are designed to help students:

- deepen their comprehension by enabling them to apply the skills they are learning to texts and activities of their own choosing.
- synthesize and organize what they are learning in order to present their findings to their classmates.
- determine suitable avenues of inquiry and methods of presentation.
- become more independent and responsible about their time and efforts.
- work efficiently in collaborative groups.

Inquiry Center

The Inquiry Center should contain materials that will facilitate the students' efforts as they work together on unit explorations, including:

- Reference books such as dictionaries and encyclopedias.
- Computers—preferably with Internet access. The SRA Home Page (see www.SRA-4kids.com) includes Internet sites specifically related to the themes the students are studying.
- Books on the themes the students are studying. You may choose to order the **Classroom Library** that accompanies the program. In addition, bibliographies of additional related books can be found following each unit in the Student Anthologies.

Concept/Question Board

One of the primary goals of *SRA/Open Court Reading* is to help you and your students form a community of learners. To do this, sharing information is essential. The **Concept/Question Board** is a bulletin board or chart. The students can share their growing knowledge about a unit theme or concept by posting on the Board newspaper clippings, magazine articles, information taken from the Internet, photographs, and other items that might be of interest to or help for their classmates. As the class progresses through a unit, the Board serves as the place where common interests become evident. As these interests emerge, the students can use them as the basis for forming collaborative groups to explore ideas in greater depth.

In addition, the Board gives students an outlet for questions that arise as they read on their own. The questions can be written directly on a sheet of paper attached to the Board, or they can be written on separate slips of paper and pinned to it. Self-sticking notepads can also be used. The **Concept/Question Board** lets students know that questions are not problems but a way of learning. Questions thus become a springboard to further exploration. Collaborative groups can be formed around common questions.

The Board should change constantly, reflecting the developing and changing interests of the class. For the **Getting Started** section and for Unit 1, you may use one **Concept/Question Board.** If you choose, you can give the Board a title, such as "Reading and Writing."

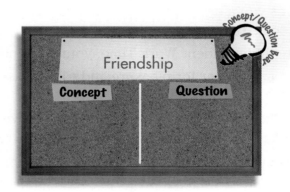

Independent Work Time

Independent Work Time is integral to ***SRA/Open Court Reading***. It is during this time, which you designate as a part of each class day, that students gain the experience of managing their own learning process. In Independent Work Time, students work on their own or collaboratively to practice and review material taught in the lessons or to complete projects of their own choosing. As the students gradually take more responsibility for their work, they learn to set learning goals, to make decisions about the use of time and materials, and to collaborate with classmates. Of equal importance, Independent Work Time gives you a designated time each day to work with students one-on-one or in small groups.

During Independent Work Time, your students can:

- read to each other for pleasure and to increase fluency.

- work independently and in small collaborative groups on their exploration projects.

- work on unfinished writing projects.

- work on any unfinished projects or assignments they have.

- assess what projects they have that need work, prioritize their time, and direct their own efforts.

During Independent Work Time, you can:

- work with individuals and small groups who have shown a need for additional instruction.

- listen to individuals read in order to assess informally their progress and help them gain fluency.

- conduct writing conferences with individual students to discuss their progress as writers.

The Reading, Listening, Writing, and Inquiry Centers will be used extensively during Independent Work Time. If possible, equip these areas with furniture that is easy to move and will allow for both independent work and small group work.

Getting Started Checklist

This checklist will help you be prepared for the school year. Look back over the Getting Started section if you have any questions about these program elements.

- ○ **Display Alphabet/Sound Cards**
- ○ **Organize Big Books and Predecodables**
- ○ **Set Up Reading Center**
- ○ **Create Word Wall**
- ○ **Establish Listening Center**
- ○ **Plan for Discussions**
- ○ **Plan for Writing Journal**
- ○ **Organize Writing Portfolios**
- ○ **Establish Writing-in-Progress Folder**
- ○ **Establish Writing Center**
- ○ **Plan for Writing Seminar**
- ○ **Establish Inquiry Center**
- ○ **Develop Concept/Question Board**
- ○ **Plan for Independent Work Time**

Exploring the Theme

Introduction

The first few weeks of kindergarten are a time of great excitement. Becoming a student is a big step in five-year-olds' lives. Every day they are introduced to new roles and routines associated with being a "student." So much is new, and the environment in which they must navigate is so very different from the cherished world where they have spent the last five years of their lives.

Kindergarten is the first time many children are expected to follow set routines — for both the classroom and the school as a whole. It is also the first time many children are expected to interact with large numbers of other children who are essentially strangers to them. These new challenges they face can be thrilling, but they can be frightening too.

Throughout Open Court Reading we give children the opportunity to reflect on themes that they care about, and can relate to their own lives. What better place to begin than with a unit about school? The present unit is designed so that children's first formal introduction to books and their first formal introduction to school can take place simultaneously, with each informing and enriching the other.

Exploration and Reflection Goals

There are three interrelated goals in this unit:

1. The first goal of the unit is to have children see books as a valuable source for learning about school – its purposes, activities and routines, and people. Achieving this goal involves:
   - giving children a forum to discuss, create, and share both trade books and original stories.

2. The second goal of the unit is to offer children an opportunity to learn more about the literary features of narrative. Achieving this goal involves introducing children to:
   - the roles of members of a literary community including listener (or audience), reader, and writer.
   - basic literary devices, picture/text relationship, and features of books such as title, author, and illustrator.

3. The third goal of the unit is to have children begin to learn how to create literary works themselves. Achieving this goal involves:
   - providing opportunity and context for children to tell stories that were read to them and stories about things that have happened to them.

Learning Goals

In this unit the children will engage in a variety of listening, speaking, reading, and writing activities that will encourage them to reflect on their own goals and expectations and those of their classmates and teachers. As they read the stories and poems, the children will view school through the eyes of story characters, offering them an opportunity to think about and discuss this new chapter of their lives. The unit's selections will extend the children's speaking and listening vocabularies and encourage the use of a variety of phonological decoding and reading comprehension strategies.

The children will work on projects that allow them to connect their past learning to the present and future. They will work independently and under teacher direction to develop their understanding of school.

Exploring the Theme

Unit Activities

Throughout this unit, you and the children will work on unit activities. The aim of the unit activities is to provide an opportunity for the children to explore their school and to become more familiar and comfortable with attending school The activities we suggest involve using a class "mascot" to scaffold the children's learning about their new social and physical environment. Because the unit's opening selection is about a dog who discovers what school is like, we have chosen a stuffed dog, which we call "Boomer," as the mascot in our lessons.

You and your students may choose to use another animal or another name.

In the suggested activities, the children will explore their classroom and school with Boomer, teaching him and learning from him. They will also engage in early literacy experiences with Boomer as one of the focal points — composing simple stories about him and their classmates, creating a class book about their school, and learning to "read" the book as they share it with their classmates, caregivers, and families.

	Boomer Goes to School	What Will Mommy Do When I'm at School?
Overview of Selection	■ This piece of realistic fiction presents the typical events of a kindergarten day, viewed through the eyes of an unlikely, yet willing student, Boomer, the dog.	■ In this piece of realistic fiction, a young girl attributes her fears and worries about separation to her mother, and works through them with the help of her understanding family.
Link to the Theme	■ For the novice, a day at school can be a bit confusing but exciting and fun.	■ Starting school can mean no longer being with someone you love, but it can also mean having new things to share with those you love.
Unit Activity ■ Create picture/story book about school	■ Children teach Boomer about classroom activity and routines, learn names of some classmates, and begin work on the picture/story book.	■ Students learn about important locations in the school and meet members of the school staff. They continue to create and "read" the class picture/story book.
Supporting Student Explorations	■ Teachers introduce the Unit Project Activity and begin the picture/story book. Teachers also take children's pictures with Boomer while they are engaged in various classroom activities and routines and begin to assemble a class picture/story book.	■ Teachers organize searches for Boomer who goes missing. They take pictures of school staff and continue assembling the picture/story book.

Supporting Student Explorations

Unit activities are meant to be motivated by the students' interests and concerns. However, at the kindergarten level, the children will need considerable support articulating their interests and questions. The following general activities are suggested to assist them:

- introduce a variety of textual material dealing with school so that children can learn from the experiences of story characters.

- encourage the children to read books about school with their parents and to share the books by placing them in the classroom library.

- give children an opportunity to express their expectations and anxieties in relation to school and to think about how they fit into this new community.

- structure time for sharing ideas and problems related to activity work throughout the unit.

- encourage children to use the Concept/Question Board to share their thoughts and explore their questions.

More specific activities that teachers might use to support students' Unit Activity work are summarized in the chart below and an elaborated version is offered in each lesson.

I Brought a Worm	Annabelle Swift, Kindergartner (Read-Aloud)
■ This poem captures a humorous sharing time moment in a kindergarten class.	■ This third piece of realistic fiction offers a perceptive look at the ups and downs of life in the Kindergarten classroom.
■ Sharing things from a kindergartner's "other life" is an opportunity for fun.	■ Kindergarten can be challenging, but having a big sister to help you helps – sometimes.
■ Children paste photographs in the unit activity book and compose accompanying text. They also visit another area of the school and learn about the person who works there.	■ Children practice group "readings" of the picture/story book and take it home to share with parents.
■ Help children generate and write text. Arrange class visit with school personnel.	■ Teachers arrange large group "readings" of the picture/story book, and schedule a time for each child to take the book home to share with his or her family.

Program Resources

Student Materials

Little Big Book, School
Pages 1–48

Pre-Decodable Books
Books 1–5

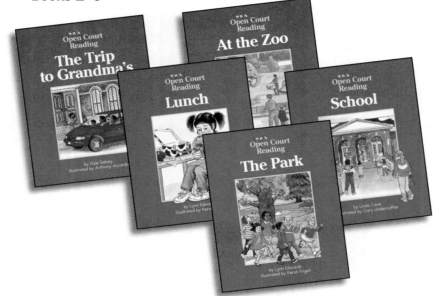

Pre-Decodable Takehome Stories
Pages 9–28

Reading and Writing Workbook
Pages 1–7

Teacher Materials

Teacher's Edition, Book 1

Pickled Peppers

Big Book School

Pages 1–48

Alphabet Book

Pictures Tell Stories

Read-Aloud Book Annabelle Swift, Kindergartner

Willy the Wisher

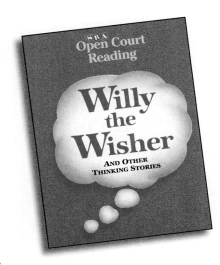

Skills Assessment

Pages 1–14

ESL Supplement

Additional Materials

- **Home Connection** Pages 1–22

Program Resources

Classroom Library*

Bea and Mr. Jones

BY AMY SCHWARTZ, ALADDIN, 1994

Bea and her father decide they would prefer to be in each other's shoes, so they trade places. Bea goes to work, and her father goes to kindergarten. (**Advanced**)

Mouse Views: What the Class Pet Saw

BY BRUCE MCMILLAN, HOLIDAY HOUSE, 1994

In this beginning reader, the classroom and the classroom objects are viewed through the eyes of the class pet mouse. (**Easy**)

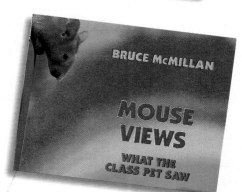

School Bus: For the Buses, the Riders and the Watchers

BY DONALD CREWS, GREENWILLOW, 1984

Crews takes readers on a day in the life of a school bus. (**Easy**)

School Days

BY B.G. HENNESSY, PICTURE PUFFINS, 1990

Simple, rhyming text describes school days. (**Average**)

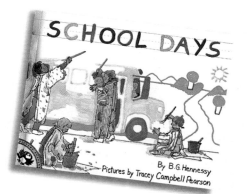

＊ These books, which all support the unit theme School, are part of a 20-book Classroom Library available for purchase from SRA/McGraw-Hill.
Note: Teachers should preview any trade books for appropriateness in their classrooms before recommending them to students.

 How to Conduct Yourself at School
PIED PIPER

In this video for K–3 students, children are taught how to handle themselves in the classroom and at play. Videocassette; 13 min.

*Just Like Abraham Lincoln

A young boy's neighbor, who looks like Abraham Lincoln, goes to school with him, and the students celebrate Lincoln's birthday in a memorable way. Videocassette; 12 min.

Morris Goes to School
CHURCHILL FILMS, 1989

This video is based on the book by Bernard Wiseman. Morris goes to school and learns a number of new things, including how to read, count, and paint. Videocassette; 15 min.

Arthur's Teacher Trouble
BRODERBUND

This interactive program is based on the book by Marc Brown. Find out what happens when Arthur is selected to compete in the school spellathon. CD-ROM.

Multisensory Kindergarten CD
ORANGE CHERRY NEW MEDIA

Students explore a schoolroom and click on various objects that "come to life," providing multisensory experiences that reinforce skills such as sequencing, classification, and animal identification. CD-ROM.

*Listening Library: School
SRA/MCGRAW-HILL, 2000

Students will enjoy listening to the selections they have read. Encourage them to use the audiocassette during Independent Work Time. Audiocassette.

*Lesson Planner
SRA/MCGRAW-HILL, 2000

Use the Lesson Planner to adjust and refine lessons to meet the specific needs of your students. CD-ROM.

*Phonics
SRA/MCGRAW-HILL, 2000

See the Phonics CD-ROM for activities to support the phonemic awareness activities in these lessons.

*Research
SRA/MCGRAW-HILL, 2000

As students continue their exploration of school, encourage them to use the Research program to help them organize and share their findings. CD-ROM.

School Web Sites

Check the Reading link of the **SRA** Web page for links to theme-related Web sites. **http://www.sra-4kids.com**

The Computer Basics unit of the **SRA Basic Computer Skills** program can be used to help students develop computer skills within the context of the unit theme. The **Applying Computer Skills in Reading** activity contains a computer skills application specific to this unit.

Titles preceded by an asterisk (✱) are available through SRA/McGraw-Hill. Other titles can be obtained by contacting the publisher listed with the title. See the appendix of this book for ordering information.

Unit Skills Overview

	PHONEMIC AWARENESS	LETTER RECOGNITION & PRINT AWARENESS	COMPREHENSION SKILLS & STRATEGIES
Boomer Goes to School **Genre:** **Realistic Fiction**	■ Listening ■ Rhythm	■ Directionality of Print ■ Page Numbers ■ Table of Contents/ Page numbers ■ Letter Names/Shapes: Aa ■ Letter Names/Shapes: Bb	■ Clarifying ■ Predicting ■ Drawing Conclusions
What Will Mommy Do When I'm at School? **Genre:** **Realistic Fiction**	■ Listening ■ Oral Blending	■ Word Boundaries ■ Directionality of Print ■ Letter Names/Shapes: Cc ■ Letter Names/Shapes: Dd ■ Letter Names/Shapes: Ee ■ Letter Names/Shapes: Ff ■ Letter Names/Shapes: Gg ■ Letter Names/Shapes: Hh	■ Clarifying ■ Making Connections ■ Compare and Contrast ■ Predicting
I Brought a Worm **Genre: Poetry**	■ Oral Blending ■ Listening	■ Letter Names/Shapes: Ii ■ Italic Type ■ Letter Names/Shapes: Jj	■ Visualization
Annabelle Swift, Kindergartner **Genre:** **Realistic Fiction** **Unit Wrap-Up**	■ Oral Blending ■ Listening	■ Letter-Word Distinction ■ Word Length ■ Letter Names/Shapes: Kk ■ Picture/Text Relationship ■ Letter Names/Shapes: Ll ■ Letter Names/Shapes: Mm ■ Letter Names/Shapes: Nn ■ Word Length ■ Letter Names/Shapes: Oo ■ Letter Names/Shapes: Pp	■ Asking Questions ■ Predicting ■ Drawing Conclusions

🍞 Phonics

VOCABULARY	WRITING	LISTENING, SPEAKING, VIEWING	GRAMMAR	STUDY & RESEARCH SKILLS	ACROSS THE CURRICULUM
■ Comparing Word Meanings ■ Rhyming Words ■ Comparing Word Meanings ■ Time of Day Words ■ Color Words	■ Choose a Pet ■ Writing Ideas ■ Sequencing ■ Opposites ■ Journal Writing	■ Listening Attentively ■ *Pictures Tell Stories* ■ Reading Words and Pictures ■ Dramatizing		■ Maps	■ Drama *Act Out a Scene* ■ Social Studies *Follow a School Map; Transportation* ■ Music *Singing About School* ■ Movement *Following Directions* ■ Math *Colors Graph*
■ Opposites ■ Rhyming Words ■ High-Frequency Words: *here, is, a, an* ■ Position Words ■ Names of Days of the Week	■ Journal Writing ■ Being a Student ■ My Classroom ■ My Friends and I ■ What I Like to Do in School ■ Seminar	■ Asking/Answering Questions ■ Listening Attentively (to appreciate) ■ Left/Right Directionality ■ Following Directions	■ Words that Name (Nouns) ■ Capitalization	■ Parts of a Library	■ Social Studies *Categorizing and Classifying; Morning and Afternoon; Staff Members* ■ Movement *What We Do Together* ■ Music *Sing About the Morning* ■ Math *Create a Schedule*
	■ Poetry ■ Journal Writing	■ Listening (to Appreciate) ■ Listening Skills	■ Words that Show Action (Verbs)		■ Social Studies *Classifying* ■ Dramatization *Act Out Characters' Feelings*
■ Names of Classroom Objects ■ High-Frequency Words: *we, and* ■ Color Words ■ Review	■ Journal Writing ■ First Day of School ■ Proofreading ■ Seminar ■ Collaborative Writing	■ Asking/Answering Questions ■ Listening Attentively (to Get Information) ■ *Pictures Tell Stories* ■ Making Introductions		■ Charts	■ Social Studies *Classroom Jobs; Telephone Numbers; Classifying* ■ Math *Travel to School* ■ Math *Compare Numbers* ■ Art *Make a School Collage*

Meeting the Needs of All Children

Meeting Individual Needs

	Reteach	ESL	Challenge
Boomer Goes to School **Genre: Realistic Fiction**		■ Sing Along ■ Sound Sequence ■ Rhyming ■ Numbers Help ■ Articles ■ Rereading ■ Native Language Use ■ Background Information ■ Preread the Story ■ Comparing Words ■ Summarizing ■ Relationship Words ■ Word Sequence	■ Independent Reading
What Will Mommy Do When I'm at School? **Genre: Realistic Fiction**	■ Identifying Letters ■ Identifying *a-e*	■ Preteach ■ This Ship Is Loaded With _____ Game ■ Simon Says ■ Vocabulary ■ Relationship Words ■ Opposites ■ Parts of a Library ■ Position Words ■ High-Frequency Words	■ Letters *A-F* ■ Letters *a-e*
I Brought a Worm **Genre: Poetry**	■ Letters *a-h*	■ Oral Blending ■ Vocabulary ■ Visual Clues	■ Letters *a-h*
Annabelle Swift, Kindergartner **Genre: Realistic Fiction** **Unit Wrap-Up**	■ Capital and Lowercase Letters ■ Letters *Ll*, *Mm*, and *Nn* ■ Alphabet Sequence	■ Oral Blending ■ Selection Vocabulary ■ Identifying Colors ■ Activities ■ Signs ■ Teamwork ■ Number Sequence	■ Capital and Lowercase Letters ■ Letters *Ll*, *Mm*, and *Nn* ■ Hop Along ■ Alphabet

Assessment

Intervention	✓ Informal	✓ Formal
■ Letter Names ■ Forming Letters	■ Line Formation ■ Listening ■ Letter Strokes/Pencil Control ■ Fluency/High-Frequency Word (*the*) ■ Monitoring	**Skills Assessment** ■ Matching Letters, p. 1
■ Pencil Control ■ Letter Recognition ■ Letter Formation	■ Monitoring ■ Letter Formation ■ Responding to Literature ■ Rhyming ■ Letter Recognition ■ Phonemic Awareness ■ Discussing the Selection	■ Picture Vocabulary: High-Frequency Words, p. 2 ■ Rhyming Words, p. 3
■ Letter Recognition ■ Letter Formation		■ Words and Letters, p. 4
■ Letter Recognition ■ Letter Formation ■ Long Vowel Sounds		■ Matching Upper- and Lowercase Letters, p. 5 ■ The Alphabet, p. 6

Previewing the Unit

Kindergarten Overview

The goals of the kindergarten program of Open Court Reading are:

- to introduce the children to the alphabet and how it works;
- to provide the children with an introduction to how the sounds of the language work together;
- to give the children early reading and writing experiences at which they can be successful;
- to help the children focus not only on the importance of learning but also on the joy that learning brings to our lives.

To accomplish these goals, kindergarten instruction focuses on:

Phonemic Awareness activities give the children practice in discriminating the sounds that make up words. Across the year, it is taught by two complementary techniques: oral blending and segmentation. At the beginning of the year, the children use oral blending to put sounds together to make words. Later they use segmentation to separate words into sounds. The phonemic awareness activities are purely oral and do not involve the teaching of sound/spelling relationships.

Letter Recognition and Sounds and Letters
Large *Alphabet Cards* are used first to familiarize the children with the names and shapes of the letters of the alphabet, and, later, to remind the children of sound/letter relationships. The name of the picture on each card contains the target sound at the beginning of words for most consonants and in the middle for most vowels. In addition, the picture associates a sound with an action, which is introduced through a short, interactive story in which the pictured object or character makes the sound of the letter.

Big Books and Read-Alouds engage the children in listening, familiarize them with print and book conventions, and introduce them to the behaviors good readers engage in as they read.

Writing includes a range of activities: class books, journals writing, individual writing.

Independent Work Time is integral to the success of the entire program. Independent Work Time gives the children an early experience of managing their own learning process. For this reason, you should designate a time each day for the children to work independently, with partners, in small groups, or with you to reinforce learning. Independent Work Time is also the time for you to provide extra help for those children who need it and to assess and monitor the progress of individuals or of the whole class. At this point in the school year, you will take the lead in directing Independent Work Time; reinforcing and reviewing learning for the children or providing extra help to those children who need it.

Lesson Format

Unit 1, *School*, contains twenty lessons. Activities in each lesson are presented in three major divisions:

Part I, Sounds and Letters

The activities in the Sounds and Letters part of the lesson in Unit 1 begin with listening and gamelike activities to develop the children's phonemic awareness and to familiarize them with the names and shapes of the letters of the alphabet.

Activities in Sounds and Letters are arranged as follows:

Sounds Letters and Language activities in Unit 1 grow from the rhymes, poems, and songs in the *Big Book Pickled Peppers*. Language games and word play add opportunities for the children to apply their increasing knowledge of sounds, letters, and language. In *First-Step Story 1*, the children create their own illustrations for the poem "Sleeping Outdoors" by Marchette Chute.

Phonemic Awareness exercises focus on rhyming activities and introduce oral blending.

Letter Recognition takes the children through the alphabet, letter by letter. Songs, games, and *Alphabet Card* activities help the children learn and remember the name and shape of each letter.

Part 2, Reading and Responding

Each selection in the *School* unit provides children with a variety of shared reading, writing, listening, and speaking experiences. Activities following the reading focus on developing print awareness, literature appreciation, and reading/writing connections. Theme Connection Activities and the unit project are presented here as well. The activities in Part 2 combine to provide the children opportunities

- to explore interesting and familiar themes that help them expand their knowledge and examine new ideas;
- to experience a variety of types of authentic literature, including fiction, non-fiction, and poetry;
- to expand and develop their print awareness;
- to engage in collaborative learning activities;
- to practice important reading, speaking, and listening behaviors.

Part 3, Integrating the Curriculum

Part 3 of each lesson contains an array of language arts activities including independent and collaborative writing exercises; vocabulary, grammar, literary, and study skills activities; *Pictures Tell Stories* activities that link reading to fine art; and *Willy the Wisher Thinking Stories,* which provide opportunities for the children to engage in listening, speaking, and thinking activities.

Home Connection

Distribute *Home Connection* page 1 that tells families about the School unit. This letter is avaliable in English and Spanish.

Research in Reading

Marilyn Jager Adams on Phonemic Awareness

Preschool-age children's awareness of phonemics—of the speech sounds that correspond roughly to individual letters—has been shown to hold singular predictive power, accounting for as much as 50% of the variance in their reading proficiency at the end of first grade. A child's level of phonemic awareness on entering school is widely held to be the strongest single determinant of the success that she or he will experience in learning to read.

Measures of preschool-age children's level of phonemic awareness strongly predict their future success in learning to read. Measures of schoolchildren's ability to attend to and manipulate phonemes strongly correlate with their reading success through the twelfth grade. Indeed, among readers of alphabetical languages, those who are successful invariably have phonemic awareness, whereas those who lack phonemic awareness are invariably struggling.

Knowing that so many children lack phonemic awareness and that phonemic awareness is critical to learning to read and write an alphabetic script, we begin to see the importance of making a place for its instruction. In fact, developing phonemic awareness through instruction significantly accelerates children's subsequent reading and writing achievement.

Lesson Planner

	DAY 1	DAY 2
Part 1 **Sounds and Letters**	**Sounds, Letters, and Language,** pp. 18–19 ■ Reading the Big Book *Pickled Peppers,* pp. 6–7 **Phonemic Awareness**  ■ Listening for Sounds, p. 20 ■ Feeling the Rhythm, pp. 20–21 **Letter Recognition** ■ Letter Names, p. 22 ✓■ Letter Shapes, p. 23	**Sounds, Letters, and Language,** p. 46 ■ Reading the Big Book *Pickled Peppers,* pp.6–7 **Phonemic Awareness** ✓■ Listening for the First, Middle, or Last Sounds, p. 47 ■ Feeling the Rhythm, p. 47 **Letter Recognition** ✓■ Letter Names, p. 48 ✓■ Letter Shapes, p. 49

Part 1 Materials
- 1 Name Necklace per child (see Lesson 1)
- Big Book *Pickled Peppers,* pp. 6–7, 26–27, 24–25
- Listening Library Audiocassette: School
- Alphabet Cards
- Picture Cards (see lessons)
- Pre-Decodable Book 1: *The Park*
- Word Cards (see lessons)
- *Alphabet Book,* p. 4
- Blackline Masters 1, 2, 3, 5
- Transparency 1
- Pocket Chart

	DAY 1	DAY 2
Part 2 **Reading and Responding**	**Exploring the Theme,** p. 25 ■ Build Background, p. 26 ■ Preview and Prepare, p. 27 **Vocabulary** ■ Selection Vocabulary: *bus,* p. 28 **Reading Recommendations,** p. 29 **Comprehension Strategies** ■ Clarifying, pp. 30, 32, 34, 36 ■ Predicting, pp. 30, 32, 36, 38 **Comprehension Skills** ■ Discussing the Selection, p. 39 ■ Purposes for Reading, p. 39 **Responding to Literature** ■ Print Awareness, p. 40 **Exploring the Theme,** p. 41	**Activate Prior Knowledge,** p. 50 **Preview and Prepare,** p. 50 **Vocabulary** ■ Concept Vocabulary: Words About School, p. 50 **Reading Recommendations,** p. 51 **Comprehension Strategies** ■ Predicting, pp. 52, 54 ■ Clarifying, pp. 52, 54 **Comprehension Skills** ■ Drawing Conclusions, p. 53, 55 ■ Discussing the Selection, p. 55 **Responding to Literature** ■ Literature Appreciation, p. 56 **Exploring the Theme,** p. 57

Part 2 Materials
- Big Book *School,* pp. 4–21, 48
- Unit Activity Materials (see lessons)
- Home Connection, pp. 3, 5, 7
- Listening Library Audiocassette: School
- Blackline Master 6

	DAY 1	DAY 2
Part 3 **Integrating the Curriculum**	**Independent and Collaborative Writing** ■ Writing Activities, p. 42 **Listening, Speaking, Viewing** ■ Listening Attentively, p. 43 **Vocabulary** ■ Comparing Word Meanings, p. 44 **Across the Curriculum: Drama,** p. 45	**Independent and Collaborative Writing** ■ Choose a Pet, p. 58 **Vocabulary** ■ Rhyming Words, p. 58 **Across the Curriculum: Social Studies,** p. 59

Part 3 Materials
- Big Book *School*
- Big Book *Pictures Tell Stories,* pp. 16, 17
- Word Cards (see lessons)
- Picture Cards (see lessons)
- Blackline Master 4
- Transparency 32
- Across the Curriculum: see activities, pp. 45, 59, 75, 89, 103

Independent Work Time

Materials
Big Books: School, Pickled Peppers, Alphabet Book, Pictures Tell Stories
Willy the Wisher
Skills Assessment page 1
Intervention Guide Unit 1, Lessons 1–5
ESL Supplement Unit 1, Lessons 1–5
Pre-Decodable Book 1

DAY 1	DAY 2
Preteach ■ Selection Vocabulary ■ *School* "Boomer Goes to School" (*Listening Library Audiocassette*) ■ *Pickled Peppers* "I'm a Little Teapot" (*Listening Library Audiocassette*) **Unit Project:** Class picture book about School	**Reteach** ■ "Boomer Goes to School" ■ "I'm a Little Teapot" **Writing: Choose a Pet** **Skills Assessment** "Matching Letters" **Unit Project continued**

  Phonics ✓ Informal Assessment Available ✓ Formal Assessment Available

DAY 3	DAY 4	DAY 5

Sounds, Letters, and Language, p. 60
- Reading the Big Book *Pickled Peppers*, pp. 26–27

Phonemic Awareness
- Listening for the First, Middle, or Last Words, p. 61
- Word Substitution, p. 62

Letter Recognition
- ✓ Letter Names, p. 63
- Letter Shapes, p. 63

Sounds, Letters, and Language, p. 76
- Reading the Big Book *Pickled Peppers*, pp. 26–27

Phonemic Awareness
- Listening for Missing Sounds, p. 77
- Word Substitution, p. 77
- Rhyme, p. 77

Letter Recognition
- Letter Names, p. 79
- ✓ Letter Shapes, p. 79

✓ **Reading Pre-Decodable Book I: The Park,** pp. 80–81

Sounds, Letters, and Language, p. 90
- Reading the Big Book *Pickled Peppers*, pp. 24–25

Phonemic Awareness
- Listening for Missing Words, p. 91
- Word Substitution, p. 91
- ✓ Rhyme, p. 91

Letter Recognition
- Letter Names, p. 92
- ✓ Letter Shapes, p. 92

Activate Prior Knowledge, p. 64
Preview and Prepare, p. 64
Vocabulary
- Selection Vocabulary: *share, paint, play,* p. 64

Reading Recommendations, p. 65
Comprehension Strategies
- Clarifying, pp. 66, 68

Comprehension Skills
- Drawing Conclusions, p. 67
- Discussing the Selection, p. 69

Responding to Literature
- Literature Appreciation, p. 70

Exploring the Theme, p. 71

Activate Prior Knowledge, p. 82
Preview and Prepare, p. 82
Vocabulary
- Selection Vocabulary: *wiggled, squirmed,* p. 82

Reading Recommendations, p. 83
Comprehension Strategies
- Confirming Predictions, p. 84
- Clarifying, p. 84

Comprehension Skills
- Discussing the Selection, p. 85

Responding to Literature
- Reading/Writing Connection, p. 86

Exploring the Theme, p. 87

Activate Prior Knowledge, p. 94
Preview and Prepare, p. 94
Vocabulary
- Selection Vocabulary: *still,* p. 94

Reading Recommendations, p. 95
Comprehension Strategies
- Predicting, p. 96

Comprehension Skills
- Discussing the Selection, p. 97

Responding to Literature
- Reading/Writing Connection, p. 98
- Using the Audiocassette, p. 98

Exploring the Theme, p. 99

Independent and Collaborative Writing
- Writing Ideas, p. 72

Listening, Speaking, Viewing, p. 73
- *Pictures Tell Stories,* p. 16

Vocabulary
- Comparing Word Meanings, p. 74

Across the Curriculum: Social Studies, p. 75

Independent and Collaborative Writing
- Sequencing, p. 88

Listening, Speaking, Viewing, p. 88
- *Pictures Tell Stories,* p. 17

Across the Curriculum: Music, p. 89

Independent and Collaborative Writing
- Opposites, p. 100

Listening, Speaking, Viewing
- Reading Words and Pictures, p. 101

Study and Research Skills
- Make a Classroom Map, p. 101

Vocabulary
- Time of Day Words, p. 102

Across the Curriculum: Movement, p. 103

Reteach
- "Boomer Goes to School"

Preteach
- *Pickled Peppers* "One, Two, Buckle My Shoe"
- *Pictures Tell Stories*

Writing Ideas

Unit Project continued

Reteach
- "Boomer Goes to School"
- "One, Two, Buckle My Shoe"

Preteach
- *Pictures Tell Stories*

Partner-read Pre-Decodable Book I

Unit Project continued

Reteach
- "Boomer Goes to School"

Preteach
- *Pickled Peppers* "Houses (Casitas)"
- *Alphabet Book Aa*

Writing: Sequencing

Study and Research: Make a classroom map

Unit Project continued

Meeting Individual Needs
Independent Work Time

Sounds and Letters

Meeting Individual Needs

ESL
- Sing Along, p. 18
- Sound Sequence, pp. 20, 47
- Rhyming, p. 46
- Numbers Help, p. 60
- Articles, p. 80
- Rereading, p. 80
- Native Language Use, p. 90

Intervention
- Letter Names, pp. 22, 48
- Forming Letters, p. 92

Reading and Responding

Meeting Individual Needs

ESL
- Background Information, p. 26
- Preread the Story, p. 29
- Comparing Words, p. 82

Integrating the Curriculum

Meeting Individual Needs

ESL
- Opposites, p. 100

Formal Assessment Options

Use this assessment page along with your informal observations to gauge the students' progress.

Name _____ Date _____

Matching Letters

(Teacher: Look at each group of letters. Draw a line under the letter that is different.)

1. a   <u>s</u>   a

2. b   b   <u>d</u>

3. a   <u>s</u>   a

4. <u>m</u>   n   n

5. o   o   <u>c</u>

Skills Assessment   1

**Skills Assessment, p. 1
Matching Letters**

Teacher's Observation Log

Student _____

Date _____ Unit _____

Activity _____

General Comprehension
Concepts Discussed _____

Behavior Within a Group
Articulates, expresses ideas _____

Joins discussions _____

Collaboration (such as works with other students, works alone) _____

Role in Group
Role (such as leader, summarizer, questioner, recorder, critic, observer, non-participant) _____

Flexibility (changes roles when necessary) _____

Use of Reading Strategies
Uses strategies when needed (either those taught or student's own)/Describe strategies used _____

Changes strategies when appropriate _____

Changes Since Last Observation
_____

If more space is needed, write on the back or use another sheet.

18   Copyright © SRA McGraw-Hill. Permission is granted to reproduce this page for classroom use.   Assessment Guide

**Teacher's Observation Log,
Assessment Master**

1 Sounds and Letters

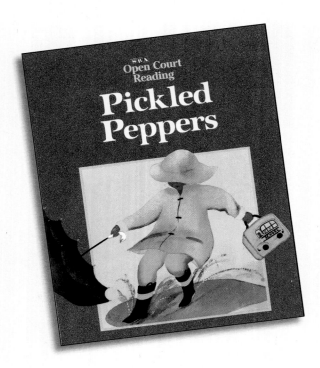

SRA
Open Court
Reading

Pickled Peppers

Sounds, Letters, and Language

Names

- Prepare a Name Necklace for each child and one for yourself. Each necklace should have the child's first name written on an oak tag rectangle, with yarn tied through holes at each end so the necklaces can be worn.

- Explain that every person has a name. Put on your Name Necklace and introduce yourself. Go around the room and ask the children to state their names, including their last names if they choose to do so.

- Then provide each child with his or her own Name Necklace. Hold up each necklace, read the name aloud as you point to the word, and have the child come up and get the necklace. Encourage them to put on the necklace and say their names aloud as they point to their written name.

- When all the children have their necklaces on, demonstrate how to turn to the *right* and have the children introduce themselves to the person on the right. Then demonstrate turning to the *left*, and have the children repeat the procedure.

Reading the Big Book *Pickled Peppers*
"I'm a Little Teapot," pages 6–7

- Gather children around the **Big Book.** Point out the front and back covers and the title, and read the title with children. Let them know that this is the "name" of the book. Discuss briefly that we read books for fun and also to learn things. Mention quickly other things that people read: newspapers, magazines, signs, lists, newsletters, and labels on food packages. Then have the children tell why they think this book is so big.

- Turn to the selection "I'm a Little Teapot." Point to the title and read it aloud. If some children already know the song, let them sing it for the class. Some children may automatically perform the motions in the song as well. Tell these children that they can be your "helpers" when the whole class learns the motions tomorrow, but that for now you want to read the words to "I'm a Little Teapot." Read the song slowly, accentuating the rhyming words and moving your finger from line to line. Explain that you are going to read the song once more and that you will point to each word as you read it. Read the song once more, pointing word by word.

Teacher Tip

Name Necklaces Tell the children to keep their Name Necklaces in front of them when they are at their desks. Encourage them to wear the necklaces when they move around the classroom.

Meeting Individual Needs

ESL

Sing Along For English-language learners who are not familiar with the song "I'm a Little Teapot": Conduct a practice session with them before the whole group sings it. Read each sentence to them, and then have them repeat it after you, making sure they understand the words and their connection to the actions. Use rhythm and pantomime to help them memorize the song.

■ Now sing the song, or you may prefer to use the ***Listening Libraries Audiocassette.*** Refer to the Appendix for the music. Sing the song several times, pointing to each line as the children sing along. Clarify unfamiliar words such as *stout, shout, steam.*

■ Point to the pictures and explain that pictures are different from words but that they also help give meaning to the song. Name and point to the word *handle*, and then to the girl making the handle with her arm. Name and point to the word *spout*, and ask a child to point to the boy making the spout. Point to the words *tip me over*, one by one, and say each word. Ask a child to find the picture that illustrates *tip me over*.

Research in Action

Throughout this program, the children are asked to think about topics well before they are offered real instruction on them. This is done in recognition that, in order for any new lesson to be worth learning or even learnable, it is important for children to have wondered about it already. Teaching any lesson is most effective when it answers a question that the children have already asked themselves.   *(Marilyn Jager Adams)*

1 Sounds and Letters

Phonemic Awareness

Listening for Sounds

Gather materials to make sounds, or play recorded familiar sounds, such as dropping a book, bouncing a ball, or closing the door, for children to identify.

- Ask children to close their eyes and listen to a sound. Make (or play) one sound.
- Ask children to identify the sound, using the sentence "I heard the sound of a _____."
- Make (or play) another sound. Ask the children, "What sound did you hear?" Call on individual children and encourage them to answer in complete sentences: "I heard the sound of a _____."
- After children have identified each sound, play two sounds at a time. Ask, "How many sounds did you hear?" After they answer "two," review the sounds. "Yes. First we heard a _____, and last we heard a _____."
- If children are ready, repeat the game with a series of three sounds. As you play the three sounds, take the opportunity to model using *first*, *middle*, and *last*: "First we heard a _____, in the middle we heard a _____, and last we heard a _____.
- Repeat the activity with three more sounds.

Meeting Individual Needs

ESL

Sound Sequence To teach *first*, *middle*, and *last* (or *beginning*, *middle*, and *end*) word sounds to English-language learners, use a book, a list, or a row of people or objects to demonstrate, Point to the first object as you say, "first." Ask the students to repeat the word. Then continue with "middle" and "last." Do the sequence again with other objects.

Teacher Tip The suggestions for teaching the concepts *first*, *middle*, and *last* for English-language learners can be used for the entire group if those concepts are unfamiliar. You will find that many kindergartners of every background need help with the word *middle*.

Research in Action

Listening games help children learn to listen for sounds in general. This, in turn, sharpens their ability to attend selectively to single sounds. In later lessons, the children will transfer this skill to listening for separate words in sentences, parts of words, and individual phonemes in words. *(Marilyn Jager Adams)*

Feeling the Rhythm

Teach children the following rhyme:

Polly put the kettle on	Sukey take it off again
Polly put the kettle on	Sukey take it off again
Polly put the kettle on	Sukey take it off again
We'll all have tea	They've all gone away

- When children are comfortable with the rhyme, substitute a child's name for *Polly*. Have children join in saying the rhyme with the new name and clapping each time the new name is said.
- Substitute another child's name for *Sukey*.

■ Repeat the rhyme several times with new names, and have the children join in reciting and clapping with you.

Research in Action

Children naturally play with language. Their repetitive playground songs and rhymes attest to this. Extending children's natural love of rhythm into classroom instruction will allow you to help them focus on the form of language. Clapping, singing, and "feeling" the pattern of language are fun, but more importantly, they provide a learning framework. Through familiar poems and "ditties," children will learn to distinguish meaning and form. Following a natural progression, children will be able to see that sentences are made up of words, words are made up of separate parts, and that these parts are made up of individual sounds.   *(Marilyn Jager Adams)*

Phonemic Awareness activities related to the lessons can be found at **http://www.sra-4kids.com**

Sounds and Letters

Letter Names

Alphabet Song

- Arrange the *Alphabet Cards* across the board or in another spot in the classroom where all the children can easily see them. Point to the whole row of cards and tell the children that this is the *alphabet*. Invite volunteers to identify any letters they know.

- Ask the children why it is so important to know the alphabet. Help them understand that all the writing around us is made up of the letters of the alphabet.

- Tell children that they are going to learn the "Alphabet Song," which names every letter. Point out that this version of the "Alphabet Song" is just a little different from the other versions they may already know. (The music can be found in the Appendix.)

- Have the children listen as you sing the song or play it on the *Listening Libraries Audiocassette*. Pronounce each letter clearly.

- Sing the song together several times, clapping on each letter that comes before a pause. (*G, N, Q, T, W, Z*)

  ABCDEFG

  HIJKLMN

  OPQ

  RST

  UVW

  XYZ

  Now I never will forget

  How to say the alphabet.

Alphabet Tap

- Tell the children that they are going to sing the "Alphabet Song" again, but they are going to mark the pauses a little differently.

- Have each child hold a pencil or marker. Then invite the children to sing the "Alphabet Song" with you, and this time tap the pencil at the "pause" letters. (*G, N, Q, T, W, Z*)

- You might vary this activity by designating different groups of children to tap when they hear a certain letter.

Intervention

Letter Names If the children are having difficulty remembering the Alphabet Song, you might have them repeat the letters *after* you sing each line. Repeat this method once or twice until they are ready to sing along as you point to the letters in turn.

 Teacher Tip

Many teachers put a symbol of a hand on the *G, N, R, T, W,* and *Z Alphabet Cards* to remind children to stop and clap when they come to these letters.

Letter Shapes

Use either an overhead projector or the chalkboard so that all children can see. Have children mimic your strokes in the air with their fingers.

Up-and-down Lines

- Make a small dot for a starting point and have the children hold up their fingers. Then make a downward stroke with your finger.
- Repeat the stroke several times and watch to be sure the children are moving their fingers from top to bottom.
- Then place your marker or chalk at the starting dot. Have the children place their crayons at the top of their papers. Tell them to watch as you move your marker from top to bottom. Then have them make a downward stroke as you say, "Start at the top and move straight down."

Across Lines

- Repeat the procedure for horizontal lines, first demonstrating on the overhead projector or chalkboard and having the children do their strokes in the air.
- Have the children place their crayons at the left side of their papers. Have them watch as you make a horizontal line.
- Then have them do the same as you say, "Start here and move across to the right."

Teacher Tip

Letter Formation Making straight lines on the chalkboard (or small chalkboard) or at easels may be helpful for children who have difficulty with pencil or crayon control. You may also want to make a class set of *Blackline Master 1* and have the children practice up-and-down and across lines.

Assessment

✓ **Informal** Note children who are having difficulty following the line formation exercise. Plan to work with these children during independent work time.

② Reading and Responding

This selection is taught in six lessons:

Lesson 1	Lesson 3	Lesson 5
Lesson 2	Lesson 4	Lesson 6

Selection Summary

Genre: Realistic Fiction

In this selection, children view the activities of school through the eyes of Boomer, a dog. Boomer has a lot of fun participating in school activities in his own way.

About the Author

Constance (Connie) McGeorge was born in Akron, Ohio, and lived primarily in the Akron/Cleveland area until she attended the Ohio State University. After graduating from OSU, she settled in Columbus to teach.

Connie now spends her time with her creative interests—mostly writing children's picture books—and with her husband, James, their two dogs and a horse. In addition to riding her horse, Connie enjoys gardening. She has a collection of polar bears and still has her favorite stuffed animals from childhood.

Other Books by Constance W. McGeorge
- *Boomer's Big Day*
- *The Snow Riders*
- *Waltz of the Scarecrows*

About the Illustrator

Mary Whyte "Art has always been a major focus of my life. I sold my first drawing when I was fourteen years old and had my first solo art exhibition when I was sixteen." Mary Whyte is best known for her unique watercolors. Her golden retriever, Boomer, inspired *Boomer's Big Day*, her first children's book. Whyte says, "I generally spend forty hours per week in my studio, illustrating books, painting portraits, and writing for artists' magazines. Boomer is always by my side . . ."

Other Books Illustrated by Mary Whyte
- *Boomer's Big Day*
- *The Snow Riders*
- *I Love You the Purplest*

Exploring the Theme

Selection Concepts

"Boomer Goes to School" is realistic fiction that describes a day in school—with a twist. Even though Boomer is a dog, he shares one important feature with most kindergartners—he doesn't know much about school. But in spite of not knowing what will happen next, he faces each event with enthusiasm. What better role model for apprehensive beginners? The key concepts to be explored are:

- School can be fun, even though it is sometimes confusing.
- School has a unique set of routines that we need to learn.

Supporting Reflection

Introduce "Boomer" (or whatever stuffed toy you choose as your class mascot) and explain that he will be learning all about school with them. Pass Boomer around the class and let the children introduce themselves to him.

- Have them guess what Boomer might think he will do in school and what he may want to learn.
- Ask them if they think Boomer might be a little scared just starting school and what some of his fears might be.
- Invite them to guess what questions Boomer might have about school.

Concept/Question Board

Set up a bulletin board or other display board in the classroom and tell the children that this is their "Concept/Question Board." Say that the Concept/Question Board will be a place for displaying their ideas about school.

- Start the Concept/Question Board display by making a border, using the children's names.
- Show the children's name strips that you have pre-prepared. Call out each child's name, and have him or her help you tack the name onto the board.
- Tell the children that you will be taking their pictures and putting them on the Concept/Question Board to show who is in their classroom.

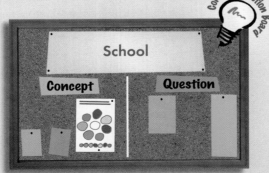

Teacher Tip If you do not have a stuffed animal to use as your mascot, consider using the *Lion Puppet* for these activities.

Teacher Tip Although children will not be working on the unit activity during this lesson, you will need to prepare a book with covers and blank pages. Consider using heavy sheets of paper that are bound together with ribbon or yarn. Print the title on the cover page–*Our Classroom and School.*

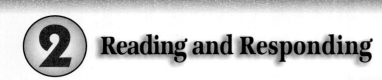

2 Reading and Responding

Meeting Individual Needs

ESL

Background Information Help English-language learners who are unfamiliar with school buses to understand what they are. Show them pictures and explain that buses are used by many schools to transport children who live too far away to walk safely to school.

Build Background

Activate Prior Knowledge

Invite the children to name some of the things they have done in school so far, such as learn where things are in the classroom and meet new friends. Then ask them if they think the story might tell about some of these things. If necessary, help children give complete responses by paraphrasing and clarifying some of their statements; for example if a child says "numbers," you might say, "At school we learn about numbers and counting at math time."

Background Information

Tell the children about a dog you know, or invite children who have dogs to tell about some of the kinds of things dogs like to do. Ask children to share what they think might happen if a dog came to spend the day in your class.

Preview and Prepare

Previewing the Big Book

Display the **Big Book** *School*. Call the children's attention to the title and read it aloud. Ask the children to say the title with you. Turn to the table of contents and explain that this page contains the names of all the stories and the poem in the **Big Book.** Point to the title of each selection and to the page number where each begins.

- Tell the children that the stories and the poem in the **Big Book** are all about school.
- Ask them what they think they might learn from the book.

Browse

- Open the **Big Book** *School* to pages 4–5, "Boomer Goes to School." Point to each word as you read aloud the title, the name of the author, and the name of the illustrator. Explain to the children that the first line tells who wrote the story and the second line tells who drew the pictures.
- Turn through several pages of the story and have the children discuss what they see in the pictures. Ask them to identify Boomer and to predict what they think the story might be about.

Set Purposes

Let the children know that there are many reasons to read a story, such as for entertainment or to get information. Ask them to think of good reasons for reading "Boomer Goes to School." Invite them to listen as you read the story aloud both to enjoy the story and to find out what happens to Boomer at school.

Boomer was just settling down after his morning walk, when suddenly, someone called his name. Then, Boomer saw his leash.

4

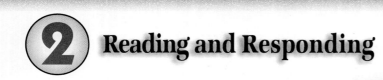

2 **Reading and Responding**

Vocabulary

Selection Vocabulary

■ This selection gives specific information about school and the school experience. Write the following word on the board and say it:

bus

■ Ask the children what they know about buses and to talk about any experiences they want to share about riding a bus. Explain that there are different types of buses—city buses, school buses, and so on.

Reading Recommendations

Read through as much of the story as possible without interruption. However, during reading, you may wish to stop occasionally to model some simple reading strategies to show the children what good readers do as they read. This will introduce the children to the thoughtful thinking process in which we all engage as we try to make sense of what we read. Before, during, and after reading, invite the children to ask questions and share what the selection makes them wonder about. The left-hand column contains suggested stopping points and ideas for modeling during reading and responding to text. Use these strategies as the need arises.

Meeting Individual Needs

ESL

During independent work time, you may want to preread the story with small groups of English-language learners. This will help them participate in the discussion more fully.

Using Reading Strategies

Modeling

During the first reading of "Boomer Goes to School," you will introduce and model the use of the following reading strategies:

- Clarifying
- Predicting

Through modeling you will think through the reading strategies aloud. Always encourage children to share their ideas as well. Remember that predicting should always be done during the first reading, and you should always stop to clarify words or ideas that the children find confusing.

Research in Action

One of the most effective ways to help young children begin to use and understand the strategies of good readers is to model these strategies. Modeling these strategies and encouraging children to articulate questions and to think aloud as they attempt to understand text can demonstrate, even to kindergarten children, how these strategies are put into practice by good readers. The most effective models you can offer, however, will be those that come from your own reading experiences. What kind of things did you wonder about? What kinds of things surprised you the first time you read a story? Drawing on such questions and on your students' questions and comments as they read will make both the text and the strategic reading process more meaningful to the students.

② Reading and Responding

Comprehension Strategies

Introducing Strategy Use

Modeling

❶ Predicting *Good readers predict, or think about what's going to happen in a story. Boomer thinks he might be going for a walk when he hears his name and sees the leash. I predict Boomer is right. He is going for a walk. What do you think? Let's read on and see if Boomer is right.*

Modeling

❷ Clarifying *What kind of bus is Boomer on? I'll look at the pictures again to help me. Oh, yes, I see. It's a school bus. The words and pictures help me clarify, or figure out what is confusing me or what I don't understand.*

 Teacher Tip Confirming Prediction Be sure to confirm all predictions when you reach the appropriate place in the text. Consider writing down all predictions so you can refer to them throughout the selection.

Boomer Goes to School

Constance W. McGeorge
illustrated by Mary Whyte

Boomer was just settling down after his morning walk, when suddenly, someone called his name. Then, Boomer saw his leash.

4

But instead, Boomer and his owner raced outside, down the driveway, and onto a big yellow bus. Boomer was going for a ride!

6

Boomer was very excited—he thought he was going for another walk. **1**

5

Comprehension Skills

During the rereading of this selection, the children will focus on specific techniques, tools, and skills to help them better understand what they read. Comprehension skill activities are provided in this column in Lessons 2 through 5.

The bus stopped again and again. Boomer had never been on a ride with so many children. The ride was very noisy. **2**

7

② Reading and Responding

Comprehension Strategies

Introducing Strategy Use

Modeling

③ Clarifying *This picture is a little confusing. I'm not quite sure what I'm looking at. Oh, when I look again I see that it is the inside of the school. When I hear the words and look at the picture, I can see where Boomer was going. Looking at it this way, from overhead, lets me see more. Its like looking down from upstairs.*

Modeling

④ Predicting *Boomer seems to be a little confused, but I predict he'll feel better as soon as he figures out he's going to have fun. Do you have any predictions?*

Modeling

⑤ Clarifying *I need to clarify something. This says, "A grownup started talking." But I don't know who. I know that Boomer is at school. I know that teachers, the principal, custodians, and others are grownups. They are in a classroom. A teacher talks in the classroom. This grownup must be the teacher.*

Teacher Tip Remind the children that in the unit activity they will be creating a picture/story book about their own school. Encourage children to think about what they would show Boomer in their school.

After a while, the bus stopped in front of a big building. The children climbed out. Boomer climbed out, too. He was quickly led inside, up some stairs, around a corner, and down a hallway. ④

8

Boomer was led to the back of the room, a loud bell rang. A grownup started talking. Everyone sat down and listened. ⑤

10

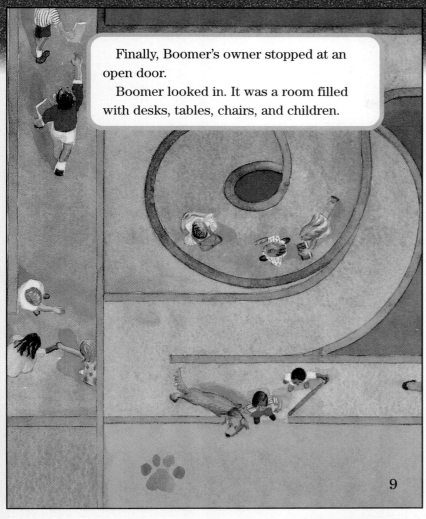

Finally, Boomer's owner stopped at an open door.

Boomer looked in. It was a room filled with desks, tables, chairs, and children.

9

When the grownup finished talking, the children jumped up from their seats. Boomer was let off his leash. He didn't know what to do first!

11

Comprehension Skills

During the rereading of this selection, the children will focus on specific techniques, tools, and skills to help them better understand what they read. Comprehension skill activities are provided in this column in Lessons 2 through 5.

2 Reading and Responding

Comprehension Strategies

Introducing Strategy Use

Modeling

6 Clarifying *There are toys to share, games to play, and pictures to paint. How can Boomer share and paint and play? The pictures help me understand or clarify this for me—they help me see what Boomer is doing in the classroom. I see that Boomer is running around and playing with the children as they share and paint.*

Does anyone else need to clarify something? Does anyone have any questions about the story?

 Clarifying Tell the children that when we read, it is important to understand what is happening in the story. Sometimes, a story can be confusing. When anything is confusing, we need to stop to clarify, or figure out what is happening.

There were toys to share . . .

12

. . . games to play . . . **6**

14

. . . pictures to paint . . .

13

and best of all . . . there was lunch!

15

Comprehension Skills

During the rereading of this selection, the children will focus on specific techniques, tools, and skills to help them better understand what they read. Comprehension skill activities are provided in this column in Lessons 2 through 5.

② Reading and Responding

Comprehension Strategies

Introducing Strategy Use

Modeling

❼ Predicting *So far Boomer has played with toys, gotten into paint, played games, and gotten into the lunches. I wonder what is going to happen next? I predict he'll keep on getting into trouble in school. Let's read on and see.*

Modeling

❽ Clarifying *Boomer seems to understand why he's in school, but I'm not sure. Let me think about what's happened and try to clarify this. He had to sit still while his owner shared stories and showed Boomer to the class. I see now. Boomer's owner brought Boomer to school to show to his classmates during sharing time.*

Teacher Tip

Predicting Tell the children that predicting helps to keep them involved in the story. Their predictions are not wild guesses. They are based on clues in the story.

After lunch, Boomer watched as the children gathered together and sat in a circle. Boomer was ready for the next game. But this time, all the children sat quietly. ❼

16

Boomer barked and barked. He was told to be quiet.

Boomer was very confused.

18

Boomer started to get up, but he was told to sit down.

Boomer wiggled and squirmed. He was told to sit still.

17

Then, Boomer was led to the center of the circle. He still wiggled and squirmed. Boomer's owner started talking—sharing stories about Boomer and showing him to the class. **8**

Finally, Boomer understood. He sat still and stayed very quiet. Boomer's owner smiled and gave Boomer a big pat on the head!

19

Comprehension Skills

During the rereading of this selection, the children will focus on specific techniques, tools, and skills to help them better understand what they read. Comprehension skill activities are provided in this column in Lessons 2 through 5.

② Reading and Responding

Comprehension Strategies

Introducing Strategy Use

Modeling

⑨ Predicting *The story seems to say that because a loud bell rang, it was time for Boomer to take another bus ride. From what we already know about how school works, what will happen next? Does anyone have a prediction? (I predict that the bell is the dismissal bell for the day, and that Boomer is going to ride the school bus home.)*

Suddenly, a loud bell rang and it was time to take another bus ride. At each bus stop, Boomer's new friends patted him good-bye. ⑨

Then, the bus stopped at Boomer's house. Boomer wagged his tail and bounded off the bus for home.

20

Teacher Tip

Because strategies are tools for understanding text, be sure to explain why you are using the strategies as you are reading and thinking aloud.

21

Discussing the Selection

Have the children share their thoughts about the selection. Have them tell about all the things that happened to Boomer at school. Encourage them to tell what they liked best about the story and to ask any questions about school the story might have sparked. Write these questions on strips of paper and place them on the Concept/Question Board. Remind the children that throughout the unit, you will try to find answers to these questions.

Purposes for Reading

Remind the children that we read both for entertainment and to get information. Ask them what information they found out from "Boomer Goes to School." If any children gave purposes for reading this story, ask them to recall those purposes and to tell if they were pleased with how the story turned out.

Reading and Responding

Home Connection, p. 3

Responding to Literature

Print Awareness

Directionality of Print

Invite volunteers to come to the **Big Book** and point to the first word on page 11 and the last word on the page.

Have other volunteers show how words are read from left to right by pointing to each word in a line of print.

Page Numbers

Have volunteers come to the **Big Book** and point to the page numbers. Say each number as the child points to it.

Home Connection

Distribute **Home Connection** page 3, a letter that tells families about "Boomer Goes to School." The letter also suggests activities that can be done at home. This letter is available in English and Spanish.

Exploring the Theme

Theme Connections

Think About It

Tell the children that you are going to ask them some questions that you want them to think about. Explain that thinking about something is different from talking about it. Tell them to close their eyes as you ask a question and think about the answer. Read each question aloud.

- What did Boomer like about school?
- Why do you think Boomer got mixed up at school?

Compliment the children for not telling their answers out loud.

Talk About It

Invite the children to share their thoughts about the questions now. Tell them about appropriate group discussion routines. For example, tell them not to answer until they are called on and to listen attentively when their classmates are speaking.

Supporting Reflection

Explain to the children that they will be making a picture/story book about their class and school. Tell them they will be:

- getting their pictures taken with Boomer and their classmates and discovering the school with him.
- working together to compose a story about them and their school.

Teacher Tip **Unit Activity** If you do not have access to a camera, consider having the children draw pictures of the people they meet and the places they find Boomer.

Check the Reading link of the **SRA** Web page for links to School-related Web sites.
http://www.sra-4kids.com

③ Integrating the Curriculum

Teacher Tip Early writing activities should be tailored to meet the needs of your group. Many children feel very comfortable with the idea of "writing" at this stage. Others may not feel that they know how to write yet. What is important at this level is simply to integrate writing into their daily activities.

Language Arts

Independent and Collaborative Writing

Writing Activities

Set aside some time each day for writing. Talk with children about some things that people write. What kinds of things would they like to write? Make a list of ideas. This might include letters, stories, lists, postcards, poems, and so on. Be sure that the children understand that they can use pictures, letters, words, and so on, in their writing.

If you are doing the picture/story book as a unit activity, explain to the children that they will be working together with you to compose a story that *tells* about what the photographs or pictures *show*.

Listening, Speaking, Viewing

Listening Attentively

Through this activity, the children will discover that, if they listen attentively, they can hear many things they might not otherwise notice.

- Ask the children to sit with closed eyes and just listen for a few moments. Tell them that if they listen carefully, they will find they can hear sounds from outdoors, indoors, and even sounds they are making themselves.

- Name two or three sounds that you can hear, and ask the children if they can hear them, too. (*Sounds they might hear might include the sounds of the wind or the rain; of cars or trucks driving by on the street outside; of children's voices or footsteps in the hall, or the sound of their own rustling.*)

- Tell the children keep their eyes covered and that you will make some sounds now.

- Explain that they should raise their hands if they think they know what they've heard. Repeat their answer in a complete sentence: "John heard the sound of a _____."

- Call on several children to describe something they can hear, inviting the others to listen for each sound described.

Integrating the Curriculum

Vocabulary

Comparing Word Meanings

- Explain that one way to figure out *exactly* what a word means is to compare it to other words that mean almost the same thing. Say that when we compare two things, we think about the ways the things are alike and the ways that they are different.

- Help the children to explore and refine their understanding of each of the words below by asking them to discuss, first, how the meanings of the two words are similar and, then, how they are different. For example, ask them first about the ways in which a *bus* and a *car* are the same as each other; then ask them how a *bus* and a *car* are different from each other.

bus	car	table	desk
bus	truck	book	page
table	chair	pages	paper

Research in Action

Vocabulary

Although children pick up words quickly, they are often satisfied with meanings that are inappropriately specific or overly vague. Examining the specific differences in meaning that set one word apart from another serves not only to refine children's understanding of the words in study but to lay the foundations for more productive and powerful vocabulary in general. *(Marilyn Jager Adams)*

Across the Curriculum

Drama

Act Out a Scene

The children might enjoy acting out scenes from "Boomer Goes to School." Assign children to be Boomer, his owner, the teacher, and other children in the school.

- Reread a scene and have the actors dramatize it.
- Encourage all children to participate in at least one scene.

Sounds and Letters

 If any of the children seem less than confident with the meaning of the words *stout*, *teapot*, or any other word in the song, take time to revisit those words and their meanings. Whether children learn a word is strongly influenced by the number of times and contexts in which they hear it. *(Marilyn Jager Adams)*

Meeting Individual Needs

ESL

Rhyming Explore with English-language learners words in their own languages that rhyme. Ask them to recite the rhyming words they know. Then move to rhyming words in English.

Sounds, Letters, and Language

Names

- Tell the children to come to the front of the room with their Name Necklaces when they hear you call their names. Working with three names at a time, call children to the front of the room.
- As the children arrive, have them form a row and announce their names to the class. Then have them be seated.

Reading the Big Book *Pickled Peppers*
"I'm a Little Teapot," pages 6–7

- Gather children around the ***Big Book*** *Pickled Peppers*. Point to the words on the front and say, *"Pickled Peppers."*
- Turn to "I'm a Little Teapot" on pages 6–7, and read the title to the children. Review the song by singing it through once and pointing to each line of the text.
- Ask the children to stand up. Tell them you want them to pretend they are short, stout teapots. Make sure the children have enough elbow room. Teach them the motions for the song so that they can mimic you.
- Sing and mime the song once or twice with the children.
- Sing the song again, touching each word as you say it. When you get to each word that you have mimed, ask the children to show the action that goes with the word.
- Have the children gather around you and the ***Big Book*** again. Explain to them that there are some rhyming words in the song. Name and point to the word *stout*. Name and point to the word *spout*. Explain that when all but the very beginnings of words sound alike, like *stout* and *spout*, we say that they *rhyme*.
- Ask the children if they can hear the rhyme, and ask them to repeat after you: *stout, spout*. Explain that *stout* and *spout* rhyme because they both end in *out*.
- Read the song through again. Ask if anyone hears more words that sound like or rhyme with *stout* and *spout*. If anyone suggests a nonrhyming word, such as *teapot*, say the two words together: *teapot, stout*. Say, "I don't hear the same sound, *out*, in these two words."
- Say the rhyming words again and ask the children to listen for the rhyme and to stop you when you come to a rhyming word. Recite the song slowly, emphasizing *stout, spout, shout,* and *out*.

Phonemic Awareness

Listening for the First, Middle, or Last Sounds

- Tell the children to close their eyes. Explain that you are going to play another listening game with sounds.

- Play or make two sounds. Remind the children to raise their hands if they think they know what they have heard. Encourage them to answer in complete sentences: "First I heard a _____ , then I heard a _____ ."

- Next, play two sounds, and then ask the children, "What was the *first* sound you heard?" Repeat this three or four times, and help the children answer using the word *first*.

- Play two sounds and ask the children, "What was the *last* sound you heard?" Repeat several times, this time helping the children answer using the word *last*.

- When the children are comfortable with identifying the first and last sounds of a sequence, add a third sound. For several rounds, ask them, "What was the *middle* sound?" Again, help them answer using the word *middle*.

Feeling the Rhythm

- Gather the children around you in a circle and review "Polly Put the Kettle On," emphasizing the names *Polly* and *Sukey*.

Polly put the kettle on	**Sukey take it off again**
Polly put the kettle on	**Sukey take it off again**
Polly put the kettle on	**Sukey take it off again**
We'll all have tea	**They've all gone away**

- Ask children to help you say the rhyme. Recite the first line, and point to individual children to say the second and the third lines. As they say their lines, clap softly along with them.

- Then have the group together say, "We'll all have tea." Encourage the children to clap along as everyone says this last line.

- Repeat for the second verse, saying the last line together. Invite the children to clap the rhythm with you throughout the second verse.

- Then say the rhyme again. For the second verse, choose a child to say his or her name in place of "Sukey." Continue a few more times with other children, encouraging the rest of the class to keep clapping in rhythm.

Teacher Tip Along with learning to listen for and isolate single sounds, children need to learn how to describe and analyze these sounds. Listening for the first, middle, and last sounds in a series; learning to identify those sounds; and using the words *first, middle,* and *last* (or *beginning, middle,* and *end*) will help them to do this.

Assessment

✓ **Informal** Notice which students seem confused by the listening exercise. Assess whether the children understand the concepts *first, middle,* and *last*. Plan to meet with children who are having difficulty during Independent Work Time.

Meeting Individual Needs

ESL

Sound Sequence To teach *first, middle,* and *last* (or beginning, middle, and last) word sounds to English-language learners, use a book, a list, or a row of people or objects to demonstrate. Point to the first object as you say, "first." Ask the students to repeat the word. Then continue with "middle" and "last." Do the sequence again with other objects.

Phonics CD-ROM

Use the ***Phonics*** CD-ROM for activities that support the Phonemic Awareness Lessons.

Sounds and Letters

Letter Recognition

Letter Names

Alphabet Song

■ Remind the children that they learned this version of the "Alphabet Song", and that it is just a little different from other versions they might know. Invite the children to tell what they remember about why it is important to learn the letters of the alphabet *(Every word is made up of letters)*.

■ Have the children listen as you sing the song or play it on the ***Listening Libraries Audiocassette.***

■ Tell the children that you will be singing the "Alphabet Song" again, but that this time they will be looking at the ***Alphabet Cards*** as you point out each letter and sing its name. Ask them to follow along closely and listen as you point to each letter.

■ Sing the song through once as the children listen. Point to each letter on the ***Alphabet Cards*** as you sing its name. To reinforce the rhythm of the song, clap as you sing the letters that come before each pause: *G, N, Q, T, W,* and *Z.* If necessary, see instructions in the Appendix.

■ Ask the children to sing with you. Continue to point to the letters and clap at the appropriate times as the children sing. Sing the song through in this manner several times.

ABCDEFG

HIJKLMN

OPQ

RST

UVW

XYZ

Now I never will forget

How to say the alphabet.

Intervention

Letter Names Have pairs of children listen together to the ***Listening Libraries Audiocassette*** of the "Alphabet Song." Encourage them to sing along quietly, until they feel more comfortable with the order of letters in the song.

Assessment

✔ **Formal Matching Letters** To assess the children's ability to match letters, have them complete ***Skills Assessment*** page 1.

Letter Shapes

Slanting Lines

Make sure that all the children can see you write, either on the chalkboard or on an overhead projector. Have children mimic your strokes in the air with their fingers.

- Tell the children they are going to practice making slanting lines. Write several slanting lines to demonstrate.

- Ask the children to use their fingers to draw slanting lines with you. Make a small starting dot and draw a slanting line. Have children mimic your line in the air. Repeat the stroke several times, slanting both right and left and saying "slant right" or "slant left." Watch to be sure children are moving their fingers on a slant with you.

- Have children use pencils and paper to make slanting strokes as you say "start at the top and slant down (right or left)."

Practice

Tell the children that they are going to practice making slanted lines because many letters have slanted lines in them. On **Blackline Master 3,** point to the complete *A.* Then point to the incomplete *A* and note that it is missing a line. Tell the children to place their pencils at the dot and draw a slanted line and so complete the letter.

 Teacher Tip **Letter Formation** Some children may do better at forming letters if they write on a chalkboard or on large chart paper at first.

 Teacher Tip **Slanted Lines** You may want to use *Blackline Master 2* to have children practice tracing slanted lines.

Assessment

✔ **Informal** Continue to observe the children making letter strokes. Plan to work with small groups that may be having difficulty.

Reading and Responding

"Boomer Goes to School"
Pages 4–9 of *School*

This selection is taught in six lessons:

Lesson 1	Lesson 3	Lesson 5
Lesson 2	Lesson 4	Lesson 6

Boomer Goes to School

Constance W. McGeorge
illustrated by Mary Whyte

Boomer was just settling down after his morning walk, when suddenly, someone called his name. Then, Boomer saw his leash.

4

Activate Prior Knowledge

Ask the children to tell what they remember about Boomer from the previous reading of the story.

Preview and Prepare

Browse

- Open the **Big Book** *School* to pages 4–5. Read and point to the title and to the names of the author and illustrator.
- Turn through the first six pages of "Boomer Goes to School," letting the children discuss the pictures. Ask them if they notice anything new or different from the first time they looked at these pictures.
- Do the same with the print.

Vocabulary

Concept Vocabulary
Words About School

To help the children understand some of the things that are new for Boomer, discuss the following words, which tell about some of the ways children behave in school:

listen   sit   read   stand up

Talk with the children about when they might hear those words in the classroom. Then ask volunteers which of these words Boomer might know. *(sit)*

Reading Recommendations

- Point to the first word on the first page of the story. Be sure children understand that when we read, we start with the first word on the first page of a story. We then read from left to right and top to bottom. Point to each word as you read.

- Encourage the children to point out parts of this story section that they especially like.

Using Reading Strategies

During the first reading of "Boomer Goes to School," you modeled the use of the following reading strategies:

- Clarifying
- Predicting

For your convenience, the strategy models from the first reading of the selection are reproduced in this lesson in the form of reminders. You may choose not to use these reminders with your class, or to use them only with children who need extra help or who missed the first reading of the selection.

Teacher Tip In the next four lessons you will be rereading portions of the story "Boomer Goes to School." In these rereads it is important to continue to emphasize the things good readers do when they read.

Building Comprehension Skills

Rereading a selection allows readers to apply skills that give them a more complete understanding of what they read. Some of these follow-up comprehension skills, such as *Clarifying and Categorizing, Cause and Effect, Sequence,* and *Compare and Contrast,* help readers to organize the information in a selection. Other skills, such as *Drawing Conclusions,* lead them to a deeper understanding of the selection, or to a "reading between the lines."

In this lesson, you will introduce the children to the comprehension skill *Drawing Conclusions.*

② Reading and Responding

Comprehension Strategies

Introducing Strategy Use

Modeling

❶ Predicting *Remind the children of the predictions they made at this point in the story. Were they correct? How did they find out if their predictions were correct? Reinforce the idea that good readers make predictions about what will happen in a story. Then, as they read, they check to see if their predictions were correct.*

Modeling

❷ Clarifying *Ask the children how they clarified, or figured out what kind of bus Boomer was on. Remind them that, as they read, they can often figure out something that confuses them by looking at the pictures in the story.*

Teacher Tip Remind the children of the picture/story big book they are creating. Invite them to think about which center or activity they would like to explain to Boomer.

Boomer Goes to School

Constance W. McGeorge
illustrated by Mary Whyte

Boomer was just settling down after his morning walk, when suddenly, someone called his name. Then, Boomer saw his leash.

4

But instead, Boomer and his owner raced outside, down the driveway, and onto a big yellow bus. Boomer was going for a ride!

6

Boomer was very excited—he thought he was going for another walk. **1**

5

The bus stopped again and again. Boomer had never been on a ride with so many children. The ride was very noisy. **2**

7

Comprehension Skills

Drawing Conclusions

- Tell the children that when we read, the author tells us many things. We learn about the characters, about where they are, and about what they do. However, authors do not always tell us everything.

- Explain that sometimes readers have to use clues from the story, and information they already know themselves, to figure out things in a story. Tell the children that we call this "drawing conclusions," or using the clues the author provides, and what we know already, to understand what we read.

- Reread page 7 and ask the children if the words tell them that Boomer is on a school bus. *(no)* Point out that the author and the illustrator give clues that Boomer is on a school bus. Have the children identify some of the clues. *(children, color of the bus)*

- Remind the children that they know that a school bus makes several stops and that children get on the bus at every stop. They also know that a school bus is always yellow, just like the one in the picture. They used what they know about school buses, and the clues in the words and pictures, to conclude that Boomer was on a school bus.

Reading and Responding

> After a while, the bus stopped in front of a big building. The children climbed out. Boomer climbed out, too. He was quickly led inside, up some stairs, around a corner, and down a hallway. ④

Comprehension Strategies

Introducing Strategy Use

Modeling

❸ **Clarifying** *Pause to remind the children that looking at the picture closely and rereading the text helped you to clarify, or figure out what this picture showed. Reinforce the idea that this is a strategy used by good readers to help them understand what they read.*

Modeling

❹ **Predicting** *Call on volunteers to tell their predictions and ask if they were correct and how they found out if they were correct.*

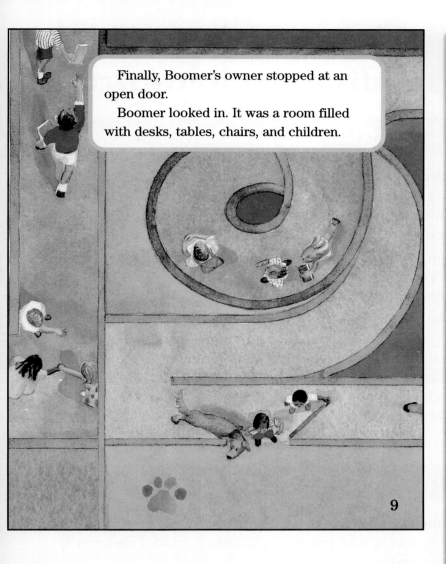

Finally, Boomer's owner stopped at an open door.

Boomer looked in. It was a room filled with desks, tables, chairs, and children.

9

Comprehension Skills

Drawing Conclusions

■ Reread the last sentence on page 9 and ask where Boomer was. Ask the children to identify the clue words the author used that helped them guess that Boomer was in a classroom. *(desk, chairs)*

Discussing the Selection

Have children retell what has happened to Boomer so far. Ask them to tell about what Boomer's owner has been doing during the day.

Teacher Tip The children will have many opportunities to learn about drawing conclusions. Don't expect mastery or complete understanding at this stage.

Reading and Responding

Responding to Literature

Literature Appreciation

Have the children examine the illustrations in "Boomer Goes to School" to identify the various feelings Boomer has throughout the story. Ask them if they can tell how Boomer feels about school from looking at the pictures.

Invite the children to make facial expressions that show how Boomer felt. Ask the children what other feelings students might have about school. Invite them to share their "feeling faces" with their classmates.

Boomer may be a new character for the children, but they may be aware of another storybook animal who went to school with its owner. Ask the children if they know the rhyme "Mary Had a Little Lamb." Call on volunteers to recite the rhyme. Recite the rhyme until all the children can say it. Invite the children to share what feelings Mary and her lamb might have had when they found out that a lamb was not allowed in school.

Home Connection

Distribute **Home Connection** page 5 which encourages families to take part in the process of teaching their children to read. This letter is available in English and Spanish.

Home Connection, p. 5

Exploring the Theme

Theme Connections

Think About It

Ask the children to think about how they get to the classroom each day. Encourage them to use directions such as *through the door, down the hall,* and *past the office.*

Supporting Reflection

Remind the children that you will be working together to make a class book about school.

- Show then the book you have constructed for this purpose (large heavy sheets of paper bound together with ribbon or yarn). Read the title, *Our Classroom and Our School*, and have the children read it with you.

- Display Boomer, and remind the children that he is new to school. Suggest that they show Boomer what he can do in school.

- Call on the children to introduce Boomer to some classroom activity *(such as identifying colors or counting)*, or explain some routine to him *(such as cleaning up after snack time)*. Have the class listen and ask questions about anything they might wonder about.

- Take each child's picture with Boomer. If possible, use a camera that produces instant pictures.

 Teacher Tip If necessary, get the permission of families to take children's photographs.

 Teacher Tip **Unit Activity** If you do not have access to a camera, consider having the children draw pictures of the people they meet and the places they find Boomer.

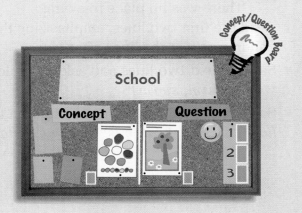

 Check the Reading link of the **SRA** Web page for links to School-related Web sites.
http://www.sra-4kids.com

③ Integrating the Curriculum

Teacher Tip Allow those children who do not want to draw to bring in pictures of pets they would like or provide magazines for the children to cut up. Have them paste the pictures on *Blackline Master 4.*

Language Arts

Independent and Collaborative Writing

Choose a Pet

Distribute ***Blackline Master 4.*** Tell the children that the words at the bottom of the page say, "I would like a _____ for a pet at _____ ."

■ Have the children draw a picture of the animal that would be their choice for a pet at home or at school.

■ After each child has completed his or her drawing, read the sentence as you point to each word. Have each child dictate words to fill in the blank spaces. Print his or her word choices on the writing lines and read the sentence once more, inviting the child to join in.

■ Have the children share their pictures with the rest of the class.

Vocabulary

Rhyming Words

■ Remind the children of "I'm a Little Teapot." Repeat the rhyme, inviting the children to chime in whenever they feel comfortable. Then review the words that rhyme *(stout, spout, shout, out).*

■ Tell the children that they are going to listen to a silly rhyme. Then read aloud this rhyme:

> Fishy went to school,
> But he thought it was a pool.
> What a surprise for him…
> There was no place to swim!

■ Read the first two lines, emphasizing the rhyming words. Then have the children repeat the lines after you.

■ Say the next two lines and ask the children to identify the rhyming words. *(him, swim)*

■ Say some word pairs and ask children to clap if the words rhyme: *stop, hop; car, star; boat, bus; bug, rug; whale, top; fish, wish.*

Across the Curriculum

Social Studies

Follow a School Map

Purpose
To familiarize students with school locations on a map.

Materials
chart paper, markers, **Big Book** *School*

Procedure
- Before beginning the activity, draw the outline of the classroom on the chart paper. Indicate the doors and your desk. Include any other important areas, such as coat rack and activity centers.
- Ask the children if they have ever seen or used a map. Explain that a map can be used to show where things are and how to get from place to place.
- Explain that the map you have drawn is a map of the classroom. Help the children identify all the areas on the map and suggest labels such as door, play area, and so on.
- Then invite several children to come up to the map and finger-trace the path they take from the door of the classroom to the area where the "morning opening routines" are completed. Prompt them with questions such as:

  Where do you go first? What do we do there?
- You might ask the children to also finger-trace routes they take to their favorite activity center.

Sounds and Letters

Meeting Individual Needs

ESL

Numbers Help To help English-language learners memorize the rhyme, "One, Two, Buckle My Shoe," write the numerals on self-stick notes and put them next to the equivalent words. Pantomime and act out each verse. Point to each numeral as you say the word aloud, and ask the children to repeat the number word. Continue until the children feel comfortable with the rhyme.

Sounds, Letters, and Language

Reading the Big Book *Pickled Peppers*
"One, Two, Buckle My Shoe," pages 26–27

- Gather the children around the ***Big Book*** *Pickled Peppers*. Turn to "One, Two, Buckle My Shoe" on pages 26–27 and help children say the title with you.

- Then read *"illustrated by Ju-Hong Chen."* Tell them that the illustrator drew the pictures that go with the rhyme.

- Read the rhyme aloud, pointing to each word from left to right and each line from top to bottom, emphasizing the rhyming words. Say *two* and *shoe*, and remind the children that both words end with the /oo/ sound. Invite children who know the rhyme to join in.

- Draw the children's attention to the illustrations. Point to the word *shoe* and say it. Ask children to find the picture of the shoe. Have a child point to the picture. Continue with *door, sticks, straight* (ask them, "Are the sticks lined up straight?"), and *hen.*

- Now read the poem again, pointing word by word. Remind children that words are groups of letters. Ask children to point to a word or count the number of words in a line.

- Reread the rhyme, pointing to each number as it is named. Say the number, then have the children say it with you.

- Write the numerals *1* and *2* on the chalkboard. Read the next line, and write the numerals *3* and *4* on the board. Continue through the rhyme in this way.

- After finishing the rhyme, point to each number on the board and say it, inviting the children to join you. Then below each numeral, write the number name. Tell the children that these are the names for these numbers. Point to each numeral, say it, then point to each number word and say it. Point again and have the children repeat everything with you. You might then ask volunteers to come to the board and touch the numeral or the number word that you say, for example, "Touch the name of *three*," or "Touch the number *two*."

Phonemic Awareness

Listening for the First, Middle, or Last Words

Now that the children have had some practice listening for the position of sounds, repeat the exercise as described in Lesson 2, only this time use words and pictures instead of sounds. Use the **Pocket Chart Picture Cards** *door, hen, shoe, sticks,* to have children identify *first, middle,* and *last.*

- First have the children listen for two words as you display each word's picture on the **Pocket Chart.** Next, place three words in the **Pocket Chart** and have the children identify the words as the *first, middle,* and *last* words.

- Rearrange the pictures and ask children to identify the *middle* picture, the *last* picture, and the *first* picture now. Encourage children to respond with complete sentences, for example: *Shoe is the middle picture.* Keep changing the set of pictures and their positions, and continue the activity.

Research in Action

Children want to be read to, and they have an unstoppable desire to make rhymes and sing. Combining this aural/oral work with the printed word is an excellent way to help children learn the form of language. Use of the **Pocket Chart** will allow you to create a visual environment for the study of words and sentences. You can use this chart to display **Pocket Chart Letter Cards, Word Cards,** and **Picture Cards.** In addition, use of the **Pocket Chart** allows you and the children to easily manipulate letters, words, and pictures which aids in print awareness and letter recognition and engages the children in learning.

(Marilyn Jager Adams)

1 Sounds and Letters

PHONEMIC AWARENESS

Word Substitution

Through the use of an activity such as a name poem, you can reinforce the idea that sentences are made up of separate words. When one word in the poem changes (in this case, a name), the sentence changes. In addition, the name poem causes the entire focus of the children's attention to change—a new name calls for a new child to respond.

■ Play the game Who Ate the Cookie from the Cookie Jar? Repeat the lines with the children several times, helping them to remember the lines, until everyone knows the words. Then try it with one child.

■ Collect all the Name Necklaces and place them in front of you. Take a Name Necklace and hold it up. Wait for that child to recognize his or her name and say it. If no one recognizes the name, point to it, say it, and then start the game with that child participating:

Teacher: Karey ate the cookie from the cookie jar.

Karey: Who me?

Teacher: Yes, you!

Karey: Couldn't be.

Teacher: Then who?

■ Stop here, hold up another necklace, and wait for the child to recognize his or her name and say it. Then continue the game as above. Give several children a chance to recognize their names and play the game.

Phonics CD-ROM

Use the *Phonics* CD-ROM for activities that support the Phonemic Awareness Lessons.

Letter Recognition

Letter Names

"Alphabet Song"

Introduce the **Lion Puppet** and tell children that this puppet will be helping the class learn more about letters. Remind children that the "Alphabet Song" will help them remember the names of the letters in the alphabet.

- Review the song by asking the class to teach it to the puppet. Tap your foot as children reach the letters G, N, Q, T, W, and Z.
- Sing the song again, but only up to G as the children listen. Clap on G. Repeat singing the line slowly, pointing to each letter.
- Ask volunteers to point to each letter as the class sings the line. You might have the puppet point along with each volunteer.
- For further reinforcement, have the puppet sing the song, but pause at the end of each line. Encourage the children to supply the missing letter for the puppet, and then have everyone sing the line together.

Letter Shapes

Curves

Make sure that all children can see you write, and have them mimic your strokes in the air with their fingers.

- Make **Blackline Master 5** into a transparency and project the "curve" shape on the chalkboard or a piece of chart paper.
- Tell children they are going to practice making curves. Write several curves to demonstrate.
- Ask children to use their fingers to draw curves with you. Make a small starting dot and draw a curve. Have children mimic your curve in the air. Repeat the stroke several times, curving both right and left and saying "curve right" or "curve left."
- Have children use crayons and paper to make curves as you say, "Start here and curve around this way to the right." Repeat, curving to the left.

Assessment

✓ **Informal** Continue to observe the children making letter strokes. Plan to work with those children having trouble during independent work time.

② Reading and Responding

"Boomer Goes to School"
Pages 10–15 of *School*

This selection is taught in six lessons:

| Lesson 1 | Lesson 3 | Lesson 5 |
| Lesson 2 | Lesson 4 | Lesson 6 |

Boomer was led to the back of the room, a loud bell rang. A grownup started talking. Everyone sat down and listened. ⑤

10

Activate Prior Knowledge

Discuss the routine your class follows first in the morning. Ask the children to tell which things are done every day and which things are done only on certain days. Then invite the children to tell which of these things was new to them and which things they already knew; for example, some children may already have known how to walk in a line, but did not know how to sing a "good morning" song.

Ask volunteers to summarize what has happened in the story so far.

Preview and Prepare

Browse

- Display the *School* **Big Book,** opened to pages 4–5. Point to and read aloud the title of the selection and the names of the author and illustrator. Turn to pages 10–11, and have the children discuss what they see Boomer doing in the pictures.

Vocabulary

Selection Vocabulary

Write the following words on the chalkboard and say them aloud:

share   paint   play

- Tell children these words all name things to do in school.
- Ask children to stand with a partner and to pantomime actions as you say each word. Then have them listen for these words as you read this section. Encourage them to also be alert for other "doing" words they might hear.

Reading Recommendations

- To reinforce children's awareness of print, point to each word as you read. Remind children that we read the words from left to right and then we move down the page from top to bottom.
- Encourage the children to stop you if they have questions or want to comment on what is happening.

Reading Strategies

During the first reading of "Boomer Goes to School," you modeled the use of the following reading strategies:

- Predicting
- Clarifying

For your convenience, the strategy models from the first reading of the selection are reproduced in this lesson in the form of reminders. You may choose not to use these reminders with your class, or to use them only with children who need extra help or who missed the first reading of the selection.

Building Comprehension Skills

In this lesson you will continue to work with the comprehension skill *Drawing Conclusions*.

② Reading and Responding

Comprehension Strategies

Introducing Strategy Use

Modeling

❺ Clarifying *Remind the children that you were confused about which grownup was talking at this point in the story. Tell them that when good readers are confused by something they read, they stop to clarify, or figure out what is going on. Sometimes they do this by thinking about what they already know and applying that knowledge to what they read.*

 Teacher Tip Remind the children to think about which class activity or center they will describe to Boomer for the picture story book.

Boomer was led to the back of the room, a loud bell rang. A grownup started talking. Everyone sat down and listened. ❺

10

There were toys to share . . .

12

When the grownup finished talking, the children jumped up from their seats. Boomer was let off his leash. He didn't know what to do first!

11

. . . pictures to paint . . .

13

Comprehension Skills

Drawing Conclusions

■ Remind the children how to use what they know and clues in the story to *draw conclusions* to figure out on page 9 that Boomer was in school.

Reading and Responding

Comprehension Strategies

Introducing Strategy Use

Modeling
6 Clarifying *Ask the children how you clarified, or figured out what the text says here.*

. . . games to play . . . **6**

14

and best of all . . . there was lunch!

15

Comprehension Skills

Drawing Conclusions

■ Reread the sentence on page 15: "and best of all . . . there was lunch!" Discuss what children know about dogs and what they see in the picture. How does this help them know that Boomer thinks lunch is the best time of all?

Discussing the Selection

■ Have the children tell about what they think is the funniest or most interesting part of the story.

■ Remind the children to tell why they feel this way, and help them identify specific items in the text or illustrations to support their ideas.

Reading and Responding

Home Connection, p. 7

Responding to Literature

Literature Appreciation

Talk to the children about good storytelling and listening practices, including speaking in a voice loud enough to be heard by their audience and listening carefully with their eyes on the storyteller. Invite volunteers to take the part of Boomer's owner and to tell the class about Boomer. Remind them to use some of the good storytelling techniques that you just described.

Home Connection

Distribute **Home Connection** page 7 which asks families to help you identify the reading interests of their children. This letter is available in English and Spanish.

Exploring the Theme

Theme Connections

Talk About It

Invite the children to think about the way Boomer behaved in this part of the story. Then have them tell about their pet or a pet they know. Ask volunteers to tell how their pet might behave in class. Prompt the discussion with questions such as:

What would happen if you brought a pet to school?
How do you think your pet would behave?
What would happen if everyone brought their pets on the same day?

③ Integrating the Curriculum

Language Arts

Independent and Collaborative Writing

Writing Ideas

Choose one or more of the following independent and collaborative writing activities, according to the interests and needs of your students:

- Make a list of all the things that went wrong for Boomer during his day in school.

- Review Boomer's problems in school and invite the children to talk about any problems they may have with school routines. Write a group story about the problems and how they can be solved.

- Remind them that they will be writing about the pictures in their picture/story big book.

 Teacher Tip All writing activities should be geared to the needs and development level of the children. Adapt or change the suggested ideas accordingly.

Listening, Speaking, Viewing

Pictures Tell Stories

Explain to the children that they are going to look at an art selection from the **Big Book** *Pictures Tell Stories*. Tell them that, just like reading words on a page, art can tell stories about many different things.

- Show the children the two fine art pieces on page 16: ***Dynamism of Dog on a Leash*** by **Giacomo Balla** and ***Two Children with Their Dogs*** by **Francisco de Goya y Lucientes.** Ask them what each painting makes them think about. Have them predict what "story" each picture might tell. Give all the children a chance to participate.

- Read the text for each painting to the children. Ask them if they can remember a time in the selection "Boomer Goes to School" when Boomer was going fast. Can they remember a time when he was standing still?

Pictures can tell stories about animals.

This little dog is in a hurry.

Here are two big dogs standing still. Can you find both dogs?

Dynamism of a Dog on a Leash. 1912. Giacomo Balla. Oil on canvas. 35.4 x 43.25 in. Albright-Knox Art Gallery, Buffalo, NY. Bequest of A. Conger Goodyear and gift of George F. Goodyear, 1964. ©1999 Giacomo Balla/Licensed by VAGA, New York, NY.

Two Children with Their Dogs. Francisco de Goya y Lucientes. Museo del Prado, Madrid, Spain. Photo: Scala/Art Resources, NY.

16

Pictures Tell Stories page 16

③ Integrating the Curriculum

Teacher Tip You may find it necessary to lead the children through many examples until they catch on.

Vocabulary

Comparing Word Meanings

■ Remind the children that one way to understand what is special about any word is to compare it to other words with similar meanings. Ask them if they recall what it means to compare two things. If necessary, remind them that when we compare two things, we think about the ways that they are like each other and the ways that they are different from each other.

■ Help the children to explore and refine their understanding of each of the words below by asking them first to discuss how the meanings of the two words are similar and then how they are different.

pages/cover	cover/title
title/story	title/author
word/letter	author/illustrator

Across the Curriculum

Social Studies

Transportation

Boomer and his owner take a bus to school. Ask the children how they get to school. Discuss with them other methods of transportation that might be used to get to school.

- Help them make a large classification chart showing "ways of traveling." Headings on the chart might include:

    To school
    To the store
    On vacation

- Have the children bring in pictures from old magazines or newspapers showing different ways to get places, and paste them on the chart under the appropriate heading.

- As an extension, the children might enjoy discussing how children who live in very different places from them might get to school. For example, how might children in a snowy land get to school? Children in the desert? Children on the moon? In addition, you might discuss how weather affects transportation.

1 Sounds and Letters

Sounds, Letters, and Language

Reading the Big Book *Pickled Peppers*
"One, Two, Buckle My Shoe," pages 26–27

Display the **Big Book** *Pickled Peppers*, and have the children gather around the book with you. Turn to "One, Two, Buckle My Shoe," pages 26–27, and ask a volunteer to say the name of the rhyme. If necessary, say the title aloud and then ask the children to repeat it. Point to and read the line *"illustrated by Ju-Hong Chen,"* and ask if anyone remembers what this means. Remind the children that the illustrator drew the pictures that go with the poem.

- Remind the children that they have already heard this rhyme, and invite them to join in. Read the rhyme aloud, tracking the print with your hand. Then reread the rhyme, having the children chime in on the number words.

- Tell the children that you will be putting "One, Two, Buckle My Shoe" on the **Pocket Chart**. Explain that some of the cards you will be using will have words on them, some will have numbers on them, and some will have pictures.

- Set out the following **Pocket Chart Picture Cards**, face up on a desk near the **Pocket Chart**: *shoe, door, straight sticks,* and *hen.* Place *1/2/Buckle/my* on the chart. Ask a child to locate the **Picture Card** that completes the line. When a child picks up the *shoe* **Picture Card**, ask him or her to place it in the correct spot on the chart. Then read the first line over again.

- Encourage the children to make some nonsense rhymes for *two: One, two, Buckle my goo, blue, flew, boo,* and so on. If necessary, help them create rhymes by supplying the beginning sound.

- Repeat the steps for the second line of the poem. This time, leave out *4* and ask the children for the correct number to complete the line. Remember to reread the line, and then pause and have the children think of nonsense rhymes for the number.

- Go through the third through fifth lines of the poem, leaving out a number or picture and asking the children to supply it.

Phonemic Awareness

Listening for Missing Sounds

- Ask the children to close their eyes and listen carefully to some sounds. Make (or play) two sounds and have the children identify them.
- Then have them close their eyes and listen again. This time, make just one of the sounds. Have the children tell which sound is missing. Continue with other pairs of sounds.
- Then move on to three sounds, making sure that the children identify each one. Again, have them close their eyes and listen. This time, play only two of the sounds. Have the children identify the missing sound.

Word Substitution

Repeat the game "Who Ate the Cookie from the Cookie Jar?" as a group, using the Name Necklaces. See pg T62

1 **Sounds and Letters**

Teacher Tip **Rhyming Words** Remember that the purpose of these lessons is to develop the children's attention to the *sounds* of language. With that in mind, there is no need to attend to the spellings of words and, indeed, unless the rhyming words are similarly spelled, it may even be confusing to do so.

Teacher Tip If the children supply a word that is essentially correct but doesn't rhyme, for example *home* instead of *house,* ask if *home* and *mouse* rhyme. Lead the children to discover the correct word.

Phonics CD-ROM

Use the **Phonics** CD-ROM for activities that support the Phonemic Awareness Lessons.

PHONEMIC AWARENESS

Rhyme

In this game, you will say all but the last word of a rhyming phrase—
A *cat* is wearing a _____(hat).

Hold up a **Picture Card** for the last word in each of the following phrases and ask the children to complete the phrase with a word that rhymes and that names the picture. Some suggestions are:

A *mouse* who lives in a _____(house).

A *moose* who is drinking some _____(juice).

A *flea* who is in love with a _____(bee).

Some *kittens* wearing some _____(mittens).

A *bug* who crawled under a _____(rug).

I *wish* I had a _____(fish).

A *gnat* who who wore a _____(hat).

Some *mice* who like _____(ice).

Research in Action
Phonemic Awareness

Phonemic awareness is the ability to think about the sounds of words as distinct from their meanings. Because sensitivity to rhyme comes quite easily to most children, rhyme play is an excellent first step toward capturing children's interest in the similarities and differences in the sounds of individual words.   *(Marilyn Jager Adams)*

Letter Recognition

Letter Names

Sing Your Way to *G* Game

Bring out the ***Lion Puppet*** and remind the children that this puppet will be helping the class learn more about letters.

- Before playing the Sing Your Way to *G* game, have the puppet point to the letter *G*, but pretend that it does not know the letter name. Ask the children to help the puppet by singing the Alphabet Song to this letter.

- When the class has sung and stopped at *G*, have the puppet point to other letters between *A* and *G* and have the class sing to each one.

- Let the children know that they can play this game by choosing any letter and singing to it.

Letter Shapes

Curves and Circles

Make sure that all children can see you write, and have them mimic your strokes in the air with their fingers.

- Remind the children that they have already made curves and ask them to use their fingers to draw curves with you.

- Have them look closely at the overhead projector or the chalkboard. Then make a small starting dot and draw a curve. Have the children mimic your curve in the air. Repeat the stroke several times, curving both right and left as you say "curve right" or "curve left."

- Then tell children that they can make circles. Continuing with the curve on the overhead projector or on the chalkboard, show them how to continue a curve all the way around to make a circle.

- Repeat the motion, and have the children mimic your movements in the air. Then have them write circles on sheets of paper.

Assessment

✓ **Informal** Continue to observe the children making letter strokes. Plan to work with those children having difficulty during independent work time.

1 Sounds and Letters

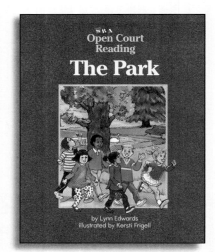

The Park

by Lynn Edwards
illustrated by Kersti Frigell

Pre-Decodable Book 1

Meeting Individual Needs

ESL

Articles Some English-language learners have no experience with the articles *a, an,* and *the* because their languages (for example, Russian) do not use articles. Work with them ahead of time to grasp the use of articles before discussing the high-frequency word *the* with the entire class.

ESL

Rereading Pair English-language learners with English-speaking children to reread the *Pre-Decodable Book.* Ask the English-language learners to teach their partners the name in their own language of the rebus picture.

Teacher Tip

Nondecodable Words Always refer to the inside back cover of the *Pre-Decodable Book* for the words that need to be taught before the students read the book.

Reading a Pre-Decodable Book

About *Pre-Decodable Books*

Each *Pre-Decodable Book* contains a story that engages children's interest as it provides them with opportunities to practice what they are learning in their lessons. These stories each contain *high-frequency words* that most children already have in their spoken vocabularies and that are a basic part of all meaningful stories. Learning to identify high-frequency words quickly, accurately, and effortlessly is a critical part of children's development as fluent, independent readers. Finally, several of the stories introduce children to position words, color words, and number words.

For your convenience, the inside back cover of each book contains a list of the high-frequency words and phonograms and, when appropriate, the position, color, or number words used in the book.

Book 1: *The Park*

High-Frequency Words

The high-frequency word introduced in this story is *the*. Write the word on the board, point to and say it, then have the children say it with you.

Reading Recommendations

- Give each child a copy of the book. Explain that you will read the book together.

- Hold up your book. Read the title aloud, then have the children read it with you. Point to and read the author's name and explain that this is the name of the person who wrote the book. Then point to and read the illustrator's name and explain that this is the name of the person who drew the pictures in the book.

- Allow children to page through the book, commenting on what they see in the pictures and making predictions about what they think the book will tell them.

- Help children find page 3. Hold up your copy of the book and sweep your hand under each line of text. Then read each line, pointing to each word or rebus as you say it. Encourage children to move their hands from left to right across the text as you read together.

- Continue through the book, following the same procedure.

- Reread the book, this time pointing to the picture on each page and asking children to tell what is happening in the picture.

- Invite children to discuss the book as a group.

- Provide many opportunities for children to partner–read.

Responding

- Have the children tell about a park that they like to go to. Invite them to describe what is there and to compare it to the park in the story.

- To review the high-frequency word, write *the* on the chalkboard and say the word. Have children look for *the* in their books and put a finger on the word when they find it. Call on volunteers to "read" the word and show it to the class. Call attention to the spaces before and after the word.

Practice

- For additional practice, you may want to use **Book 1** of the supplemental set of ***Open Court Reading Decodable Books***.

- You may want to make copies for the children of the black-and-white version of this story which is available in the ***Pre-Decodable Takehome Book***.

Research in Action

Pre-Decodable Books play an important role in children's early literacy development by providing them with meaningful "reading" experiences before they are actually reading on their own and by expanding their awareness of the forms and uses of print.

When used with a solid program of instruction in sounds and letters, the books provide children with opportunities to apply their growing knowledge of print concepts, letter names and sounds, and to become familiar with individual words.

Through retelling the story in a ***Pre-Decodable Book,*** predicting or wondering about what will happen, and asking and responding to questions about the book, children not only learn about the relationship between spoken and written language, they learn to think about what they have read and begin to use reading strategies. *(Jan Hirshberg)*

Phonemic Awareness and Phonics Videodisc   Reading a Pre-Decodable Book

Level K – Disc 1 – Side A – Chapter 2

Use the **Phonemic Awareness Videodisc** to preview lessons on *Pre-Decodable Books*. Unit 1 Lesson 4.

Assessment

✓ **Informal** Meet with individual children. Have them read the ***Pre-Decodable Book***. Observe the children's ability to "read" the book fluently. Note whether they recognize the high-frequency word *the*.

② Reading and Responding

"Boomer Goes to School"
Pages 16–19 of *School*

This selection is taught in six lessons:

| Lesson 1 | Lesson 3 | Lesson 5 |
| Lesson 2 | **Lesson 4** | Lesson 6 |

After lunch, Boomer watched as the children gathered together and sat in a circle. Boomer was ready for the next game. But this time, all the children sat quietly. **7**

16

Meeting Individual Needs

ESL

As volunteers act out these words, encourage English-language learners to tell an equivalent word in their language. Tell the children that these two words mean almost the same thing.

Activate Prior Knowledge

Invite the children to talk about what they have learned about Boomer. Ask volunteers to summarize the main events in the story so far.

Preview and Prepare

Browse

- Display the *School* **Big Book.** Turn to the table of contents and read the titles as you point them out. Have a volunteer find and point to "Boomer Goes to School." Invite another volunteer to find the page number next to the title, say the number, and help you turn to that page.
- Turn to pages 16–17 of "Boomer Goes to School." Have children quickly identify anything in the pictures that is familiar to them.

Vocabulary

Selection Vocabulary

Write the following words on the chalkboard and say them aloud:

> wiggled   squirmed

- Tell the children these words name ways to move.
- Ask some volunteers to stand and demonstrate the movements as you read each word.

Reading Recommendations

- Pointing to each word as you read each line reinforces the children's awareness of print. Remind the children that we read the words from left to right and move down the page from top to bottom.
- Encourage children to stop you if they have questions or if there are words they do not understand.

Using Reading Strategies

During the first reading of "Boomer Goes to School," you modeled the use of the following reading strategies:

- Predicting
- Clarifying

For your convenience, the strategy models from the first reading of the selection are reproduced in this lesson in the form of reminders. You may choose not to use these reminders with your class, or to use them only with children who need extra help or who missed the first reading of the selection.

Building Comprehension Skills

In this lesson you will continue to work with the comprehension skill *Drawing Conclusions*.

② Reading and Responding

After lunch, Boomer watched as the children gathered together and sat in a circle. Boomer was ready for the next game. But this time, all the children sat quietly. ❼

16

Comprehension Strategies

Introducing Strategy Use

Modeling

❼ **Confirming Predictions** *At this point, remind the children that you predicted that Boomer would keep on getting in trouble. Ask them if your prediction was correct. Explain that sometimes even good readers make incorrect predictions, and that they learn to see when they are wrong and to correct any misunderstandings they might have.*

Modeling

❽ **Clarifying** *Remind the children that as we read, it is important to make sure that we understand what we are reading. When we are confused, we need to stop and clarify, or figure out what is going on. Ask the children to clarify how they know that Boomer understands what is going on around him at this point in the story.*

Boomer barked and barked. He was told to be quiet.
Boomer was very confused.

18

Boomer started to get up, but he was told to sit down.

Boomer wiggled and squirmed. He was told to sit still.

17

Then, Boomer was led to the center of the circle. He still wiggled and squirmed. Boomer's owner started talking—sharing stories about Boomer and showing him to the class. **8**

Finally, Boomer understood. He sat still and stayed very quiet. Boomer's owner smiled and gave Boomer a big pat on the head!

19

Comprehension Skills

Discussing the Selection

■ Call on children to retell the story through this part. Encourage them to use the familiar "and then" phrase.

② Reading and Responding

Responding to Literature

Reading/Writing Connection

Point out to the children that the events in "Boomer Goes to School" follow a time line, starting when Boomer leaves home on the school bus in the morning, and ending with his return home on the bus after school. Turn through the pages of the story and invite volunteers to identify key events in sequence. Have them use the familiar "and then" phrase to connect the events in a time line.

Distribute **Blackline Master 6,** "Boomer Goes to School."

■ Point to the first frame and say "One day Boomer heard someone call his name. He saw his leash and he thought he was going for a walk."

■ Then continue through the story, pointing to the frames and inviting volunteers to tell the story, using the "and then" phrase.

■ Tell the children that stories can be told in either print or pictures as well as in print and pictures together.

If time permits, make class sets of the following picture frames from **Blackline Master 6:** 2, 3, 6, 8, 9, and 10. Cut out and distribute a set to each child. Have the children arrange the frames on their desks to create their own story of what Boomer did in school. Invite volunteers to share their stories with the class, using good storytelling practices, such as speaking in an audible voice and displaying facial expressions.

Teacher Tip
Be sure to save the cards that you made from *Blackline Master 6* to use in Lesson 5.

 Exploring the Theme

Theme Connections

Talk About It

Have the children discuss how Boomer's classroom is different from their classroom.

Supporting Reflection

Continue to work on the class book about the things they do in school.

- Continue to take each child's picture with Boomer and to show the picture to the class.

When each picture is developed, show it to the children and discuss who is in the picture. Review the activity or routine that was explained to Boomer. Paste the picture on a page in the class picture/story book and compose a simple sentence describing the event—for example, *"Chrissy and Boomer are playing in the dress-up center."*

- Have the children "read" the sentence as a group and highlight the left to right flow of the print.

- Point out individual words such as *Boomer*, and *Chrissy*.

- Ensure that children understand that a word is a group of letters and that they are separated by spaces.

- Explain that the printed words are a way of showing what we say and think.

- Print the word *Boomer* on the chalkboard and have the children identify it in isolation.

- Have them read it in a sentence.

- Count out the number of letters in the word *Boomer*, with the children. Make six dashes and print the letters on them.

- Repeat the process with the children's names as time permits.

 Teacher Tip Invite children to help you to print the letters and words as appropriate.

 Teacher Tip **Unit Activity** If you do not have access to a camera, consider having the children draw pictures of the people they meet and the places they find Boomer.

 **Web Connection** Check the Reading link of the **SRA** Web page for links to School-related Web sites. **http://www.sra-4kids.com**

③ Integrating the Curriculum

Teacher Tip Writing activities should meet the needs of your group. Some children may prefer whole-class projects for some time before they are ready to write independently.

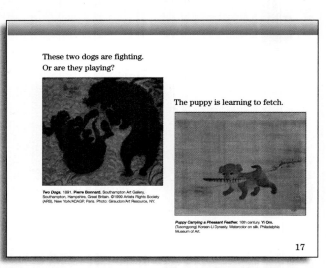

These two dogs are fighting. Or are they playing?

The puppy is learning to fetch.

Two Dogs. 1891. **Pierre Bonnard.** Southampton Art Gallery, Southampton, Hampshire, Great Britain. ©1999 Artists Rights Society (ARS), New York/ADAGP, Paris. Photo: Giraudon/Art Resource, NY.

Puppy Carrying a Pheasant Feather. 16th century. **Yi Om.** (Tusongyong) Korean-Li Dynasty. Watercolor on silk. Philadelphia Museum of Art.

17

Pictures Tell Stories, **p. 17**

Language Arts

Independent and Collaborative Writing

Sequencing

Show **Transparency 32** and invite children to talk about what they do first, next, and so on in their school day. Print a sentence in each frame. Read each sentence with the children, emphasizing the sequence of the activities.

Listening, Speaking, Viewing

Pictures Tell Stories

Explain to the children that they are going to look at another art selection from the **Big Book** *Pictures Tell Stories.* Ask them to recall some of the things that were said about art in Lesson 3 of this unit.

■ Show the children the two fine art pieces on page 17 of *Two Dogs* by **Pierre Bonnard** and *Puppy Carrying a Pheasant Feather* by **Yi Om.** Ask them what each painting makes them think about. Then have them predict what "story" each might tell.

■ Read the text for *Puppy Carrying a Pheasant Feather* to the children. If necessary, explain that *fetch* means to go after something and bring it back. Point to the feather in the puppy's mouth.

■ Read the text for *Two Dogs* to the children. Ask them to discuss whether they think the two dogs are playing or fighting and have them tell why.

■ Have the children find pictures from "Boomer Goes to School" that show him playing, and some that show him with things in his mouth.

Across the Curriculum

Music

Singing About School

Purpose

To create lyrics about what happens at school every day.

Procedure

■ Teach the children the song "Early in the Morning." If children know the song, have them join in. Repeat the song once or twice, or until the children are familiar with the melody and the repeated final line.

■ Then tell the children that they are going to write new words to the song. Explain that their new words will tell about things they do at school every day.

■ Invite the children to name some of the things they do in class, such as listening, sharing toys, and so on. Tell the children that the last line always will be *In our class each day.*

■ You might begin with this verse to get the children started:

This is the way we read and write,

read and write, read and write.

This is the way we read and write,

In our class each day.

Other verses might include the following:

■ *share and talk*

■ *ask and tell*

■ *think and learn*

① Sounds and Letters

Parts of Books It is important that students become familiar with the parts of books. Take every opportunity to point out the titles of *Big Books,* the titles of individual selections in them, and the names of the authors and illustrators.

Pronunciation If you are uncertain of how to pronounce any of the Spanish words in the poem, you may want to listen to the poem on the *Listening Libraries Audiocassette.*

Meeting Individual Needs

ESL

Native Language Use Ask English-language learners who speak Spanish to repeat the Spanish words after you to allow the class to hear the words spoken by a native speaker.

Sounds, Letters, and Language

Reading the Big Book *Pickled Peppers*
"Houses/Casitas," pages 24–25

This poem is presented in both English and Spanish. Read first the version that you and your students are most comfortable with.

■ Display pages 24–25 of *Pickled Peppers* and read the title of the poem, "Houses." Point to and read the name Tony Johnson. Explain that a person who writes poetry is called a *poet.* Then point to and read the name of the illustrator, *F. John Sierra.* Remind the children that a person who draws the pictures for a selection is called an *illustrator.*

■ Read the poem aloud. Then read each line and ask volunteers to point to a picture that goes with the line.

■ If you read the English version first, point out the Spanish version. Then read the Spanish version. Reread the poem and then point out the color words in each version. (*azul* [ah-ZOOL]/blue, *naranja* [Nah-RAHN-hah]/orange, *amarilla* [ah-mah-REE-yah]/yellow, and *verde* [VAYR-day]/green). You may note that the word in the text is *anaranjada* [an-nah-rahn-HAH-dah], which translated directly from Spanish means "to be tinted with orange."

■ If you read the Spanish version first, read the English version and point out the English color names.

■ Have the children look at the illustrations on the pages and identify any squares or circles they see. If necessary, point to windows in the houses, walls, and the door handles.

Phonemic Awareness

Listening for Missing Words

- Ask the children to listen carefully as you say some words. Say three words, such as *cat, man, fish,* and place each **Word Card** in the **Pocket Chart** as you say it. Have the children listen again, and then say just two of the words, covering or removing one of the cards. Ask the children which word is missing.

- Encourage the children to respond in a complete sentence. (*The missing word is _____.*)

- Repeat the activity several times, using different combinations of words.

Word Substitution

- Use the Name Necklaces again to play the Who Ate the Cookie from the Cookie Jar? game. If more than one child has a name beginning with the letters *A-D,* select one of these names to use in the game. Then say, for example, "David's name begins with *D.* Does anyone else have a name that begins with *D?*"

- After you have repeated the game a few times, ask the children to take off their Name Necklaces and place them on the floor in front of them. Tell them to use their fingers to trace over the letters in their names. Circulate and ask each child to name the first letter in her or his name.

Rhyme

Continue the rhyming activity from yesterday's lesson.

- Hold up **Picture Cards** of a *mouse* and a *house,* and say:

  Did you ever see a *mouse* in a _____?

- Continue, using phrases with the following pairs of words:

fish	dish (wish)
ants	pants (dance)
fox	socks (rocks)
dog	log (frog, hog)
cat	bat (mat)
fly	pie (sky)

Teacher Tip Remind the children not to call out their answers until you give the signal or call on someone.

Assessment

✓**Informal Monitoring** Research affirms that sensitivity to rhyme is a valuable step in the right direction towards understanding sounds in words. For that reason, it is important to identify children who are having difficulty and to work with them separately or in small groups until they catch on.

Phonics CD-ROM

Use the **Phonics** CD-ROM for activities that support the Phonemic Awareness Lessons.

① Sounds and Letters

Teacher Tip

Starting Points Although the children will be writing letters free-form, it is a good idea to put starting points on the overhead projector or chalkboard before you begin, as a model for later lessons. Developing a common stroke sequence for each letter hastens learning and reduces reversals.

Intervention

If children are having problems forming letters, project the transparency on the chalkboard and have children trace the letter and then write their own letter, a. Or make a copy of **Transparency 01** and have children trace the letter and then write their own letter a.

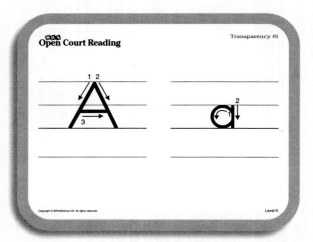

Transparency 01

Letter Names

Sing Your Way to G Game

Play Sing Your Way to *G*. Give several children a chance to use the puppet to point out a letter. Then have the class sing to that letter.

Letter Shapes

Exploring *Aa*

- Point to the *Aa* **Alphabet Card**. Explain that this letter is red because it is a special kind of letter called a vowel. Tell the children that they will learn more about this and other vowels later. Name the capital letter *A* and the small letter *a*.

- Tell the children they will be writing these letters with you. Begin by placing your pen or chalk on the overhead projector or chalkboard. Have children place their fingers in the air. As you write the letter, describe what you are doing, saying "Start at the top and slant down this way. Start at the top again and slant down this way. Then make a line across. Capital *A*."

- Repeat your actions several times, having the children copy your actions in the air.

- Then have the children make the letter on paper as you make it on the overhead or chalkboard.

- Repeat the steps for small *a*.

- When the children are done, ask them to look at their Name Necklaces. Have children identify any capital or small *a*'s that appear in their names. Explain that a capital letter is used at the beginning of a name, and that small letters are used for all the other letters.

Alphabet Big Book — Aa

Display the *Alphabet **Big Book*** and open it to page 4. Tell the children that you are going to read to them a silly poem about an anteater. Ask if anyone knows what an anteater is.

- Read the rhyme, pointing to each word as you say it.
- Call on volunteers to come to the book and to touch words that begin with capital *A* and small *a.*

An anteater can't eat a thing but an ant,
though an anteater would if he could,
it should be understood that an anteater would
but an ant-eating anteater can't.

An Anteater
Jack Prelutsky

4   5

Alphabet Big Book, pp. 4–5

② Reading and Responding

"Boomer Goes to School"
Pages 20–21 of *School*

This selection is taught in six lessons:

Lesson 1	Lesson 3	**Lesson 5**
Lesson 2	Lesson 4	Lesson 6

Suddenly, a loud bell rang and it was time to take another bus ride. At each bus stop, Boomer's new friends patted him good-bye. ❾
Then, the bus stopped at Boomer's house. Boomer wagged his tail and bounded off the bus for home.

20

Teacher Tip The concept of multiple meanings for words is quite abstract, although likely to be part of the children's intuitive knowledge of language. Do not belabor the point.

Activate Prior Knowledge

Have the children share what they have learned about Boomer. Call on volunteers to summarize the events that have happened so far in the story.

Preview and Prepare

Browse

■ Display the ***Big Book*** *School*, open to pages 4–5. Point to and say the title and the names of the author and illustrator. Have the children say each with you.

■ Turn through pages 20–21 and have the children quickly identify anything in the pictures or text that is familiar to them.

Vocabulary

Selection Vocabulary

Write the following word on the board and read it aloud.

Tell the children that this word can mean more than one thing. Ask them if they can use the word in a sentence. If no one volunteers, say the following:

still

I haven't been coming to school for many days. I still like to come to school.

Explain that in this sentence, *still* means "something that happens over and over": I continue to like to come to school.

Now say the following:
We sit very still during story time.
Explain that in this sentence, the word *still* means very quiet.

Tell the children that in this part of the selection, the word *still* is used to mean both "something that happens over and over" and "very quiet." Ask them to listen for the word as you read.

Reading Recommendations

- Running your hand under each line as you read reinforces children's awareness of print. Remind the children that we read the words from left to right and from top to bottom.
- During rereading, encourage the children to say quietly any words they recognize as they follow along with you.
- Encourage the children to participate in rereadings by inviting volunteers to retell what is happening on a specific page.

Using Reading Strategies

During the first reading of "Boomer Goes to School," you modeled the use of the following reading strategies:

- Predicting
- Clarifying

For your convenience, the strategy models from the first reading of the selection are reproduced in this lesson in the form of reminders. You may choose not to use these reminders with your class, or to use them only with children who need extra help or who missed the first reading of the selection.

Building Comprehension Skills

In this lesson you will continue to work with the comprehension skill *Drawing Conclusions*.

② Reading and Responding

Comprehension Strategies

Introducing Strategy Use

Modeling

❾ Predicting *The story seems to say that because a loud bell rang, it was time for Boomer to take another bus ride. From what we already know about how school works, What will happen next? Does anyone have a prediction? (I predict that the bell is the dismissal bell for the day, and that Boomer is going to ride the school bus home.)*

Suddenly, a loud bell rang and it was time to take another bus ride. At each bus stop, Boomer's new friends patted him good-bye. ❾

Then, the bus stopped at Boomer's house. Boomer wagged his tail and bounded off the bus for home.

20

21

Comprehension Skills

Discussing the Selection

- Invite children to comment on the characters and the events. (*Do they like Boomer? Do they do some of the same activities in their class?*)
- Ask whether children would like to have Boomer visit the class. Encourage them to explain why they think it would or would not be a good idea.

Reading and Responding

Responding to Literature

Reading/Writing Connection

Using heavy paper, make a copy of **Blackline Master 6,** Boomer, and cut out the frames. Arrange them in sequence along the chalkboard ledge, with the children's help. Have volunteers select the frames that depict activities that they do during their school day.

If you are comfortable drawing stick figures, consider creating cards depicting some of your class activities and routines. Have the children use the cards to tell stories to each other about all the things they do throughout the school day.

Using the Audiocassette

Have children sit with partners or in small groups and listen to the audiotape recording of "Boomer Goes to School." Suggest that they may stop the tape at certain points and discuss what is happening in the story so far.

Exploring the Theme

Theme Connections

View Fine Art

Display page 48 of the **Big Book** School. Invite children to look at the pictures and to comment on what they see.

■ Point out the picture **Singing the Corrido** by **Diego Rivera**. Explain that the artist who painted this picture lived in Mexico, where people speak Spanish. Some children may recall that the poem "Houses" ("Casitas") was written in Spanish.

■ Ask them to tell about what they see in the picture. Point out that the children in the picture are being schooled while their mother works.

■ Encourage children to tell what they like about this picture and others on the page.

Supporting Reflection

Finish taking the children's pictures with Boomer, as they explain various class activities and routines.

Continue discussing the photographs of Boomer and the children. Paste each in the big book and write a sentence describing the activity. Encourage the children to "read" the sentences as appropriate.

Remind the children to ask their parents if they have any pictures of their school days. Have them share the pictures of their parents with the class and display them on the Concept/Question Board for the duration of the unit.

Suggest to the children that they read story books about school with their parents and that they consider lending the books to the classroom library.

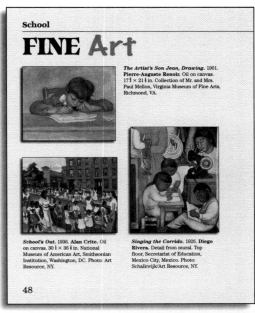

School

FINE Art

The Artist's Son Jean, Drawing. 1901. Pierre-Auguste Renoir. Oil on canvas. 17 1/2 × 21 1/2 in. Collection of Mr. and Mrs. Paul Mellon, Virginia Museum of Fine Arts, Richmond, VA.

School's Out. 1936. Alan Crite. Oil on canvas. 30 1/2 × 36 1/2 in. National Museum of American Art, Smithsonian Institution, Washington, DC. Photo: Art Resource, NY.

Singing the Corrido. 1926. Diego Rivera. Detail from mural. Top floor, Secretariat of Education, Mexico City, Mexico. Photo: Schalkwijk/Art Resource, NY.

48

Big Book School, p. 48

Check the Reading link of the **SRA** Web page for links to School-related Web sites.
http://www.sra-4kids.com

③ Integrating the Curriculum

Language Arts

Independent and Collaborative Writing

Opposites

On the chalkboard, write the following words from pages 18–20 of "Boomer Goes to School":

    big (p. 19)
    loud (p. 20)
    new (p. 20)
    off (p. 20)

- Point to and read each word, then ask the children to say each word with you.

- Ask the children to name something in their classroom that is big *(chalkboard, teacher's desk)*. Then ask them to name something that is small *(chalk, pencils)*. Explain that big is the opposite of small.

- Ask them to think of a word that is the opposite of *loud (quiet, soft)*. Continue with the remaining words until the children understand what opposites are.

- Have them draw pictures that show two things that are opposites: draw something big/small, tall/short, loud/quiet, old/new, sad/happy, and so forth.

- Encourage them to dictate sentences about their drawings.

- Provide time for the children to show their drawings to the class and to explain what they show.

Meeting Individual Needs

ESL

Meet with English-language learners to review the concept of opposites. Use pictures and words, in their language when possible, to teach this concept.

Listening, Speaking, Viewing

Reading Words and Pictures

- Have ready the *Word Cards* or *High-Frequency Word Cards Here, is, a, A, an, An* and the *Picture Cards* dog, elephant, kangaroo, mouse, octopus, pig.
- Display the *Word Cards* in a row in this order: *Here is a.* Say each word as you place it. Next, add the *Picture Card dog*, and read the sentence *Here is a dog.* Point to each word as you say it. Next, have the children read the sentence as you point to each word.
- Repeat several times, replacing the *Picture Card* and substituting the *an* card when the picture begins with a vowel.
- Rearrange the cards to read: *A _____ is here.* Place a *Picture Card* after *A*, then challenge the children to read as you point to each card.
- Repeat several times, replacing the *Picture Card* and the *A* card with *An*, as appropriate.

Study and Research Skills

Make a Classroom Map

- Display the class map you created in Lesson 2. Have the children locate and identify the activity centers that are pictured in the class book. Have them find the center in the classroom, as well.
- Then have the children help you draw in additional objects from the classroom, such as bookcases or tables, on the map. Have the children dictate labels for you to write on the objects.

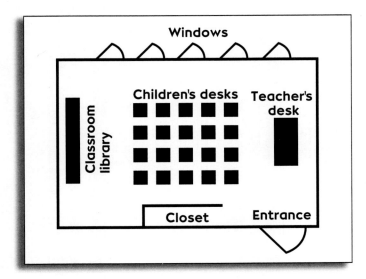

Integrating the Curriculum

Vocabulary

Time of Day Words

Make three paper strips with the following sentences or write them on the chalkboard.

> **Boomer and the children had lunch.**
> **Boomer's owner was getting ready to go to school.**
> **Boomer got back on the bus and went home.**

■ Read the sentences, then have the children help you put them in the correct sequence, according to the time of day each event described in a sentence occurred. Tell them to use the terms *first*, *middle*, and *last*, and to explain their decision about where each goes in the sequence.

■ Write the words *morning*, *noon*, and *afternoon* on the chalkboard. Ask the children what the words mean. If necessary, explain that noon is the very middle of the day—the time when many people eat lunch; *morning* is the part of the day before noon or before lunch; *afternoon* comes after noon or after lunch.

■ Produce sentences about other things Boomer did and ask the children to decide if they happened in the morning or in the afternoon by deciding if they happened before or after lunch.

■ Review the words *morning*, *noon*, and *afternoon* with the children by asking them questions about classroom activities, for example: **What do we do first thing in the morning? What else do we do in the morning? Where do we go at noon?**

Across the Curriculum

Movement

Following Directions

Purpose

To practice listening carefully to follow directions in class.

Procedure

- Remind the children that it is very important to listen to and follow directions in school. Point out that by following directions in class, they know which book to use or when it is time to line up for lunch.

- Explain that they are going to follow your directions to play a game. Explain that you will give a direction and call on one or two volunteers to follow it.

- Give common directions such as "go to the Listening Center" and "line up to go to lunch."

- Invite the children to give some directions as well and have volunteers follow the directions.

Lesson Planner

		DAY 1	DAY 2
Part 1	**Sounds and Letters** **Materials** ■ Big Book *Pickled Peppers*, p. 24–25, 12, 42 ■ Word Cards (see lessons) ■ *Alphabet Book*, p. 6–7, 8–9, 12–13, 14–15 ■ Picture Cards (see lessons) ■ *Reading and Writing Workbook*, p. 1 ■ Pre-Decodable Book 2: *Lunch* ■ Blackline Master 7 ■ Transparencies 2–6	**Sounds, Letters, and Language, p. 108** ■ Reading the Big Book *Pickled Peppers*, pp. 24–25 **Phonemic Awareness** 🍔 ✓ ■ Listening, p. 109 ■ Rhythm, p. 109 **Letter Recognition** ■ Letter Names, p. 110 ✓ ■ Rhyme, p. 110 ✓ ■ Letter Shapes, p. 111	**Sounds, Letters, and Language, pp. 120–121** ■ Reading the Big Book *Pickled Peppers*, p. 12 **Phonemic Awareness** 🍔 ■ Listening, p. 122 ✓ ■ Word Substitution, pp. 122–123 ■ Rhyme, p. 123 **Letter Recognition** ■ Letter Names, p. 124 ✓ ■ Letter Shapes, pp. 124–125
Part 2	**Reading and Responding** **Materials** ■ Big Book *School*, p. 4–21, 22–43, 48 ■ Listening Library Audiocassette: School ■ Home Connection, p. 9, 11 ■ Transparency 33	**Activate Prior Knowledge, p. 112** **Vocabulary** ■ Selection Vocabulary, p. 112 **Reading Recommendations, p. 113** **Responding to Literature** ■ Discussing the Selection, p. 114 ■ Purposes for Reading, p. 114 **Exploring the Theme, p. 115**	**Exploring the Theme, p. 127** **Build Background, p. 128** **Preview and Prepare, p. 129** **Vocabulary** ■ Selection Vocabulary: *tomorrow, alone*, p. 130 **Reading Recommendations, p. 131** **Comprehension Strategies** ■ Making Connections, pp. 132, 136, 138, 140 ■ Clarifying, pp. 134, 138, 142 **Comprehension Skills** ■ Discussing the Selection, p. 143 ■ Purposes for Reading, p. 143 **Responding to Literature** ■ Print Awareness, p. 144 **Exploring the Theme, p. 145**
Part 3	**Integrating the Curriculum** **Materials** ■ Big Book *Pickled Peppers*, p. 24 ■ *Willy the Wisher Thinking Story 1* ■ Blackline Masters 8, 9 ■ Picture Cards	**Independent and Collaborative Writing** ■ Journal Writing, p. 116 **Listening, Speaking, Viewing** ■ Dramatizing, p. 117 **Vocabulary** ■ Color Words, p. 117 *Willy the Wisher Thinking Story I*, p. 118 **Across the Curriculum: Math, p. 119**	**Independent and Collaborative Writing** ■ Journal Writing, p. 146 **Listening, Speaking, Viewing** ■ Asking and Answering Questions, p. 147 **Vocabulary** ■ Opposites, p. 148 **Across the Curriculum: Social Studies, p. 149**

Independent Work Time

Materials
Big Books: School, Pickled Peppers, Alphabet Book, Pictures Tell Stories
Willy the Wisher
Skills Assessment pages 2–3
Reading and Writing Workbook page 1

Reteach, Challenge page 1
Intervention Guide Unit 1, Lessons 6–10
ESL Supplement Unit 1, Lessons 6–10
Pre-Decodable Book 2

Reteach
■ "Boomer Goes to School"
■ "Houses (Casitas)"

Preteach
■ *Alphabet Book* Bb
■ *Willy the Wisher Thinking Story 1*

Writing: Journal Writing

Unit Project

Preteach
■ *School* "What Will Mommy Do When I'm at School?"
■ *Pickled Peppers* "Hickory, Dickory, Dock"
■ *Alphabet Book* Cc

Writing: Journal Writing

Unit Project continued

DAY 3	**DAY 4**	**DAY 5**
Sounds, Letters, and Language, p. 150 ■ Reading the Big Book *Pickled Peppers*, p. 12 **Phonemic Awareness** ☁ ■ Listening, p. 151 **Letter Recognition** ■ Letter Names, p. 152 ✓ ■ Letter Shapes, p. 153 ✓ Reading Pre-Decodable Book 2: *Lunch,* pp. 154–155	**Sounds, Letters, and Language, p. 168** ■ Reading the Big Book *Pickled Peppers*, p. 12 **Phonemic Awareness** ☁ ■ Listening, p. 169 ✓ ■ Rhyme, p. 170 **Letter Recognition** ✓ ■ Letter Names, p. 171 ■ Letter Shapes, pp. 172–173	**Sounds, Letters, and Language, p. 186** ■ Reading the Big Book *Pickled Peppers*, p. 42 **Phonemic Awareness** ☁ ✓ ■ Listening, p. 187 **Letter Recognition** ✓ ■ Letter Names, p. 187 ✓ ■ Letter Shapes, pp. 188–189
Build Background, p. 156 **Preview and Prepare, p. 156** **Vocabulary** ■ Selection Vocabulary: *eat, sing, watch, read*, p. 156 **Reading Recommendations, p. 157** **Comprehension Strategies** ■ Making Connections, p. 158 ■ Clarifying, p. 160 **Comprehension Skills** ■ Compare and Contrast, p. 159 ■ Discussing the Selection, p. 161 **Responding to Literature** ✓ ■ Literature Appreciation, p. 162 **Exploring the Theme, p. 163**	**Build Background, p. 174** **Preview and Prepare, p. 174** **Vocabulary** ■ Selection Vocabulary: *Mom, Daddy, Grandma,* p. 174 **Reading Recommendations, p. 175** **Comprehension Strategies** ■ Making Connections, pp. 176, 178 **Comprehension Skills** ■ Compare and Contrast, p. 177 ■ Discussing the Selection, p. 179 **Responding to Literature** ■ Literature Appreciation, p. 180 **Exploring the Theme, p. 181**	**Build Background, p. 190** **Preview and Prepare, p. 190** **Vocabulary** ■ Selection Vocabulary: *today, tomorrow*, p. 190 **Reading Recommendations, p. 191** **Comprehension Strategies** ■ Clarifying, p. 192 ■ Making Connections, p. 192 **Comprehension Skills** ■ Compare and Contrast, p. 193 ■ Discussing the Selection, p. 193 **Responding to Literature** ■ Reading/Writing Connection, p. 194 **Exploring the Theme, p. 195**
Independent and Collaborative Writing ■ Being a Student, p. 164 **Study/Research** ■ Parts of the Library, p. 165 **Vocabulary** ✓ ■ Rhyming Words, p. 165 **Grammar** ■ Words that Name, p. 166 **Listening** ■ Listening Attentively, p. 166 **Across the Curriculum: Movement, p. 167**	**Independent and Collaborative Writing** ■ My Classroom, p. 182 **Listening, Speaking, Viewing** ■ Left/Right Directionality, p. 183 **Vocabulary** ■ Position Words, p. 184 **Across the Curriculum: Social Studies, p. 185**	**Independent and Collaborative Writing** ■ My Friends and I, p. 196 **Listening, Speaking, Viewing** ■ Following Directions, p. 197 **Vocabulary** ■ Position Words, p. 198 **Across the Curriculum: Movement, p. 199**

Reteach
■ "What Will Mommy Do When I'm at School?"
■ "Hickory, Dickory Dock"
Preteach
■ *Alphabet Book* Dd
  Skills Assessment page 2
Partner-read ***Pre-Decodable Book 2***
Writing: Being a Student
Unit Project continued
	Reteach
	■ "What Will Mommy Do When I'm at School?"
	Preteach
	■ *Alphabet Book* Ee
	■ Vocabulary: Position words
	Writing: My Classroom
	Unit Project continued
		Reteach
		■ "What Will Mommy Do When I'm at School?"
		■ Vocabulary: Position words
		Preteach
		■ *Pickled Peppers* "The Top and the Tip"
		■ *Alphabet Book* Ff
		  Skills Assessment page 3
		Reading and Writing Workbook,
		  Reteach, Challenge page 1
		Writing: My Friends and I
		Unit Project continued

Meeting Individual Needs
Independent Work Time

Sounds and Letters

Meeting Individual Needs

Reteach
- Identifying Letters *A-F, Reteach*, p. 189

ESL
- Word Sequence, p. 109
- Preteach, p. 151
- This Ship Is Loaded With _____ Game, p. 169
- Simon Says, p. 187

Intervention
- Letter Recognition, p. 124
- Pencil Control, pp. 153, 188
- Letter Formation, p. 172

Challenge
- Letters *A–F, Challenge*, p. 189

Reading and Responding

Meeting Individual Needs

ESL
- Summarizing, p. 112
- Native Language Use, p. 113
- Vocabulary, pp. 130, 156, 190
- Relationship Words, p. 174

Challenge
- Independent Reading, p. 114

Integrating the Curriculum

Meeting Individual Needs

ESL
- Opposites, p. 148
- Parts of the Library, p. 165
- Position Words, p. 184

Formal Assessment Options

Use this assessment page along with your informal observations to gauge the students' progress.

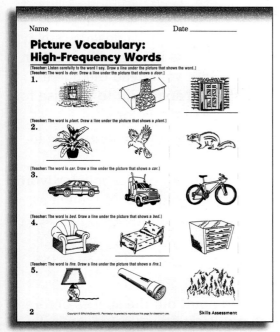

Skills Assessment, p. 2
Picture Vocabulary: *High-Frequency Words*

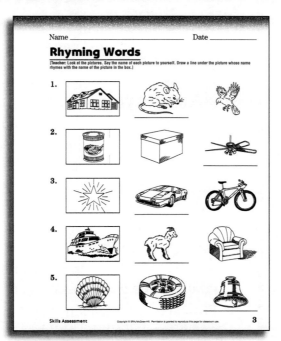

Skills Assessment, p. 3
Rhyming Words

Teacher's Observation Log, p. 18
Assessment Master

① Sounds and Letters

SRA
Open Court
Reading

Pickled Peppers

Sounds, Letters, and Language

Reading the Big Book *Pickled Peppers*
"Houses/Casitas," pages 24–25

■ Display pages 24–25 and read the title of the poem in English and then in Spanish, "Houses/Casitas." Point to and say the names of the author and illustrator. Have the children say each with you. Read the poem aloud. On a second reading, read the first word and point to a house for each line. Have the children supply the name of the color.

■ Then name a color and have the children find and touch something in the classroom that is each color.

■ Read the Spanish version. Then reread it and point out each color word. Ask the children to repeat each color word after you, as you touch an object in the picture that is the color. Then have children supply the English color word.

■ Reread the entire English version of the poem again and examine the color words *blue, orange, yellow, green*.

■ For each one, explain that it is a word and point out the spaces before and after it. Tell the children that each word gets a space before and a space after when it is written to keep it separate from other words.

■ Clarify the idea of word by reading the line "A blue house," and pointing to the words one by one. Ask if anyone can figure out how many words are in the line. Count the words while pointing to confirm that the line has three words, each separated from the others by spaces. Repeat with other lines.

Home Connection

Distribute *Home Connection* page 9 which tells families about the letter formation activities the children have been doing and offers suggestions for furthering letter formation at home. This letter is available in English and Spanish.

Letter Formation

A message from _____

At this time, your child is beginning to work on letter formation. Starting slowly, your child will practice writing straight and slanted lines, curves, and circles. Letter formation will progress very slowly, and only later in the year will children make a serious attempt to refine letter formation. In fact, this first introduction is just an overview of the basic shapes of the letters.

Your child will practice forming a different letter daily. This letter formation activity is intended to act as one more way to help your child recognize letters. Learning the names of the letters and being able to tell them apart is much more important at this time than whether or not your child can make an *s* with the curves going in the right direction.

Your child will, however, benefit greatly from being able to write his or her name. Practice time will be provided in class, but any additional practice you can give your child at home will be helpful. You might try writing your child's name on a piece of cardboard and putting it on the desk or table where he or she normally writes, colors, or plays. Ask your child to write his or her name. Praise your child's efforts no matter how imperfect they may be. Then, ask him or her to compare the name he or she has written to the name tag you have made. You might ask your child to check the order of the letters, to point out a letter that could be improved upon, and then to point out his or her very best letter. Remember, more work on letter formation will occur later in the year.

Big Book/School   9

Home Connection, p. 9

PHONEMIC AWARENESS

Phonemic Awareness

Listening for First, Middle, and Last Words

Now that the children have had quite a bit of practice locating sounds and words within a sequence, you might ask them to identify the entire sequence.

- Ask the children to listen carefully as you say some words. Then say *open the door*. Model the response you are looking for by saying, "The first word is *open*, the middle word is *the* and the last word is *door*."

- Continue with several other three-word phrases, such as *big green tree, in my house, walk to school*. Ask the children for the first, middle, and last word in each phrase. Remind them to use complete sentences in their responses.

- Open *Pickled Peppers* to "Houses/Casitas."

- Using the **Word Cards** for "Houses/Casitas," continue with the phrase "A blue house." Put the **Word Cards** in the **Pocket Chart**.

- Ask the children to listen again. Say longer sequences of words from the poem. Begin with "Just look down the street!" and enunciate each word in the sequence strongly and clearly. Ask children to say the last word.

- Choose another sequence such as "The green one is ours," and ask children to say the first word. If the children suggest *green* was the first word, ask them to listen again. Say the words slowly and remind them that *the* is a word, and that it is the first word in the sequence.

- When children give correct answers, point to the sequence of words in the **Big Book** to show the position of the words. When they make a mistake, show the word they have chosen and explain why it is the wrong answer.

Rhythm

Clapping out the rhythmic beat of a poem and then segmenting it line by line will help the children to hear language in parts rather than as one stream of sound.

- Teach the children this simple poem:

Rain, rain, go away

Come again another day!

- First clap out the poem word by word until all the children have learned it. Then put the poem in the **Pocket Chart**, saying each word as you place it. Now, repeat the poem slowly, one line at a time, and clapping word by word.

Meeting Individual Needs

ESL

Word Sequence To teach first, middle, and last word sequence to English-language learners, use a row of objects such as books, toys, or blocks to demonstrate. Point to the object as you say, "first." Ask the students to repeat the word. Then continue with "middle" and "last." Do the sequence again with different objects.

Phonemic Awareness activities related to the lessons can be found at **http://www.sra-4kids.com**

Assessment

✓ **Informal Monitoring** Pay particular attention to those children who are confused by identifying words in a sequence. Plan to work with these children in small groups or individually as necessary.

Sounds and Letters

Letter Recognition

Letter Names

Sing Your Way to *G* Game

Have the children play the Sing Your Way to *G* game. Allow several children to use the puppet to touch each letter. When the class has sung and stopped at *G*, point to other letters between *A* and *G* and have the class sing to each one. If a child is using the puppet and forgets the letter, ask "What is the letter?" and wait for the class or volunteers to answer.

Find a Letter

Explain that words are made by putting together the letters of the alphabet.

- Tell the children they can find letters in words all over the room. Walk around the room and touch words on such items as posters and calendars. Then ask volunteers to name any letters they recognize in each word.

- Encourage the children to take turns finding words around the classroom. Remind them to look carefully at their Name Necklaces and their classmates' necklaces also. As they find each word, have them identify any letters they recognize. Keep a list of the words and the letters that the children identify.

- Ask the children to do the same. Then tell them that you will point to a group of children who will say and clap the line you indicate. Continue until every child has had a chance to recite and clap one line.

Rhyme

Making Rhymes

- Say *see* and ask them to say a word that rhymes with it.
- Repeat *see* and say the word suggested by the children, then ask for another word that rhymes with *see*.
- Repeat all three words and ask if they all rhyme.
- If the children have difficulty thinking of a rhyming word, provide a clue, such as "I'm thinking of an insect that stings." Accept nonsense words, provided that they rhyme.
- Other words to use are: *please, cat, house, jar, new, boy, fan.*

Assessment

✓ **Informal Monitoring** Observe the children closely during the Find a Letter activity. Note those children who seem confused and unable to identify any letters in words. Plan to meet with these children in small groups.

Letter Shapes

Exploring *Bb*

- Point to the *Bb Alphabet Card*, name the letter, and tell the children they will be writing this letter today.

- Place your pen or chalk at a starting point on the overhead projector or chalkboard. Have the children place their fingers in the air. As you write the letter, describe what you are doing, saying:

  Start at the top and go straight down. Start at the top again and go around to the middle, then around again to the bottom. Capital *B*.

  Repeat several times, having children mimic you in the air.

- Have children make the letter on paper as you make it on the overhead or chalkboard.

- Repeat the steps for small *b*.

- When children are done, ask them to look at their Name Necklaces. Have children identify any capital or small *b*'s that appear in their names. Remind them that a capital letter is used at the beginning of a name, and that small letters are used for all the other letters.

Alphabet Big Book *Bb*

Display the *Alphabet **Big Book***, open to pages 6–7. Read the rhyme "Busy Busy Busy" pointing to each word as you say it. Then tell the children to look carefully as you read the poem again a bit more slowly, pointing to each word. Have them call out "B!" every time they see you point to a word that has a capital *B* or a small *b*.

Alphabet Big Book, pp. 6-7

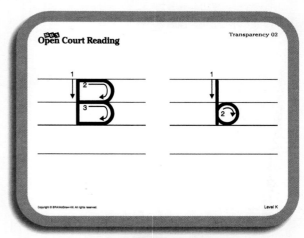

Transparency 02

Teacher Tip When working with children who find letter formation difficult, work at the chalkboard or use large sheets of paper. Then have them use pencil and paper to form the letters.

Teacher Tip **Letter Formation** For those children having difficulty with letter formation, project the letter formation transparency on the chalkboard or a piece of chart paper and have the child trace over the letter. Or make a copy of the transparency and have them practice on their own.

Assessment

✓ **Informal** While we don't expect young children to be proficient with letter formation at this time, it is important to keep track of the children's progress. Note those children who seem confused and plan to work with them to help them learn to form letters.

② Reading and Responding

"Boomer Goes to School"
Pages 4–21 of *School*

This selection is taught in six lessons:

Lesson 1	Lesson 3	Lesson 5
Lesson 2	Lesson 4	**Lesson 6**

Meeting Individual Needs

ESL

Encourage English-language learners to give summaries of the stories, providing help as necessary. The children are quite familiar with the story by now and should be encouraged to participate.

Selection Concepts

In "Boomer Goes to School," the children explored:
- School activities are many and varied.
- School is fun, even though it is sometimes confusing.
- School has a unique set of routines that we need to learn.
- We make friends at school.

Activate Prior Knowledge

Have the children tell what they remember about "Boomer Goes to School." Call on volunteers to summarize the main events in the story, using the familiar "and then" phrase.

Vocabulary

Selection Vocabulary
- Review all the selection vocabulary words for the story.

bus	play	listen
share	wiggled	sit
paint	squirmed	stand
	still	

- Write them on the chalkboard and invite the children to identify any that they recognize. Then say the words aloud as you point to them.
- Have the children use different words in sentences. Then have them be alert for the words during the rereading.

Reading Recommendations

- Running your hand under each line and pointing to the words as you read reinforces children's awareness of print. Remind the children that we read the words from left to right and from top to bottom.

- During rereading, encourage the children to say quietly any words they recognize as they follow along with you.

- Ask the children to come up to read a word with you. Ask them to point out the spaces before and after the word, and to point to the first and last letters in the word.

- Allow the children to comment on favorite parts of the story or parts they found amusing.

Using Reading Strategies

Review the Reading Strategies *Clarifying* and *Predicting* and remind the children how good readers use these strategies.

Building Comprehension Skills

Review *Drawing Conclusions* with the children.

Teacher Tip

Using the Audiocassette Have children sit with partners or in small groups to listen to the *Listening Libraries Audiocassette* recording of "Boomer Goes to School." If your class is using the small book, invite the children to use them to follow along as they listen to the recording.

Meeting Individual Needs

ESL

Native Language Use Encourage English-language learners to offer vocabulary words in their own languages. Invite them to talk about their experience or knowledge of what the words mean in their home countries.

Reading and Responding

Meeting Individual Needs

Challenge

Independent Reading Invite the children to come to the **Big Book** and point to words or lines that they feel they can read. If no one volunteers, reread a section of the selection, pointing to each word, and then ask again for volunteer readers.

Responding to Literature

Discussing the Selection

Have the children share their thoughts about the selection. Have them tell about all the things that happened to Boomer at school. Encourage them to tell what they liked best about the story. Review each of the questions the children placed on the Concept/Question Board after the first reading and ask them if each question has been answered. Remind the children that not all questions about school will be answered by "Boomer Goes to School," and that throughout the unit, you will try to find answers to these questions.

Purposes for Reading

Remind the children that we read both for entertainment and to get information. Ask them what information they found out from "Boomer Goes to School." If any children gave purposes for reading this story, ask them to recall those purposes and to tell if they were pleased with how the story turned out.

Exploring the Theme

Theme Connections

Think About It

Tell the children that you are going to ask them some questions to think about. Explain that you asked them these same questions after the first reading of the selection.

Remind them that thinking about something is different from talking about it. Suggest to them that they close their eyes as you ask a question and think about the answer. Read each question below aloud:

- What did Boomer like about school?

- Why do you think Boomer got mixed up at school?

Compliment each child for not telling their answers out loud.

Talk About It

Invite the children to share their thoughts about the questions now. Ask them if the answers are the same ones they gave earlier. If the answers have changed, ask them why. Explain that our thoughts about something can change as we learn more about it.

③ Integrating the Curriculum

Teacher Tip There are 4 stories in this school unit. You may want to make a multi page journal for children to write their reactions to each story and what they have learned in the unit. Children can take these home at the end of the unit to share with their families.

Language Arts

Independent and Collaborative Writing

Journal Writing

Today's lesson introduces journal writing. Journals provide a writing option for children. You may want to read the entries with children periodically as you conference during writing time. Do not feel obligated to read and respond to every entry. Also, children may choose to share their journal entries with the class or with small groups. Each child should have a journal. This can be a spiral notebook brought from home or a simple journal made in class by stapling a number of blank pages inside a cover. The children will be able to work in their journals by drawing pictures, making letters, writing words or phrases using invented spellings, and eventually writing in complete sentences. Explain to the children that it does not matter how they write. It is important only that they try and that they put their ideas down on paper in whatever way they can. Reassure them that their writing will get better and better as they learn more about writing throughout the year.

If you have prepared a journal for this unit, have children share their reactions to "Boomer Goes to School." Begin by writing the title of the story on the chalkboard and having children copy it. They can then draw their favorite part or character or how the story made them feel.

Listening, Speaking, Viewing

Dramatizing

Pose the following question to the children: "If an animal were to go to school with you one day, what animal would it be and what might happen?" Have them consider this question for a moment. Then allow volunteers to tell their story to the rest of the group.

This could lead to a role-playing activity in which the children choose others to accompany them in acting out their stories, showing various behaviors and the consequences of each behavior.

Vocabulary

Color Words

Post the color *Picture Cards* along the chalkboard ledge.

- Divide the children into groups and assign each group a color.

- Have the children cut pictures out of magazines or catalogs that show the color they are working on.

- You may wish to provide each group with a large piece of newsprint to paste the pictures onto. Then you could label each group's finished product with the color name and display these "color posters" in the classroom.

③ Integrating the Curriculum

Teacher Tip

Willy the Wisher In the first twelve *Willy the Wisher* stories, each character is introduced in a manner that establishes his or her individualized way of thinking. Later stories contain situations and problems that are more subtle or complex than those found in earlier stories.

Willy the Wisher

Thinking Story 1: "Willy the Wisher"

Willy has one of the most consistent and easily identified peculiarities of any of the characters in the *Thinking Stories*—his tendency to deal with problems by wishing for solutions rather than by figuring out what to do. Stories in which Willy appear are designed to have the children think about how things really happen.

In this story, Willy wishes for a lot of things to happen, but he doesn't do anything to make them happen.

Reading Recommendations

- Tell the children that you are going to read them a story about a character named Willy and that you want them to listen closely as you read to see if they can find out Willy's way of thinking.
- Read the story to the children.
- Through discussion, help the children to understand Willy's particular way of thinking.

Extending the Activity

- After reading the story, ask the children, "Are you ever like Willy? What should you do instead of just wishing?"

Research in Action

Thinking Stories

The ***Thinking Stories*** are intended to be interactive, with the children both listening as you read and participating by responding to questions included with the story text and anticipating what characters will do.

The activities present many opportunities for you to model thinking for the children. For example, some activities ask you to think aloud about how you would answer a question in a story, then ask the children to tell you how they went about deciding on their answers.

The introduction to *Willy the Wisher and Other Thinking Stories* explains more fully the nature and purpose of the ***Thinking Stories*** and offers additional teaching suggestions.

Approach *Willy the Wisher* with a spirit of fun. Many of the stories are farcical. They do not have a serious message, and they should be read and discussed in a light-hearted way that makes them enjoyable for the children. *(Marilyn Jager Adams)*

Across the Curriculum

Math

Colors Graph

Purpose

To identify colors in the classroom.

Materials

large-square graph paper, crayons or markers

Procedure

- Display graph paper and make a column for each color mentioned in the poem "Houses/Casitas." *(blue, orange, yellow, green)* Use appropriately colored markers to label the columns, and say the words. Then add columns for the other colors the children have learned in earlier lessons: red, white, black

- Have the children identify classroom items with these colors. As the children supply items for each color, fill in a box in the appropriate column. After a while, encourage the children to tell you in which column you should fill in the square.

- When all children have selected some items, discuss the graph and ask which color has the most items filled in and which has the fewest.

 Sounds and Letters

Sounds, Letters, and Language

Reading the Big Book *Pickled Peppers*
"Hickory, Dickory, Dock," page 12

- Open the ***Big Book*** *Pickled Peppers* to the table of contents. Remind the children that you have already read selections from *Pickled Peppers* called "I'm a Little Teapot," "One, Two, Buckle My Shoe," and "Houses/Casitas." Point to these titles in the table of contents and read them.

- Tell the children that today you are going to read "Hickory, Dickory, Dock." Find the title in the table of contents and read it, then point to the numeral *12* and say it. Let the children know that this number tells you that you can find the poem on page 12. Turn to page 12 and point to the page number.

- Point to the title of the poem and read it. Then read *"illustrated by"* and ask if anyone remembers what this means. Remind the children that the illustrator drew the pictures that go with the poem.

- Read the rhyme several times, emphasizing the rhyming words *hickory/dickory* and *dock/clock*. Read the rhyme again and ask the children to name the word that rhymes with *hickory* and the word that rhymes with *dock*.

- Tell the children to listen to see if you do something wrong as you read the rhyme once again. Start at the bottom of the page and read the rhyme backward. When children tell you to start at the top, begin with the last word of the first line. When the children tell you to begin with the first word, read the first word of each line. Ask the children what you should do. Emphasize that reading moves left-to-right and top-to-bottom.

- Point to and read Line 3 ("The clock struck one"). Ask the children what the first word of this line is. Confirm that it is *The*. Next, read Line 4 ("The mouse ran down") and ask the children to identify the first word again. If necessary, say that these two words are spelled the same, asking them to say the letters of each with you as you slowly move your finger from one letter to the next. Repeat the procedure with the words *mouse* and *ran*.

- Remind the children that words are separated by spaces, and call on volunteers to come to the **Big Book** and point first to the words *mouse* and *ran* and then to the spaces before and after each word.

- Have the children mime the rhyme.

1 Sounds and Letters

 These, and all phonemic awareness activities, should be fast-paced. Do not expect mastery or drill children. The activities will be repeated many times and the children will have ample opportunities to become proficient.

Listening

Listening for Word Changes

- Read "Hickory, Dickory, Dock" correctly, inviting the children to join in on the words.

- Reread the poem, substituting wrong words. Read *Hickory, dickory dock, the mouse ran up the rug.* Tell the children to listen carefully and to raise their hands as soon as they hear you make a mistake and correct your mistake.

- Continue substituting other words and having children correct you.

- You can continue to sharpen your student's listening skills by having them listen to familiar poems that you recite incorrectly. You might go back and reread other familiar rhymes such as, "One, Two, Buckle My Shoe," or "I'm a Little Teapot."

- Remind children to listen very carefully to catch wrong words when you say them. When they identify a mistake, compare the incorrect line to the correct line of the rhyme.

 Phonics CD-ROM

Use the *Phonics* CD-ROM for activities that support the Phonemic Awareness Lessons.

Research in Action

Listening for Word Changes

By having children listen for mistakes in your reading, such as lines or words that are substituted or out of order, you will help them to develop their awareness of words as well as their ability to listen to language carefully and analytically. Both are key literacy skills. This kind of listening activity can be done with poems that the children are already familiar with, and it can also serve as a review of past selections from *Pickled Peppers.*   *(Marilyn Jager Adams)*

Word Substitution

Any practice in which children are becoming more aware of words as separate units will help them prepare for listening to separate sounds as units within words. In the last lesson, the children broke a rhyme down into lines. In this lesson, they will break it down into words and work again with word substitution.

- Review the rhyme "Rain, rain, go away" and clap it out, word by word.

- Have the children sit in a circle. Move around the circle and recite the rhyme slowly, one word at a time. Tap a different child on the shoulder for each word you say. Now choose a child to go around the circle,

Assessment
✓ **Informal Monitoring** Notice children for whom word substitution is difficult and plan to provide extra practice during independent work time.

tapping others on the shoulder. This time, the child who is tapped says the word. The child who says *day* then takes the place of the child who tapped him or her. Allow four or five children to have a turn as the "tapper."

■ Ask the children to substitute a word for *rain*. Give an example first, such as, "Skunks, skunks, go away. Come again another day!" Play the game again with *skunks*. When a child becomes the tapper, she or he can substitute another word for *rain*. Be prepared to help the child think of a word to use.

Rhyme

Along the chalkboard ledge, make a row of three ***Picture Cards***, two of which show things that rhyme. Name each picture as you point to it.

Tell the children to raise their hands, and then say the names of the two pictures that rhyme.

1 Sounds and Letters

Letter Recognition

Letter Names

Alphabet Song

Review the "Alphabet Song" by singing it all the way through twice. Point to each letter as you say its name, and remind the children to clap when they reach the last letter in a line.

Sing Your Way to *N* Game

Extend the Sing Your Way to _____ Game to include the letters between *A* and *N*. Touch any letter between *G* and *N*. Have children sing to that letter. Repeat with other letters between *G* and *N*.

Find a Letter

- Review the list of letters that the children found yesterday.
- Point to an **Alphabet Card** such as *Pp* and have the children find examples of matching letters around the room. Have them point out and name their letters. Add these to the list.

Letter Shapes

Exploring *Cc*

- Display the **Alphabet Card** *Cc* and point to the capital letter *C* and the small letter *c*.
- Tell children they will be writing the capital letter *C*. Say:
  Start here and go around this way (left), then stop.
- Repeat the stroke several times and have the children imitate it in the air with their fingers.
- Demonstrate the letter again, and then have the children use pencil or crayons and paper to make a capital *C*.
- Repeat the procedure for small *c*.
- Ask children to point out any capital or small *c*'s in their Name Necklaces.

Transparency 03

Letter Formation For those children having difficulty with letter formation, project the letter formation transparency on the chalkboard or a piece of chart paper and have the child trace over the letter.

Alphabet Big Book — Cc

Display the *Alphabet **Big Book*** and open it to pages 8–9. Read "Crusty corn bread," pointing to the words as you say them. Then have one group of children count how many capital *C*'s there are, and have another group count how many small *c*'s there are.

Flaky biscuits,
crunchy toast,
cracks in the crackers
crumble the most.

Eve Merriam

Crusty corn bread,
crumbly crumbs,
mumbly muffins,
buttery thumbs.

8

9

Alphabet Big Book, pp. 8–9

Assessment

✓ **Informal Monitoring** Continue to observe children's attempts at letter formation. Provide extra help for children who are having difficulty.

② Reading and Responding

"What Will Mommy Do When I'm at School?"
Pages 22–43 of *School*

This selection is taught in six lessons:

| Lesson 7 | Lesson 9 | Lesson II |
| Lesson 8 | Lesson 10 | Lesson I2 |

What Will Mommy Do When I'm at School?
by Dolores Johnson

I worry about my mother, 'cause I'm starting school tomorrow. As long as I've known my mom, I've never left her alone.

22

Selection Summary

Genre: Realistic Fiction

As part of the new experience of going to school, a little girl worries how her mother will feel at home all by herself while she is away at school all day.

About the Author/Illustrator

Dolores Johnson Author/Illustrator Dolores Johnson writes, "When I was young, I always knew I could draw, but I didn't think I was an artist." Johnson had a brother whom she considered a real artist. While her brother concentrated on art, she had many other interests. Johnson eventually went to art school. After graduation, Johnson says, "I floundered about." She worked as a production artist for a while. She then became a production manager for the art department of a mail-order company. It wasn't until a friend saw some of her work and suggested Johnson write and illustrate children's books that Johnson even considered doing so.

Writing and illustrating children's books gives Johnson a real sense of satisfaction. "I welcome the opportunity to write and illustrate books because it is a wonderful means to communicate with the most important segment of our society—the children. I like to write about the basic issues that are critical to the typical child's life ..."

**Other Books
by Dolores Johnson**
- *What Kind of Baby-Sitter Is This?*
- *The Best Bug to Be*
- *Your Dad Was Just Like You*

 Exploring the Theme

Selection Concepts

"What Will Mommy Do When I'm In School?" is realistic fiction about a girl who is about to start kindergarten. The girl's close, loving relationship with her mother is clearly illustrated by the child's unmistakable enjoyment of their past times together and her worries that her mother will be lonely when she goes to school. With the understanding and support of her family, the girl is able to resolve her conflict and go the school with an easy mind. Key concepts to be explored are:

■ It is hard to leave warmth and certainty for something new and unknown.

■ Love and understanding can build bridges to the future.

■ School holds the promise of new experiences that can be shared with loved ones at home.

Supporting Reflection

Throughout this selection, the children will continue to work on their unit activity about school. Because the selection "What Will Mommy Do When I'm at School" is read in its entirety during this lesson, there will be little time to work on the class picture/story big book. Over the subsequent lessons that focus on the selection, however, children will:

■ explore and discover their school as they search for Boomer who is missing from the classroom. They will learn about important locations in the school and will meet members of the school staff.

■ continue working with you and their classmates to make a class book about themselves and their school so that they can show their families what their school is like.

■ learn how to "read" the class book and share with others.

2 Reading and Responding

Build Background

Activate Prior Knowledge

Remind the children that the theme of this unit is school. Ask them to think about how they felt before they started school. Discuss any fears they might have had, and how they overcame those fears.

Background Information

Discuss what kinds of things the children do at home when they are not in school. Make a list of these on the chalkboard. After reading the story compare what the children do at home with what the little girl did.

Preview and Prepare

Browse

■ Display the **Big Book** *School*, opened to the table of contents. Tell the children that they have read one selection in this book, "Boomer Goes to School." Point to the title on the page. Explain that today they will read another selection called "What Will Mommy Do When I'm at School?" Point to the title and read it. Then point to the page number where the story begins and say it. Turn to pages 22–23, and point to and read aloud the name of the author/illustrator. Explain that Dolores Johnson wrote the story and drew the pictures.

■ Have the children discuss what they see in the pictures. Ask them to tell what they think the story might be about.

Set Purposes

Remind the children that they can read stories to find things out or just to enjoy them. Tell them that they can also read or listen to stories for other reasons, such as to discover new ideas.

Invite them to listen to find out what the little girl thinks about going to school. As they listen, ask them to think whether they are at all like the little girl in the story.

2 Reading and Responding

Vocabulary

Selection Vocabulary

- Tell the children that *tomorrow* is when the little girl will go to school for the first time. Point out that when she goes to school, she thinks her mother will be afraid being all *alone*. Let them know that they will hear these words as you read the different parts of the story.

- Write each of the following words on the chalkboard, touch it, and read it aloud:

tomorrow   alone

- Ask which word tells about the day after today. (*tomorrow*)
- Ask which word means "all by yourself"? (*alone*) Invite volunteers to try to make sentences using these words.
- Invite the children to compose a complete sentence using the word "Alone," and starting with "Tomorrow the little girl . . ."

Meeting Individual Needs

ESL

If possible, find out the equivalent words in the native language of the English-language learners to help them participate in the vocabulary lesson.

Reading Recommendations

- Read the story through completely, pausing only to model reading strategies and answer the children's questions.

- Ask the children if they remember where to start reading the story. Be sure all children know that we start reading at the first word on the first page of the selection.

- Run your hand under each line as you read, and point to the words. Remind children that the words they hear as you read are the words that are written on the page.

- Encourage the children to ask questions about words or ideas they do not understand.

Using Reading Strategies

During the reading of "What Will Mommy Do When I'm at School?", you will model the use of the following reading strategies:

- Clarifying
- Making Connections

Stop to clarify words or ideas that the children find confusing. Be sure that the children understand *why* you are using the strategies *(to help understand the story)*. Whenever possible, have children model the strategies for their classmates.

Reading and Responding

Comprehension Strategies

Introducing Strategy Use

Modeling

1 **Making Connections** *The little girl is worried because she's afraid to leave her mother all alone. I know that when I have to go someplace new, I often worry before I get there. I think this little girl is worried about how she'll feel at school as well as how her mother will feel at home. One of the ways people make sense of what they read is to make connections between what is written in the story and something in their own lives.*

Modeling

2 **Making Connections** *Who can tell how the little girl might feel? (I know just how the little girl feels. I had to hurry to eat breakfast in the morning, too. What about you?)*

 Teacher Tip Beginning kindergarten children may not respond readily to prompts. However, with a great deal of encouragement, they will eventually catch on and respond.

What Will Mommy Do When I'm at School?

by Dolores Johnson

I worry about my mother, 'cause I'm starting school tomorrow. As long as I've known my mom, I've never left her alone.

22

No more cooking muffins together. No more taking time with breakfast. I'll have to hurry and eat cold cereal. It never tastes as good. **2**

24

Do you think she'll miss me? I hope she won't be scared without me. But school starts tomorrow, and I really have to go. **1**

23

We used to sing lots of songs together, like "The Fuzzy Wuzzy Bear" and "I'm a Little Teapot." Who'll remind her of the words when I'm gone?

25

Comprehension Skills

During the rereading of this selection, the children will focus on specific techniques, tools, and skills to help them better understand what they read. Comprehension skill activities are provided in this column in Lessons 8 through 11.

Reading and Responding

Comprehension Strategies

Introducing Strategy Use

Modeling

3 Clarifying *I'm beginning to think that the little girl is not telling us the complete story. If I look at the pictures, I can clarify a bit. On page 26, I see that it's the little girl who is watching cartoons and Mommy who straightens up the living room in the morning. On page 28, it says that Mommy has never shopped for groceries alone. Do you think that's true? How do you think the little girl feels about going to school? Do you think she wants to go? I'm beginning to think that it's really her who doesn't want to be alone.*

Now Mom can't watch cartoons with me while we straighten up the living room. She'll have to spend the mornings all alone.

26

No more helping her with the groceries. You know she's never done it alone. **3**

28

No more time for her to comb my hair in the morning. I won't have time to comb her hair for her, either.

27

No more picture books. Mom loves to hear me read them. No more tea for two at three o'clock. But my bear, Miss Muffin, will still be there.

29

Comprehension Skills

During the rereading of this selection, the children will focus on specific techniques, tools, and skills to help them better understand what they read. Comprehension skill activities are provided in this column in Lessons 8 through 11.

Reading and Responding

Comprehension Strategies

Introducing Strategy Use

Modeling

4 **Making Connections** *This is the first time we've seen the little girl's father. What do you think is happening here? How can we figure it out? (It looks as if he is trying to comfort her. I know that sometimes it helps if someone takes the time just to tell me that everything will be all right.)*

Oh, I've been to day-care centers. And I've stayed overnight with Grandma. But Mom and I have never been apart for very long.

30

My daddy tells me Mom will be all right by herself. But I tell him, "She won't be happy." He tells me Mom will make other friends. I say, "None as good as me." **4**

32

31

33

Comprehension Skills

During the rereading of this selection, the children will focus on specific techniques, tools, and skills to help them better understand what they read. Comprehension skill activities are provided in this column in Lessons 8 through 11.

② Reading and Responding

Comprehension Strategies

Introducing Strategy Use

Modeling
❺ Making Connections *I remember when I was little. Sometimes my mother knew so many things, I thought she knew about everything in the whole world.*

Modeling
❻ Clarifying *I'm not sure what the little girl is doing. Let's try to figure this out. Does anyone want to clarify it? (It seems like she is telling about what she thinks will happen when she starts school.) From what you see in the picture, do you think Mommy will still pick out the clothes the little girl wears?*

I tell him, "Mom teaches me lots of things. My ABC's, how to write my name." I tell him, "She knows everything, except how to get along without me." ❺

34

Now I'll have to wake Mom in the morning. Then I'll have to pick out my clothes every day. My mom really loves to do that. Maybe I'll still let her. ❻

36

I say, "Maybe you can stay home. If I can't stay here, why not you?" He said he would if he could, 'cause he misses Mommy, too.

35

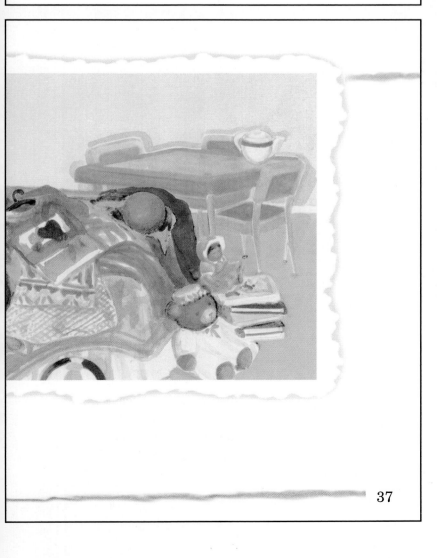

37

Comprehension Skills

During the rereading of this selection, the children will focus on specific techniques, tools, and skills to help them better understand what they read. Comprehension skill activities are provided in this column in Lessons 8 through 11.

2 Reading and Responding

Comprehension Strategies

Introducing Strategy Use

Modeling

7 Making Connections *How does it feel when someone makes you feel better when you're sad? Who can tell us? Is that the same feeling as the little girl has? By making connections we can really understand how the girl is feeling.*

Modeling

8 Making Connections *Well, finally the little girl is talking to her mother. How does she feel? (the little girl looks relieved) When you talk to someone about something that is bothering you, how do you feel?*

So Mom will walk me to school tomorrow. It will be like when we used to walk to the park together. But then I'll kiss her and hug her and tell her good-bye.

38

My mom said, "I don't want you to leave me, baby, but school is such a great new adventure. You're going to be able to learn so much and do so much. There will be so many new things you can even teach me." **8**

40

But I'll still worry about my mother. What will she do without me? Today she asked me to come closer so she could wipe my tears away. **7**

39

Comprehension Skills

During the rereading of this selection, the children will focus on specific techniques, tools, and skills to help them better understand what they read. Comprehension skill activities are provided in this column in Lessons 8 through 11.

"Well, I'm not going to let you be lonely, Mom. When I come home, I'll tell you everything I've learned. I will bring you pictures I've drawn. I can bring over all my new friends. Maybe they can become your new friends, too."

41

2 Reading and Responding

Comprehension Strategies

Introducing Strategy Use

Modeling

9 Clarifying *Well, all this time we've been wondering what the little girl's mother would do at home all alone. Now the story tells us that her mother is not going to be staying home at all. How interesting!*

"Well, you don't have to worry about me, sweetheart," said my mother. "Though I'll miss you, I won't be lonely. I'll be starting my own new adventure. While you're at school tomorrow, I'll be beginning a brand-new job." **9**

42

"You know, Mom, maybe school won't
be so bad after all. Think of all the great
new things we can tell each other when
we get home."

"I can hardly wait, baby."

43

Discussing the Selection Be
prepared with questions about the
story to prompt the children. Many
kindergarten children may be
reluctant to ask questions without
prompting.

Discussing the Selection

Have the children share their thoughts about the
selection. Encourage them to tell what they liked best about
the story and to ask any questions about school the story
might have sparked. Write these questions on strips of paper
and place them on the Concept/Question Board. Remind the
children that throughout the unit, you will try to find
answers to these questions.

Purposes for Reading

Remind the children that we read both for entertainment
and to get information. Ask them what information they
found out about the little girl from "What Will Mommy Do
When I'm at School?"

Reading and Responding

Responding to Literature

Print Awareness

Word Boundaries

As you read, touch individual words. Ask volunteers to point to the first word on a page and to the last word on the page. Then ask the children to frame an individual word with their fingers. Have them point to the spaces before and after the word.

Directionality of Print

Call on volunteers to move their fingers under lines on the pages left to right as you read the words. Remind the children that readers follow the words from left to right on a page.

Home Connection

Distribute **Home Connection** page 11 which tells families about the selection "What Will Mommy Do When I'm at School" and offers suggestions for activities to do at home. This letter is available in English and Spanish.

Home Connection, p. 11

Exploring the Theme

Theme Connections

Talk About It

■ Sit with the children and ask them to try to remember what they thought about on the night before their first day of school. Prompt them with a question such as:

Did you think about what your home would be like during the day?

Supporting Reflection

Although students will not have time to work on the class picture/story big book during this lesson, over the next few lessons they will be exploring the school and meeting some of the members of the staff.

To make this activity more fun for the children, we suggest that you continue to have Boomer visit other parts of the school so the children have to search for him. During the searches, children will visit various locations in the school and learn what happens there. Arrange these visits—for example, to the library, school office, custodian's office, and so on ahead of time.

Check the Reading link of the **SRA** Web page for links to School-related Web sites.
http://www.sra-4kids.com

③ Integrating the Curriculum

Teacher Tip When the children begin to recognize some words, you might post a list of ideas they can refer to as they choose subjects for journal writing. Later, you can invite the children to add their own suggestions.

Language Arts

Independent and Collaborative Writing

Journal Writing

Invite the children to record any thoughts they want in their journals. Circulate as they write or draw their entries. Confer with as many children as possible. Conferences should be brief, providing reassurance and support for children. If students are unsure as to what to write or draw in their journals, talk with them about ideas discussed earlier with the whole class; let them decide which of these, or what other idea, they would like to draw or write about.

Tell the children that they might choose to write in their journals during writing time each day, or they might choose to write in their journals during Independent Work Time. Make sure they understand that they can also write in their journal at other times—for example, if they learn something interesting in math or learn a new song they want to remember, they can write it in their journal.

Listening, Speaking, Viewing

Asking and Answering Questions

Tell the children that one way we can find out things is to ask questions.

■ Point out to the children that questions often begin with the words *who*, *what*, *why*, *when*, or *where*. Talk with them about polite ways to ask questions. Have children take turns asking questions, perhaps about what their classmates did before school this morning, who helped them, and so on.

■ Remind the children that when someone asks them a question, they should listen very carefully so they can give a good answer. Explain also that when someone is answering their question, they should also listen very carefully so they can get all the information.

Teacher Tip

There are ways to encourage the children to ask questions. Choose a subject area or topic and model question asking. Have the students ask questions using the same model but a different topic. Switch and have children ask different types of questions about the same topic.

Integrating the Curriculum

Vocabulary

Opposites

- Say the word *hot*, and ask the children to think of the word that would mean *not hot*. If necessary explain that *cold* is the *opposite* of *hot*. Continue with other words from "What Will Mommy Do When I'm at School?", and ask the children to say the opposite word: start (*stop*), never (*always*), day (*night*), long (*short*), good (*bad*).

Meeting Individual Needs

ESL

Opposites Ask English-language learners to offer pairs of words that are opposites in their primary languages first, to verify that they understand the concept of opposites, before working with the class on English words.

Across the Curriculum

Social Studies

Categorizing and Classifying

Purpose

To group items and activities into *Home* and *School* categories.

Materials

two construction paper strips labeled *Home* and *School*, drawing paper, crayons, markers

Procedure

- Ask the children to name some things they like to do at school. Invite them to tell why it is something they enjoy.
- Then invite the children to suggest some activities they like to do at home and tell why these activities are fun.
- On the bulletin board, attach the two construction paper strips side by side to create two columns. Point to each word and say it aloud. Then encourage the children to say them with you.
- Then invite the children to draw one picture of themselves engaged in a favorite home activity and one picture of themselves in a favorite school activity.
- When the pictures are completed, invite the children to tell about the activities they have illustrated and whether they are things to do at home or at school. Then have them fasten their pictures in the correct columns on the bulletin board.

① Sounds and Letters

Open Court Reading
Pickled Peppers

Teacher Tip

Clap along to keep the rhythm as the children substitute their own rhyming words in "Hickory, Dickory, Dock."

Phonemic Awareness and Phonics Videodisc

Reading the Big Book

Level K – Disc 1 – Side A – Chapter 4

Use the **Phonemic Awareness Videodisc** to preview the Big Book. Unit 1 Lesson 8.

Sounds, Letters, and Language

Reading the Big Book *Pickled Peppers*
"Hickory, Dickory, Dock," page 12

- Open *Pickled Peppers* to the table of contents and point to "Hickory, Dickory, Dock." Ask the children if someone can point to the page number. Say the number and then turn to it. Read the title, pointing to each word. Read the author's name and then read *illustrated by Steve Henry*. Remind the children that illustrators are people who draw pictures to go along with stories and poems.

- Read through the poem slowly, running you finger under each word as you do so. Ask the children to look at the picture as you read. Then ask them to listen for any words that are depicted in the picture. Have the children repeat the word as they point to the picture.

- Invite volunteers to recite the rhyme with you. Then read the rhyme and have the children mime the actions of the mouse running up and down the clock. Review the rhyming words *hickory/dickory* and *dock/clock*.

- Put **Word Cards** in the **Pocket Chart** to make the rhyme. Say each word as you place it in the chart. Then have children say the rhyme with you as you touch each card.

- Tell the children that you can make the rhyme sound different. Hold up **Picture Cards** *sock*, *rock*, and *lock*. Place one picture over the first word clock in the chart. Then have the children help you read to the second word *clock*. Ask a volunteer to replace that *clock* with the second picture of a *sock*. Reread the rhyme with the new words. Continue in the same manner with the other pictures, substituting them for the word *clock*.

- Review the rhyming words by having children say them with you: *clock, rock, sock, lock*. Ask them to suggest other words that rhyme with *clock*. Recite the rhyme, substituting the children's words.

- Remind the children that every word gets a space before it and a space after it when it is written. Clarify by pointing to words one by one as you read the title "Hickory, Dickory, Dock" from left to right.

- Ask the children to figure out how many words are in the title. To confirm, recite them slowly as you point to each. After pointing to each word, point to the space in front of it and the space after it.

- Read the title again, followed by the first line of the rhyme. Have the children notice that the title and the first line have the same words. Clarify by pointing to *Hickory* in the title, then in the first line. Do the same for the remaining two words.

- Have children find the high-frequency word *the*.

PHONEMIC AWARENESS

Phonemic Awareness

Listening

Substituting Rhyming Words

- Tell the children that you can change the poem by changing the word *dock*.
- Display **Picture Cards** *cat*, *moon*, and *lamp*.
- Recite the first two lines, substituting the nonsense word *dat* for *dock* and stopping before the last word:

  Hickory, dickory, dat
  The mouse ran up the _____.

- Have children find the picture that completes the new rhyme. *(cat)*
- Continue in the same way, substituting the nonsense word *doon* then *damp* for *dock*.
- Once the game is established, continue substituting *dock*, but play without picture clues.

Word Substitution

- Recite the rhyme "Rain, Rain, Go Away" again. Hold up a classroom object and have a child name it. Now ask the class or the child to recite the rhyme, substituting the name of the object in place of *rain*.
- Continue, using other classroom objects. To give many children a chance to participate, you may return to this game another day.

Rhyme

Tell the children to listen carefully as you say some words. Explain that all but one of the words you say will rhyme. Tell them that as soon as they hear the word that does *not* rhyme, they are to raise their hands.

- Read the following words. If any hands are slow to go up when you read the non-rhyming word, read the list again.

mark	shark	dark	park	**steam**	lark	hark

- To confirm the children's response, you may want to read the list again.
- Continue the activity with the following lists:

wink	drink	blink	stink	**smell**	think	ink	pink
op	hop	stop	mop	**go**	chop	flop	drop
real	wheel	feel	seal	**soap**	meal	kneel	deal
are	car	bar	star	**store**	jar	far	scar
aim	came	same	name	tame	**time**	fame	blame
soon	moon	spoon	noon	**shoe**	room	broom	boom

Remember that some children may not be ready to make rhymes on their own, even if they can listen for them and identify them. Giving them a visual clue will allow them to make new rhymes that match the changes you make in a familiar verse.

Meeting Individual Needs

ESL

Preteach Work with the English-language learners beforehand by asking them for rhyming words in their own languages. Explain the use of nonsense words such as *dat* and *doon*.

Phonics CD-ROM

Use the **Phonics** CD-ROM for activities that support the Phonemic Awareness Lessons.

Sounds and Letters

Letter Recognition

Letter Names

Sing Your Way to *N* Game

- Ask the class to sing the letters to *N*, having the puppet touch each letter.
- Have a child use the puppet and touch any letter between *G* and *N*. Then have the class sing to the letter in order to identify it. Repeat with other children and other letters between *G* and *N*.

Find a Letter

- Review the list of letters that the children have found in previous lessons. Then have the children refer to the ***Alphabet Cards*** and find other examples of matching letters around the room.
- Make a new list with the children's names. Call on a child whose name is on the list and ask him or her to tell what letter he or she found. Note the letters on the list.

Letters *Hh* to *Mm*

- Give each child a set of ***Letter Cards*** for the letters *Hh-Jj* or *Kk-Mm*. Ask children to look for a card with *H* and to hold it up when you give a signal. When the letters are found, have the children show the small *h* to the person next to them.
- If the children need help, sing the "Alphabet Song" for them and tap your foot when you reach the letter they should find. Then have the children sing again with you, and tap the card itself when they reach that letter.
- Continue naming other letters for children to find.

Letter Shapes

Exploring *Dd*

- Direct the children's attention to the *Dd* **Alphabet Card**.

- Point to the capital letter *D* and the small letter *d*. Tell the children that they will be writing these letters. Say:

  Start at the top and go straight down. Then start here and go around this way (right), then stop at the bottom. Capital *D*.

- Repeat the stroke several times and have children imitate it in the air with their fingers.

- Then have the children use pencils and paper to make the letter.

- Repeat the procedure for small *d*. Tell them where to start and how to make the curve to the left. Then show them where to start the line that goes straight down.

- Ask children to point out any capital or small *d*s in their Name Necklaces. You might also have them find *Dd* in the name list from the Find a Letter game they played earlier.

Alphabet Big Book—Dd

Display the *Alphabet* **Big Book** and open it to pages 10–11. Read "Ducks in the Rain," pointing to the words as you say them. When the children see you touch words that begin with capital *D* or small *d*, tell them to flap their arms like ducks.

Ducks are dabbling in the rain,
Dibbling, dabbling in the rain.
Drops of water from each back
Scatter as ducks flap and quack

Ducks in the Rain
James S. Tippett

10   11

Alphabet Big Book, pp. 10–11

Teacher Tip

Letter Formation For those children having difficulty with letter formation, project the letter formation transparency on the chalkboard or a piece of chart paper and have the child trace over the letter. Or copy the transparency and have them practice on their own.

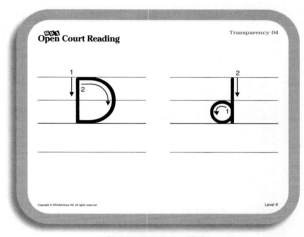

Transparency 04

Intervention

Be aware if children are having difficulty with pencils or crayons. If necessary, have them work on the chalkboard or with chart paper. Repeating the strokes may be helpful.

Assessment

✓**Informal** Continue to observe children writing letters. Plan to give help during Independent Work Time.

1 Sounds and Letters

High-Frequency Word Wall Add the words from this book to the High-Frequency Word Wall.

Nondecodable Words Always refer to the inside back cover of the *Pre-Decodable Book* for the words that need to be taught before the students read the book.

Pre-Decodable Book 2

Assessment

✔ **Formal Picture Vocabulary** To assess the children's ability to identify certain high-frequency words through pictures, have them complete **Skills Assessment** page 2.

Reading a Pre-Decodable Book
Book 2: *Lunch*

High-Frequency Words

The new high-frequency words in this story are *here*, *is*, *a*, and *an*.

Reading Recommendations

■ Introduce the new high-frequency words listed at the top of the page. Write each word on the chalkboard. Point to and say each word, then have the children say each word with you.

■ Give each child a copy of the **Pre-Decodable Book**. Explain that you will read the book together.

■ Discuss each rebus picture to be sure the children understand what each is.

■ Hold up your book. Read the title aloud, then have the children read it with you. Point to and read the author's name and explain that this is the name of the person who wrote the book. Then point to and read the illustrator's name and explain that this is the name of the person who drew the pictures in the book.

■ Allow children to page through the book, commenting on what they see in the pictures and making predictions about what they think the book will tell them.

■ Help children find page 3. Hold up your copy of the book and sweep your hand under each line of text. Then read each line, pointing to each word or rebus as you say it. Encourage children to move their hands from left to right across the text as you read together.

■ Continue through the book, following the same procedure.

■ Reread the book, this time pointing to the picture on each page and asking children to tell what is happening in the picture.

■ Invite children to discuss the book as a group.

■ Provide many opportunities for children to partner-read.

For a complete discussion of how to use **Pre-Decodable Books**, see the Appendix.

Responding

- Help the children find page 8 in their books. Read the text, *Here is lunch*, and ask the children to say the first word. Then ask them for the middle word, and then ask for the last word. Have them respond in complete sentences such as, "The first word is *here*." "The middle word is *is*." and "*Lunch* is the last word."

- Review the high-frequency words introduced in this book. Write *is* on the chalkboard and say the word. Ask children to look for *is* in their books and to touch the word when they find it. Call on volunteers to "read" the word and show it to the class. Repeat the procedure for *an*, *a*, and *here*.

During the time you set aside each day for individual and small-group work, encourage the children to review previous *Pre-Decodable Books* with a partner.

is	a
an	here

- Call on individual children to retell the story by looking at the illustration on each page.

- For additional practice, you may want to use *Book 2* of the supplemental set of *Open Court Reading Decodable Books*.

- You may want to make copies for the children of the black-and-white version of this story which is available in the *Pre-Decodable Takehome Book*.

② Reading and Responding

"What Will Mommy Do When I'm at School?"

Pages 22–29 of *School*

This selection is taught in six lessons:

Lesson 7	Lesson 9	Lesson II
Lesson 8	Lesson 10	Lesson 12

What Will
Mommy Do When
I'm at School?

by Dolores Johnson

I worry about my mother, 'cause I'm
starting school tomorrow. As long as I've
known my mom, I've never left her alone.

22

Meeting Individual Needs

ESL

Preteach the Selection Vocabulary to English-language learners so that they can participate in the class discussion.

Build Background

Activate Prior Knowledge

Ask the children what they remember about "What Will Mommy Do When I'm at School?" from previous readings.

Preview and Prepare

Browse

■ Display the *School **Big Book***, opened to the table of contents. Point to and read the title, "What Will Mommy Do When I'm at School?" Point to and say the page number on which the story begins. Turn to pages 22–23 and point to and read the names of the author/illustrator. Turn through pages 22–29 and ask the children to tell about anything that interests them in the pictures or the print.

Vocabulary

Selection Vocabulary

Write each of the following words on the chalkboard, touch them, and read them aloud:

eat   sing   watch   read

■ Tell children that each word names an action or something someone can do.
■ Have groups of three children at a time pantomime each word. Then ask the children to listen carefully for these words as you read this part of the story.

Reading Recommendations

- Run your hand under each line of print as you read. Remind children that the words they hear as you read are the words that are written on the page.

- Encourage the children to ask questions about words or ideas they do not understand as you reread pages 22–29.

Using Reading Strategies

During the first reading of "What Will Mommy Do When I'm at School?", you modeled the use of the following reading strategies:

- Clarifying
- Making Connections

For your convenience, the strategy models from the first reading of the selection are reproduced in this lesson in the form of reminders. You may choose not to use these reminders with your class, or to use them only with children who need extra help or who missed the first reading of the selection.

Building Comprehension Skills

Rereading a selection allows readers to apply skills that give them a more complete understanding of what they read. Some of these follow-up comprehension skills, such as *Clarifying and Categorizing, Cause and Effect, Sequence,* and *Compare and Contrast,* help readers to organize the information in a selection. Other skills, such as *Drawing Conclusions,* lead them to a deeper understanding of the selection, or to a "reading between the lines."

In Lessons 8–11 you will be working with the comprehension skill *Comparing and Contrasting.* Consider using **Transparency 33** to help illustrate this graphically.

Transparency 33

② Reading and Responding

Comprehension Strategies

Introducing Strategy Use

Modeling

❶ Making Connections *Remind the children that you knew how the little girl felt about being afraid to go to a new place because of your own experiences. Tell them that good readers often stop to make connections, or figure out what is going on. Sometimes they do this by making a connection with something they have experienced in their own lives.*

Modeling

❷ Making Connections *Remind the children that good readers often stop to make connections, or figure out what is going on in a story. Sometimes they do this by making a connection with something they have experienced in their own lives.*

Teacher Tip Beginning kindergarten children may not respond readily to prompts. However, with a great deal of encouragement, they will eventually catch on and respond.

What Will Mommy Do When I'm at School?

by Dolores Johnson

I worry about my mother, 'cause I'm starting school tomorrow. As long as I've known my mom, I've never left her alone.

22

No more cooking muffins together. No more taking time with breakfast. I'll have to hurry and eat cold cereal. It never tastes as good. ❷

24

Do you think she'll miss me? I hope she won't be scared without me. But school starts tomorrow, and I really have to go. **1**

23

We used to sing lots of songs together, like "The Fuzzy Wuzzy Bear" and "I'm a Little Teapot." Who'll remind her of the words when I'm gone?

25

Comprehension Skills

Compare and Contrast

■ Explain to the children that writers often make their stories more interesting by telling how things or people are alike and how they are different from one another.

■ Have the children look at the illustrations on pages 23 and 25. Ask them how the pictures are the same *(they both show the little girl and her mom)*. Ask them how the two pictures are different *(one shows the little girl looking sad while the other shows her looking happy)*. Have the children explain why the 2 pictures show different feelings. *(In one the little girl is remembering happier times and in the other she's thinking about sad times ahead.)*

■ Read pages 22–25 again and have the children compare their thoughts about starting school to those of the girl in the story.

② Reading and Responding

Comprehension Strategies

Introducing Strategy Use

Modeling

❸ Clarifying *Remind the children that you stopped to look at the pictures in the story to better understand what is actually happening. Tell them that good readers sometimes stop to clarify, or figure out what is going on. Sometimes they look at a story's illustrations to help them better understand a story.*

Now Mom can't watch cartoons with me
while we straighten up the living room.
She'll have to spend the mornings all alone.

26

No more helping her with the groceries.
You know she's never done it alone. ❸

28

Teacher Tip

When you reread the story, model the strategies only if your children need additional help. Otherwise, focus on Comprehension Skills such as Comparing and Contrasting.

No more time for her to comb my hair in the morning. I won't have time to comb her hair for her, either.

27

No more picture books. Mom loves to hear me read them. No more tea for two at three o'clock. But my bear, Miss Muffin, will still be there.

29

Comprehension Skills

Discussing the Selection

Have the children discuss what the little girl says she is worried about in this part of the story. Ask them if they think the little girl should be worried about these things, or if they think her mother will be fine.

Reading and Responding

Responding to Literature

Literature Appreciation

In a typical children's story, the events follow a simple time line sequence: first this happens, then that happens, and so forth. However, the author of "What Will Mommy Do When I'm at School?" uses two separate time lines. One time line occurs in the past, and is shown in some of the pictures of the little girl and her mother doing fun things together. A second time line tells what is happening in the present—the little girl is worried about her mother. This time line is conveyed in pictures and in the text.

Although keeping two time lines in mind simultaneously is usually very difficult for children, this selection makes it understandable for them by the effective use of illustrations.

Some of the events in the past and present time lines are:

Past	*Present*
■ cooking muffins with mom for breakfast	■ worrying about having to eat a cold hurried breakfast
■ singing songs with mom	■ worrying about mom not remembering the words
■ watching cartoons with mom	■ worrying about mom spending all morning alone

Review each time line of events with the children. One occurs in the past, and tells of the fun things the little girl and her mother did together; the other tells what is happening in the present—the little girl is worried about her mother and fears their "fun times" are over.

Assessment

✔ **Informal** Note how the children are responding to the stories. Some children may need to discuss the stories in smaller group settings.

Exploring the Theme

Theme Connections

Talk About It

■ Have the children discuss how their routines have changed since they started going to school. Prompt them with questions such as:

What do you like most about your day since you started going to school?

What do you miss most about your day that you don't do any more?

Supporting Reflection

Display the class picture/story big book and remind the children that they have explained almost everything about the class to Boomer. Stop suddenly and draw the children's attention to the fact that you haven't seen Boomer today. Ask them to look for him.

Organize a search by having the children identify an activity center or classroom location where they will look. After a brief search is completed have the children report to the whole group where they looked unsuccessfully.

Suggest to the children that since Boomer isn't in the classroom that he might have gotten out and is looking around the school. Take a picture of the whole group as you start the search. Take the children to some school location, such as the library, and ask the librarian if she or he has seen Boomer. Invite the librarian to help the children search for Boomer throughout the library. As she looks, she can briefly and informally acquaint the children with the layout of the library and her responsibilities. Have the librarian find Boomer in the young children's section of the library, with some books about school. Arrange for the librarian to suggest the children take the books back to their classroom to read with Boomer. Take her picture with Boomer in the library. Suggest to the children that they ask her any questions they might have.

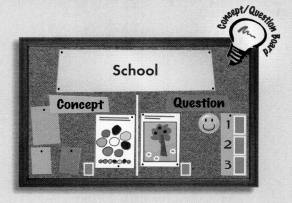

Check the Reading link of the **SRA** Web page for links to School-related Web sites. **http://www.sra-4kids.com**

③ Integrating the Curriculum

Language Arts

Independent and Collaborative Writing

Being a Student

■ Write the word *student* on the chalkboard and say it. Invite the children to talk about themselves in their new roles as students. How does being a student make them feel? Encourage the children to draw a picture of themselves as students, or with a few words dictate a sentence; then invite volunteers to share their work with the class.

Study/Research

Parts of the Library

As part of the *Our Classroom and School* unit activities, the children will visit the school library. Encourage the school librarian to

- point out that the library groups the same kinds of books and materials in sections to make things easier to find.

- help the children understand many kinds of materials can be found at the library in addition to books, such as magazines, recordings, videotapes.

- help the children understand that all of the story books are in one place, magazines are in another place, books about real people and things are in still another place. Travel around the library identifying each special section.

Vocabulary

Rhyming Words

Remind the children that words rhyme when they have the same ending sounds.

- Have the children listen as you say some words. Ask them to clap when they hear two words that rhyme. Use these word pairs: *hop, top*; *book, bag*; *boat, coat*; *hand, sand*; *moon, mouse*; *rake, cake.*

- Then tell the children that you will say a word and that you will ask a volunteer to name a rhyming word. Some words to give are: *hot, cat, lace, ride, bug.*

Meeting Individual Needs

ESL

Parts of the Library Take the English-language learners to the school library ahead of the class visit, and identify the areas where different types of books and materials are placed. Then ask the children to make simple labels for each of these areas: story books, magazines, books about real people and things. Have the children place the labels in the appropriate places in the library.

Assessment

✓ **Informal Monitoring** Monitor the children's ability to do the rhyming activities. Plan to work in small groups with children who do not seem to understand rhyming.

Integrating the Curriculum

Grammar

Words that Name

- Display **Pocket Chart Picture Cards** *sock*, *rock*, *mouse* along the chalk ledge and have children name each picture. Write the name of the picture on the chalkboard above the card.

- Touch and read the word *sock* and tell children that this word names the picture. Repeat with each picture name.

- Have children hold up their Name Necklaces. Explain that these words are the names of people. Tell children that some words, called nouns, name things, other words name people, and other words name places.

- Ask children to suggest some words that name things in the classroom. Then have them go over and touch the item as you write the noun on the chalkboard. Continue the activity with the names of places in your school.

Listening, Speaking, Viewing

Listening Attentively

Remind the children that when they ask and answer questions, they must listen carefully to get all the information.

- Explain that listening carefully is important even when they are just listening to enjoy something. Ask the children to tell what might happen if someone told a riddle and they weren't listening closely. Help them realize that they might miss the best part of the riddle, the part that makes you laugh!

- Point out that it is always important to be attentive when they listen, so they can enjoy all the songs, poems, and stories they can. Review that good listeners sit quietly, look at the speaker, and don't interrupt. Tell a few riddles and have the children demonstrate good listening skills. Periodically lower your voice to focus the children's listening.

Across the Curriculum

Movement

What We Do Together

Purpose

To act out activities that children used to do at home.

Procedure

- Ask the children to think about some things the girl and her mother did together before she started school. Have them work with a partner to discuss some of the things and to choose an activity that they would like to act out.

- Allow some time for the children to practice. Then invite partners to pantomime the activity. Remind them that pantomime means "acting out silently."

- Then have the children think of an activity that they used to do before they started going to school. Have them again work with a partner to decide how they will show their activity. Then invite the partners to pantomime this new scene.

1 Sounds and Letters

Sounds, Letters, and Language

Reading the Big Book *Pickled Peppers*
"Hickory, Dickory, Dock," page 12

Gather the children around you and open *Pickled Peppers* to "Hickory, Dickory, Dock."

- Read the poem through several times, emphasizing the rhyming words, *hickory/dickory* and *dock/clock*. Read the poem again and ask the children, "What rhymes with *hickory*? What rhymes with *dock*?"

- Tell the children you might do something wrong and that you want them to raise their hands when they see or hear you do something wrong. Read the poem once, following the words with your fingers. Now start reading it backward from the last word at the bottom of the page. When children say you must start at the top, start with the last word of the first line. When children say you must start with the first word, read the first word of each line. Ask children what you should do. Emphasize that reading moves from top to bottom, left to right.

- Read the poem through again several times. If the children know the poem well enough, you can ask them to recite it slowly as you point to each word. Model this for them first. Remind them to wait until you point to a word before saying it.

- Ask if anyone notices a difference between the way the word *Dock* is written in the title and in the first line (*dock*). Call on volunteers to explain the capital and small *Dd*. If no one recognizes the difference, point to the **Alphabet Card** *Dd* and affirm that *Dock* begins with a capital *D* in the title and a small *d* in the first line.

- Affirm that important words such as names begin with a capital letter. Have them notice the capital letters on their Name Necklaces. Point out that a title is the name of a poem or story.

- Point to the words *The*, *mouse*, and *ran* each time they appear in the rhyme and have the children notice that the word is spelled the same way each time it appears.

 Teacher Tip   Before playing the game, go over a list of rhyming words to get the children ready.

Phonemic Awareness

The Ship is Loaded with _____ Game

- Have the children sit in a circle on the floor and tell them they will play a rhyming game. Hold up a ball and say, "The ship is loaded with cheese." Then roll the ball to a child, who must repeat the sentence, ending it with a word that rhymes with *cheese*. For example, "The ship is loaded with peas."

- Continue rolling the ball around the circle, having each child who receives the ball repeat the sentence and replace the last word with a new rhyme.

- When children can no longer think of rhymes, begin again with a new cargo, such as logs, stars, mats.

Listening

Word and Number Substitution

Teach the children the following rhyme:

> Five little monkeys, jumping on the bed.
> One fell off and bumped his head.
> Four little monkeys, jumping on the bed.
> One fell off and bumped his head.
> Three little monkeys, jumping on the bed.
> One fell off and bumped his head.
> Two little monkeys, jumping on the bed.
> One fell off and bumped his head.
> One little monkey, jumping on the bed.
> One fell off and bumped his head.
> No more monkeys, jumping on the bed.

- When children can recite the rhyme with you, use **Word Cards** and **Picture Cards** to create the following rebus line in the **Pocket Chart**:

  [5] little [monkeys] jumping on the [bed].

- Give each child a set of number cards, created from **Blackline Master 7**, and have them select the cards for 1–4. Review the numbers by counting and having children hold up the card when their number is called.

- Recite the first line of the poem, touching each card in the chart. Ask the children to tell how many monkeys would be on the bed if one fell off and bumped his head.

Meeting Individual Needs

ESL

The Ship is Loaded with _____ Game Play this game beforehand with the English-language learners, asking for rhyming words in their own languages.

Teacher Tip Generating rhyming words is more challenging than recognizing rhyming words. If children cannot think of a rhyming word, give help and go on with the game.

Teacher Tip **Phonemic Awareness** Remember to move quickly through the phonemic awareness activities. Do not hold the class back until all the children catch on. Individual progress will vary, but often moving on to other activities is more helpful than continued drilling on one activity.

Phonics CD-ROM

Use the **Phonics** CD-ROM for activities that support the Phonemic Awareness Lessons.

Sounds and Letters

- When children identify the correct number, have a child with that number come place it in the chart, replacing the 5. Read the new line.
- Continue in the same manner with the other numbers. Repeat the activity as time allows.

Rhyme

Continue the listening for rhyme activity, using the following lists of words:

rhyme	climb	dime	lime	**like**	time	chime
flat	bat	cat	**coat**	rat	sat	hat
eat	seat	feet	**tease**	beat	street	greet
race	lace	place	space	case	**paste**	face
will	still	hill	fill	bill	**pick**	chill
one	fun	run	sun	**rug**	done	bun
rice	ice	slice	spice	nice	**piece**	twice

Have the children raise their hand when they hear a word that doesn't rhyme.

Assessment

✓ **Informal** Monitor the children during the rhyming activity. Note those children who are having difficulty and plan to meet with small groups during Independent Work Time.

Letter Recognition

Letter Names

Alphabet Song

- Review the "Alphabet Song" by singing it all the way through once with the class. Then ask volunteers to sing it with partners as the class claps on the letters *G, N ,Q, T, W, Z*.

Sing Your Way to *T* Game

- Extend the Sing Your Way to _____ Game. Point to, but do not name, any letter between *Nn* and *Tt*. Ask the children to sing the "Alphabet Song" with you and the puppet until you reach the letter and then stop to identify the letter. Then have the puppet touch other letters between *Nn* and *Tt* and ask individual children to sing their way to these letters and stop.

Find a Letter

- Review letters that have been found previously. Have the children find the letters around the room. Then add the letters to the list of letters that each child has found.

Letters *Hh* to *Mm*

- Give each child a set of **Letter Cards** for the letters *Hh–Jj* or *Kk–Mm*. Try to give them different sets than they had in Lesson 8.
- Name letters for children to find and hold up.

Sounds and Letters

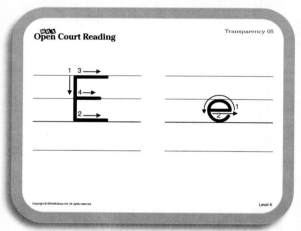

Transparency 05

Letter Formation For those children having difficulty with letter formation, project the letter formation transparency on the chalkboard or a piece of chart paper and have the child trace over the letter.

Letter Shapes

Exploring *Ee*

- Point to the capital letter *E* and the small letter *e* on the **Alphabet Card**. Note that the *Ee* card is red. Say that *a* and *e* are special letters called vowels. Tell the children that you have a cheer that will help them remember which letters are vowels:

  A (clap) E (clap) I, O, U (clap)

  I can name the vowels for you.

  A (clap) E (clap) I, O, U (clap)

  You can name them, too. Hoo!

- Point to the capital *E* and the small *e*. Tell the children that they will be writing these letters with you, beginning with capital *E*. Say:

  Start at the top and go down. Start here and go straight out. Start here and go straight out. Start here and go straight out. Capital *E*.

- Repeat the strokes several times and have children imitate you in the air with their fingers.

- Have children use pencils and paper to make the letter.

- Repeat the procedure for small *e*, saying:

  Start here, go around like this (left). Then go straight out. Small *e*.

- Ask children to point out any capital or small *E*'s in their Name Necklaces.

Alphabet Big Book — Ee

Display the *Alphabet **Big Book*** and open it to pages 12–13. Read "Eletelephony," pointing to the words as you say them. Call on volunteers to make up silly words of their own using the beginning sound of one word and the ending sound of another. Have them tell what each new word might mean.

Have volunteers come to the book and point out capital *E*'s and small *e*'s.

Once there was an elephant,
Who tried to use the telephant—
No! no! I mean an elephone
Who tried to use the telephone—
(Dear me! I am not certain quite
That even now I've got it right.)

Howe'er it was, he got his trunk
Entangled in the telephunk;
The more he tried to get it free,
The louder buzzed the telephee—
(I fear I'd better drop the song
Of elephop and telephong!)

Eletelephony
Jack Prelutsky

12   13

Alphabet Big Book, pp. 12–13

② Reading and Responding

"What Will Mommy Do When I'm at School?"
Pages 30–35 of *School*

This selection is taught in six lessons:

Lesson 7	Lesson 8	Lesson 9
Lesson 10	Lesson 11	Lesson 12

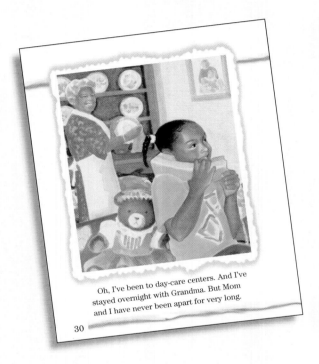

Oh, I've been to day-care centers. And I've stayed overnight with Grandma. But Mom and I have never been apart for very long.

30

Meeting Individual Needs

ESL

Relationship Words To help English-language learners understand the meaning of words such as *Mom, Daddy,* and *Grandma,* make simple stick drawings depicting the family members. Write and then say the matching word under each figure. Ask the children to repeat the words.

Build Background

Activate Prior Knowledge

Call on children to tell what they remember about "What Will Mommy Do When I'm at School?" from previous readings.

Preview and Prepare

Browse

■ Open the *School Big Book* to the table of contents and point to "What Will Mommy Do When I'm at School?" Ask the children if someone can point to the page number. Then turn to it. Read the title, pointing to each word. Read the author and illustrator name, Dolores Johnson. Remind the children that illustrators are people who draw pictures to go along with stories and poems.

■ Turn a few pages and ask the children to tell what other people and things they see in these pictures.

Vocabulary

Selection Vocabulary

■ Write each of the following words on the chalkboard, touch them, and read them aloud:

Mom   Daddy   Grandma

■ Tell the children that each word names a person in a family.

■ Then ask children to make up sentences using the words. If they like, have them make up sentences about these members of their own families.

Reading Recommendations

- Run your hand under each line of print as you read pages 30–35.
- Invite the children to join in when they see any words they recognize.
- Encourage the children to ask questions about anything they do not understand.

Using Reading Strategies

During the first reading of "What Will Mommy Do When I'm at School?", you modeled the use of the following reading strategies:

- Clarifying
- Making Connections

For your convenience, the strategy models from the first reading of the selection are reproduced in this lesson in the form of reminders. You may choose not to use these reminders with your class, or to use them only with children who need extra help or who missed the first reading of the selection.

Building Comprehension Skills

In this lesson you will continue to work with the comprehension skill *Comparing and Contrasting*.

② Reading and Responding

Comprehension Strategies

Introducing Strategy Use

Modeling

❹ Making Connections *Making a connection to my own life helped me understand why her dad would need to comfort her.*

Teacher Tip Ensure that students understand when and why specific strategies are used.

Oh, I've been to day-care centers. And I've stayed overnight with Grandma. But Mom and I have never been apart for very long.

30

My daddy tells me Mom will be all right by herself. But I tell him, "She won't be happy." He tells me Mom will make other friends. I say, "None as good as me." ❹

32

31

33

Comprehension Skills

Compare and Contrast

- Reread page 32. Discuss what the girl is comparing when she says, "None as good as me."

- Have two children stand and hold up an object such as a book, a crayon, a pencil, and so on. Compare the two objects in a sentence using *as* _____ *as* _____. "Paco's book is *as* big *as* Liz's book."

- Continue naming pairs of objects in the room. Call on volunteers to compare the objects, using sentences with *as* _____ *as* _____. Provide help as needed.

Teacher Tip Kindergarten children are likely to need considerable support to make these comparisons. It will help if you make the two objects very similar in color, size, weight, function, and so on. Do not labor the issue, only point out that you can compare two things in this way.

② Reading and Responding

Comprehension Strategies

Introducing Strategy Use

Modeling

❺ Making Connections *Did anyone make a connection with this part of the story? Who can model* Making Connections *for us? (When I read this the first time, it made me remember how I felt about my own mother. Making connections with the story helps keep me involved with my reading.)*

I tell him, "Mom teaches me lots of things. My ABC's, how to write my name." I tell him, "She knows everything, except how to get along without me." ❺

34

I say, "Maybe you can stay home. If I can't stay here, why not you?" He said he would if he could, 'cause he misses Mommy, too.

35

Discussing the Selection

Ask the children to discuss how the girl's father tries to cheer her up. How would they have done things differently? How have people tried to cheer them up?

Reading and Responding

Responding to Literature

Literature Appreciation

Turn through pages 22–29 and have the children notice what the author says about how the little girl feels (*she is worried about going to school because her mother will be lonesome*). Have them look at the illustrations and notice the expressions on the characters' faces. If necessary, remind them that some of the pictures on these pages show sadness and worry while others show happiness.

Invite the children to explain why some of the pictures show the characters smiling when the text states that she is worried (*because the pictures show what happened before—when the little girl and her mother were doing fun things together*). Explain that the pictures show what the little girl was remembering: She was thinking about what they *used to do*. Have the children think about and talk about how the illustrations complement and add to the story text.

Turn through pages 30–35 and have the children reflect on the little girl's feelings on each page. Invite them to express her feelings with facial expressions.

Encourage them to show how they felt on the first day of school and how they feel now. Help them see the similarity between their experience and that of the story character, the little girl.

Tell them that one of the reasons that stories are so interesting to us is that the characters, or people in the stories, sometimes act and feel just like us.

 Exploring the Theme

Theme Connections

View Fine Art

- Display page 48, *Fine Art*, in the **Big Book** *School.* Point to the picture *School's Out* by **Alan Crite**.

- Ask the children to discuss what is happening in the picture.

- Ask them to discuss any questions they might have about the picture. For example, you may ask "Why do you think this is called *School's Out*?"

Supporting Reflection

In the suggested unit activity, the children are exploring the school, becoming familiar with the staff and the building. If you are doing the suggested activity:

- tell the children that Boomer is missing again, and have them search for the mascot in the school nurse's office.

- involve the nurse in the search and ask him or her to briefly explain what a nurse does in a school.

- take the nurse's picture with Boomer and place it in the *Our Classroom and School* class book.

- with the children, continue assembling the pictures in the class book and compose a brief sentence about the new picture.

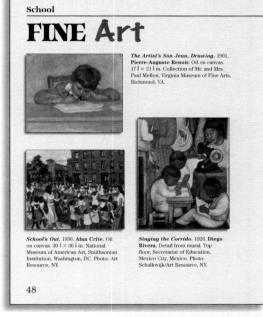

School

FINE Art

The Artist's Son Jean, Drawing, 1901. **Pierre-Auguste Renoir.** Oil on canvas. 17¾ × 21¼ in. Collection of Mr. and Mrs. Paul Mellon, Virginia Museum of Fine Arts, Richmond, VA.

School's Out, 1936. **Alan Crite.** Oil on canvas. 30¼ × 36¼ in. National Museum of American Art, Smithsonian Institution, Washington, DC. Photo: Art Resource, NY.

Singing the Corrido, 1926. **Diego Rivera.** Detail from mural. Top floor, Secretariat of Education, Mexico City, Mexico. Photo: Schalkwijk/Art Resource, NY.

48

Big Book School, p. 48

Check the Reading link of the **SRA** Web page for links to School-related Web sites. **http://www.sra-4kids.com**

③ Integrating the Curriculum

Teacher Tip Some kindergartners may still have difficulty drawing representationally. You can have these children find pictures in magazines or they can dictate sentences about what is in the classroom.

Language Arts

Independent and Collaborative Writing

My Classroom

- Distribute **Blackline Master 8**. Tell the children that the words at the bottom of the page are *My Classroom*. Have the children point to the words as you read them again.

- Ask them what they think the picture on the page should show. Have them look around the classroom and then discuss some of the things they might include in a picture of their classroom.

- Provide crayons and encourage the children to complete their pictures independently.

- Have the children share their drawings with you and the rest of the class during sharing.

- Remind the children to continue writing in their journals during Independent Work Time.

Listening, Speaking, Viewing

Left/Right Directionality

- Have a volunteer stand with you, with your backs to the class. Raise your left hands and say, "This is my left hand." Have the children raise their left hands as well. Remind them that they should always begin reading from this side of the page.

- Then, with the volunteer copying your action, move your hand across, keeping it in view, until it touches your right hand. Say, "I moved my hand from left to right. This is my right hand." Show the children your right hand, and have them raise their right hands. Point out that when they move their fingers along the page as they read, they move from left to right.

③ Integrating the Curriculum

Meeting Individual Needs

ESL

Teach position words used in this exercise to English-language learners doing the activity with the class. Have the children use the position words from their native language to help them understand the English equivalents.

Vocabulary

Position Words

- Place a book on a table and ask the children to tell you where the book is. Help them answer in a complete sentence, such as, "The book is on the table," and say *on* is a word that tells where something is.

- Move the book and hold it under the table. Ask children to tell where it is now. Emphasize that *under* tells where something is. Move the book to other places and have children tell where it is, using position words and complete sentences.

- Tell the children that you will play Simon Says.

- Provide each child with a small object, such as a block. You will give directions for what to do with the object. Explain that they should follow the instructions only if they hear the words *Simon says*.

- Have the children stand in a line in front of you. Explain that you will give them a direction but they are to follow the direction only if you say, "Simon says" first.

- Start with very easy directions and use "Simon says" for the first few so you can be sure the children understand that they are to perform certain actions. For example say "Simon says take a step toward me." Wait for the children to respond and then say, "Simon says take a step back."

- When you are sure the children understand this part, try giving a direction without saying "Simon says." For example, "Step forward." Help the children understand that they are not to respond if you don't say "Simon says."

- Give directions using position words, such as:

  Simon says put the block on your head.

  Simon says put the block under your foot.

  Put the block in front of you.

  Simon says hold the block in front of your face.

  Move the block around in a circle.

  Simon says put the block between your hands.

Across the Curriculum

Social Studies

Morning and Afternoon

Purpose

To group school activities into morning and afternoon.

Materials

chart paper, markers

Procedure

■ Remind the children that the little girl in the story talked about some of the things she did in the morning and in the afternoon with her mother.

■ Talk with the children about what they do in the morning at home. Then ask what else they do in the morning. Ask them what they usually do in the afternoon.

■ Begin a discussion to determine when certain school activities are done. Prompt the discussion with questions such as:

> **When do we always have story time?**
>
> **Is quiet time always in the afternoon or in the morning?**
>
> **When we go to the gym, is it morning or afternoon?**

■ Then give the children a sentence frame and have them contribute to a cumulative sentence as you point to them. Begin with "In the morning, we…" and have a child name a morning activity. Continue building the sentence by adding "and we…" and asking another child to contribute. Before using the sentence frame for the afternoon ("In the afternoon, we…"), recall some of the activities that were mentioned in the discussion.

■ If you have a half-day kindergarten class, discuss what to do in school and then at home after school.

1 Sounds and Letters

Teacher Tip

Print Directionality If the children have trouble focusing on the left-to-right movement as you work with the *Big Book* page, write a line of text from either "Hickory, Dickory, Dock" or "The Top and the Tip" on the chalkboard and demonstrate the left-to-right movement as you read.

Sounds, Letters, and Language

Reading the Big Book *Pickled Peppers*
"The Top and the Tip," page 42

- Open *Pickled Peppers* to the table of contents and point to "The Top and the Tip." Ask the children if someone can point to the page number. Say the number and then turn to it. Read the title, pointing to each word. Read the author's name and then read *illustrated by Cynthia Fisher*. Remind the children that illustrators are the people who draw pictures to go along with stories and poems.

- Read through the poem slowly, running your finger under each word as you do so. Ask the children if they see anything in the picture that the words describe and have them point out these pictures. Explain that all illustrators choose to draw pictures about a story or poem in their own way.

- Read through the poem slowly, pointing to each word. As children listen to the words, ask them to look in the picture for the things the words describe.

- Reread the poem, one line at a time. Call on volunteers to point to each part of the picture that is described by the words.

- Read the poem once more. Have the children place their hands on their heads when you read Line 1 *Hair is the top of a person.*

- Have volunteers come to the **Big Book** and point to the words in the title of the poem, moving from left to right.

- Point to the word *Top* in the title and again in the first line of the poem. Ask the children to find and point to the word in other places in the poem. Remind them that the word is spelled the same way each time it appears. Repeat with the word *Tip*.

- Focus attention on the difference in the capital *T* and small letter *t* of *Top* and *Tip* in the title and in the text of the poem. Ask volunteers to tell when capital letters are used. Point to the **Alphabet Card** *Tt* to remind the children of the capital and small versions of the letter.

Phonemic Awareness

Listening

Simon Says

Tell the children that they are going to play the Simon Says game with you.

Remind the children that they played this game in the previous lesson. Invite a volunteer to explain it to the rest of the class.

In order to help the children in listening and following the directions, you should take the part of Simon until you are sure that all the children know and are comfortable with what they are to do.

■ When you are sure all the children understand what to listen for, try easy Simon Says routines focusing on the position words *behind, over, after, first, middle,* and *last.* Then have the children take turns being Simon. See the Appendix for complete instructions for this game.

Word Substitution

■ Continue working on word substitution, this time breaking down a sentence and then changing it using the children's names.

Meeting Individual Needs

ESL

Simon Says For English-language learners, demonstrate the meanings of *first, middle, last, before, after, behind,* and *over* using classroom objects. For instance, hold a pencil over a book as you say, *over.* Ask the English-language learners to repeat the word. Follow this procedure with the other words.

Letter Recognition

Letter Names

Sing Your Way to _____ Game

Play the Sing Your Way to _____ Game to the letter *T.* Have one child wear the puppet and point to a letter (*Nn–Tt*), as the other children sing to the letter and stop. If the child with the puppet forgets, then you ask, "What is the letter?" and wait for the other children to answer. Give several children a chance to play.

Secret Passletter

■ Each day, choose a Secret Passletter. Establish some way of letting the children know early in the day what the Secret Passletter is. For example, you might post it outside the classroom door before the children arrive each morning. This activity will reinforce recognition of a particular letter.

■ Choose a letter between *A* and *G* to be the secret passletter. Give several clues about the letter, such as "The secret passletter has a big curve. It is not a *C*," and so on. Throughout the day, invite individual children to guess the letter. Be sure to reveal the day's letter at the end of the day.

Assessment

✓**Informal** Monitor the children during the phonemic awareness activities. Plan to give extra support to those who are having difficulty with these activities.

Sounds and Letters

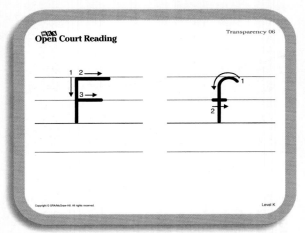

Transparency 06

Teacher Tip

Letter Formation For those children having difficulty with letter formation, project the letter formation transparency on the chalkboard or a piece of chart paper and have the child trace over the letter. Or make a copy of the transparency and have them work independently.

Alphabet Cheer

Tell the children that they are going to learn a different version of the "Alphabet Song."

■ First, have the children sing the "Alphabet Song" to be sure they are comfortable with it. Then have them listen as you call out this cheer:

Boom, boom [CLAP]

■ Repeat the "Boom, boom [CLAP]" line, and invite the children to chime in as soon as they are ready, beginning with the clap after "Boom, boom." Have them practice the cheer completely a few times. Then tell them that they are going to say this cheer before each line of the "Alphabet Song."

■ Then have them sing the "Alphabet Song," as you add the cheer before each line. Tell them to wait until they hear you say the cheer before singing the next line of the song. Practice once or twice this way, and then invite the children to add the cheer themselves and sing the whole new version.

Letter Shapes

Exploring *Ff*

■ Point to the capital letter *F* and the small letter *f* on the **Alphabet Card**. Tell the children that they will be writing these letters with you, beginning with the capital *F*. Say:

Start at the top and go down. Start here and go straight out. Start here and go straight out. Capital *F*.

■ Repeat the strokes several times and have children imitate you in the air with their fingers.

■ Have children use pencils and paper to make the letter.

■ Repeat the procedure for small *f*, saying,

Start here, go up and around and down. Then start here and go straight out. Small *f*.

Alphabet Big Book — *Ff*

Display the *Alphabet Big Book* and open it to pages 14–15. Read "It's Fun to Be a Fire Dog," pointing to each word as you say it. Ask volunteers to come up and touch the left side of the first line and then move their hands to the right. Then ask the volunteers to find words that begin with capital *F* and small *f*.

Alphabet Big Book, pp. 14-15

Reading and Writing Workbook

Distribute copies of *Reading and Writing Workbook* to each child. Explain to the children that these books will be theirs to work in for the rest of the year. Show them the place where they are to keep their books when they are not using them and talk to them about how to take care of the books.

Tell the children to open *Reading and Writing Workbook* to page 1. Tell them to look closely at the picture. Say, "In this picture, all of the letters from *A* to *G* are hidden. Take your pencil and circle as many of them as you can find."

Reading and Writing Workbook, p. 1

② Reading and Responding

"What Will Mommy Do When I'm at School?"

Pages 36–39 of *School*

This selection is taught in six lessons:

Lesson 7	Lesson 9	Lesson 11
Lesson 8	Lesson 10	Lesson 12

Now I'll have to wake Mom in the morning. Then I'll have to pick out my clothes every day. My mom really loves to do that. Maybe I'll still let her. ❻

36

Meeting Individual Needs

ESL

Vocabulary Encourage English-language learners to offer vocabulary words in their own languages. Invite them to talk about their experience of knowledge of what the words mean in their home countries.

Build Background

Activate Prior Knowledge

Call on volunteers to tell what they remember about "What Will Mommy Do When I'm at School?" from previous readings.

Preview and Prepare

Browse

■ Open the *School* **Big Book** to the table of contents and point to "What Will Mommy Do When I'm at School?" Ask the children if someone can point to the page number. Say the number and then turn to it. Read the title, pointing to each word. Turn a few pages, to page 39, and ask the children what they remember about this part of the story. Have the children tell how the pictures help them remember the events in this section.

Vocabulary

Selection Vocabulary

Write each of the following words on the chalkboard, touch it, and read it aloud:

today   tomorrow

■ Tell children that each word tells about a day.

■ Discuss what day *today* is. Then ask what day is *tomorrow*. Remind the children that the little girl starts school the day after today, *tomorrow*.

■ Call on volunteers to say the word that names the day before today. (*yesterday*)

Reading Recommendations

- Run your hand under the words as you read.
- Pause occasionally to have children point out illustrations that match the text.
- As you turn to a new page, periodically ask a volunteer to come up and show you which word to read first.

Using Reading Strategies

During the first reading of "What Will Mommy Do When I'm at School?", you modeled the use of the following reading strategies:

- Clarifying
- Making Connections

For your convenience, the strategy models from the first reading of the selection are reproduced in this lesson in the form of reminders. You may choose not to use these reminders with your class, or to use them only with children who need extra help or who missed the first reading of the selection.

Building Comprehension Skills

In this lesson you will continue to work with the comprehension skill *Comparing and Contrasting*.

Reading and Responding

Comprehension Strategies

Introducing Strategy Use

Modeling

6 Clarifying *When I first read this I wasn't sure what the little girl was doing. By looking at the pictures and rereading the words, I was able to clarify what was happening.*

Modeling

7 Making Connections *By making connections to my own life, I was able to understand how the little girl felt when someone tried to make her feel better.*

Now I'll have to wake Mom in the morning. Then I'll have to pick out my clothes every day. My mom really loves to do that. Maybe I'll still let her. **6**

36

So Mom will walk me to school tomorrow. It will be like when we used to walk to the park together. But then I'll kiss her and hug her and tell her good-bye.

38

37

But I'll still worry about my mother.
What will she do without me? Today
she asked me to come closer so she
could wipe my tears away.

39

Comprehension Skills

Compare and Contrast
■ Reread pages 36 and 38. Have the children *compare* and *contrast* the things the girl did with her mother in the morning before with the things they will do now.
■ Use **Transparency 33** to help illustrate this graphically.

Discussing the Selection
Discuss the girl's plans for the morning. Ask the children how the little girl plans to let her mother help her in the morning. (*She will still let her mother pick out her clothes, and she will let her mother walk her to school.*)

Teacher Tip
Be prepared to lead these comprehension discussions for some time. In time the children will take more initiative. Your models will let the children know what is expected of them.

Reading and Responding

Responding to Literature

Reading/Writing Connection

Have the children notice that the story describes many activities that the little girl and her mother do together. Invite them to look at the illustrations and tell what the activities are.

Invite the children to brainstorm the various activities the little girl might be involved in when she begins school. Make a list on the chalkboard, recording each child's name by his or her contribution.

Review with the children some of the people the little girl will meet when she goes to school. Print the titles of school staff members on cards (*Teacher, Principal, Custodian, Librarian, Secretary, Nurse, and so on*) and display the cards on the Concept/Question Board, along with photographs of each. (If you are doing the suggested unit activities, you may want to use the photographs taken during the children's searches for Boomer.)

Suggest to the children that they pick a card and try to read the word on it as they consult the photograph. Have them "pretend play" that they are members of the school staff and student body, including students in higher grades.

Exploring the Theme

Theme Connections

Talk About It

- Invite children to discuss what they do to help their families before they come to school. Prompt them with questions such as:

  Do you feed your pets?
  Do you help with a younger brother or sister?
  Do you make your own breakfast?

Supporting Reflection

With the children, continue assembling pictures in the class picture/story big book and compose a brief caption for each picture—for example, for the "search party" picture you might print the following:

  Boomer is missing.
  Where is Boomer?
  Let's look for him.

- Have the children practice "reading" the class big book. Highlight early-literacy skills such as top to bottom and left to right flow of the text and remind the children of good oral reading practices, such as voice volume and expression. Additional activities with the book might include sentence strip matching, discussing the pictures, and identifying individuals and school locations.

Check the Reading link of the **SRA** Web page for links to School-related Web sites.
http://www.sra-4kids.com

③ Integrating the Curriculum

Continue to provide alternatives for those children who do not want to draw. They can cut out pictures from magazines or dictate sentences stating their ideas.

Language Arts

Independent and Collaborative Writing

My Friends and I

- Distribute **Blackline Master 9**. Read aloud the words on the bottom of the page, *My Friends and I*. Discuss what children might draw on the sheet, mentioning the kinds of things they do together at school. Remind them that everyone in the room could be a friend, but they may choose to draw just a few in the picture.

- Have the children work on their pictures independently. They might want to include their name and their friends' names on the picture.

- Invite volunteers to share their pictures with the class.

Listening, Speaking, Viewing

Following Directions

- Explain to the children that it is important to listen carefully when someone tells how to do something. Point out that it could cause problems if they miss a step in the directions.

- Remind the children that they have already listened to directions when they played Simon Says. Let them know that most directions are given in a certain order, from the first thing to do to the last.

- Tell the children that you are thinking about an item in the classroom. Then invite the children to find the object as you recite the directions. For example, "Please find the big brush that is on the easel." Remind them to listen carefully for position words to find the exact spot. Continue with other children and objects. Invite children to give directions, as well.

Integrating the Curriculum

Vocabulary

Position Words

- Remind the children of the importance of listening carefully to follow directions that tell where to put something. Hold up a chalkboard eraser or other small object. Tell children that you will ask volunteers to put this object in various places in the classroom.
- Give the object to a child and say, "Put this on my desk." When the child has done so, call on volunteers to tell where it is.
- Hand the object to other children and give them instructions, such as, "Put the erasers under a book," or "Put the erasers behind the door."
- Call on volunteers to give directions to their classmates.

Across the Curriculum

Music

Sing About the Morning

Purpose

To substitute words about morning routines in a familiar song.

Procedure

- Review with the children the song, "Early in the Morning," which they sang in Lesson 4. Sing a verse once or twice until the children become familiar with it again.
- Then talk about the things they do to get ready for school each morning. For example:

  This is the way we *brush our teeth, brush our teeth, brush our teeth.*

  This is the way we *brush our teeth,*

  Early in the morning.

- After they have spoken the new verse, have the children sing the song with that verse. Then invite volunteers to take turns substituting new morning activities and singing the verse again.

Lesson Planner

	DAY 1	DAY 2
Part 1 **Sounds and Letters** **Materials** ■ Book *Pickled Peppers*, p. 42, 41 ■ Word Cards (see lessons) ■ *Alphabet Book*, p. 16, 17, 18, 20–21, 22 ■ Pre-Decodable Book 3: *School* ■ Sounds and Letters First-Step Story 1, "Sleeping Outdoors" ■ *Reading and Writing Workbook*, pp. 2–4 ■ Transparencies 7–11	**Sounds, Letters, and Language, p. 204** ■ Reading the Big Book Pickled Peppers p, 42 **Phonemic Awareness** 🌥 ■ Listening, pp. 204–205 **Letter Recognition** ■ Letter Names, p. 206 ■ Letter Shapes, pp. 206–207	**Sounds, Letters, and Language, p. 216** ■ Reading the Big Book *Pickled Peppers*, p. 41 **Phonemic Awareness** 🌥 ■ Oral Blending: Word Parts, p. 217 **Letter Recognition** ■ Letter Names, p. 218 ✓ ■ Letter Shapes, pp. 218–219 **Reading Pre-Decodable Book 3:** *School,* pp. 210-221
Part 2 **Reading and Responding** **Materials** ■ Big Book *School* p. 22–43, 44–47 ■ Listening Library Audiocassette: School ■ Home Connection, p. 13, 15, 17, 19 ■ Read-Aloud Book: *Annabelle Swift, Kindergartner* ■ Transparency 33 ■ Unit Project Materials (see lessons)	**Build Background, p. 208** **Preview and Prepare, p. 208** **Vocabulary** ■ Selection Vocabulary: *adventure*, p. 208 **Reading Recommendations, p. 209** **Comprehension Strategies** ■ Clarifying, p. 210 ■ Making Connections, p. 210 **Comprehension Skills** ■ Compare and Contrast, p. 211 ■ Discussing the Selection, p. 211 **Responding to Literature** ■ Reading/Writing Connection, p. 212 Exploring the Theme, p. 213	**Build Background, p. 222** **Vocabulary** ■ Selection Vocabulary, p. 222 **Reading Recommendations, p. 223** **Responding to Literature** ✓ ■ Discussing the Selection, p. 224 ■ Purposes for Reading, p. 224 **Exploring the Theme, p. 225**
Part 3 **Integrating the Curriculum** **Materials** ■ Blackline Masters 10, 11 ■ Picture Cards (see lessons) ■ Word Cards (see lessons) ■ Big Book *Pictures Tell Stories*, p. 25 ■ *Willy the Wisher Thinking Story 2* ■ *Willy the Wisher Thinking Story 3* ■ Across the Curriculum Materials, see pp. 215, 229, 245, 255, 285	**Independent and Collaborative Writing** ■ What I Like to Do in School, p. 214 **Grammar** ■ Capitalization, p. 214 **Across the Curriculum: Social Studies, p. 215**	**Independent and Collaborative Writing** ■ Seminar, p. 226 **Vocabulary** ■ Days of the Week, p. 227 *Willy the Wisher Thinking Story 2*, p. 228 **Across the Curriculum: Math, p. 229**

Independent Work Time

Materials

Big Books: School, Pickled Peppers, Alphabet Book
Annabelle Swift, Kindergartner (Read-Aloud)
Willy the Wisher
Skills Assessment pages 4–5
Reading and Writing Workbook pages 2–4

Reteach, Challenge pages 2–4
Intervention Guide Unit 1, Lessons 11–15
ESL Supplement Unit 1, Lessons 11–15
First-Step Story 1
Pre-Decodable Book 3

Reteach
■ "What Will Mommy Do When I'm at School?"
■ "The Tip and the Top"
Preteach
■ *Alphabet Book* Gg
Writing: What I Like to Do in School
  Reading and Writing Workbook, Reteach, Challenge page 2
Unit Project

Reteach
■ "What Will Mommy Do When I'm at School?"
Preteach
■ *Alphabet Book Hh*
■ *Willy the Wisher Thinking Story 2*
■ Vocabulary: Days of the Week
Partner-read Pre-Decodable Book 3
Writing: Seminar
Unit Project continued

DAY 3	DAY 4	DAY 5
Sounds, Letters, and Language, p. 220 ■ **Reading the Big Book** *Pickled Peppers*, **p. 41** ■ **Sounds and Letters First-Step Story 1, p. 230** **Phonemic Awareness** ☁ ✓ ■ **Oral Blending: Word Parts, p. 232** ■ **Listening, p. 233** **Letter Recognition** ■ **Letter Names, p. 234** ■ **Letter Shapes, pp. 234–235**	**Sounds, Letters, and Language, p. 246** ■ **Reading the Big Book** *Pickled Peppers*, **p. 41** ■ **Sounds and Letters First-Step Story 1, p. 246** **Phonemic Awareness** ☁ ■ **Oral Blending, p. 247** ■ **Listening, p. 247** **Letter Recognition** ■ **Letter Names, p. 248** ■ **Letter Shapes, pp. 248–249**	**Sounds, Letters, and Language, p. 256** ■ **Reading the Big Book** *Pickled Peppers*, **p. 41** ■ **Sounds and Letters First-Step Story 1, p. 256** **Phonemic Awareness** ☁ ■ **Oral Blending, p. 257** ■ **Listening, p. 257** **Letter Recognition** ■ **Letter Names, p. 258** ■ **Letter Shapes, p. 259**
Exploring the Theme, p. 237 **Build Background, p. 238** **Preview and Prepare, p. 238** **Vocabulary** ■ **Selection Vocabulary:** *brought, showed*, **p. 239** **Reading Recommendations, p. 239** **Comprehension Strategies** ■ **Visualization, p. 240** **Comprehension Skills** ■ **Discussing the Selection, p. 241** **Responding to Literature** ■ **Literature Appreciation, p. 242** **Exploring the Theme, p. 243**	**Activate Prior Knowledge, p. 250** **Preview and Prepare, p. 250** **Vocabulary** ■ **Selection Vocabulary, p 251** **Reading Recommendations, p. 251** **Responding to Literature** ■ **Discussing the Selection, p. 252** ■ **Purposes for Reading, p. 252** ■ **Print Awareness, p. 252** ■ **Using the Audiocassette, p. 252** **Exploring the Theme, p. 253**	**Exploring the Theme, p. 263** **Build Background, p. 264** **Preview and Prepare, p. 264** **Vocabulary** ■ **Selection Vocabulary:** *mother, father, sister*, **p. 265** **Reading Recommendations, p. 265** **Comprehension Strategies** ■ **Asking Questions, pp. 266, 268, 272, 274, 276** ■ **Predicting, pp. 270, 278, 280** **Comprehension Skills** ■ **Discussing the Selection, p. 281** **Purposes for Reading, p. 281** **Responding to Literature** ■ **Print Awareness, p. 282** **Exploring the Theme, p. 283**
Independent and Collaborative Writing ■ **Write a Poem, p. 244** **Listening, Speaking, Viewing** ■ **Listening to Appreciate, p. 244** **Across the Curriculum: Social Studies, p. 245**	**Independent and Collaborative Writing** ■ **Journal Writing, p. 254** **Grammar** ■ **Words that Show Action (Verbs), p. 254** **Listening, Speaking, Viewing** ■ **Listening Skills, p. 254** **Across the Curriculum: Dramatization, p. 255**	**Independent and Collaborative Writing** ■ **Journal Writing, p. 284** *Willy the Wisher Thinking Story 3*, **p. 384** **Across the Curriculum: Social Studies, p. 285**
Preteach ■ *School* "I Brought a Worm" ■ *Pickled Peppers* "Sleeping Outdoors" ■ *Alphabet Book Ii* **First-Step Story I** *Reading and Writing Workbook, Reteach, Challenge* page 3 *Skills Assessment* page 4 **Writing: Poetry** **Unit Project continued**	**Reteach** ■ "I Brought a Worm" ■ "Sleeping Outdoors" **Preteach** ■ *Alphabet Book Jj* **First-Step Story I** **Writing: Journal Writing** **Unit Project continued**	**Reteach** ■ "Sleeping Outdoors" **Preteach** ■ *Annabelle Swift, Kindergartner* (Read-Aloud) ■ *Alphabet Big Book Kk* ■ *Willy the Wisher Thinking Story 3* **First-Step Story I** *Reading and Writing Workbook, Reteach, Challenge* page 4 **Writing: Journal Writing** **Unit Project continued**

Meeting Individual Needs
Independent Work Time

Sounds and Letters

Meeting Individual Needs

Reteach
- Identifying *a–e, Reteach,* p. 207
- *a–h, Reteach,* p. 235
- Capital and Lowercase Letters, *Reteach,* p. 261

ESL
- Simon Says, p. 204
- High-Frequency Words, p. 220
- Oral Blending, pp. 232, 247, 257

Challenge
- *a–e, Challenge,* p. 207
- *a–h, Challenge,* p. 235
- Capital and Lowercase *Challenge,* p. 261

Intervention
- Letter Recognition, pp. 206, 248, 258
- Letter Formation, pp. 207, 234, 249, 259
- Pencil Control and Letter Formation, p. 219

Reading and Responding

Meeting Individual Needs

ESL
- Vocabulary, pp. 222, 239
- Visual Clues, p. 250
- Selection Vocabulary, p. 265
- Identifying Colors, p. 268

Integrating the Curriculum

Formal Assessment Options

Use this assessment page along with your informal observations to gauge the students' progress.

Name _____ Date _____

Words and Letters

[Teacher: Look at each group of letters and words. Draw a line under the answer that is a word, not just a letter.]

1. d　　　　n　　　　<u>and</u>

2. <u>was</u>　　　s　　　　w

3. g　　　<u>from</u>　　　m

4. b　　　<u>not</u>　　　t

5. e　　　k　　　<u>she</u>

4　　Copyright © SRA/McGraw-Hill. Permission is granted to reproduce this page for classroom use.　　Skills Assessment

Skills Assessment, p. 4
Words and Letters

Teacher's Observation Log

Student _____

Date _____ Unit _____

Activity _____ ⊛

General Comprehension
Concepts Discussed _____
_____

Behavior Within a Group
Articulates, expresses ideas _____
_____
Joins discussions _____
Collaboration (such as works with other students, works alone) _____

Role in Group
Role (such as leader, summarizer, questioner, recorder, critic, observer, non-participant)
_____
_____
Flexibility (changes roles when necessary) _____

Use of Reading Strategies
Uses strategies when needed (either those taught or student's own)/Describe strategies used
_____
_____
Changes strategies when appropriate _____

Changes Since Last Observation
_____
_____
If more space is needed, write on the back or use another sheet.

18　　Copyright © SRA/McGraw-Hill. Permission is granted to reproduce this page for classroom use.　　Assessment Guide

Teacher's Observation Log, p. 18
Assessment Master

1 Sounds and Letters

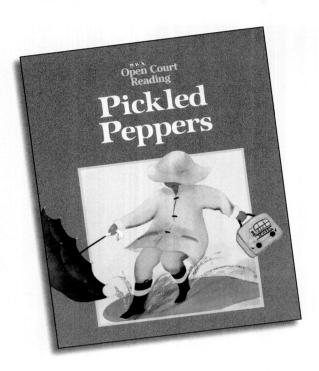

Sounds, Letters, and Language

Reading the Big Book *Pickled Peppers*
"The Top and the Tip," page 42

■ Open *Pickled Peppers* to the table of contents and point to "The Top and the Tip." Ask the children if someone can point to the page number. Say the number and then turn to it.

■ Read the title, pointing to each word. Read the author's name and then read *illustrated by Cynthia Fisher*.

■ Read through the poem, running your finger under each word.

■ Place the **Word Cards** *is, the, top, of,* and *a* in the **Pocket Chart**, leaving a space at the beginning of the line.

■ Point to and read the words, and ask the children to think of objects that are on the top of something. Use their objects to complete the sentence. For example, *Hair is on the top of my head.*

■ Repeat, changing the word *top* in the **Pocket Chart** to *tip.*

Phonemic Awareness

Listening

Simon Says

■ Play the Simon Says game with the class. Remind the children to follow your directions only if they hear the words *Simon says*.

■ Give directions, using position words such as *over, under, in front of, behind,* and *on.*

> **Simon says put your hands over your head**
>
> **Turn around**
>
> **Simon says put your hands on your knees.**

■ When the children feel comfortable with the game, invite volunteers to be "Simon."

Meeting Individual Needs

ESL

Simon Says During Independent Work Time, play the game with English-language learners to review the position words learned in earlier lessons, and to help them learn the meanings of the new position words.

Rhythm

Return to the poem "Rain, Rain, Go Away."

- Clap out the words.
- Clap out any playground chants popular at your school.
- Invite the children to mime the actions as they say the words.

Rhymes

Continue the listening for rhymes activity, using **–ing** forms of action verbs.

chopping	hopping	popping	stopping	**jumping**
singing	ringing	stinging	**reading**	bringing
racing	facing	**raining**	bracing	pacing
feeling	kneeling	squealing	**sneezing**	dealing

Miming Action Words

Tell the children that words such as *go*, *read*, and *ring* are action words. Explain that it is harder to make a picture of action words than of words such as *dog*, *cat*, and *house*, but that these words can be acted out. Explain that action words are things we do.

Tell the children to act each action as you read each line exaggerating the meter. The children should anticipate the second rhyme of each couplet.

a bird that's flying	(flap arms)
a baby that's crying	(rub eyes with knuckles)
a hand that's waving	(wave)
a Daddy shaving	(pretend to shave)
a student learning	(pretend to read)
some pages turning	(pretend to turn a page)
a camera clicking	(pretend to snap pictures)
a foot that's kicking	(kick)
a horse prancing	(high step)
a dancer dancing	(wave arms gracefully)

Phonemic Awareness activities related to the lessons can be found at **http://www.sra-4kids.com**

1 Sounds and Letters

Intervention

Letter Recognition During Independent Work Time, have children work with **Letter Cards** if they are having difficulty with some of their letters. Encourage them to look at their **Letter Cards** and to say them aloud one at a time as you listen.

Exploring Letters — Gg Remember at this point, children are not expected to master writing the letter g. Later lessons will focus on the letter g. This exposure is to give children more work with the letter so that they will learn to recognize it.

Letter Formation For those children having difficulty with letter formation, project the letter formation transparency on the chalkboard or a piece of chart paper and have the child trace over the letter.

Letter Recognition

Letter Names
Sing Your Way to Z Game
- Extend the Sing Your Way To _____ Game to include all of the letters to Z. Have the children use the puppet to point to letters between *T* and *Z*.

Secret Passletter
- Choose a Secret Passletter for the day, and write it on an index card, and prepare three or four other index cards with other letters. At various times, ask individual children "What is the secret passletter?" as you hold out the card. Vary the activity by holding out one of the other cards and asking, "Is this the secret passletter?" Then ask the child to identify the correct letter.

Practice
Ordering Letters Game If children have not yet worked as partners during Independent Work Time, establish the rules for partner work and have the children play **Ordering Letters *Aa–Nn.*** (see the Appendix for a full description)
- Tell children that they will each find a set of **Letter Cards** *Aa–Nn* in the materials area. (The cards in each set should be shuffled out of order and facing different ways.)
- Tell the children they should do two things with these cards. First, they should turn all of the cards so that they are showing either all capitals or all small letters. Then they should show the set to their partner to check.
- Next, have each child work with a partner and match each capital letter with a small letter.

Letter Shapes
Exploring Gg
- Direct children's attention to the *Gg* **Alphabet Card**. Point to the capital letter *G* and the small *g*. Form the capital *G* on the overhead projector or chalkboard. Say,

  Start here, go all the way around this way (left), and then up. Start here and go straight across. Capital *G*.
- Have children make the letter in the air with their fingers and then on blank paper with their pencils.
- Make the letter several times.

- Repeat the steps for small *g*. Say,

  Start here, go around this way (left) all the way. Start here, go straight down, touching the circle, and down around this way (left). Small *g*.

- Make sure you say the name of the letter each time you write it.

- Find capital G's and small g's in children's names and in objects around the room.

Alphabet Big Book — Gg

Display the *Alphabet **Big Book*** and open it to page 16, "Gazelle." Tell the children that a gazelle is a very fast and graceful animal—one that moves smoothly. If you choose, model *graceful* movement. Read the poem, pointing to the words as you say each one. On the second reading, have the children raise their hands as you touch words that begin with capital *G* and small *g*.

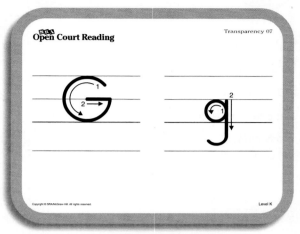

Transparency 07

O gaze on the graceful gazelle as it grazes
It grazes on green growing leaves and on grasses
On grasses it grazes, so gaze as it passes
It passes so gracefully, gently, O gaze!

Gazelle
Mary Ann Hoberman

Alphabet Big Book, pp. 16–17

Reading and Writing Workbook

Have the children complete page 2 of the ***Reading and Writing Workbook*** for additional practice identifying a–e. Have them find the letters in the picture and circle them.

Meeting Individual Needs

Reteach
For children having trouble identifying a–e, provide ***Reteach*** page 2 and have them practice finding these letters.

Intervention
There are likely to be children for whom letter formation is difficult. Encourage these children to use the chalkboard or large chart paper. For those with serious difficulty, have them trace over letters on the board. Repeating the strokes is also helpful for some children

Challenge
a–e For a challenging activity on *a–e*, have children complete ***Challenge*** page 2.

② Reading and Responding

"What Will Mommy Do When I'm at School?"

Pages 40–43 of *School*

This selection is taught in six lessons:

Lesson 7	**Lesson 9**	**Lesson II**
Lesson 8	**Lesson 10**	**Lesson 12**

My mom said, "I don't want you to leave me, baby, but school is such a great new adventure. You're going to be able to learn so much and do so much. There will be so many new things you can even teach me." **8**

40

Build Background

Activate Prior Knowledge

Invite volunteers to tell about some new things they found when they first came to school. Have them tell who helped them understand what these things were. Ask the children what they remember about "What Will Mommy Do When I'm at School" from previous readings.

Preview and Prepare

Browse

■ Display the *School **Big Book***, opened to pages 40–41. Turn through the story to page 43 and ask what the children remember about this last part of the story. Help them see that this is the first time the little girl's mother talks to her about school.

Vocabulary

Selection Vocabulary

■ Write the following word on the chalkboard, touch it, and read it aloud:

adventure

■ Ask the children what the word "adventure" means. Invite a volunteer to use it in a sentence. If necessary, explain that an *adventure* is doing something new and exciting.

■ Discuss why going to school for the first time might be an *adventure*. Invite other volunteers to use the word in a sentence that tells why starting school might have been an *adventure* for them.

Reading Recommendations

- Run your hand under the words and point to them as you read.
- Invite the children to tell how the expressions on the characters' faces help readers understand the story better.
- Draw their attention to how you use vocal expression as you read— lowering your voice as you read about the little girl's sadness and changing voice tone as various characters speak.
- Encourage the children to ask questions and to comment on the action as you read.

Using Reading Strategies

During the first reading of "What Will Mommy Do When I'm at School?", you modeled the use of the following reading strategies:

- Clarifying
- Making Connections

For your convenience, the strategy models from the first reading of the selection are reproduced in this lesson in the form of reminders. You may choose not to use these reminders with your class, or to use them only with children who need extra help or who missed the first reading of the selection.

Building Comprehension Skills

In this lesson you will continue to work with the comprehension skill *Comparing and Contrasting*.

2 Reading and Responding

Comprehension Strategies

Introducing Strategy Use

Modeling
8 Making Connections *Remind the children that good readers often stop to make connections, to help them figure out what is going on in a story. Sometimes they do this by making a connection with something they have experienced in their own lives.*

Modeling
9 Clarifying *Ask the children why readers sometimes stop to clarify (to figure out what is going on in a story). Invite a volunteer to tell about a time he or she needed to clarify.*

My mom said, "I don't want you to leave me, baby, but school is such a great new adventure. You're going to be able to learn so much and do so much. There will be so many new things you can even teach me." **8**

40

"Well, you don't have to worry about me, sweetheart," said my mother. "Though I'll miss you, I won't be lonely. I'll be starting my own new adventure. While you're at school tomorrow, I'll be beginning a brand-new job." **9**

42

"Well, I'm not going to let you be lonely, Mom. When I come home, I'll tell you everything I've learned. I will bring you pictures I've drawn. I can bring over all my new friends. Maybe they can become your new friends, too."

41

"You know, Mom, maybe school won't be so bad after all. Think of all the great new things we can tell each other when we get home."

"I can hardly wait, baby."

43

Comprehension Skills

Compare and Contrast

- Reread page 43 and discuss how the girl feels at the end of the story.
- Then ask children to find clues in the story and in the pictures that help them *compare* and *contrast* the way the little girl felt earlier in the story.
- Consider using ***Transparency 33*** to help with comparing and contrasting.

Discussing the Selection

- Discuss how the author/illustrator lets the readers know how the girl feels about going to school at the beginning of the story and how she felt at the end. *(She shows through pictures and tells through the text.)*
- Have the children tell whether their feelings have changed about going to the school from the beginning of the year to this point.

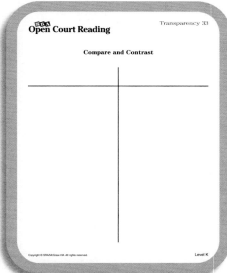

Transparency 33

② Reading and Responding

Responding to Literature

Reading/Writing Connection

Make a feelings chart using the familiar icon faces. Ask the children to review for you the feelings the little girl showed in the story. Tell them that you have made a chart of "feeling faces." Point to the faces on the chart and have the children identify each feeling. Point to the word above the feeling face and say, for example, "and this word says 'happy.'"

happy	sad	scared	surprised

Distribute **Blackline Master 10** "Feeling Faces" on which the feelings are printed. Have children print their names on the sheet. Read each feeling word with the children and have them draw their own feeling face. Offer assistance as needed. Have the children bring their work home—with an accompanying note explaining that the children are learning to understand how story characters feel at various points in the story.

Exploring the Theme

Theme Connections

Sing It   TEKS K.1C; K.3A, C; K.15A; K.16B

Review the tune to "Early in the Morning" with the children. Then let them know that they are going to change the words to tell about what happens in school.

- Demonstrate an opening verse, using lyrics such as:

    This is what I did at school today,

    School today, school today.

    This is what I did at school today,

    I'll tell you all about it.

- Brainstorm with the children ideas about how to the change the last line. Then have them sing the first three lines, and then change the last line to tell about something that happened at school, such as *we read a good story.*

Supporting Reflection

TEKS K.3A; K.5B; K.15A; K.16B

Continue to explore the school as the children search for Boomer. Arrange a class visit to some special part of the building, such as the principal's office.

- As the children look around, have the principal briefly explain the area and what they do to help the children. Take the principal's picture with Boomer and the children.

- Have the children practice "reading" the class book. Emphasize such print awareness skills as the top-to-bottom and left-to-right directionality of print, and remind the children of good oral reading practices, such as voice volume and expression. Additional activities with the book might include sentence strip matching, discussing the pictures, and identifying individuals and school locations.

Teacher Tip **Unit Activity** If you do not have access to a camera, consider having the children draw pictures of the people they meet and the places they find Boomer.

Check the Reading link of the **SRA** Web page for links to School-related Web sites.
http://www.sra-4kids.com

③ Integrating the Curriculum

Teacher Tip

As in the previous lessons, provide alternatives for the children for whom drawing representationally is difficult.

Language Arts

Independent and Collaborative Writing

What I Like to Do in School

- Distribute **Blackline Master 11**. Read aloud the words on the bottom of the page, *In school I like to* _____. Discuss some of children's favorite school activities and ask what they might like to draw on this page. Tell them that you will help them complete the sentence to tell about their picture.
- Have children work on their pictures independently. Circulate and print the words they dictate to complete the sentence on the page.
- As you help them "write" their sentences, encourage them to help you write from left-to-right and top-to-bottom when appropriate.
- Invite volunteers to share their pictures with the class.
- Remind the children that they can write in their journals about anything that interests them.

Grammar

Capitalization

- Have the children take out their Name Necklaces. Hold up and read several names, pointing out that each name begins with a capital letter.
- Explain that special names, like the names of people, books, and places like the town or city you live in, begin with a capital letter. Provide some examples, such as the name of your town, a school staff member, and a well-known building or other landmark in your area.
- Display the **Big Book** *School* and point out the title on the cover. Explain that the title is the special name of a book. That is why the important words of a title begin with capital letters.
- Have children find book titles, children's names, or other names around the room and identify the capital letter at the beginning of each word.

Across the Curriculum

Social Studies

School Staff Members

Purpose

To identify school workers and their jobs.

Materials

drawing paper, crayons

Procedure

- Discuss with children the various adults they have met at school or on their way to school, such as the crossing guard, bus driver, principal, school secretary, librarian, and nurse.

- Talk about the ways each person helps children every day.

- Print the name of each person and print his or her job on sentence strips—for example, *Ms. McGurn is our principal.* Cut off the job title from each strip and mix them up. Have volunteers locate the correct job title for each person.

1 Sounds and Letters

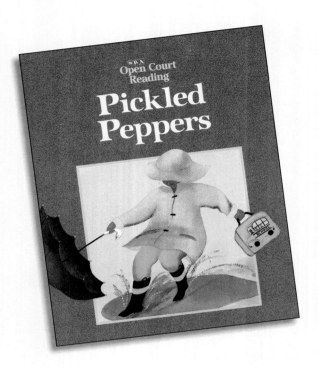

Sounds, Letters, and Language

Reading the Big Book *Pickled Peppers*
"Sleeping Outdoors," page 41

■ Open the ***Big Book*** *Pickled Peppers* to the table of contents. Remind the children that you have already read selections from *Pickled Peppers* called "I'm a Little Teapot," "One, Two, Buckle my Shoe," "Houses/Casitas," and "Hickory, Dickory Dock." Point to these titles in the table of contents and read them.

■ Tell the children that today you are going to read "Sleeping Outdoors." Find the title in the table of contents and read it, then point to the numeral *41* and say it. Let the children know that this number tells you that you can find the poem on page 41. Turn to page 41 and point to the page number.

■ Point to the title of the poem and read it. Then read *illustrated by* and ask if anyone remembers what this means. Remind the children that the illustrator drew the pictures that go with the poem.

■ Read the poem slowly, running your finger underneath each word. Point to the parts of the picture that match the text.

■ Reread the second and fourth lines, emphasizing the words *tree* and *me*. Point to the words and ask if anyone can point to the word that rhymes with *tree*.

■ Ask other children to volunteer words that rhyme with *tree* and *me*. Give them a beginning sound if they need help.

PHONEMIC AWARENESS

Phonemic Awareness

Oral Blending

Word Parts

- Explain to the children that as they learn to read and write, they must learn to listen carefully to how words sound. Tell them that they will now play a listening game. You will say a word in two parts. They must listen carefully and tell you what the word is.

- Read each word, pronouncing each part distinctly and pausing cleanly at the breaks indicated (…). Then say that you will put the two parts together and say the whole word. Begin with the following:

| Teacher: | Dino. . .saur. I'll say the parts again. Dino. . .saur. Now I'll put the parts together: *dinosaur* |

- Continue with the following words:

  alpha. . .bet
  butter. . .fly

- Now ask the children to join you as you put the parts together. Continue to say the word parts, but only once, and then ask the children to say the whole word with you. Try these words:

  tele. . .vision   ele. . .phant   lolli. . .pop   birth. . .day
  astro. . .naut   valen. . .tine ani. . .mal

Research in Action

The goal of oral blending is to lead the children to understand that spoken words are made up of smaller units of sound. Because children are accustomed to producing and hearing whole words, the challenge is to find ways to get them to notice that words contain smaller units of sound—syllables and phonemes.

Because syllables are easier to distinguish than individual phonemes, blending syllables is a good first step in leading children to become aware of the units of sound that make up speech. Developing this sort of awareness of speech sounds—*phonological awareness*—will prepare the children to learn phonics easily in later lessons.   (*Marilyn Jager Adams*)

Teacher Tip

Remember to move quickly through the oral blending activities, even if all children do not catch on. It is often more helpful to move on to other activities, rather than continue drilling on one activity.

Phonics CD-ROM

Use the *Phonics* CD-ROM for activities that support the Phonemic Awareness Lessons.

Phonemic Awareness and Phonics Videodisc

Oral Blending: Word Parts

Use the **Phonemic Awareness Videodisc** to preview the lessons on Oral Blending. Unit 1 Lesson 12

Level K – Disc 1 – Side B – Chapter 2

Sounds and Letters

Teacher Tip For the "What is the Letter?" activity, vary the mode of response. Ask for responses from the whole group, from individuals, "everyone wearing red," and so on.

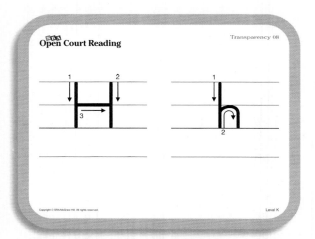

Transparency 08

Teacher Tip **Letter Formation** For those children having difficulty with letter formation, project the letter formation transparency on the chalkboard or a piece of chart paper and have the child trace over the letter.

Letter Recognition

Letter Names

Sing Your Way to Z Game

- Include the whole alphabet in the game this time. Have children use the puppet to point to letters and then call on specific classmates to sing their way to the letter. Encourage the children to take turns using the puppet.

Secret Passletter

- Determine and identify the Secret Passletter for the day and give clues to what it is. Then, throughout the day, ask children whether or not they have the Secret Passletter in their names.

- Have the children use their Name Necklaces to check if the Secret Passletter is there. If they have the letter in their names, have them point to it and say it. Then have those children ask other classmates to check if the Secret Passletter is in their names.

What Is the Letter?

- Hold up *Alphabet Flash Cards* for the letters *Aa—Mm* and ask the children to respond as a group to name the letter.

Letter Shapes

Exploring *Hh*

- Direct the children's attention to the *Hh* **Alphabet Card**. Point to the capital letter *H* and the small letter *h* . Tell the children that they will be writing these letters with you, beginning with the capital *H*. Say:

    Start here and go straight down. Start here and go straight down. Start here and go straight across the middle. Capital *H*.

- Have the children make the letter in the air with their fingers and then on blank paper with their pencils. Make the letter several times.

- Have children use pencils and paper to make the letter.

- Repeat the steps for small *h*. Say:

    Start here, straight down, back up, around this way (right), and straight down. Small *h*.

- Have the children look for capital *H*'s and small *h*'s in objects in the classroom or in their names.

Alphabet Big Book — Hh

Display the *Alphabet **Big Book*** and open it to page 18. Read "I'll Walk Half-way to Your House," pointing to the words as you say them. Have the children stand as you read, and tell them to "walk" in place whenever you read and point to a word that has a capital *H* or a small *h*. Be sure to read at a rate that allows the children to respond in this way.

I'll walk halfway to your house
if you walk halfway to mine.
We'll decide about the other half
when we come to the halfway line.

Charlotte Pomerantz

Alphabet Big Book, pp. 18–19

Home Connection

Distribute ***Home Connection*** page 13 which describes the work you are doing in Letter Recognition and suggests activities for families to do at home with their children. This letter is available in English and Spanish.

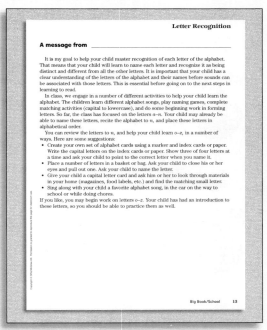

Home Connection, p. 13

Assessment
✓ **Informal** Continue to monitor children's ability to form letters. Note those children who need extra help.

1 Sounds and Letters

Pre-Decodable Book 3

Teacher Tip During independent work times, encourage the children to choose one of the previous *Pre-Decodable Books* to read on their own.

Teacher Tip **High-Frequency Word Wall** Add the words from this book to the High-Frequency Word Wall.

Meeting Individual Needs

ESL

High-Frequency Words Review the high-frequency words with English-language learners to make sure they know the meanings. Use pictures, objects, pantomime, the **ESL Visual Glossary,** and bilingual dictionaries as needed.

Reading a Pre-Decodable Book
Book 3: *School*

High-Frequency Words

The high-frequency words introduced in this story are: *I, see*

Reading Recommendations

For a complete discussion of the procedure for using **Pre-Decodable Books**, see the Appendix.

■ Introduce the new high-frequency words listed at the top of the page. Write each word on the chalkboard. Point to and say each word, then have the children say each word with you.

■ Preview the rebus pictures with the children to be sure they understand what each represents.

■ Give each child a copy of the **Pre-Decodable Book**. Explain that you will read the book together.

■ Hold up your book. Read the title aloud, then have the children read it with you. Point to and read the author's name and explain that this is the name of the person who wrote the book. Then point to and read the illustrator's name and explain that this is the name of the person who drew the pictures in the book.

■ Allow children to page through the book, commenting on what they see in the pictures and making predictions about what they think the book will tell them.

■ Help children find page 3. Hold up your copy of the book and sweep your hand under each line of the text. Then read each line, pointing to each word or rebus as you say it. Encourage children to move their hands from left to right across the text as you read together.

■ Continue through the book, following the same procedure.

■ Reread the book, this time pointing to the picture on each page and asking children to tell what is happening in the picture.

Responding

- Call on children to tell what they like best about the story.

- Write the high-frequency words *I*, *see*, and *the* on separate index cards (or use **Word Cards**) and make a punctuation card for the period (.). Place the cards on the **Pocket Chart** in random order. Give each child a blank index card and tell children to look around the room and find one thing to draw on the card, such as the class hamster, the door, or the globe. Call on a child to arrange the words on the **Pocket Chart** in order as he or she says, "I see the," and finishes the sentence with the drawing and the period. Scramble the cards on the chart and call on other volunteers to make and say a sentence using the high-frequency words.

- For additional practice, you may want to use **Book 3** of the supplemental set of *Open Court Reading Decodable Books*.

- You may want to make copies for the children of the black-and-white version of this story which is available in the *Pre-Decodable Takehome Book*.

② Reading and Responding

What Will Mommy Do When I'm at School?

Pages 22–43 of *School*

This selection is taught in six lessons:

Lesson 7	**Lesson 9**	**Lesson II**
Lesson 8	**Lesson 10**	**Lesson 12**

Meeting Individual Needs

ESL

Vocabulary Review the selection vocabulary with English-language learners to help them understand the usage and meaning of the words.

Selection Concepts

Remind the children of the key concepts explored in "What Will Mommy Do When I'm at School?":

■ It is hard to leave warmth and certainty for something new and unknown.

■ Love and understanding can build bridges to the future.

■ School holds the promise of new experiences that can be shared with loved ones at home.

Invite them to discuss how each of these concepts is illustrated by the story.

Build Background

Activate Prior Knowledge

Ask the children what they remember about in "What Will Mommy Do When I'm at School?" Call on volunteers to summarize the main events in the story, using the familiar "and then" phrase.

Vocabulary

Selection Vocabulary

■ Review the vocabulary words the children learned through the selection.

adventure	eat	read	tomorrow
alone	grandma	sing	
daddy	mom	today	

■ Have the children listen for the vocabulary words as you reread the story.

Reading Recommendations

- Reread the story through, pausing only for the children's comments.
- As you get to certain pages, encourage the children to explain how the pictures help show exactly what is happening and what the words are saying. On other pages, have them tell how the pictures show what the girl remembers about what happened a while ago. Ensure that they understand that the words don't tell about her memory.

Using Reading Strategies

As you reread, review *Clarifying* and *Making Connections* with the children. Remind them how good readers use these strategies to help them understand what they read.

Building Comprehension Skills

Review *Comparing and Contrasting* with the children. Answer any questions they might have.

Reading and Responding

Responding to Literature

Discussing the Selection

■ Ask the children to share how they feel about the way the little girl handled her fears. Have them tell whether they would have done the same things, or whether they would have done things differently.

■ Have them describe their favorite part of the story. Why do they like this part so much?

Purposes for Reading

Have the children review their purposes for reading.

Assessment

✓ **Informal** Note those children who have not participated in any of the discussion of the story. Plan to meet with them in a small group to assess if they have understood the story and the follow-up discussion.

 Exploring the Theme

Theme Connections

Talk About It

Invite the children to discuss how going to school could be an adventure. Prompt the discussion with questions such as:

What did you do by yourself for the very first time when you started school?

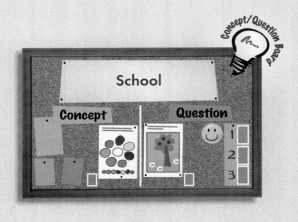

③ Integrating the Curriculum

Teacher Tip Kindergarten children are likely to be reluctant to participate in Seminar. It will take some time for children to ask questions or offer positive criticism. Time and exposure should make it easier.

Language Arts

Independent and Collaborative Writing

Seminar

Introduce *Seminar*, during which all the children will have a chance to talk about their writing.

In general, during Seminar the children should have enough room to sit in a circle on the floor without touching one another. Establish a rule that children who wish to ask a question or make a comment must first raise their hands and be called on, either by you as leader or by the child presenting his or her work. Seminar participants must also listen carefully and provide constructive comments.

Invite a child to share a piece of his or her work from previous lessons.

As the children share their work, invite their classmates to respond to it. First, though, provide a model for appropriate questioning and commenting in these introductory stages. Lead the questioning and commenting until the children are comfortable. Focus on questioning to find out more and comment on positive features. Encourage children to tell something about themselves as they show their pictures, such as something that they have done or would like to do.

If you have prepared a unit journal, invite the children to write about this selection and share that for Seminar.

Vocabulary

Days of the Week

Review the names and order of the days of the week.

Point to the name of each day on a large calendar as you say them. Then point to the name of each day again and tell the children something special about each one. For instance, Monday and Friday can be identified as the first and last days of the school week. For the other weekdays— Tuesday, Wednesday, and Thursday—you should pick school activities that occur only on those days.

Have the children say the days with you each morning for the next few days, if possible. Point to the name of each day on a large calendar as you say it.

3 Integrating the Curriculum

Guessing You may want to use this story to familiarize children with ideas about guessing—that guessing is different from knowing and that some guesses are better than others because they fit with the facts. Invite the children to come up with other things that Ferdie might guess went under the door but that they know could not have done so, or suggest some things yourself (for example, a cat, a newspaper, a cartoon character). Discuss with them why these are not good guesses.

Willy the Wisher

Thinking Story 2: "The Thing That Went Under the Door"

Ferdie and Portia are a brother and sister with very different ways of thinking and acting. Ferdie is impulsive and overconfident. Because of this, he often leaps to conclusions. Through Ferdie, children learn to identify and consider the information that he ignores. Portia is more cautious than her older brother. She tends to consider and reason before she reaches conclusions. Through Portia, children see what someone who thinks things through might say or do.

In this story, Ferdie leaps to conclusions and makes silly guesses about what went under the door. Portia points out the problems with her brother's guesses, then makes more cautious and reasonable guesses herself.

- Tell the children that in the story you are going to read to them, they will meet two characters who have very different ways of thinking and acting. Ask them to listen closely as you read to see if they can figure out how Ferdie and Portia are different in the ways they think and act.

- Read the story to the children.

- Through discussion, help the children to understand the different thinking behaviors displayed by Ferdie and by Portia.

- Ask the children to tell what they think ran under the door and why they think so.

Across the Curriculum

Math

Create a Schedule

Purpose

To arrange a schedule of events for a school morning.

Materials

chart paper, markers

Procedure

- Explain that a schedule is a way to know what to do at certain times during the day.

- Write the title "What We Do in the Morning" on the chart paper, and then write the numbers 1 to 4 down the left side of the paper. Explain that the children are going to plan a schedule for a school-day morning. They will decide what activities they will do, and in what order, between the time they arrive at school and lunchtime.

- Then ask volunteers to suggest activities that are often done in the class during the morning. Have them dictate to you the name of the activity and when they would like to do it. Enter the activity on the schedule.

- Once the schedule is completed, review the activities with the children and ask if they would like to change anything. Then agree on a day when the class will follow this schedule. On that day, have children take turns checking the order and monitoring that the correct activity is being done.

Sounds and Letters

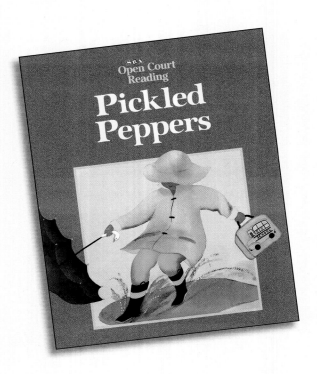

Reading the Big Book *Pickled Peppers*
"Sleeping Outdoors," page 41

Gather the children around you. Open the **Big Book** *Pickled Peppers* to the table of contents and find the poem "Sleeping Outdoors." Point to the title and to the page number. Ask a child to help you turn to that page.

- Point to and read the names of the author and illustrator.
- Read the poem slowly, running your finger under each word.
- Reread the poem until the children can say it with you.
- Talk about the meaning of *under*. Ask, "What does the poem say is *under* the dark? (*a star*) What is *under* the star? (*a tree*) What is *under* the tree? (*a blanket*) and What is *under* the blanket? (*me*)"
- Point to the child in the illustration and ask the children, "What are some things that might be under *me*?" (*grass, flowers, the ground, a pillow, another blanket, an air mattress, and so on*)

Sounds and Letters First-Step Story I
"Sleeping Outdoors"

- Distribute a copy of the **Sounds and Letters First-Step Story 1** "Sleeping Outdoors" to each child. Explain that this book does not have any pictures because they will get to draw their own pictures for the book.
- Ask the children to look at the front of the book and to read the title and author's name with you. Then read *illustrated by* and explain that the children can write their own names on the line because they will draw the pictures for this version of "Sleeping Outdoors."
- Hold up a copy of the **First-Step Story** and read one line at a time. Have children say each line with you.
- Remind the children that capital letters are used at the beginning of special words such as names, and explain that capital letters are also used for words at the beginning of each line in a poem. Point to the capital letters in the **Big Book** and ask the children to do the same in their own books.
- Tell children they can draw pictures to go with the lines of the poem. Explain that they should take care of the books, because they will be using them again in the next few days.

 Teacher Tip To make *First-Step Story 1,* copy Blackline Masters 15–18 for all students. Bind them together with a staple. Alternatively, you may have the children create their own more elaborate bindings using string or ribbon during Independent Work Time.

Research in Action

In this lesson, the children will work with their first *First-Step Story*. Each child will have his or her own book to own and take care of. Illustrating, narrating, and sharing their own stories with friends and family will give the children a sense of pride and will allow them to practice the skills and behaviors of accomplished readers and writers.

First-Step Stories are sometimes reprints of selections found in *Pickled Peppers*, sometimes new stories or poems, and sometimes picture books that the children create themselves. *First-Step Story*, "Sleeping Outdoors," is taken from *Pickled Peppers*.

Assessment

✔ **Formal Words and Letters** To assess children's ability to distinguish words from letters, have them complete *Skills Assessment* page 4.

Meeting Individual Needs

ESL

Oral Blending Review the blending words with English-language learners to make sure they know what the words mean. Use pictures, objects, pantomime, the *ESL Visual Glossary* and the *ESL Supplement* as needed.

Phonemic Awareness and Phonics Videodisc

Use the **Phonemic Awareness Videodisc** to preview the Oral Blending lessons. Unit 1 Lesson 13.

Oral Blending: Word Parts with Puppets

Level K – Disc 1 – Side B – Chapter 4

Phonics CD-ROM

Use the **Phonics** CD-ROM for activities that support the Phonemic Awareness Lessons.

Phonemic Awareness

Oral Blending

Word Parts

■ Hold up the puppet and explain that today he wants to play a new listening game. Remind the children that in the last lesson, they put together parts of words. Explain that this time the puppet will say the last part of the word and that they will put the word together.

■ Say the first part of a word, pause, and then have the puppet say the last part of the word. Then say the whole word. For example:

Teacher: alpha

Puppet: bet

Teacher: Now let's put the word together: alphabet

■ Continue with the following words, having the children say the whole word. Alternate between asking for whole-class and individual response.

alliga. . .tor	refrigera. . .tor	cinna. . .mon	dino. . .saur
televi. . .sion	hambur. . .ger	Septem. . .ber	remem. . .ber
le. . .tter	le. . .ttuce	cele. . .ry	car. . .toon

Which Word Is Longer?

■ Choose two children, one with a first name that has at least three syllables and one with a first name that has one syllable. Ask them to put on their Name Necklaces and come to front of the room. Direct everyone's attention to the two Name Necklaces, and have them notice that one name is longer than the other.

■ Tell them that the name that looks longer is also longer to say. Show them by having them clap out the syllables, or individual parts, of both children's names; for example, *E-liz-a-beth* and *Tom*.

■ Ask the rest of the class to put on their Name Necklaces, and then choose two more children to work with. Together with the class, say the names and clap the syllables. Repeat with other children's names.

Research in Action

The goal of oral blending activities is to lead the children to understand that spoken words are made up of smaller units of sound. Once the children are comfortable listening for syllables, they will be ready to turn their attention to sounds within syllables—the phonemes. *(Marilyn Jager Adams)*

Listening

Simon Says

- Play Simon Says again, emphasizing words that show position, such as *behind, over, in front of, under, on, in*. This time add *left, right, top, bottom*; for example, "Hop *on* your *left* foot."

1 Sounds and Letters

 Teacher Tip Remember that the goal of these early lessons is for the children to explore the formation of letters in order to become familiar with the letters' names and shapes. These lessons are not intended to build children's proficiency in writing the letters. Letter formation, along with proofreading, will begin in later lessons.

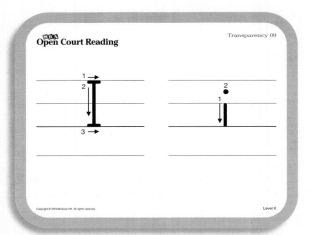

Transparency 09

Intervention

Allow time for children who find letter formation difficult to work first with crayons, the chalkboard, or on an easel. For children who are having extreme difficulty, allow them to trace letters on the chalkboard.

 Teacher Tip **Letter Formation** For those children having difficulty with letter formation, project the letter formation transparency on the chalkboard or a piece of chart paper and have the child trace over the letter. Or copy the transparency and have them work on their own.

Letter Names

"Alphabet Cheer"

■ Tell the children that they are going to do the "Alphabet Cheer" again. Review the cheer with them. As a variation, divide the class into two groups. Tell one group to say the cheer and the other group to sing the "Alphabet Song." Then have groups switch roles.

Secret Passletter

■ Have children sit in a circle with you. Whisper the Secret Passletter to a child next to you. Then have the children whisper it around the circle. Let the last child announce the letter to see if the correct letter made its way all the way around.

■ Then invite volunteers to locate the Secret Passletter on charts or posters around the room.

Letter Shapes

Exploring *Ii*

■ Direct the children's attention to the *Ii* **Alphabet Card** and point to the capital letter *I* and the small letter *i*. Explain that this letter is red because it is a special kind of letter, a vowel. Ask if anyone remembers the other special letters they have learned (*a*, *e*).

■ Tell children they will be writing these letters with you, beginning with capital *I*. Say:

> **Start here and go across. Start here and go straight down. Start here and go across. Capital *I*.**

■ Repeat the strokes several times and have the children imitate you in the air with their fingers.

■ Then have the children use pencils and paper to make the letter.

■ Repeat the procedure for small *i*, saying:

> **Start here and go straight down. Then go back to the top and make a dot. Small *i*.**

■ Find capital *I*'s and small *i*'s in children's name and in objects around the room.

Alphabet Big Book — Ii

■ Display the *Alphabet **Big Book*** and open it to page 20. Read "Lizard Longing," pointing to the words as you say them. Read the poem again, and this time have a volunteer touch words that begin with capital *I* and small *i* as you read them. Reread the poem a few more times, inviting the students to act like a lizard when they hear the word "iguana," and to act like a fish when they hear the word "piranha."

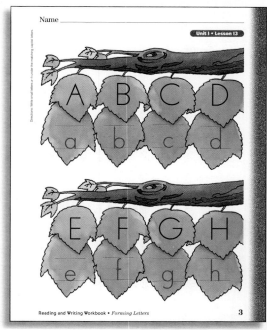

Reading and Writing Workbook, p. 3

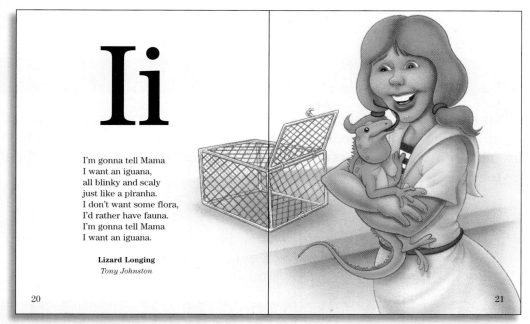

Alphabet Big Book, pp. 20–21

Within image 2:

Ii

I'm gonna tell Mama
I want an iguana,
all blinky and scaly
just like a piranha.
I don't want some flora,
I'd rather have fauna.
I'm gonna tell Mama
I want an iguana.

Lizard Longing
Tony Johnston

20   21

Reading and Writing Workbook

Children may use ***Reading and Writing Workbook*** page 3 for additional practice making the lower case letters a–h. Have the children make the appropriate letter under each capital letter.

Meeting Individual Needs

Reteach

Have the children who are having difficulty with the letters a–h complete ***Reteach*** page 3.

Challenge

a–h For a challenging activity on *a–h*, have children complete ***Challenge*** page 3.

② Reading and Responding

"I Brought a Worm"
Pages 44–47 of *School*

This selection is taught in two lessons:

Lesson 13
Lesson 14

Selection Summary

Genre: Poetry

Since sharing time, or show-and-tell, is a favorite time of day for many children, they will delight in the humorous experience of the child in this poem.

About the Author

Kalli Dakos, an elementary school teacher for many years, uses her experiences as a springboard for her poems. One of her main goals is to let "children and teachers see that there is so much to write about in their own lives."

Other Books by Kalli Dakos
- *If You're Not Here, Please Raise Your Hand* (Children's Choice Award)
- *Don't Read This Book, Whatever You Do!* (Children Choice Award)

About the Illustrator

Cynthia Fisher began her illustrating career at age 8. Since then she has illustrated many different kinds of books from a Christmas pop-up to a book about calculator riddles. Cynthia Fisher remarks that becoming a successful illustrator "requires great dedication and determination," but it is "well worth it." Cynthia Fisher currently lives in Massachusetts with her husband and two children. She enjoys reading and gardening and serves on the board of directors for a local library and preschool.

Other Books Illustrated by Cynthia Fisher
- *The Biggest Pest on Eighth Avenue*
- *The Sky is Falling*

Exploring the Theme

Selection Concepts

This poem tells about a favorite time in school, but it also shows how different sharing-time experiences can be.

Supporting Reflection

Have the children continue to work on their picture/story book about school during this lesson.

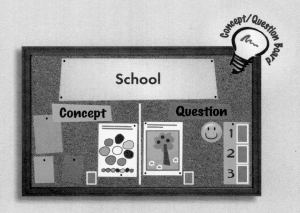

2 **Reading and Responding**

Building Background

Activate Prior Knowledge

If your class has a sharing time, discuss what children like to share. Have them tell how many different kinds of things they remember seeing during sharing time.

Background Information

If children are unfamiliar with sharing time, review "Boomer Goes to School," and discuss why the boy took his dog to school. Point out that in some classrooms, sharing time is called "show and tell." Invite the children to tell why they think this is also a good name for sharing time.

Preview and Prepare

Browse

■ Display the *School **Big Book***, opened to pages 44–45, "I Brought a Worm." Point to and read the title, then point to and read the names of the poet and illustrator. Ask children to look at the pictures and to tell about what they see. Explain that you think this might be a funny poem and ask them to explain why you might think that.

Set Purposes

Tell the children that they are going to listen to find out what happens when someone brings a worm to school.

Vocabulary

Selection Vocabulary

■ Write the following words on the chalkboard. Touch each word as you say it:

brought   showed

■ Explain that each word tells about an action that already happened. Give examples to demonstrate. You might say, "Today I bring my lunch to school." Then, touch *brought* and say, "Yesterday I brought my lunch to school."

■ Then give some examples for *showed.* You might say, "Today I show you a book. Yesterday I showed you a book."

Reading Recommendations

■ For your first reading, proceed through the poem as a whole, without pausing.

■ Have the children follow along as you read aloud the entire poem.

■ Be sure children understand that, just like in the other selections, we begin reading poems with the first word in the first stanza.

■ Run your hand under each line from left to right as you read to illustrate once more that the words on a page are read from left to right and from top to bottom.

■ When children become familiar with the line *But I brought a worm!,* ask them to join in reading it with you.

Using Reading Strategies

This poem invites the use of the reading strategy *Visualization.*

Reading and Responding

Comprehension Strategies

Introducing Strategy Use

Visualization *At each point indicated on the reduced pages, invite the children to close their eyes and visualize the scene in the poem. Explain that good readers sometimes do this when a vivid description occurs in the text.*

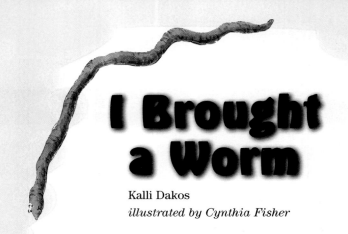

I Brought a Worm

Kalli Dakos

illustrated by Cynthia Fisher

Jane brought a baseball bat
And a ball for sharing time.

But I brought a worm! **1**

Rich brought a goldfish bowl
Without a goldfish.

But I brought a worm!

44

Jane showed us how to hit
The ball with the bat.

Rich put the class turtle
In the goldfish bowl.

Lizzy showed us how to prick an egg
And take the yolk out.

Joe tried to cut his sandwich
With his eraser knife.

46

Lizzy brought an egg with a yolk
And an egg without a yolk. ❷

But I brought a worm!

Joe brought an eraser shaped like a knife
And an olive sandwich.

But I brought a worm!

45

But I ate the worm!
Right there in front of everyone
I ate the worm!

(It was a candy worm.)

47

Comprehension Skills

Discussing the Selection

Have the children share their thoughts about the poem. Did they think the child in the poem really ate the worm? Were they surprised by the ending? If, after reading the poem, the children have any questions about school or sharing time, write their questions on strips and place them on the Concept/Question Board.

② Reading and Responding

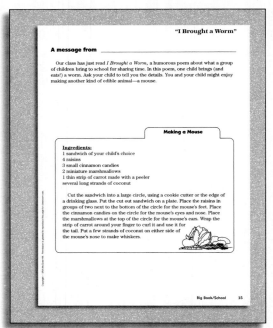

Home Connection, p. 15

Responding to Literature

Literature Appreciation

Repetitive or repeated text, such as that found in the refrain of "I Brought a Worm," is both interesting and comforting to children; it is also an effective aid both to word recognition and fluency.

Ask the children if they know other poems or stories in which a line or phrase is repeated. Invite them to share these with their classmates. You might also share with the children books with repetitive phrases, such as *Brown Bear, Brown Bear.*

Home Connection

Distribute ***Home Connection,*** page 15, which tells families about the poem "I Brought a Worm." It encourages families to reinforce children's play with songs and nursery rhymes as much as possible. This letter is available in English and Spanish.

 # Exploring the Theme

Theme Connections

Talk About It

- Invite children to discuss what kinds of things they like to bring to school for sharing time.
- Have them tell what was the most unusual thing they would like to bring for sharing time.

Supporting Reflection

- Continue assembling the pictures in the class book. Paste the pictures in the book and write captions beneath them. Encourage the children to help compose the text and to help you print, emphasizing the left-to-right direction as they print. Invite them to practice reading the book, independently, in partners, or to the whole class as time permits.
- Ask the children if they have read any books about school with their parents. Remind them that they can share their own books about school with their classmates.

 Check the Reading link of the **SRA** Web page for links to School-related Web sites.
http://www.sra-4kids.com

Integrating the Curriculum

Language Arts

Independent and Collaborative Writing

Write a Poem

■ The children might enjoy adding verses to the poem.

■ Have them use some of the verses in the *Big Book* as a "frame" or model and invite them to substitute their names and the objects they have brought to share for the ones in the poem.

■ Model this activity first by substituting your name and an object in the poem. Then allow the children to do the same.

■ Print the new poem on chart paper. Read it together.

■ Allow volunteers to illustrate the poem, as time permits.

■ Tell the children that, during Independent Work Time, they might continue to write verses for the poem in their journals.

Listening, Speaking, Viewing

Listening to Appreciate

Remind children that the class in "I Brought a Worm" was having sharing time.

■ Discuss rules for listening and for appreciating what someone is sharing during sharing time. Remind the children that good listeners sit quietly, look at the speaker, and don't interrupt. Tell them that after the speaker is finished, they may say what they liked about the things they saw or heard by raising their hands and waiting to be called upon.

■ Display chart paper and have children dictate to you their own wording for these rules. When the chart is completed, invite volunteers to read a rule. Then post the chart where everyone can refer to it.

Across the Curriculum

 **Social Studies**

Classifying

Purpose

To show how objects can be classified and identify them using pictures and labels.

Procedure

Discuss the things that the children in the poem brought to school for sharing time: a baseball bat and ball, a goldfish bowl, an egg with a yolk and an egg without a yolk, an eraser shaped like a knife. Remind the children that the baseball bat and ball go with the sport of baseball. Ask them to think of other sports that they know. Then have them name some of the equipment that goes with each sport. Continue classifying other things mentioned in the poem. For example:

■ sports that use a ball

■ school pets that could live in a goldfish bowl

■ animals that have a shell

■ animals that swim

■ foods we eat for breakfast

■ tools we use when we write

You might have the children find pictures for each category and paste them on a chart or a piece of paper, or they might make individual booklets. Invite the children to "write" or dictate labels for the objects on the chart.

1 Sounds and Letters

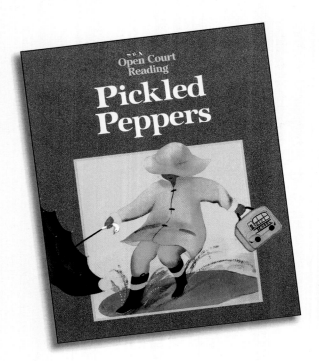

Teacher Tip If the children are having difficulty illustrating their pages, you may want to read specific lines from the poem to help them remember. You may also want to work with small groups who are having difficulty drawing pictures. Help them think of pictures that they can draw and provide tips for making illustrations.

Home Connection, p. 17

Sounds, Letters, and Language

Reading the Big Book *Pickled Peppers*
"Sleeping Outdoors," page 41

Encourage children to follow in their *First-Step Stories* as you read in *Pickled Peppers*.

- Have the children get their copies of *First-Step Story 1*, "Sleeping Outdoors," and gather around you.

- Open *Pickled Peppers* to page 41. Point to the title and read "Sleeping Outdoors." Ask the children if they can find the same title on their own books. Ask them to point to it.

- Point to the author's name and read it. Ask the children to point to the author's name in their books. Now ask them to point to their names as illustrators of their own books.

- Read the poem "Sleeping Outdoors" from *Pickled Peppers* as the children follow along in their books. Read each line slowly and pause to remind the children to turn the page. Read the poem several times.

- Ask a child to come up and point to the capital letter in the first word of each line in the poem. Say, "Yes, capital *U* is the first letter in *Under*, and it is a capital because it starts a new line in the poem," and so on.

Sounds and Letters First-Step Story I
"Sleeping Outdoors"

- Have volunteers "read" from their books, each reading one page.

- If children have not yet completed illustrating their books, invite them to continue working.

- Tell children that they will work on their books again during independent work time.

Home Connection

Distribute **Home Connection** page 17 which tells families about the various poems and songs you have been using in class. It also offers suggestions for ways to work with poems and songs at home. This letter is available in English and Spanish.

Phonemic Awareness

Oral Blending

Which Word Is Longer?

- Review with the children the Name Clapping game they played in the previous lesson. Choose two children to wear their Name Necklaces and have the class clap out the syllables of the children's names.

- Then ask the two children to say their last names. Write them on the board and determine which is longer and which is shorter. Have the class say the names with you, and then together clap the syllables of the last names.

Listening

Missing Sounds Game

- Remind the children of the Missing Sounds game they played earlier. Tell them that you are now going to play some sounds and that they must listen very carefully.

- Then play or make three different sounds. Wait a few seconds and repeat the sounds, leaving one out.

- Have the children tell which sound is missing, using words such as *first*, *middle*, and *last*. Continue with other sounds.

Meeting Individual Needs

ESL

Oral Blending Review the blending words with English-language learners to make sure they know what the words mean. Use pictures, objects, pantomime, the **ESL Visual Glossary** and the **ESL Supplement** as needed.

Tell the children to answer in complete sentences as they respond to the Missing Sound game.

Phonics CD-ROM

Use the **Phonics** CD-ROM for activities that support the Phonemic Awareness Lessons.

Sounds and Letters

Letter Recognition

Letter Names

"Alphabet Cheer"

- Do the "Alphabet Cheer." This time point to the letters on the **Alphabet Cards** as you say each one. Repeat the cheer and have children point to the letters in each line.

> Boom, boom [clap] Boom, boom [clap]
> A B C D
> Boom, boom [clap] Boom, boom [clap]
> E F G H
> Boom, boom [clap] Boom, boom [clap]
> I J K L
> Boom, boom [clap] Boom, boom [clap]
> M N O P
> Boom, boom [clap] Boom, boom [clap]
> Q R S T
> Boom, boom [clap] Boom, boom [clap]
> U V
> Boom, boom [clap] Boom, boom [clap]
> W X Y Z
> Boom, boom [clap] [clap] Boom

Secret Passletter

Choose a Secret Passletter and include it in activities throughout the day.

Letter Shapes

Exploring *Jj*

- Direct the children's attention to the *Jj* **Alphabet Cards**. Point to the capital letter *J* and the small letter *j* and tell children they will be writing these letters with you, beginning with capital *J*.

- Using the established procedure, form the capital *J* on the chalkboard. Say:

  > **Start here and go straight down. Then curve to the left and go back up a little bit. Capital J.**

- Have the children imitate the strokes in the air with their fingers as you give the directions and write the letter.

Intervention

Letter Recognition During Independent Work Time, pair children who are having trouble recognizing letters with partners who are more proficient. Give the children a **Letter Card,** have them name it, and then match it to a small **Letter Card.** Repeat with other letters, making sure to do them out of order. Remind the children to sing the "Alphabet Song" to help them remember the letters.

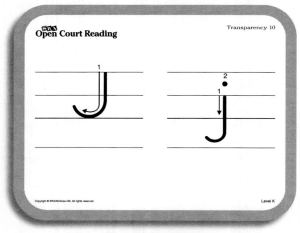

Transparency 10

- Then have the children use pencils and paper to make the letter.
- Repeat the procedure with small *j*. Say:

  Start here and go straight down. Then curve to the left and go back up a little bit. Go back to the top and make a dot. Small *j*.

- Have the children look for capital *J*'s and small *j*'s around the classroom and in their names.

Alphabet Big Book — Jj

- Display the *Alphabet **Big Book*** and open it to pages 22–23. Read "Jack Was Nimble," pointing to the words as you say them. Tell the children to jump once in place as you touch words that begin with capital *J* and small *j*.

Intervention

Allow children who are having difficulty to work on the chalkboard or on chart paper.

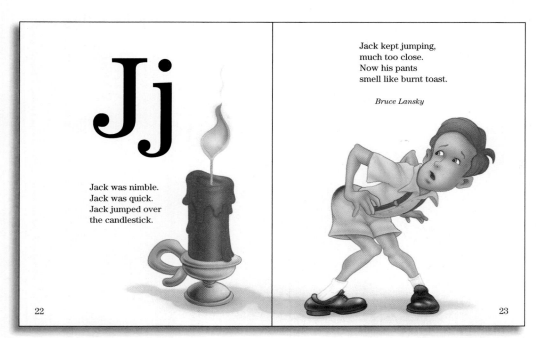

Jack was nimble.
Jack was quick.
Jack jumped over
the candlestick.

Jack kept jumping,
much too close.
Now his pants
smell like burnt toast.

Bruce Lansky

22

23

Alphabet Big Book pp. 22–23

② Reading and Responding

"I Brought a Worm"
Pages 44–47 of *School*

This selection is taught in two lessons:

Lesson 13
Lesson 14

Meeting Individual Needs

ESL

Visual Clues Before reading a selection, talk to the English-language learners about the illustrations in it. Associating the words in the text with the illustrations helps the English-language learners learn to think of English words before translating them first from their native languages.

Activate Prior Knowledge

Ask the children to tell what they remember about the poem from yesterday's reading.

Preview and Prepare

Browse

- Open the **Big Book** *School* to pages 44–45. Read and point to the title and the name of the author and illustrator.
- Turn through pages 44–47, letting the children discuss what they see in the pictures.

Vocabulary

Selection Vocabulary

■ Review the selection vocabulary that the children learned earlier. Invite volunteers to create sentences using the words.

brought   showed

Reading Recommendations

■ As you reread, keep tracking the print with your hand.

■ Reread the entire poem, indicating to the class to join in on the line *But I brought a worm!*

■ During one rereading, you might pause from time to time to invite children to act out what is happening in the poem.

Using Reading Strategies

Remind the children to *visualize* the poem as you read it.

Reading and Responding

Responding to Literature

Discussing the Selection

- Discuss whether children think the girl in the poem liked to joke with her friends. Ask the children whether they would like to have this girl as their friend.

Purposes for Reading

Remind the students that in the last lesson you decided to read to find out what happened when someone brought a worm to school. Tell the children that another reason we read poetry is for enjoyment.

Print Awareness

Italic Type

- Focus the children's attention on the italic type on each page. Explain that this slanted kind of print is called *italic type*.
- Point out that the italic words and the regular words have the same letters, but that they look a little different. Tell the children that writers sometimes use italics when they want to show that the words are special.

Using the Audiocassette

- Have the children work with partners and listen to the recording of "I Brought a Worm" on the ***Listening Library Audiocassette.*** Encourage them to read along with their books, and follow the print from left to right as they listen.

Exploring the Theme

Theme Connections

Talk About It

Sit with children and discuss having a special sharing time. Have them choose a topic and suggest that they bring in objects that are related to that topic. Some topics that might come from the poem include sports, favorite foods, tools, and hats.

Supporting Reflection

Review the class picture/story book with the children. Invite volunteers to read a page of the book—with your help—and explain the photograph. Comment that they have learned a lot about their class and school.

- Arrange with the school custodian to bring Boomer to his or her office. Ask him or her to come to your class and inform the class that there's a dog in his or her office. Bring the class to the custodian's office to get Boomer. Have the custodian explain his or her work and take the custodian's picture with the class.

- At some point in the unit, have a staff member take a photograph of you to include in the class book.

Check the Reading link of the **SRA** Web page for links to School-related Web sites.
http://www.sra-4kids.com

③ Integrating the Curriculum

Language Arts

Collaborative Writing

Journal Writing

If you have prepared a special "school" journal, have the children "write" on the third page.

■ Tell them they should write about the poem they just read.

■ Let them know that they can write about any part of the poem they want.

■ If some children have difficulty coming up with an idea, suggest that they draw or write about something they would like to bring to school for sharing time.

Grammar

Words that Show Action (Verbs)

■ Write the sentence *I ate the worm.* on the chalkboard and read it. Ask what the girl did.

■ When the children respond "ate the worm," point out that the word *ate* tells what she did. Explain that some words name actions.

■ Write each of the following words on the board, one at a time. When you write it, touch and read the word. Call on a volunteer to perform each action: *jump, clap, smile, stand, hop.*

■ Call on a child to say a sentence with each action word on the board.

Listening, Speaking, Viewing

Listening Skills

Call on small groups to role play sharing time. Have one child "present" a classroom object and have the group members demonstrate good listening skills. Remind them also to observe any sharing time rules the class has discussed.

Across the Curriculum

Dramatization

Act Out Characters' Feelings

Purpose

To help children identify the feelings of story characters.

Procedure

- Have children look at the illustration at the bottom of page 46 and discuss how the class feels about the girl eating a worm (when they think it is real).

- Discuss how people can show their feelings using facial expression and movement. Then have children take turns acting out various feelings or emotions. For example, they might like to pretend to be the children in the poem and show surprise, or to be parents watching their child eat a worm.

1 Sounds and Letters

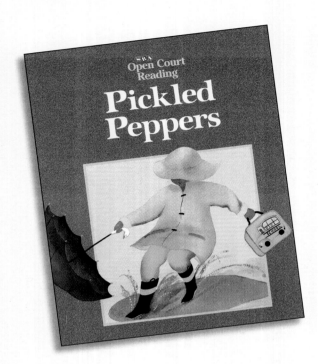

Teacher Tip

Position Words You might want to have the children watch you construct the pile of objects, and listen as you say, "I put the book on *top* of the eraser. Now the eraser is *under* the book." Then continue with the activity.

Sounds, Letters, and Language

Reading the Big Book *Pickled Peppers*
"Sleeping Outdoors," page 41

- Open the *Pickled Peppers* **Big Book** to page 41, "Sleeping Outdoors" and have children take out their copies of the ***First-Step Story*** "Sleeping Outdoors."

- Read each line slowly and have children follow along in their books pointing to each word as you read if they are able to do so. Remember to tell them when to turn the page.

- Call on a volunteer to come up to the **Big Book** page and point to any word in "Sleeping Outdoors." Read the word and then read the entire line. Repeat with other words.

- Point to the word *Under* and read it. Then point to an appropriate object in the room and ask what is under it. Or, make a pile of several objects and ask, "What is under the paper?" *(eraser)* "What is under the eraser." *(pencil)*

- Then reverse the question and ask: "What is on top of the eraser?" *(paper)* "What is on top of the pencil?" *(book)*

Sounds and Letters First-Step Story I
"Sleeping Outdoors"

- If the children have not completed their ***First-Step Story*** books, tell them to continue working on their pictures.

- Circulate and have children "read" their completed pages to you.

Phonemic Awareness

Oral Blending

Word Parts

- Hold up the puppet and explain that you will say a part of a word and the puppet will say another part. When the puppet asks what the word is, have the children put the parts together and say the word.
- Practice with the following word:

Teacher: de

Puppet: light. What's the word?

Everyone: delight

- When children demonstrate their understanding, continue with the following words. Alternate between whole-class and individual response.

les. . .son	per. . .fect	kitch. . .en
lem. . .on	grand. . .ma	tar. . .get
gro. . .ceries	ba. . .nana	pum. . .pernickel

Which Word Is Longer?

- Remind the children of the clapping game they have played with classmates' names in Lessons 13 and 14.
- Tell them that they are going to play the same game, but with other words. Direct their attention to the chalkboard as you write two words, one of which has more syllables than the other, such as *bat* and *banana*. Say both words aloud and then ask the children which they think is longer. (*banana*)
- Then say the words again, and clap the syllables. Have the children confirm that the word that looks longer is also the one that has more syllables and takes longer to say. Invite them to clap these two words.
- Continue with other word pairs, such as *toe/tomato*, *bird/birthday*, and *pop/lollipop*, *macaroni/map*, *watermelon/word*, and *cat/calendar*.

Listening

Simon Says

- Play "Simon Says" again. This time, emphasize descriptive words, for example, take a *big* step or tap your head *very gently*. After a few tries, encourage volunteers to be the leader.

Teacher Tip For the next five days, observe four or five children a day during the lesson. Call on individual children to determine if they can orally blend word parts. Do this each day until you have checked every child. Record observations on the Observation Log.

Teacher Tip Take care that the word you write or ask about first is sometimes the shorter and sometimes the longer so that the children really have to think to answer the question.

Meeting Individual Needs

ESL

Oral Blending Review the oral blending words with English-language learners to make sure they know what the words mean. Use pictures, objects, pantomime, the *ESL Visual Glossary*, and the *ESL Supplement* as needed.

 Phonics CD-ROM

Use the *Phonics* CD-ROM for activities that support the Phonemic Awareness Lessons.

Sounds and Letters

Letter Recognition

Letter Names

Vowel Song

- Remind the children that some special letters of the alphabet are called vowels. Ask volunteers to tell which vowels they remember learning about. (*a, e, i*) Explain that sometimes you can hear the names of these vowels in words, such as *a* in *acorn*. Point to each vowel on the **Alphabet Cards** and say its name.

- Remind the children of the Vowel Poem they learned in Lesson 9. Then tell them that they will hear a vowel song. Sing the song to the class, pointing to the **Alphabet Cards** for *a, e, i, o,* and *u* as you sing them. Consult the Songs Teacher Resources in the Appendix.

  A (clap) E (clap) I, O, U (clap)

  I can name the vowels for you

  A (clap) E (clap) I, O, U (clap)

  And you can name them too! Hoo!

  And you can name them too! Hoo!

- Sing the song together several times until all the children have caught on to the rhythm and remember the names of the vowels.

Research in Action

For children to understand how the alphabet works, they must appreciate that the vowels behave differently than other letters, in both spelling and sound. You can initiate this understanding by introducing the vowels as a special subset among letters. In the upcoming lessons, the children will pay special attention to the vowels, learning to name them and to listen for their long sounds in words. This is important preparation for the How the Alphabet Works activities that begin in Unit 2. Note, too, that extra attention to the names and sounds of the vowels is especially valuable for children for whom English is not the first language. *(Marilyn Jager Adams)*

Secret Passletter

Choose a vowel as the Secret Passletter for the day. Place the Secret Passletter and the other vowels on your index cards, so that the children are focusing on the vowels when you ask them for the Secret Passletter.

Letter Shapes

Exploring *Kk*

- Using the *Kk Alphabet Card*, point to the capital letter *K* and the small letter *k* and tell children they will be writing these letters with you, beginning with capital *K*.

- Follow the established procedure to form the capital letter on the overhead or on the chalkboard. Say:

    Start here and go straight down. Then start here and draw a line down to the middle. Start down here and draw a line down. Capital *K*.

- Have the children form the letter in the air with their fingers. Then have the children use pencils and paper to make the letter.

- Repeat the procedure for small *k*. Say:

    Start here and go straight down. Then start down here and draw a line to this spot on the first line. Now start here and draw a line down. Small *k*.

Open Court Reading   Transparency 11

Copyright © SRA/McGraw-Hill. All rights reserved.   Level K

Transparency 11

Teacher Tip **Letter Formation** For those children having difficulty with letter formation, project the letter formation transparency on the chalkboard or a piece of chart paper and have the child trace over the letter.

1 Sounds and Letters

Alphabet Big Book — Kk

■ Display the *Alphabet **Big Book*** and open it to page 24. Read "Keepsakes," and point to the words as you say them. Call on two volunteers to come up to the ***Big Book*** page. Have one child touch each word that has a letter *K*, ask the class "O*K*?" and have the class respond "O*K*!" Invite pairs of children to go on a Word Hunt. Have them go around the room to find words—on charts, signs, and in books—that begin with the letter *Kk*.

Alphabet Big Book pp. 24–25

Reading and Writing Workbook

All of the animals pictured on page 4 of **Reading and Writing Workbook** sleep outdoors: the bird, crab, dog, frog, hen, insect. Point out this connection between the picture and the poem. Then have the children draw a line from the animal to its home and match small letters with capitals. Tell them that they can trace over the capital and small letters for practice.

Reading and Writing Workbook, p. 4

Meeting Individual Needs

Reteach

Help children who are having trouble matching capital and lower case letters complete **Reteach** page 4.

Challenge

Capital and Lowercase For a challenging activity on capital and lowercase letters, have children complete **Challenge** page 4.

② Reading and Responding

Annabelle Swift, Kindergartner (Read-Aloud)

This Read-Aloud selection is taught in five lessons:

Lesson 15 **Lesson 17** **Lesson 19**
Lesson 16 **Lesson 18**

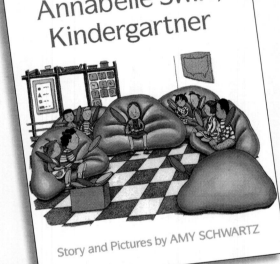

Annabelle Swift, Kindergartner

Story and Pictures by AMY SCHWARTZ

Selection Summary

Genre: Realistic Fiction

When Annabelle's older sister, Lucy, tries to prepare her for her new school experience, not all of Lucy's advice is helpful. In the end, however, Lucy's tutoring finally pays off.

About the Author and Illustrator

Amy Schwartz Growing up in California, Amy Schwartz knew from an early age that she wanted to write and illustrate children's books. Amy draws from her family experiences and says "all of my stories begin with something real and important to me." Although she has written as well as illustrated many books, Amy Schwartz considers herself an illustrator first because, she says, "I do more illustrating than writing. And I've drawn and painted since I was a child, whereas writing still feels fairly new to me."

Other Books by Amy Schwartz
- *A Teeny Tiny Baby*
- *The Magic Carpet*
- *The Lady Who Put Salt in Her Coffee*

Exploring the Theme

Selection Concepts

Annabelle Swift, Kindergartner, is the story of Annabelle's first day at school and how her big sister, Lucy, tried to ease the fears of the younger, less-experienced child. Although not everything Lucy teaches Annabelle is helpful to her, in the end the tutoring pays off, and Annabelle feels the kind of pride that comes from excelling. The key concepts explored in the selection are:

- Entering school for the first time is rather scary for many kindergartners.

- Older brothers and sisters can sometimes help their younger siblings get ready to attend school.

- Although people who give advice try to be helpful, they don't always tell us the right thing.

- When we're given advice, it's important to think carefully about whether to follow it or not.

- In school, students sometimes feel good about what they have done and, at other times, not so good. But it is important to keep trying, anyway, so that we can feel good about ourselves in the end.

Supporting Reflection

Although there is no school picture/story book activity for this lesson, you should prepare whatever material you will need ahead of time. In these final lessons, you will complete and bind the unit activity book.

2 Reading and Responding

Building Background

Activate Prior Knowledge

Some children may have older brothers or sisters. Ask them if their older brothers of sisters helped them get ready for kindergarten in any way. Other children may have talked to older cousins or friends. Allow volunteers to share any stories they may have.

Background Information

Invite children to tell about times when someone may have tried to tell them what to do at school. Discuss whether the advice was helpful.

Preview and Prepare

Browse

Display the book *Annabelle Swift, Kindergartner*, read the title, and show the children the first few pages. Have them tell if they have any idea of what the story is about by just looking at the first pictures. Remind the children that good readers often browse before they read to get an idea of what the story is about. Invite them to ask any questions they might have—another strategy of good readers.

Set Purposes

Remind the children that an important purpose for reading is to find out information. Invite them to listen carefully to find out if Lucy has good advice for Annabelle.

Vocabulary

Selection Vocabulary

- Write the following words on the chalkboard. Touch each word as you read it aloud:

mother   father   sister

- Explain that each word names a person in a family.
- Ask volunteers to say a sentence with each word. Suggest that they create their sentences about their own families, if they feel comfortable doing so.

Reading Recommendations

The complete text of *Annabelle Swift, Kindergartner* is reproduced in this lesson. You may want to read the entire selection today, pausing only to model the reading strategies for the story. If you feel the selection is too long for one reading, you may want to use today for pre-reading activities only, then read the selection in sections. If so, you can use the story division that appears in Lessons 16–18.

Using Reading Strategies

During the reading of *Annabelle Swift, Kindergartner*, you will model the use of the following reading strategies:

- Asking Questions
- Predicting

You should always stop to clarify words or ideas that the children find confusing or difficult.

Meeting Individual Needs

ESL

Selection Vocabulary Encourage English-language learners to offer vocabulary words in their own languages. Invite them to talk about their experience or knowledge of what the words mean in their native countries.

Reading Recommendation
The Read-Aloud *Annabelle Swift, Kindergartner* does not have numbered pages. The text for this story starts on the actual page 5.

Reading and Responding

Comprehension Strategies

Introducing Strategy Use

Modeling

❶ Asking Questions *Does anyone have any questions about what is happening here? (Why is Lucy showing Annabelle where they are on a globe? It must be awfully hard to see exactly where their town is. I wonder if Annabelle is confused?) Even if our questions might not get answered, the questions help us think more about the story and that helps us understand the story even better.*

Modeling

❷ Asking Questions *Does anyone have a question? Invite volunteers to model "asking questions" for the class. (Why would Lucy use make-up to teach colors to Annabelle? Annabelle won't be wearing make-up to kindergarten.) Maybe we'll find out as we keep reading.*

Lucy stood by the globe.
"This is the world, Annabelle. *This* is geography."
She peered at the globe and put her finger on a certain spot.
"And this is *us.* Got that?" ❶
Annabelle nodded.
"Good! On to colors!"

Lucy taped the name tag onto her little sister's blouse.

"Annabelle Swift, Kindergartner!" she read. "I remember my first day of kindergarten, Annabelle," Lucy said importantly. "I didn't have a big sister to train me."

Annabelle straightened her name tag.

"I'm going to teach you the fancy stuff, Annabelle. Tomorrow they'll know you're *my* sister."

Annabelle followed Lucy into the den.

Comprehension Skills

During the rereading of this selection, the children will focus on specific techniques, tools, and skills to help them better understand what they read. Comprehension skill activities are provided in this column in Lessons 16 through 18.

Next they went to their mother's dressing table. Lucy coated her lips with lipstick.

"What color's this, Annabelle?"

"Red!"

"*This* is not red," Lucy replied. She read the lipstick label.

2 "This is Raving Scarlet."

She smeared powder under her eyebrows. "And *this* is Blue Desire. Now that you've gotten that, we'll do arithmetic before dinner."

Reading and Responding

Comprehension Strategies

Introducing Strategy Use

Modeling

❸ Asking Questions *I'm a little confused. Is anyone else? Why did Annabelle put her name tag in her pocket? How will the other kids be able to read her name when it's in her pocket? Why did she rub her finger over it? Let's keep these questions in mind as we continue to read. We may not find the answers, but asking questions helps us think about the story.*

Lucy emptied their father's change dish onto the rug.

"Remember to ask lots of questions, Annabelle. Teachers like that. Are there numbers less than zero? And what's the number after infinity, anyway?"

Annabelle didn't answer. She was already counting the pennies on the rug. Annabelle loved to count.

Lucy had already taught her the numbers past 100.

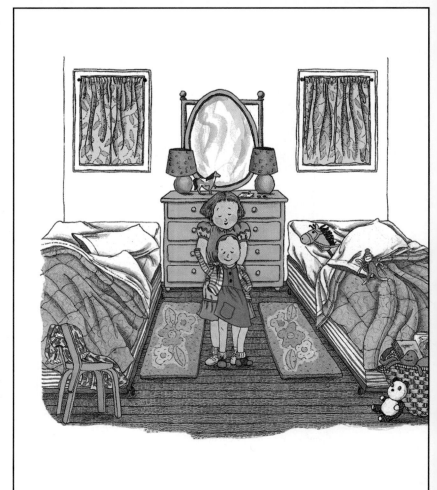

Meeting Individual Needs

ESL

Identifying Colors Give English-language learners practice learning the English names of colors. Point to items in the story illustrations and ask the children to name each. Then help them identify classroom items by color.

Annabelle came to a nickel. Lucy had taught Annabelle about nickels. "Remember, a nickel's worth five pennies," Lucy said. She picked up a penny. "One," she counted. Then she took Annabelle's nickel. "Two, three, four, five, six. A nickel and a penny. Six cents."

"Annabelle, call your sister to dinner," their mother called from the kitchen.

Annabelle stood up. She cleared her throat and moved close to Lucy. "Dinner!" she shouted.

Annabelle woke up early the next morning. She practiced counting the nickels and pennies in her father's change dish until her mother told her it was time to get ready. Annabelle ate breakfast and put on the red dress she'd helped pick out for her first day of kindergarten.

Lucy helped Annabelle on with her sweater. "Remember your milk money." Lucy gave Annabelle the nickel and the penny that were lying on the dresser. "And don't forget your name tag. It'll bring you luck."

Annabelle smiled. She put the name tag in her pocket and rubbed it with her finger. **3**

Comprehension Skills

During the rereading of this selection, the children will focus on specific techniques, tools, and skills to help them better understand what they read. Comprehension skill activities are provided in this column in Lessons 16 through 18.

② Reading and Responding

Comprehension Strategies

Introducing Strategy Use

Modeling

④ Predicting *Lucy seems to know what she is doing. I predict that her advice will help Annabelle. Making predictions while reading helps you to think about the story.*

Modeling

⑤ Predicting *Lucy told Annabelle what to do and say in school. I think Lucy's advice will not help Annabelle, though. I predict Annabelle will be unhappy. What do you think?*

Confirming Predictions Be sure to confirm all predictions when you reach the appropriate place in the text. Also, consider writing down all predictions so you can refer to them throughout the selection.

The girls' mother walked with them to school. They dropped Lucy off at her third grade classroom.

"Good luck, honey," her mother said. "Let the teacher know who's boss."

Lucy hugged her mother. She turned to her little sister and shook her hand. "Annabelle, remember, you're my sister!" ④

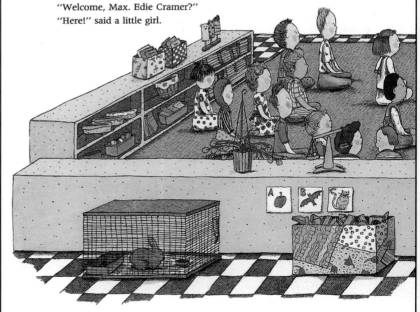

Mr. Blum took Annabelle's hand. "Come join your classmates on the green rug. I'm just calling roll. Watch the other children and you'll know ⑤ what to do."

Annabelle sat down like the other kids and folded her hands.

"Max Adams?" Mr. Blum called.

A red-haired boy waved his hand.

"Welcome, Max. Edie Cramer?"

"Here!" said a little girl.

Annabelle and her mother walked past the second grade room, past the first grade room, and up to the kindergarten. A tall man opened the door.

"Hello, there. I'm Mr. Blum, the kindergarten teacher."

"Annabelle, Mr. Blum will look after you." Annabelle's mother kissed her good-bye. "I'll be back at noon to pick you up."

Annabelle folded and refolded her hands. Her mouth was dry.

"Lucy," she whispered. "What do I do?" Then she saw the corner of her name tag sticking out of her pocket and remembered. "My sister told me how to do this," she said to the chubby boy sitting next to her.

Comprehension Skills

During the rereading of this selection, the children will focus on specific techniques, tools, and skills to help them better understand what they read. Comprehension skill activities are provided in this column in Lessons 16 through 18.

Reading and Responding

Comprehension Strategies

Introducing Strategy Use

Modeling

6 **Asking Questions** *How can Annabelle crawl under the rug? Let me try to figure out what this means. When everyone laughed at her, she felt embarrassed. I'll bet she wanted to hide . . .* crawl under the rug *must mean that Annabelle felt very embarrassed.*

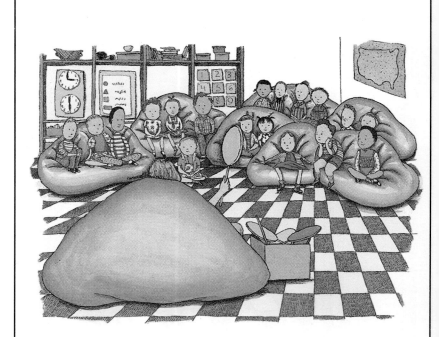

"Now let's go to the concept corner for the colored lollipop game," Mr. Blum said. He pulled a construction paper lollipop out of a box.

"Who knows what color this is?"

"Annabelle Swift?" Mr. Blum called.
Annabelle jumped up. She cleared her throat.
"Annabelle Swift, Kindergartner!"
All the kids on the green rug started laughing. Except the chubby boy.
Annabelle sat down. She wanted to crawl under the rug. **6**

Comprehension Skills

During the rereading of this selection, the children will focus on specific techniques, tools, and skills to help them better understand what they read. Comprehension skill activities are provided in this column in Lessons 16 through 18.

"Raving Scarlet," Annabelle whispered to the chubby boy.
"Red!" Edie Cramer called out.
"That's right, Edie," said Mr. Blum.
Annabelle rubbed her name tag with her finger. She counted the buttons on Mr. Blum's shirt.

Mr. Blum pulled out another lollipop. "And this one?"
Annabelle jumped to her feet.
"Blue Desire!" she shouted.

Mr. Blum cleared his throat. "It's light blue, Annabelle."
Annabelle sat down. "Drat that Lucy," she whispered to herself.

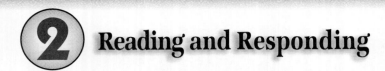

2 Reading and Responding

Comprehension Strategies

Introducing Strategy Use

Modeling

7 Asking Questions *Is Annabelle talking to a bush? Why would she do that? Who could be hiding in the bush? We might find the answers as we read on.*

Modeling

8 Asking Questions *What's a Milk Monitor? That's not something I've ever heard of. When we read more we'll probably find out. Does anyone have any ideas?*

During recess Annabelle and the chubby boy dragged sticks along the fence.

"Annabelle!" a bush outside the fence said.

Annabelle jumped. Then she recognized the voice.

"Don't worry," she said to the chubby boy. "It's just my sister."

All the kids sat down again on the green rug. Mr. Blum said, "Now we'll have arithmetic. Any questions before we begin?"

Annabelle decided *not* to ask about zero, or infinity.

Mr. Blum pointed to some big numbers on a felt board. "We'll practice counting together first."

The class counted to ten. To herself, Annabelle counted past 100.

"And now . . . snacktime!" Mr. Blum announced. "I'd like all of you to take out your milk money and put it in the middle of the rug."

Everyone piled nickels and pennies on the rug.

Mr. Blum picked up some coins. "A nickel is five cents and a penny is one," he said. "During the year, we'll study nickels and pennies. In June, whoever can count all the money will get to be Milk Monitor. For now, I'll add up the coins myself." **8**

"How's kindergarten?" the bush asked. "Isn't my training a big help?"

Annabelle glared at the bush. "Not exactly," she said. Annabelle dropped her stick. Her lower lip quivered. "Everything I say is wrong."

"Oh, Annabelle," the bush said. "Don't cry. Remember, Annabelle, you're not just any kid. You're Annabelle Swift, Kindergartner!" **7**

The bell rang. Recess was over.

"Put on your name tag," the bush whispered. "It'll help."

The chubby boy helped Annabelle stick on her name tag as they walked inside.

Comprehension Skills

During the rereading of this selection, the children will focus on specific techniques, tools, and skills to help them better understand what they read. Comprehension skill activities are provided in this column in Lessons 16 through 18.

2 Reading and Responding

Comprehension Strategies

Introducing Strategy Use

Modeling

9 Predicting *Annabelle has counted all of the coins. I predict that she will get to do something special and then feel very proud.*

But many of the kindergartners decided to start counting the milk money right away. Most kids didn't get past ten cents. Max Adams ran out of fingers. Edie Cramer got the nickels mixed up with the pennies.

"Annabelle!" Mr. Blum exclaimed. "That's wonderful! In all my years of teaching, I've never seen a kindergartner count all the milk money on the very first day!"

He shook Annabelle's hand.

"Class, today Annabelle will take the milk money to the cafeteria."

The chubby boy cheered, "Hooray for Annabelle!"

Mr. Blum put all the nickels and pennies in a big yellow envelope. He wrote "$1.08" on the corner and handed it to Annabelle.

"That big pink building at the end of the walkway is the cafeteria," he said. "I'll watch from the window to make sure you get there. Just give the envelope to one of the cafeteria ladies inside."

Annabelle took the envelope. She opened the door and headed for the cafeteria. She walked past the first grade room, and the second grade room.

Clearing her throat rather loudly, she walked past her sister's third grade.

Soon Annabelle was the only kindergartner counting.

"One hundred and five," Annabelle said. "One hundred and six . . . one hundred and seven . . . one . . . hundred . . . and . . . eight!"

The class was stunned. **9**

Comprehension Skills

During the rereading of this selection, the children will focus on specific techniques, tools, and skills to help them better understand what they read. Comprehension skill activities are provided in this column in Lessons 16 through 18.

2 Reading and Responding

Comprehension Strategies

Introducing Strategy Use

Modeling

⓾ Predicting *Annabelle still seems a little worried when she goes into the cafeteria. But I think she is happier now than she was before. I predict that she will do just fine carrying the tray of milk.*

Annabelle carried the tray to the cafeteria door.

"Honey, I need to mark down the Milk Monitor for our records," the hairnet lady called after her. "What's your name, dear?"

She opened the door to the cafeteria. **10**
"Why, thank you, dear," a big lady wearing a scary red hairnet said.
She took the envelope and handed Annabelle a tray holding eighteen little
cartons of milk and eighteen straws.

"My name's Annabelle," Annabelle said.
She slowly opened the door.
Then she carefully turned around, balancing the big tray.
"My name's Annabelle," she repeated. "Annabelle Swift, Kindergartner!"

Comprehension Skills

During the rereading of this selection, the children will
focus on specific techniques, tools, and skills to help them
better understand what they read. Comprehension skill
activities are provided in this column in Lessons 16
through 18.

Reading and Responding

Comprehension Strategies

Introducing Strategy Use

Modeling

⓫ **Predicting** *Annabelle looks happy in the picture. What do you predict will happen in the story now? (I predict that she will have a good day and not make the same mistakes tomorrow as she did today.) Explain that even though the story is over, good readers often make predictions about what will happen to story characters later on.*

Then past the third grade room, past the second grade, and past the first, Annabelle Swift, Kindergartner, proudly walked back to rejoin her class. ⓫

Comprehension Skills

Discussing the Selection

Discuss what Lucy had told Annabelle about school. How do the children feel about this information? Invite them to tell what they might say to Lucy.

Purposes for Reading

■ Remind the children that they were listening to find out about Annabelle. Discuss what they have found out about her, such as what she did, what she thought, and what she felt. Have them identify the places in the story where they heard their information.

2 Reading and Responding

Responding to Literature

Print Awareness

Letter/Word Distinction

- Show the title of the story book *Annabelle Swift, Kindergartner*. Point to the title and read it aloud. Remind the children that words are made up of individual letters. Then ask the children to tell what words have around them. (*spaces*)

- Read the title again and ask the children how many words they see. Then have a volunteer come up and frame one word. Invite volunteers to count the individual letters in the framed word.

- Continue with other words within the text, periodically identifying the word *I*. Help the children recognize it as a capital letter and as a word. Point out that when there are spaces around capital *I*, it is a word all by itself. Point out that spaces mark the end of one word and the beginning of another.

Word Length

- Write *Swift* and *Annabelle* on the chalkboard. Tell children one of these words is *Swift* and one is *Annabelle*. Have children say each word with you and clap the syllables.

- Ask which word looks longer. When children identify *Annabelle*, call on a volunteer to touch the word *Annabelle* on the board. Explain that this is the correct word because it has more letters.

- Erase the words and write *kindergarten* and *school* on the board. Tell children, without touching the words, that one word is *school* and one is *kindergarten*. Have them say and clap the words. Then ask them to identify the word *school*.

Home Connection

Distribute **Home Connection** page 19 which provides information about *Annabelle Swift, Kindergartner* and suggests activities to do at home. This letter is available in English and Spanish.

"Annabelle Swift, Kindergartner"

A message from _____

We have been reading a story called *Annabelle Swift, Kindergartner*. It is about a girl whose first day of school wasn't exactly as her sister told her it would be. Annabelle's third-grade sister, Lucy, tried to be helpful, but it was Annabelle herself who discovered that each person has to find her own way. Ask your child to tell you what happens in the story.

One of the activities Annabelle's class did during her first day of school was identifying colors. You and your child might enjoy creating your own color identification book. Here are directions for a book that is easy to make.

Book of Colors

You will need:
several sheets of white paper
different colored sheets of construction paper
glue or paste
pen or marker
crayons
stapler
scissors

What to do:
1. To make a book, fold the sheets of white paper in half and staple them together on the fold.
2. Cut a square from each piece of construction paper.
3. Glue or paste a different colored square on each page of the book.
4. Write the name of the color under the square.
5. Have your child decorate the front of the book and write his or her name on it.
6. Encourage your child to add pages to the color book each time he or she learns a new color.
7. You can enhance this idea by adding to the pages items that correspond with the color on each page, such as candy wrappers or pictures of items from old magazines.

Big Book/School   19

Home Connection, p. 19

 Exploring the Theme

Theme Connections

Think About It

Invite the children to review how thinking about something is different than talking about it. *(When you think, you just do it in your head. Talking means you have to use your voice.)*

- Tell them that you have one question for them to think about. Read the question aloud: "What was Annabelle good at in school?"
- When they have finished, praise them for thinking about the question and not talking.

Talk About It

- Ask the students to recall how Annabelle felt at various points in the story (*excited, scared, embarrassed, sad,* and *proud*).
- Help them see that many new students, as well as "veterans," experience this range of feelings.

③ Integrating the Curriculum

Language Arts

Independent and Collaborative Writing

Journal Writing

Invite the children to use their journals to write about school. Ask them to reflect on what they learn in school.

Willy the Wisher

Thinking Story 3: "The Bucket in the Basement"

Ferdie and Portia take turns making guesses about what the apartment building manager is going to do with the bucket he is taking to the basement. Through Ferdie's silly guesses and Portia's more reasoned ones, the children learn the difference between inappropriate guesses and educated guesses.

- Before reading this story to the children, tell them that it is about Ferdie and Portia and ask them what they know about these characters.

- The story ends with an unsolved problem: What could the apartment building manager be doing with the bucket in the basement? After reading, invite the children to suggest reasonable explanations, discussing why they think their explanations are reasonable. For example, could the manager be fixing a leak in the pipes? Is he getting ready to bail out a flooded basement?

Teacher Tip

Willy the Wisher Thinking Stories are built around humorous characters, each with easily recognizable ways of thinking and acting. Ferdie leaps to conclusions; while Portia, his sister, thinks things through. Each story includes questions that encourage the children to become active participants in the story as it develops.

Across the Curriculum

Social Studies

Classroom Jobs

Remind the students that Annabelle was given the job of getting milk for the class. Discuss with the children the classroom jobs that they take turns being responsible for: line leader, plant monitor, door holder, attendance taker, and so on.

- Talk about the importance of these jobs in making the classroom work and run smoothly.

- Have them compare their jobs to community jobs such as police officer, firefighter, mail carrier, trash collector, or to school jobs held by adults, such as principal, teacher, librarian, custodian.

- Discuss how we need these people to do their jobs in order for the community and the school to run smoothly.

Lesson Planner

	DAY 1	DAY 2
Part 1 — Sounds and Letters **Materials** ■ Big Book *Pickled Peppers*, p. 8 ■ Letter Cards (see lessons) ■ *Alphabet Book* p. 24, 26, 28, 30, 32 ■ Pre-Decodable Book 4: *The Trip to Grandma's* ■ Picture Cards (see lessons) ■ Listening Library Audiocassette: School ■ Pre-Decodable Book 5: *At the Zoo* ■ *Reading and Writing Workbook*, pp. 5–7 ■ Transparencies 12–16	**Sounds, Letters, and Language, p. 290** ■ Reading the Big Book *Pickled Peppers*, p. 8 **Phonemic Awareness**  ■ Oral Blending, p. 291 ■ Listening, p. 292 **Letter Recognition** ■ Letter Names, p. 293 ■ Letter Shapes, p. 293 **Reading Pre-Decodable Book 4:** *The Trip to Grandma's,* p. 295	**Sounds, Letters, and Language, p. 308** ■ Reading the Big Book *Pickled Peppers*, p. 8 **Phonemic Awareness** ■ Oral Blending, p. 309 ■ Listening, p. 310 **Letter Recognition** ■ Letter Names, p. 312 ■ Letter Shapes, pp. 312–313
Part 2 — Reading and Responding **Materials** ■ Read-Aloud Book: *Annabelle Swift, Kindergartner* ■ Big Book *School*, p. 48 ■ Home Connection, p. 21 ■ Unit Project Materials (see lessons)	**Activate Prior Knowledge, p. 296** **Preview and Prepare, p. 296** **Vocabulary** ■ Selection Vocabulary: *jumped, pulled, whispered*, p. 296 **Reading Recommendations, p. 297** **Comprehension Strategies** ■ Asking Questions, pp. 298, 300 **Comprehension Skills** ■ Drawing Conclusions, p. 299 ■ Discussing the Selection, p. 301 **Responding to Literature** ■ Literature Appreciation, p. 302 **Exploring the Theme, p. 303**	**Activate Prior Knowledge, p. 314** **Preview and Prepare, p. 314** **Vocabulary** ■ Selection Vocabulary: *coin, penny, nickel*, p. 314 **Reading Recommendations, p. 315** **Comprehension Strategies** ■ Confirming Predictions, p. 316 ■ Asking Questions, pp. 318, 320 **Comprehension Skills** ■ Drawing Conclusions, pp. 317, 319 ■ Discussing the Selection, p. 321 **Responding to Literature** ■ Reading/Writing Connection, p. 322 **Exploring the Theme, p. 323**
Part 3 — Integrating the Curriculum **Materials** ■ *Willy the Wisher Thinking Story 4* ■ Big Book *Pickled Peppers* ■ Blackline Masters 12–14 ■ Across the Curriculum Materials, see pp. 307, 327, 343, 355, 365	**Independent and Collaborative Writing** ■ First Day of School, p. 304 **Listening, Speaking, Viewing** ■ Asking and Answering Questions, p. 305 **Study and Research** ■ Charts, p. 305 **Vocabulary** ■ Names of Classroom Objects, p. 306 **Across the Curriculum: Math, p. 307**	**Independent and Collaborative Writing** ■ Proofreading, p. 324 **Listening, Speaking, Viewing** ■ Listening for Information, p. 325 **Vocabulary** ■ Color Words, p. 326 **Across the Curriculum: Social Studies, p. 327**

Independent Work Time

Materials
Big Books: Pickled Peppers, Alphabet Book, Pictures Tell Stories
Annabelle Swift, Kindergartner (Read-Aloud)
Willy the Wisher
Skills Assessment pages 5–6

Reading and Writing Workbook pages 5–7
Reteach, Challenge pages 5–7
Intervention Guide Unit 1, Lessons 16–20
ESL Supplement Unit 1, Lessons 16–20
Pre-Decodable Book 4

Reteach
■ *Annabelle Swift, Kindergartner*
Preteach
■ *Pickled Peppers* "By Myself"
■ *Alphabet Book Ll*
■ Vocabulary: Names of Classroom Objects
Partner-read *Pre-Decodable Book 4*
Reading and Writing Workbook, Reteach, Challenge p. 5
Writing: First Day of School
Unit Project

Reteach
■ *Annabelle Swift, Kindergartner*
■ "By Myself"
■ Vocabulary: Color Words
Preteach
■ *Alphabet Book Mm*
Writing: Proofreading
Unit Project continued

DAY 3	DAY 4	DAY 5
Sounds, Letters, and Language ■ Days of the Week, p. 328 **Phonemic Awareness** ■ Oral Blending, p. 328 ■ Listening, p. 329 **Letter Recognition** ■ Letter Names, p. 330 ✓■ Letter Shapes, pp. 330–331	**Sounds, Letters, and Language** ■ Days of the Week, p. 344 **Phonemic Awareness** ■ Oral Blending: Initial Consonants, p. 345 ■ Listening, p. 345 **Letter Recognition** ■ Letter Names, p. 346 ■ Letter Shapes, pp. 346–347	**Sounds, Letters, and Language, p. 356** ■ Reading the Big Book *Pickled Peppers*, p. 8 **Phonemic Awareness** ■ Oral Blending: Initial Consonants, p. 357 ■ Listening, p. 357 ✓**Letter Recognition** ■ Letter Names, p. 358 ■ Letter Shapes, p. 358 **Reading Pre-Decodable Book 5:** *At the Zoo,* p. 361
Activate Prior Knowledge, p. 332 **Preview and Prepare, p. 332** **Vocabulary** ■ Selection Vocabulary: *first, second, third,* p. 332 **Reading Recommendations, p. 333** **Comprehension Strategies** ■ Confirming Predictions, pp. 334, 336, 338 **Comprehension Skills** ■ Drawing Conclusions, pp. 335, 337 ■ Discussing the Selection, p. 339 **Responding to Literature** ■ Reading/Writing Connection, p. 340 **Exploring the Theme, p. 341**	**Activate Prior Knowledge, p. 348** **Vocabulary** ■ Selection Vocabulary, p. 348 **Reading Recommendations, p. 349** **Responding to Literature** ■ Discussing the Selection, p. 350 ■ Purposes for Reading, p. 350 **Exploring the Theme, p. 351**	**Responding to Literature** ■ Read Aloud, p. 362 ■ Whole Group Discussion, p. 362 **Exploring the Theme, p. 363**
Independent and Collaborative Writing ■ Seminar, p. 342 **Listening, Speaking, Viewing, p. 342** ■ *Pictures Tell Stories*, p. 25 **Across the Curriculum: Math, p. 343**	**Independent and Collaborative Writing** ■ Journal Writing, p. 352 **Listening, Speaking, Viewing** ■ Making Introductions, p. 353 *Willy the Wisher Thinking Story 4*, p. 354 **Across the Curriculum: Social Studies, p. 355**	**Independent and Collaborative Writing** ■ Collaborative Writing, p. 364 **Vocabulary** ■ Vocabulary Review, p. 364 **Across the Curriculum: Art, p. 365**
Reteach ■ *Annabelle Swift, Kindergartner* **Preteach** ■ *Alphabet Book Nn* *Reading and Writing Workbook, Reteach, Challenge* page 6 *Skills Assessment* page 5 **Writing: Seminar** **Unit Project continued**	**Reteach** ■ *Annabelle Swift, Kindergartner* **Preteach** ■ *Alphabet Book Oo* ■ *Willy the Wisher Thinking Story 4* **Writing: Journal Writing** **Unit Project continued**	**Reteach** ■ "By Myself" **Preteach** ■ *Alphabet Book Pp* **Partner-read** *Pre-Decodable Book 5* *Reading and Writing Workbook, Reteach, Challenge* page 7 *Skills Assessment* page 6 **Writing: Collaborative Writing** **Unit Project Celebration**

Meeting Individual Needs
Independent Work Time

 Part 1

Sounds and Letters

Meeting Individual Needs

Reteach
- **Capital and Lowercase,** *Reteach,* **p. 294**
- **Letters** *Ll, Mm,* **and** *Nn, Reteach,* **p. 331**
- **Alphabet Sequence,** *Reteach,* **p. 360**

ESL
- **Oral Blending, pp. 291, 309, 345, 357**
- **Activities, p. 293**
- **Signs, p. 295**
- **Teamwork, p.361**

Challenge
- **Capital and Lowercase,** *Challenge,* **p. 294**
- **Letters** *Ll, Mm,* **and** *Nn, Challenge,* **p. 331**
- **Hop Along, p. 313**
- **Alphabet,** *Challenge,* **p. 360**

Intervention
- **Long Vowel Sounds, pp. 292, 310**
- **Letter Formation, pp. 293, 331, 346, 358**
- **Letter Recognition, p. 312, 330, 358**

 Part 2

Reading and Responding

Meeting Individual Needs

ESL
- **Number Sequence, p. 332**

 Part 3

Integrating the Curriculum

Formal Assessment Options

Use this assessment page along with your informal observations to gauge the students' progress.

Name _____ Date _____

Matching Upper- and Lowercase Letters

[Teacher: Look at the letter in the box. Draw a line under the upper-case form of the same letter.]

1. d   <u>D</u>   O   S

2. f   E   Z   <u>F</u>

3. l   T   <u>L</u>   V

4. p   G   <u>P</u>   D

5. k   <u>K</u>   X   A

Skills Assessment   5

Skills Assessment, p. 5
Matching Upper- and Lowercase Letters

Name _____ Date _____

The Alphabet

[Teacher: Listen carefully to what I say. Draw a line under the answer you think is right.]

[Teacher: The letters in the box are a and b. Which letter comes next in the alphabet, c or l? Draw a line under the letter that comes after ab. Is it c or l?]

1. a b   <u>c</u>   l

[Teacher: The letters in the box are f and g. Which letter comes next in the alphabet, d or h? Draw a line under the letter that comes after fg. Is it d or h?]

2. f g   d   <u>h</u>

[Teacher: The letters in the box are m and n. Which letter comes next in the alphabet, k or o? Draw a line under the letter that comes after mn. Is it k or o?]

3. m n   k   <u>o</u>

[Teacher: The letters in the box are q and r. Which letter comes next in the alphabet, s or e? Draw a line under the letter that comes after qr. Is it s or e?]

4. Q R   <u>S</u>   E

[Teacher: The letters in the box are x and y. Which letter comes next in the alphabet, l or z? Draw a line under the letter that comes after xy. Is it l or z?]

5. X Y   I   <u>Z</u>

6   Skills Assessment

Skills Assessment, p. 6
The Alphabet

Teacher's Observation Log

Student _____
Date _____ Unit _____
Activity _____

General Comprehension
Concepts Discussed _____

Behavior Within a Group
Articulates, expresses ideas _____

Joins discussions _____

Collaboration (such as works with other students, works alone) _____

Role in Group
Role (such as leader, summarizer, questioner, recorder, critic, observer, non-participant) _____

Flexibility (changes roles when necessary) _____

Use of Reading Strategies
Uses strategies when needed (either those taught or student's own)/Describe strategies used _____

Changes strategies when appropriate _____

Changes Since Last Observation
_____

If more space is needed, write on the back or use another sheet.

18   Copyright © SRA/McGraw-Hill. Permission is granted to reproduce this page for classroom use.   Assessment Guide

Teacher's Observation Log, p. 18
Assessment Master

① Sounds and Letters

Sounds, Letters, and Language

Reading the Big Book *Pickled Peppers*
"By Myself," page 8

- Open the ***Big Book*** *Pickled Peppers* to the table of contents. Remind the children that you have already read several selections from *Pickled Peppers*. Point to some of these titles in the table of contents and read them.

- Tell the children that today you are going to read "By Myself." Find the title in the table of contents and read it, then point to the numeral *8* and say it. Let the children know that this number tells you that you can find the poem on page 8. Turn to page 8 and point to the page number.

- If your class is using the small version of *Pickled Peppers*, ask the children if they can find the same title on their own books. Ask them to point to it.

- Point to the author's name and read it. Ask the children to point to the author's name in their books. Now ask them to point to the name of the illustrator in their own books.

- Read each line of the poem, moving your hand as you point to each word, emphasizing the left-to-right direction of the print.

- Beginning with the line, *I'm a twin*, read each of the next four pairs of lines and ask children to name the rhyming words.

- Reread the poem and have the children chime in on the rhyming words. Encourage them to clap along with the rhythm of the stressed syllables.

Phonemic Awareness

Oral Blending

Word Parts

- This activity is similar to activities the children have done in the preceding lessons, except that the first part of the word gives little clue to the rest of the word. Because of this, the children will have to listen carefully.

- Hold up the puppet and explain that you will say a part of a word and the puppet will say another part. When the puppet asks what the word is, children should put the parts together and say the word.

- Practice with the following word:

Teacher: dy

Puppet: namite. What's the word?

Everyone: dynamite

- Continue with the following words.

li. . .brary	high. . .way	mo. . .torcycle
mi. . .croscope	go. . .pher	ge. . .ography
wai. . .ter	mi. . .crophone	lo. . .comotive
bea. . .ver	sci. . .entist	si. . .lent

Meeting Individual Needs

ESL

Oral Blending Review blending using words formed with letter-cards with English-language learners to make sure they know what the words mean. Use pictures, objects, pantomime, the *ESL Visual Glossary* and the *ESL Supplement.*

1 Sounds and Letters

Intervention

Long Vowel Sounds Practice in listening for and identifying the long vowel sounds. Developing sensitivity to the sounds of the vowels is a relatively difficult step for all young readers and more so for English-language learners. If children show signs of difficulty with the vowels, have them return to these basic exercises at a later time.

Listening

Long Vowel Sounds—Long *a*

- Tell the children that they will be listening for vowel sounds in words.
- Say, "If you listen closely, you can hear sounds in words. The set of letters called vowels are special because many times you can hear their names in words."
- Have children name the letters as you touch each vowel **Alphabet Card**. Repeat the vowel name, and give a word with the long vowel sound. Say "Can you hear *a* in *tray?*"
- Tell the children you will say some words and they should listen for *a* to say its name. The children should repeat the word and then give the thumbs-up sign if they hear /ā/.
- Use the following words:

say	**day**	**way**	**lay**
low	so	**say**	grow
gray	**age**	**ate**	toe
know	hoe	high	pie
pay	me	my	**may**

Research in Action

You have already introduced vowels as a special subset of the alphabet. And you have explained to the children that you can sometimes hear the name of the vowel in the word. The best way to demonstrate this is by having the children listen for the sounds of the long vowels within open-syllable words, that is, words in which the first or the last sound the children hear is a long vowel. Learning first to hear and categorize the sounds of the long vowels will make it easier for the children to work with the more difficult short vowel sounds later.   (*Marilyn Jager Adams*)

Phonemic Awareness activities related to the lessons can be found at **http://www.sra-4kids.com**

Letter Recognition

Letter Names

Vowel Song

- Review with the children that vowels are special letters of the alphabet. Remind them that sometimes you can hear the names of vowels in words.

- Sing the "Vowel Song" with the children. Refer to Songs Teacher Resources in the Appendix.

- Sing the song again slowly, having children take turns pointing to each vowel ***Alphabet Card.***

Secret Passletter

- Choose a Secret Passletter for the day.

Show Me Game

- Give each child a set of ***Letter Cards*** for *Ee-Ll.* Name a letter, such as capital *H.* Have children find the letter, then, on your signal, hold up the card so the letter faces you.

Letter Shapes

Exploring *Ll*

- Using the *Ll* ***Alphabet Card,*** point to the capital letter *L* and the small letter *l* and tell children they will be writing these letters with you, beginning with capital *L.* Say:

  Begin here and go straight down. Then draw a line across to the right. Capital *L.*

- Follow the established procedure to form the capital letter on the overhead or on the chalkboard. Have children form the letter in the air with their fingers.

- Have children use pencils and paper to make the letter.

- Repeat the procedure for small *l.* Say:

  Begin here and go straight down. Small *l.*

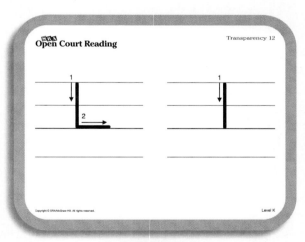

Transparency 12

 Teacher Tip **Letter Formation** For those children having difficulty with letter formation, project the letter formation transparency on the chalkboard or a piece of chart paper and have the child trace over the letter.

1 Sounds and Letters

Meeting Individual Needs

Reteach

Help children having trouble matching capital and small letters using **Reteach** page 5.

Challenge

Capital and small Letters For a challenging activity with capital and small letters, have children complete **Challenge** page 5.

Alphabet Big Book — Ll

■ Display the *Alphabet **Big Book*** and open it to page 26. Read "Lily Lee," pointing to the words as you say them. Have the children say, "Ooh, la, la" when you point to words with a capital *L* or a small *l*.

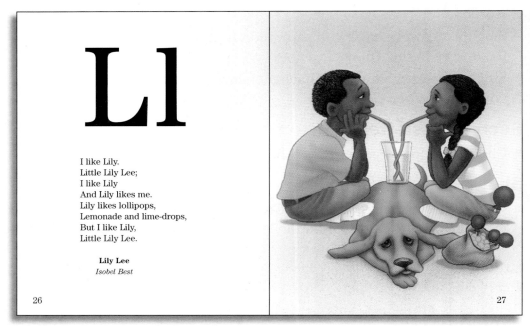

Ll

I like Lily.
Little Lily Lee;
I like Lily
And Lily likes me.
Lily likes lollipops,
Lemonade and lime-drops,
But I like Lily,
Little Lily Lee.

Lily Lee
Isobel Best

26   27

Alphabet Big Book pp. 26–27

Reading and Writing Workbook

Help the children complete **Reading and Writing Workbook** page 5 for additional practice matching capital and small letters. Have them circle the appropriate small letter for the corresponding capital letter.

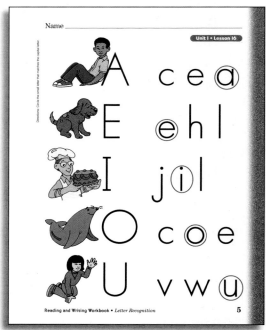

Reading and Writing Workbook p. 5

Reading a Pre-Decodable Book
Book 4: *The Trip to Grandma's*

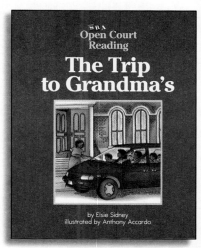

High-Frequency Words

The high-frequency words introduced in this story are: *we, and*

Reading Recommendations

- Introduce new high-frequency words listed at the top of the page. Write each word on the chalkboard. Point to and say each word, then have the children say each word with you.

- Preview the rebus pictures with the children to be sure they understand what each represents.

  For a complete discussion of the procedure for using **Pre-Decodable Books**, look in the Appendix.

- Hold up your book. Read the title aloud, then have the children read it with you. Point to and read the author's name and explain that this is the name of the person who wrote the book. Then point to and read the illustrator's name and explain that this is the name of the person who drew the pictures in the book.

- Allow children to page through the book, commenting on what they see in the pictures and making predictions about what they think the book will tell them.

Responding

- Encourage the children to ask each other questions such as, "How many people are in the picture?" "Where are they going?" and "Where does Grandma live?"

- Have children "read" the line of text on page 3 as you write it on the chalkboard. Circle and repeat the word *van*. Encourage children to think of words, real or nonsense, that rhyme with *van*. List the words on the board, then say each one and call on a child to use it to replace *van* in the line of text, for example: "The *man* is here." "The *fan* is here." and "The *pan* is here."

- Ask children to point out any words they recognize from their reading. If necessary, focus their attention on the words *the, here, a,* and *an* and call on a child to say each.

- Point to the rebus for *stop sign* on page 4 and ask children what the sign means. Have them discuss the purpose of signs and describe any signs with which they are familiar, such as other traffic signs, signs for favorite restaurants or shops, and signs showing hospitals or libraries.

- During independent work time, encourage the children to retell the story to a partner or to a small group of classmates. Have the other children follow along in their own books.

 High-Frequency Word Wall Add the words from this book to the High-Frequency Word Wall.

Meeting Individual Needs

ESL

Signs Invite English-language learners to use their primary languages to describe the signs in the story.

 For additional practice, you may want to use Book 4 of the supplemental set of *Open Court Reading Decodable Books.*

 You may want to make copies for the children of the black-and-white version of this story which is available in the *Pre-Decodable Takehome Book.*

② Reading and Responding

Annabelle Swift, Kindergartner (Read-Aloud)

This selection is taught in five lessons:

Lesson 15   Lesson 17   Lesson 19
Lesson 16   Lesson 18

Annabelle Swift, Kindergartner

Story and Pictures by AMY SCHWARTZ

Activate Prior Knowledge

Ask the students what they remember about the story. Invite them to tell how they feel when they give a correct answer to a question at school. Have them tell how they feel when someone else gives an incorrect answer.

Preview and Prepare

Browse

- Hold up the book. Point out once again the title and author.
- Flip through the first seven pages of the story. Invite the children to note details about the school and the classroom.
- Ask them what the pictures make them think of.

Vocabulary

Selection Vocabulary

- Write the following words on the chalkboard. Touch each word as you read it aloud:

jumped   pulled   whispered

- Explain that each word tells about something a person did.
- Illustrate this by saying, "I jump now; I just jumped."
- Ask volunteers to act out each word. Then have them use one of the words in a sentence.

Reading Recommendations

- To provide a listening focus, preview one thing that Annabelle does in the section you are about to read in the story.

- Pause to let children comment or ask questions.

- Encourage the children to stop you to identify any long *a* words that they hear.

Using Reading Strategies

During the first reading of *Annabelle Swift, Kindergartner*, you modeled the following reading strategies:

- Asking Questions
- Predicting

For your convenience, the strategy models from the first reading of the selection are reproduced in this lesson in the form of reminders. You may choose not to use these reminders with your class, or to use them only with children who need extra help or who missed the first reading of the selection.

Building Comprehension Skills

In lessons 16–18 you will work with the comprehension skill *Drawing Conclusions*. Remind the children that they drew conclusions when they reread "Boomer Goes to School."

Reading and Responding

Comprehension Strategies

Introducing Strategy Use

Modeling

1 Asking Questions *Remind the students that when you first read this page, you asked some questions about what you were reading. Tell them that you wondered why Lucy was showing Annabelle where they are on a globe. Tell them that, even though you really never got an answer to your questions, asking the question helped you think about the story and helped you understand the story even better.*

Modeling

2 Asking Questions *Point out that, on this page, you asked yourself why Lucy would use make-up to teach colors to Annabelle since Annabelle probably won't use make-up in school. Ask them where in the story they heard more about Annabelle talking about colors. Ask them if they found an answer to this question in that section.*

Lucy stood by the globe.
"This is the world, Annabelle. *This* is geography."
She peered at the globe and put her finger on a certain spot.
"And this is *us*. Got that?" **1**
Annabelle nodded.
"Good! On to colors!"

Lucy taped the name tag onto her little sister's blouse.

"Annabelle Swift, Kindergartner!" she read. "I remember my first day of kindergarten, Annabelle," Lucy said importantly. "I didn't have a big sister to train me."

Annabelle straightened her name tag.

"I'm going to teach you the fancy stuff, Annabelle. Tomorrow they'll know you're *my* sister."

Annabelle followed Lucy into the den.

Next they went to their mother's dressing table. Lucy coated her lips with lipstick.

"What color's this, Annabelle?"

"Red!"

"*This* is not red," Lucy replied. She read the lipstick label. "This is Raving Scarlet."

She smeared powder under her eyebrows. "And *this* is Blue Desire. Now that you've gotten that, we'll do arithmetic before dinner."

Comprehension Skills

Drawing Conclusions

■ Remind the children that writers do not always tell the reader everything about the story or about a character. Review with the children that sometimes they need to use story clues and things that they already know to figure out things in a story. This is called *Drawing Conclusions.*

■ Reread the paragraphs where Lucy tells Annabelle that she's going to teach her the *fancy stuff*. Ask the children to tell about the things Lucy tells Annabelle.

■ Then have the children think about the things they already know about kindergarten.

■ Help children conclude that Lucy may be giving Annabelle too much "fancy" information and not enough information that will really help.

At this point the goal is to expose the children to comprehension skills and how good readers use them. Keep a light touch.

Reading and Responding

Comprehension Strategies

Introducing Strategy Use

Modeling

3 **Asking Questions** Say, *"I was a little confused when I first read this passage. I didn't understand why Annabelle put her name tag in her pocket or why she rubbed her finger over it."* Invite them to discuss what answers they found to these questions, if any. Direct their attention to the illustrations on later pages that show Annabelle wearing her name tag. Tell the students that good readers use pictures as well as words to find answers to their questions.

Lucy emptied their father's change dish onto the rug.

"Remember to ask lots of questions, Annabelle. Teachers like that. Are there numbers less than zero? And what's the number after infinity, anyway?"

Annabelle didn't answer. She was already counting the pennies on the rug. Annabelle loved to count.

Lucy had already taught her the numbers past 100.

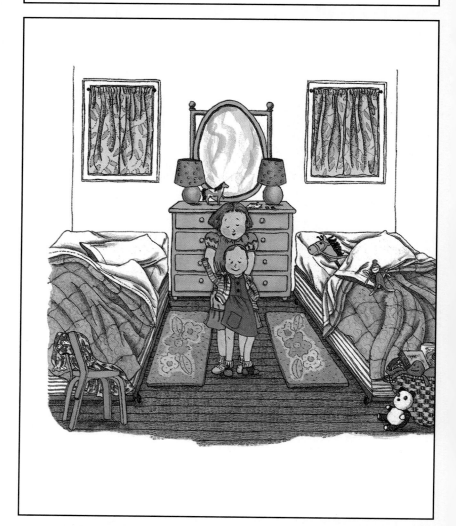

Annabelle came to a nickel. Lucy had taught Annabelle about nickels. "Remember, a nickel's worth five pennies," Lucy said. She picked up a penny. "One," she counted. Then she took Annabelle's nickel. "Two, three, four, five, six. A nickel and a penny. Six cents."

"Annabelle, call your sister to dinner," their mother called from the kitchen.

Annabelle stood up. She cleared her throat and moved close to Lucy. "Dinner!" she shouted.

Comprehension Skills

Discussing the Selection

■ Discuss how Annabelle probably feels about school now. Have the children tell what they might say to make her feel better.

Annabelle woke up early the next morning. She practiced counting the nickels and pennies in her father's change dish until her mother told her it was time to get ready. Annabelle ate breakfast and put on the red dress she'd helped pick out for her first day of kindergarten.

Lucy helped Annabelle on with her sweater. "Remember your milk money." Lucy gave Annabelle the nickel and the penny that were lying on the dresser. "And don't forget your name tag. It'll bring you luck."

Annabelle smiled. She put the name tag in her pocket and rubbed it with her finger. **3**

Reading and Responding

Responding to Literature

Literature Appreciation

Tell the children that throughout the story Annabelle experiences many different emotions such as happy, sad, scared, and proud. Tell them that the author uses many different ways to show us these emotions. Have the children notice that the author often describes an action or uses an expression that tells the feeling, rather than saying what the feeling is. Ask the children to listen for phrases and words that tell indirectly how Annabelle felt (for example, *"Annabelle smiled," "Her mouth was dry," "She wanted to crawl under the rug,"* and *"Her lower lip quivered."*)

Invite the children to show the expression that might be on Annabelle's face when each event occurred.

Exploring the Theme

Theme Connections

View Fine Art

- Display the *School Big Book* page 48 and have the children look at the picture called ***The Artist's Son*** by **Pierre-Auguste Renoir**. Tell the children that this was painted almost 100 years ago.

- Invite the children to tell what this painting makes them think of. Ask them if they think this little boy looks as if he is doing his school work.

- Have them compare this painting to the way they do their work. How is it the same? How it is different? Encourage them to make comparisons to the children they have read about in this unit so far.

Supporting Reflection

- Have the children finish pasting pictures and writing captions for the class book.

- Add any additional pictures to the class book, as appropriate, and work with the children to make a decorative cover. Have them watch as you print their names in the list of authors or, when appropriate, invite the children to print their own name on the list.

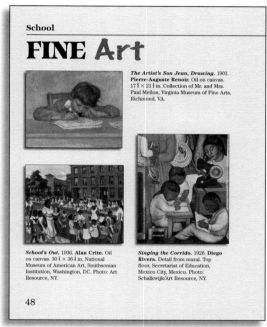

School

FINE Art

The Artist's Son Jean, Drawing. 1901. **Pierre-Auguste Renoir.** Oil on canvas. 17 1/8 × 21 1/8 in. Collection of Mr. and Mrs. Paul Mellon, Virginia Museum of Fine Arts, Richmond, VA.

School's Out. 1936. **Alan Crite.** Oil on canvas. 30 1/8 × 36 1/8 in. National Museum of American Art, Smithsonian Institution, Washington, DC. Photo: Art Resource, NY.

Singing the Corrido. 1926. **Diego Rivera.** Detail from mural. Top floor, Secretariat of Education, Mexico City, Mexico. Photo: Schalkwijk/Art Resource, NY.

48

School Big Book, p.48

Check the Reading link of the **SRA** Web page for links to School-related Web sites.
http://www.sra-4kids.com

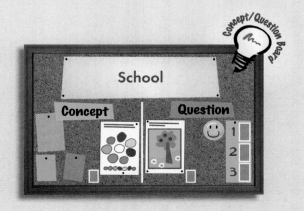

③ Integrating the Curriculum

Language Arts

Independent and Collaborative Writing

First Day of School

Teacher Tip You may wish to have the children dictate a sentence about their picture and write it on the back of the page.

- Working with the class as a whole, brainstorm activities the children did on the first day of school.

- If the children have difficulty remembering, you might prompt them with some possible activities.

- Prepare five or six sentence strips with the following sentence starter printed on them:

  On the first day of school we _____

- Read the sentence starter with the children, pointing to the words. Have the children furnish the missing word or phrase by referring to the brainstormed activities. Print the activity in the blank.

- If appropriate, invite volunteers to help you print some of the letters and words. Have the children practice rereading the sentence strips as time permits.

- During Seminar, invite children to show their pages and tell about them.

Listening, Speaking, Viewing

Asking and Answering Questions

- Remind the children that Mr. Blum asked Annabelle's class some questions and Annabelle was anxious to give the answers she knew. Point out that asking questions and finding the answers is one of the most important ways we learn new information.

- Discuss what Annabelle did when she answered a question. She jumped up and answered the question. Invite some students to pantomime this action. Ask them if this is the proper way to answer a question in school. Ask why Annabelle acted that way. (*It was her first day of school and she didn't know the school routines.*)

- Discuss what children should do to get your attention when they have a question. Have students raise their hands. Call on a student and have them stand up. Allow several students to model the correct method for answering questions.

Study and Research

Charts

- Remind the children that Annabelle and Lucy walked to school. Ask how many children in your class walk to school. Ask what other ways children come to school.

- Display chart paper that has been marked with a grid for graphing or a large sheet of graph paper. Explain that a chart is a picture that makes information easier to understand. Tell the children that they can help you make a chart to show how their classmates get to school in the morning.

- Distribute small self-stick notes to the children and ask them to print their names on them. Explain that they will use them to make a graph.

- Ask the children to suggest different ways they come to school, and draw a picture to illustrate each one at the bottom of a column on the graph. For example, draw a figure walking, a bus, and a car.

- Touch one mode of transportation and ask the children who come to school this way to stand. Have each child place the self-stick note in one of the column boxes, starting at the bottom. Continue in the same manner for each other mode of transportation.

- When the chart is completed, help children use it to determine how the most children get to school and how the fewest children come to school.

Integrating the Curriculum

Vocabulary

Names of Classroom Objects

Check the children's knowledge of classroom object names by pointing to classroom objects such as the ones listed below and asking individual children, "What's that?"

table	(We work at it. We sit at it.)
chair	(We sit on it.)
desk	(We work on it. We lay things on it. We put things in its drawers.)
floor	(We walk on it. We sit on it.)
window	(We look through it. We open it.)
pencil	(We write with it. We draw with it.)
piece of chalk	(We write with it. We draw with it.)
chalkboard	(We write on it. We draw on it.)
eraser	(We erase with it.)
scissors	(We cut with them.)

Across the Curriculum

Math

Travel to School

Display the "travel to school" chart.

- Have children count the number of names in each column, starting at the bottom.

- Explain that on charts we usually have numbers written along the sides.

- Print the numbers along the left-hand side of the chart, *starting at the bottom*. If appropriate, invite volunteers to help.

- With the children read aloud the numbers.

- Recount the names in a column and point out to the children that the final number in the count is the final number of blocks filled in.

① Sounds and Letters

Sounds, Letters, and Language

Reading the Big Book *Pickled Peppers*
"By Myself," page 8

- Open *Pickled Peppers* to the table of contents. Review with the children what information is on these pages and how to use it.

- Turn to page 8, "By Myself," and ask the children what they remember about this poem.

- Read the poem through, this time emphasizing the rhyming words. Then have the children chime in on the second rhyme of each couplet.

- After the rereading, discuss that the poem is about using our imagination. Invite the children to imagine they are something different, such as a favorite animal or a favorite character in a story. Have them share what they imagine themselves doing, or feeling.

- Have them make new imagination rhymes, following the poem pattern. Take out **Picture Cards** for *frog*, *dog*, *bat*, and *cat*. Make new couplets for "By Myself," asking the children to supply new rhyming words of each pair as you hold up the pictures. Begin as follows:

  When I'm by myself

  And I close my eyes

  I'm a little green *frog*

  I'm a furry brown *dog*

  I'm a soft gray *cat*

  I'm a great big *bat*

- Continue with other rhyming picture pairs, such as *kitten/mitten* and *fish/dish*.

Phonemic Awareness

This is similar to previous oral blending activities. In this set of words beginning with a consonant and vowel, the second part of the word does not give a strong clue to the word. Therefore, the children must listen very carefully. Do not spend a lot of time on these activities. With numerous repetitions most children will catch on.

Oral Blending

Initial Consonants

To this point, the children have been blending word parts. In this activity they will start by blending syllables, and then begin to blend words after hearing only the initial consonant and then the rest of the word.

■ Tell the children that the puppet wants to make the blending game a little bit harder. Explain that you will still say the beginning of the word and he will say the end. Let them know that they must listen carefully, because sometimes the first part will be only one sound.

Teacher: wea. . .

Puppet: sel. What's the word?

Everyone: weasel.

■ Continue with these words:

kit. . .ten   sand. . .wich   pro. . .gram   mu. . .sic

■ Then use the words again, saying only the initial consonant. Demonstrate with the puppet as follows:

Teacher: /k/

Puppet: itten. What's the word?

Everyone: kitten

■ Then continue with the remaining words, adding more if you choose.

Meeting Individual Needs

ESL

Oral Blending Review the blending with English-language learners to make sure they know what the words mean. Use pictures, objects, pantomime, the *ESL Visual Glossary* and the *ESL Supplement*.

Sounds and Letters

Intervention

Long Vowels You should note children who are consistently having difficulty with these activities, and plan to spend time with them individually or in small groups.

Phonics CD-ROM

Use the **Phonics** CD-ROM for activities that support the Phonemic Awareness Lessons.

Listening

Long Vowel Sounds—Long e

■ Remind the children that they are listening for long vowel sounds. A long vowel sound is when you can hear the vowel's name in the word.

■ Have the children name the vowels as you touch each vowel **Alphabet Card**.

■ Now tell the children that you will say some words and you want them to listen for the vowel *e* to say its name.

■ Give each child an *Ee* **Letter Card.** Tell them to hold up their card when they hear the /ē/ sound.

■ Use the following words:

see	so	bow	**bee**	pay
eat	ate	**tree**	now	me
day	**ease**	**knee**	know	my
she	**he**	hoe	**flee**	may

"Apples and Bananas"

The song "Apples and Bananas" will help children listen for and say vowels. In each verse of the song, some of the vowel sounds are replaced with a new vowel sound. (The words for the song can be found in the Appendix and on the *Listening Library Audiocassette*.)

Tell the children they are going to hear a song named "Apples and Bananas" that will help them hear and say the special letters called vowels.

- Sing or play the song for the children:

  I like to eat, eat, eat

  apples and bananas.

  I like to eat, eat, eat

  apples and bananas.

- In the next verse, some of the vowels are replaced with /ā/.

  I like to ate, ate, ate

  ayples and baynaynays.

- In the next verse, some of the vowels are replaced with /ē/.

  I like to eat, eat, eat

  eeples and beeneenees.

And so on.

- Sing the song together, announcing the vowel sound for each new verse and pointing to the *Alphabet Card*. For example, say, "And now let's sing for /ī/." Go through all the vowel sounds slowly.

Teacher Tip The vowel substitutions may be difficult and confusing for some young children. Try to explain what you are doing. However, with repeated singing, more and more students will catch on.

1 Sounds and Letters

InterVention

Letter Recognition During Independent Work Time, have children use their own sets of **Letter Cards** to play the Show Me game again, concentrating on letters that they find difficult to remember.

Letter Names

"Vowel Song"

Sing the "Vowel Song" with the children again, pointing to the **Alphabet Cards** for *a, e, i, o,* and *u* as you sing them.

Secret Passletter

Have a child choose the Secret Passletter for the day. Remind him or her to ask classmates about the Secret Passletter throughout the day.

Show Me Game

Distribute the **Letter Cards** *Ee–Ll* to each child. Say a letter such as "capital *I*" or "small *h.*" Tell the children to find the letter and then, on your signal, hold up the letter card so that the correct letter is facing you.

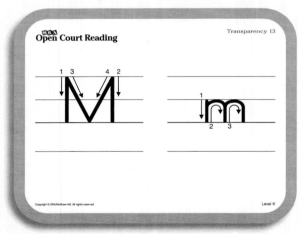

Transparency 13

Letter Shapes

Exploring *Mm*

- Point to the capital letter *M* and the small letter *m* on the **Alphabet Card**, and tell children they will be writing these letters with you, beginning with the capital *M*. Say:

  Begin here and go straight down. Now start here and draw another line straight down. Go back to the top and draw a line down this way. Then draw a line down this way. Capital *M*.

- Follow the established procedure to form the capital letter on the chalkboard. Have the children form the letter in the air with their fingers.

- After the children have practiced a few times, have them use pencils and paper to make the letter.

- Then repeat the procedure for small *m*. Say:

  Begin here and draw a straight line down. Then go back to here and curve over the top and go down. Then make another curve over the top and go straight down. Small *m*.

Letter Formation For those children having difficulty with letter formation, project the letter formation transparency on the chalkboard or a piece of chart paper and have the child trace over the letter.

Alphabet Big Book—Mm

- Display the *Alphabet **Big Book*** and open it to page 28. Read "Molly's Glasses," pointing to the words as you say them. Have volunteers frame the words that have capital *M* or small *m*. Encourage children to come forward to point to, and trace over with their fingers, capital *M*'s and small *m*'s in the poem.

Now Molly's glasses
are icky sticky gluey gooey
soppy gloopy moppy.

Molly's Glasses
Eve Merriam

Molly dropped her glasses
into molasses.
Icky sticky gluey goo.

She mopped up the muck
until the mop
got stuck.

28   29

Alphabet Big Book pp. 28–29

② Reading and Responding

Annabelle Swift, Kindergartner (Read-Aloud)

This selection is taught in five lessons:

Lesson 15	Lesson 17	Lesson 19
Lesson 16	Lesson 18	

Annabelle Swift, Kindergartner

Story and Pictures by AMY SCHWARTZ

Activate Prior Knowledge

Ask the children to tell what they remember about Annabelle from the previous readings.

Preview and Prepare

Browse

- Display the story book, turn through pages 8–19. Ask the children to comment on the details they see in the pictures and to tell where Annabelle is now.
- Ask if they notice anything new or different from the last time they looked at these pages.

Vocabulary

Selection Vocabulary

- Write the following words on the chalkboard. Touch each word as you read it aloud:

coin   penny   nickel

- Explain that each word tells about money.
- Point out that round, metal money is called a *coin*.
- Ask whether anyone knows if a *penny* is a *coin*.
- Ask if a *nickel* is a *coin*. Explain that a *nickel* is equal to five *pennies*.

Reading Recommendations

- Invite the children to comment or ask questions as you read this section of the story.
- During rereadings, you might call on children to say some of the more simple dialogue in the story.

Using Reading Strategies

During the first reading of this section of *Annabelle Swift, Kindergartner*, you modeled the use of the following reading strategies:

- Asking Questions
- Predicting

For your convenience, the strategy models from the first reading of the selection are reproduced in this lesson in the form of reminders. You may choose not to use these reminders with your class, or to use them only with children who need extra help or who missed the first reading of the selection.

Building Comprehension Skills

In this lesson you will continue to work with the comprehension skill *Drawing Conclusions*.

② Reading and Responding

Comprehension Strategies

Introducing Strategy Use

Modeling

④ Confirming Predictions *Tell the children that you predicted that Lucy seemed to know what she is doing and that her advice would help Annabelle. Ask them if your predictions came true. Discuss with the students that good readers often make predictions that turn out to be wrong and that it's all right to do that. Making predictions helps us think about the story, even if our predictions turn out to be wrong.*

The girls' mother walked with them to school. They dropped Lucy off at her third grade classroom.

"Good luck, honey," her mother said. "Let the teacher know who's boss."

Lucy hugged her mother. She turned to her little sister and shook her hand. "Annabelle, remember, you're my sister!" ④

Modeling

⑤ Confirming Predictions *Point out that when you came to this passage, you realized that your earlier prediction was wrong. After seeing Annabelle in school, you realized that the information Lucy gave her would not help her. Tell the students that good readers often make incorrect predictions, but they also change their predictions when new information arises.*

Mr. Blum took Annabelle's hand. "Come join your classmates on the green rug. I'm just calling roll. Watch the other children and you'll know ⑤ what to do."

Annabelle sat down like the other kids and folded her hands.

"Max Adams?" Mr. Blum called.

A red-haired boy waved his hand.

"Welcome, Max. Edie Cramer?"

"Here!" said a little girl.

Annabelle and her mother walked past the second grade room, past the first grade room, and up to the kindergarten. A tall man opened the door.

"Hello, there. I'm Mr. Blum, the kindergarten teacher."

"Annabelle, Mr. Blum will look after you." Annabelle's mother kissed her good-bye. "I'll be back at noon to pick you up."

Annabelle folded and refolded her hands. Her mouth was dry.

"Lucy," she whispered. "What do I do?" Then she saw the corner of her name tag sticking out of her pocket and remembered. "My sister told me how to do this," she said to the chubby boy sitting next to her.

Comprehension Skills

Drawing Conclusions

- Tell the children they can use what happened in the story, and what they know about the way people feel when they are laughed at, to *draw* a *conclusion* about Lucy's advice.

- Have children think about how they would feel if everyone laughed at them. Discuss what happened when Annabelle did the things that Lucy told her to do.

- Ask what they conclude about how Annabelle feels about what Lucy told her. (*Answers may vary, but the children should note that Annabelle seemed to think that Lucy's information was important.*)

Teacher Tip At this point, it is important that the children recognize that reading and thinking about what is read go together.

Reading and Responding

Comprehension Strategies

Introducing Strategy Use

Modeling

6 Asking Questions *Help the students recall that when you first read this passage, you did not understand how Annabelle could "crawl under the rug." Remind them that, by stopping and thinking about how Annabelle felt, you were able to determine that Annabelle must have felt embarrassed and wanted to hide from the class. Tell the students that when good readers don't understand something, they often stop to ask questions about what has happened in the story. Asking questions helps readers understand what is going on in a story.*

"Now let's go to the concept corner for the colored lollipop game," Mr. Blum said. He pulled a construction paper lollipop out of a box.
"Who knows what color this is?"

"Annabelle Swift?" Mr. Blum called.
Annabelle jumped up. She cleared her throat.
"Annabelle Swift, Kindergartner!"
All the kids on the green rug started laughing. Except the chubby boy.
Annabelle sat down. She wanted to crawl under the rug. **6**

"Raving Scarlet," Annabelle whispered to the chubby boy.
"Red!" Edie Cramer called out.
"That's right, Edie," said Mr. Blum.
Annabelle rubbed her name tag with her finger. She counted the buttons on Mr. Blum's shirt.

Mr. Blum pulled out another lollipop. "And this one?"
Annabelle jumped to her feet. "Blue Desire!" she shouted.

Mr. Blum cleared his throat. "It's light blue, Annabelle."
Annabelle sat down. "Drat that Lucy," she whispered to herself.

Comprehension Skills

Drawing Conclusions

- Reread the section in which the children are counting the money.
- Have children discuss whether or not Edie and Max are able to count all the money. Then discuss what Annabelle knows about counting. *(Eddie and Max can't count all the money, but Annabelle can.)*
- Ask how they feel when they are given an important job to do.
- Help them use the story information and what they know about classroom jobs to *draw* the *conclusion* that Annabelle probably feels very pleased and proud.

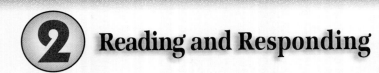

② Reading and Responding

Comprehension Strategies

Introducing Strategy Use

Modeling

❼ Asking Questions *Remind the children that when you first read this passage you were wondering why Annabelle would talk to a bush. Since you couldn't find the answer right away, you decided to read on and see what happened. Ask if any students remember why Annabelle was talking to a bush, and ask them how they know that. Point out that, as good readers, we ask questions to help us think more about the text and find more information.*

Modeling

❽ Asking Questions *Discuss with the children the confusion you had over the term* milk monitor. *Remind them that you had not heard that word before reading this passage. You decided that maybe you would find the answer later. Ask the students if they know what a milk monitor does. Help them understand that this point got clarified as you read the text.*

During recess Annabelle and the chubby boy dragged sticks along the fence.

"Annabelle!" a bush outside the fence said.

Annabelle jumped. Then she recognized the voice.

"Don't worry," she said to the chubby boy. "It's just my sister."

All the kids sat down again on the green rug. Mr. Blum said, "Now we'll have arithmetic. Any questions before we begin?"

Annabelle decided *not* to ask about zero, or infinity.

Mr. Blum pointed to some big numbers on a felt board. "We'll practice counting together first."

The class counted to ten. To herself, Annabelle counted past 100.

"And now . . . snacktime!" Mr. Blum announced. "I'd like all of you to take out your milk money and put it in the middle of the rug."

Everyone piled nickels and pennies on the rug.

Mr. Blum picked up some coins. "A nickel is five cents and a penny is one," he said. "During the year, we'll study nickels and pennies. In June, whoever can count all the money will get to be Milk Monitor. For now, I'll add up the coins myself." ❽

"How's kindergarten?" the bush asked. "Isn't my training a big help?"

Annabelle glared at the bush. "Not exactly," she said. Annabelle dropped her stick. Her lower lip quivered. "Everything I say is wrong." **7**

"Oh, Annabelle," the bush said. "Don't cry. Remember, Annabelle, you're not just any kid. You're Annabelle Swift, Kindergartner!"

The bell rang. Recess was over.

"Put on your name tag," the bush whispered. "It'll help."

The chubby boy helped Annabelle stick on her name tag as they walked inside.

Comprehension Skills

Discussing the Selection

■ Discuss how much of Lucy's advice has been helpful to Annabelle so far. Have the children tell whether they think things are looking up for Annabelle. What do they think she will tell her sister after school?

② Reading and Responding

Responding to Literature

Reading/Writing Connection

Prepare the following ahead: Draw a series of 5 stick figures, each depicting one of the following facial features – *excited*, *scared*, *embarrassed*, *sad*, and *proud* (see the Appendix for help drawing these faces). Print the feeling above each figure. Also print the following sentence starter beneath the figure: "Annabelle felt _____ ." Make a class set and distribute the sheets to the children.

Discuss the "feeling faces" with the children and point to the word above each, saying, "This word says _____ ."

Tell the children to:

- choose one of the pictures, cut it out, and paste on heavy gauge paper.
- cut out the sentence starter and paste it beneath the stick figure.

Invite the children to try to copy the appropriate word in the blank. As the children are working, circulate, helping them, as necessary, to fill in the correct word to complete the sentence.

Exploring the Theme

Theme Connections

Listen to Share Stories

Ask the children to gather stories from their families about their first day of school experiences.

- Encourage them to share any of the stories.
- Invite them to bring in photographs of their parents' school days. Have them show them to the class.
- Invite English-language learners to share stories of what going to school is like in their country.
- You may also want to engage children in a conversation about what going to school would be like in other regions, perhaps where it may rain or snow a lot.

Supporting Reflection

Remind the children of the unit activity.

- Add any additional pictures to the class book and work with the children to make a decorative cover.
- Have them watch as you print their names in the list of authors.
- Alternatively, consider inviting the children to print their own names on the list.

Check the Reading link of the **SRA** Web page for links to School-related Web sites.
http://www.sra-4kids.com

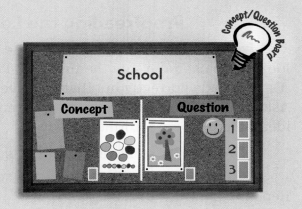

③ Integrating the Curriculum

Language Arts

Independent and Collaborative Writing

Proofreading

In today's lesson, introduce *proofreading*. Whenever the children write, whether at the board or on paper, they should proofread their work. Proofreading allows the children to learn by self-correction, and it provides an immediate second chance for success in writing. It also helps them develop the habit of looking critically at their own work, revising and rewriting when necessary. Circling, rather than erasing or crossing through, each error before writing the correction above or beside it permits them to see both the error and the correction.

First teach the children to proofread the letters they make in the Letter Recognition activities.

- Start by praising the work. Let the children tell you what is good about it. Lead them to notice the good things they might overlook.
- Ask the writer whether anything can be improved. Then have the group proofread the work (when it is on the chalkboard or projected overhead).
- If the children agree that something can be improved, have the writer (or a volunteer) circle the error and write the correction above or beside it.
- Praise the proofreading to let the children know that you are pleased they can find and correct their own mistakes.

Later you will teach the children to proofread for spelling, usage, punctuation, and content, but they should routinely proofread their letter forms.

Proofreading the Letters *A, a, B, b*

Give each child a copy of **Blackline Master 12**. Ask the children to look at the capital *A*'s on the first line. Point out that one of these capital *A*'s was made correctly but that the other could have been improved. Ask which capital *A* could have been improved. When the children have identified the poorly formed *A*, say

> **We'll draw a circle around this *A* to show that it can be improved.**

Repeat this for the remaining letters.

Listening, Speaking, Viewing

Listening for Information

Discuss with children some of the things that Lucy told Annabelle. Remind them that Lucy said many things, but Annabelle remembered exactly what Lucy told her.

- Help the children conclude that Annabelle must have been listening very carefully to what Lucy said.

- Play the Telephone Game with the children. Have all of the children line up or get in a circle.

- Tell them that you will whisper a sentence into the ear of the first child and then that child will whisper the sentence to the next child, and so on.

- Remind the children that they must listen carefully so that they hear the correct sentence, because the speaker is allowed to say it only once.

- Whisper the phrase, "I sang seven silly songs," or any other phrase you choose, to the first child. After all children have heard the phrase, have the last child say the phrase aloud.

- Determine with the children if they are good listeners or if they need to work on listening skills.

Integrating the Curriculum

Vocabulary

Color Words

Annabelle picked out a red dress for the first day of kindergarten. Play a color game with the children. Ask who's wearing a red dress. Have those children stand up together in a group. Then ask who's wearing a red shirt and have those children group together. Continue with other colors and other articles of clothing. Red socks? Blue pants? A brown belt?

Across the Curriculum

Social Studies

Telephone Numbers

Purpose

To recognize numbers in telephone numbers.

Procedure

Lucy taught Annabelle many things before she started kindergarten. Talk with the children about some of the things they learned before starting school. The children may mention learning their telephone number and address.

- Explain that it is important for everyone to know this information. Discuss with the children various situations in which such information would be helpful.

- Have those children who know their address and telephone number recite them. Then distribute **Blackline Master 13.** Read the sentence at the bottom of the page. Have the children write their telephone number on the lines. Circulate and help those who are having difficulty. Have telephone numbers available from your records for those children who don't know theirs.

- Have the children use the page to practice dialing their own phone number by touching the correct numbers on the phone. Then have them trade papers and try dialing a classmate's telephone number.

- On another day, distribute **Blackline Master 14** and have the children repeat the same procedure for writing their address.

- Circulate and help the children print their address on the line at the bottom of the page.

1 Sounds and Letters

Sounds, Letters, and Language

Days of the Week

Have the children repeat the verse for the days of the week:

Sunday, Monday,
Tuesday, Wednesday, Thursday,
Friday, Saturday, Sunday,
And back to the first day.

- Ask them if their families have a "special" family day (*such as Friday is Movie Day or Wednesday is Pizza Day*).
- Point to the names of the days on a large calendar and say them.

Phonemic Awareness

Teacher Tip **Word Choice** The purpose of these games is to develop the children's awareness of the sounds of words. Yet, they are much, much harder to the extent that the words are unfamiliar. Where a word in these lists is beyond your students' comfortable vocabulary, substitute another word or take time to make the word familiar through discussion and use.

Oral Blending

Initial Consonants

Have the puppet whisper something to you and then explain as follows: "The puppet thinks it is time to make this game harder. He wants me to say only the very first *sound* of each word."

Teacher:	/b/
Puppet:	asket. What's the word?
All:	basket
Teacher:	/t/
Puppet:	ailor. What's the word?
All:	tailor

- Continue with the following words:

    marshmallow daffodil pantomime happiness

- Tell the children that the words for today end with a long vowel sound.
- Review the long vowel sounds with the children. Say, "Sometimes vowels say their names in words: /ā/, /ē/, /ī/, /ō/, and /ū/."
- Hold up the puppet and explain that the puppet will say a part of a word and you will say another part. Then tell the children to say the whole word.

- Practice with the following word:

Puppet: pota

Teacher: to. What's the word?

Everyone: potato

- Continue with the following words:

toma. . .to	occu. . .py	avoca. . .do
Colora. . .do	chim. . .ney	chimpan. . .zee
magni. . .fy	satis. . .fy	bun. . .ny
multi. . .ply	lim. . .bo	plen. . .ty

Listening

Long Vowel Sounds—Long *i*

- Remind the children that they have been listening for the long vowel sounds in words. A long vowel sound is when you can hear the vowel's name in the word.

- Have children name the vowels as you touch each vowel *Alphabet Card*.

- Give each child an *Ii Letter Card*. Tell them to listen for *i* to say its name in some words. They should repeat the word and hold up their card when they hear the /ī/ sound.

- Use the following words:

ice	**cry**	**iron**	**I'm**
shy	show	**my**	**pie**
day	**why**	**high**	lie
die	**sly**	toe	**dry**
guy	she	play	**buy**

1 Sounds and Letters

Teacher Tip Be sure to keep the *Letter Cards* organized. You may want to separate all of the *c*'s, *f*'s, and so on. The children may keep individual sets in plastic bags and pull out the letters as needed.

Assessment

✓ **Formal Upper- and lowercase letters** To assess the children's ablility to match upper- and lowercase letters, have them complete *Skills Assessment* page 5.

Transparency 14

Letter Recognition

Letter Names

Alphabet Cheer

Lead the class in the Alphabet Cheer. You might want to distribute rhythm instruments and have the children accompany the cheer. Invite individuals to be the "band leader" and to point to the letters as the class cheers.

Secret Passletter

Have a child choose the Secret Passletter for the day. Give the child the responsibility of keeping track of how many times he or she asks for the Secret Passletter during the day.

Show Me Game

Distribute **Letter Cards** *Ee-Ll* to each child. Ask for a letter and have the children hold up the correct **Letter Card**. Then have the children say the letter.

Letter Shapes

Exploring *Nn*

- Using the *Nn* **Alphabet Card**, point to the capital letter *N* and the small letter *n* and tell children they will be writing these letters with you, beginning with capital *N*. Say:

  Start here and draw a line straight down. Then start here and go straight down. Then start here and draw a line down and to the right, this way. Capital *N*.

- Follow the established procedure to form the capital letter on the overhead or on the chalkboard. Have children form the letter in the air with their fingers.

- Have children use pencils and paper to make the letter.

- Repeat the procedure for small *n*. Say:

  Start here and draw a line straight down. Then go back here and make a curve over the top. Then go straight down. Small *n*.

Alphabet Big Book—Nn

Display the *Alphabet **Big Book*** and open it to page 30. Read "Norman Says Nelly is Noisy," pointing to the words as you say them. Have the children clap their hands once when you point to a word with a capital *N*, and stomp their feet once when you point to a word with small *n*.

Norman says Nelly is noisy
and natters all night with the nurse.
But Nelly says Norman is nosy
which Nelly says is much worse.

Nosy or noisy, which is worse?
Nobody here can choose.
Nothing else has happened.
That's the end of the news.

Michael Rosen

30   31

Alphabet Big Book pp. 30–31

Reading and Writing Workbook

Help the children complete ***Reading and Writing Workbook*** page 6 for additional practice with the letters *Ll*, *Mm*, and *Nn*. Have the children write each letter six times in the space provided.

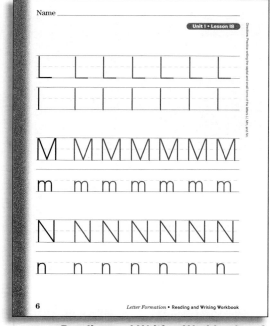

Reading and Writing Workbook p. 6

Meeting Individual Needs

Reteach

Have children who are having difficulty with the letters *Ll*, *Mm*, and *Nn* complete page 6 of **Reteach**.

Challenge

Ll, Mm, and Nn For a challenging activity on these three letters, have children complete ***Challenge*** page 6.

② Reading and Responding

Annabelle Swift, Kindergartner (Read-Aloud)

This selection is taught in five lessons:

Lesson 15   Lesson 17   Lesson 19

Lesson 16   Lesson 18

Story and Pictures by AMY SCHWARTZ

Meeting Individual Needs

ESL

Number Sequence To teach *first, second,* and *third* to English-language learners, use a row of objects to demonstrate. Point to the first object as you say *first.* Ask the students to repeat the word. Then continue with *second* and *third.* Do the sequence again with other objects.

Activate Prior Knowledge

Discuss what has happened in the story. Have the children discuss any things in your class that are different from those in the story. For example, do you have to go outside to get to the cafeteria the way that Annabelle does? What is it like in this school?

Preview and Prepare

Browse

- Display the story book, opened to the title page. Ask the children what they know about this page. Remind the children that the title is the name of the book and the author is who wrote the book. Tell the children that the author of the book also drew the pictures.

Vocabulary

Selection Vocabulary

- Write the following words on the chalkboard. Touch each word as you read it aloud:

first   second   third

- Explain that each word tells about a number.
- Draw three boxes on the chalkboard, from left to right. Touch each box as you say, "This is the first box, this is the second box, this is the third box."
- Ask children to gather three objects from around the room and place them on their desks. Then have them copy your phrase, using the appropriate words, and touching each item in the correct order.

Reading Recommendations

- Invite the children to comment or ask questions about what they are hearing.
- Be sure the children can view the illustrations after you have read a few pages. Invite them to describe what they see and how it matches what they have heard.

Using Reading Strategies

During the first reading of *Annabelle Swift, Kindergartner*, you modeled the use of the following strategies:

- Asking Questions
- Predicting

For your convenience, the strategy models from the first reading of the selection are reproduced in this lesson in the form of reminders. You may choose not to use these reminders with your class, or to use them only with children who need extra help or who missed the first reading of the selection.

Building Comprehension Skills

In this lesson you will continue to work with the comprehension skill *Drawing Conclusions*.

② Reading and Responding

Comprehension Strategies

Introducing Strategy Use

Modeling

❾ Confirming Predictions *Ask the children if their predictions about Annabelle came true. Remind them that one of the reasons we read is to gather information. Tell them that predicting is one way we focus on the information we are trying to discover.*

But many of the kindergartners decided to start counting the milk money right away. Most kids didn't get past ten cents. Max Adams ran out of fingers. Edie Cramer got the nickels mixed up with the pennies.

"Annabelle!" Mr. Blum exclaimed. "That's wonderful! In all my years of teaching, I've never seen a kindergartner count all the milk money on the very first day!"

He shook Annabelle's hand.

"Class, today Annabelle will take the milk money to the cafeteria."

The chubby boy cheered, "Hooray for Annabelle!"

Mr. Blum put all the nickels and pennies in a big yellow envelope. He wrote "$1.08" on the corner and handed it to Annabelle.

"That big pink building at the end of the walkway is the cafeteria," he said. "I'll watch from the window to make sure you get there. Just give the envelope to one of the cafeteria ladies inside."

Annabelle took the envelope. She opened the door and headed for the cafeteria. She walked past the first grade room, and the second grade room.

Clearing her throat rather loudly, she walked past her sister's third grade.

Soon Annabelle was the only kindergartner counting.
"One hundred and five," Annabelle said. "One hundred and six . . .
one hundred and seven . . . one . . . hundred . . . and . . . eight!"
The class was stunned. **9**

Comprehension Skills

Drawing Conclusions

Tell the children that we can often learn a lot about what happens in a story by observing other characters. Reread the line, "The class was stunned." If necessary, define the word *stunned* as it is used here. Have the students *draw conclusions* about why the class was stunned that Annabelle could count to 100. Answers may vary, but the class should notice that none of the other students could count to 100 and even Mr. Blum was surprised at Annabelle's counting.

② Reading and Responding

Comprehension Strategies

Introducing Strategy Use

Modeling

⑩ Confirming Predictions *Ask the students what they thought when they first read this section. Remind them that predicting makes us think about the story and about what might happen. Let them know that it doesn't matter if a prediction is right or wrong, just that you think about the story.*

Annabelle carried the tray to the cafeteria door.

"Honey, I need to mark down the Milk Monitor for our records," the hairnet lady called after her. "What's your name, dear?"

She opened the door to the cafeteria. **10**
"Why, thank you, dear," a big lady wearing a scary red hairnet said. She took the envelope and handed Annabelle a tray holding eighteen little cartons of milk and eighteen straws.

"My name's Annabelle," Annabelle said.
She slowly opened the door.
Then she carefully turned around, balancing the big tray.
"My name's Annabelle," she repeated. "Annabelle Swift, Kindergartner!"

Comprehension Skills

Drawing Conclusions

■ Point out that Annabelle felt a lot better at the end of the story than she did earlier. Discuss what happened along the way, and have the children *draw conclusions* about which events help Annabelle the most. *(For example, Annabelle made a friend, she counted the milk money, and she was chosen to go get the milk.)*

Reading and Responding

Comprehension Strategies

Introducing Strategy Use

Modeling

⑪ Confirming Predictions *Remind the children of their predictions that Annabelle will have a good day and not make the same mistakes tomorrow as she did today. Tell them that, even though the story is over, good readers often make predictions about what will happen to story characters later on.*

Then past the third grade room, past the second grade, and past the first, Annabelle Swift, Kindergartner, proudly walked back to rejoin her class. ⑪

Comprehension Skills

Discussing the Selection

■ Discuss whether or not Lucy helped Annabelle after all. How will Annabelle tell Lucy about the results of her advice? Do you think Annabelle will ever ask Lucy for help again? Why or why not?

② Reading and Responding

Responding to Literature

Reading/Writing Connection

Review the selection with the children, emphasizing the feelings that Annabelle experienced through the story. Discuss each of the feelings presented in the selection *(excited, scared, and sad)* and have the children give examples of each, both from the story and from their own personal experience.

Children may have difficulty identifying a time when they felt embarrassed or proud. Consider relating a short story about a time when you, or a previous student, experienced these emotions. Then invite the children to think of a time they felt proud or embarrassed. Because these latter emotions are complex, and not typically well understood by children until they are a bit older, do not spend too much time ensuring that all children understand them completely at this time.

Exploring the Theme

Theme Connections

Record Ideas

- Ask the children to think about what they are good at in school.
- In their journals have them draw a picture of them doing what they are good at.
- As they draw, have them explain their picture. On the child's picture, print what the picture depicts.

③ Integrating the Curriculum

Teacher Tip You will probably have to take the lead during Seminar until the children become comfortable with the activity.

Language Arts

Independent and Collaborative Writing

Seminar

Make today a seminar day.

■ Have two or more children share their work. Begin by having each child who is sharing also lead the discussion. The leader sits at the front of the group and calls on children to ask questions or make comments.

■ Continue to model good question-asking and positive comments.

■ Tell the children that they should first say something they like about another's work, then they can ask questions about it.

Listening, Speaking, Viewing

Pictures Tell Stories

■ Explain to the children that they are going to look at another art selection from the **Big Book** *Pictures Tell Stories*. Remind them that art can tell stories just like words do.

■ Direct the children's attention to the fine art piece **L'il Sis** on page 25 of *Pictures Tell Stories*. Explain that *l'il* is another way of saying *little*. Ask the children what the painting makes them think about. Have them predict what "story" the picture might tell.

■ Now ask the children to suggest some of the things that the big sister in the picture might do to help her little sister. Responses will vary, but some suggestions might be: She's holding a spatula so she might be making her dinner; the baby is in a carriage so perhaps she is going to take her for a walk. Give all the children a chance to participate.

But L'il Sis is quiet.

Shhhh, the baby is sleeping.

L'il Sis, 1944. **William H. Johnson.** ©The National Museum of American Art, Smithsonian Institution, Washington, DC. Photo: Art Resource, NY.

The Cradle, 1872. **Berthe Morisot.** Musée d'Orsay, Paris. Photo: Giraudon/Art Resource, NY.

25

Pictures Tell Stories, p. 25

Across the Curriculum

Math

Compare Numbers

Purpose

To have children compare numbers.

Procedure

- Remind the children that Annabelle got 18 cartons of milk, so there must have been 18 children in her class. Review with the children whether your class is bigger or smaller than Annabelle's. Write the number for your class size on the chalkboard.

- Then work with the children to compare other quantities. For example, count how many children are wearing something blue today and how many are wearing something green. Write both numbers on the chalkboard and ask, "Which number is larger?" Choose one of the numbers and count toward it, telling the children to call out "Stop!" when they hear the number.

- Have them compare other numbers, such as how many children drank juice at lunch and how many drank milk.

- You may need to adapt this activity to fit the level of your children. For example, if the children are only counting to 5 or 10, change the activity accordingly.

 # Sounds and Letters

Sounds, Letters, and Language

Days of the Week

- Ask the children if they know what day of the week it is. Confirm their answers, then review the verses "Days of the Week."

  Sunday, Monday,
  Tuesday, Wednesday, Thursday,
  Friday, Saturday, Sunday,
  And back to the first day.

- Check the classroom calendar for any special events that are noted there. Point to the box on the calendar and then to the name of the day. Ask a volunteer to tell you on which day this will (or did) happen. If other special days are noted, repeat the procedure with those days.

Phonemic Awareness

Oral Blending

Initial Consonants

Continue the initial consonant blending activity from the previous lesson.

- Tell the children that you will say just the first sound of a word and the puppet will say the rest of the word. When the puppet asks for the word, tell the children to say the whole word.

  Teacher: /l/

  Puppet: aundry. What's the word?

  All: laundry

- Continue with these words:

video	horse	dinner
party	silly	puppet

Listening

Long Vowel Sounds—Long o

- Remind children that they are listening for the long vowel sounds in words. A long vowel sound is when you can hear the vowel's name in the word.

- Give each child an *Oo* **Letter Card**. Tell them to listen for *o* to say its name in some words. They should hold up their card and repeat the word when they hear the /ō/ sound, and say /ō/.

- Use the following words:

may	play	**over**	**open**
so	**ocean**	**throw**	**glow**
grow	gray	**go**	**no**
new	stay	**toe**	slip
slow	tray	free	**blow**

"Apples and Bananas"

Sing "Apples and Bananas" with the children, signaling each new verse by pointing to the **Alphabet Card** that shows the corresponding vowel.

Be sure the children repeat the word before judging whether it contains the target sound.

Word Choice The purpose of these games is to develop the children's awareness of the sounds of words. Yet, that may be difficult because the words may be unfamiliar. When a word is beyond the children's vocabulary, substitute another word or take time to make the word familiar through discussion and use.

Phonics CD-ROM

Use the **Phonics** CD-ROM for activities that support the Phonemic Awareness Lessons.

Sounds and Letters

Letter Names

"Alphabet Cheer"

Lead the class in the "Alphabet Cheer." Distribute two capital and two small *Letter Cards* to each child. After the cheer, play the game of "Give Me an *N*." Children holding an *N* should stand and respond *N*. Continue with other letters.

Secret Passletter

Have a child choose a vowel as the Secret Passletter for the day. Ask that child to keep track of which children he or she asked about the Secret Passletter throughout the day.

Show Me Game

Distribute *Letter Cards Ii-Oo* to each child. Have the children hold up the correct letter as you give its name. Then invite the children to play the Show Me game in small groups.

Letter Shapes

Exploring *Oo*

- Point to the capital letter *O* and the small letter *o* on the *Alphabet Card* and tell children they will be writing these letters with you, beginning with capital *O*. Say:

     Begin here and make a circle. Go all the way around until you get back to where you started. Capital *O*.

- Follow the established procedure to form the capital letter on the overhead or on the chalkboard. Have children form the letter in the air with their fingers.

- Then have the children use pencils and paper to make the letter.

- Repeat the procedure for small *o*. Say:

     Begin here and make a small circle. Go all the way around until you get back to where you started. Small *o*.

Transparency 15

Open Court Reading · Transparency 15 · Level K · Copyright © SRA/McGraw-Hill. All rights reserved.

Transparency 15

Inter**v**ention

Letter Formation Remember to allow children who are having difficulty the opportunity to use the chalkboard or chart paper for letter formation.

Alphabet Big Book—Oo

■ Display the *Alphabet **Big Book*** and open it to page 32. Read "Saucy
Little Ocelot" pointing to the words as you say them. Reread the poem
and invite individual children to pantomime what the Ocelot might look
like when he turns and tosses and frets and fusses.

Oo

Saucy little ocelot
ocelot
ocelot
You like to turn and toss a lot
toss a lot
ocelot
You often fret and fuss a lot
fuss a lot
ocelot
Speckled, spotted
polka-dotted
Saucy little ocelot

Saucy Little Ocelot
Jack Prelutsky

32

33

***Alphabet Big Book* pp. 32–33**

② Reading and Responding

Annabelle Swift, Kindergartner (Read-Aloud)

This selection is taught in five lessons:

Lesson 15   Lesson 17   **Lesson 19**
Lesson 16   Lesson 18

Annabelle Swift,
Kindergartner

Story and Pictures by AMY SCHWARTZ

Selection Concepts

Remind the children of the selection concepts for this story:

- Entering school for the first time is rather scary for many kindergartners.
- Older brothers and sisters can sometimes help their younger siblings get ready to attend school.
- Although people who give advice try to be helpful, they don't always tell us the right thing.
- When we're given advice, it's important to think carefully about whether to follow it or not.
- In school, students sometimes feel good about what they have done and, at other times, not so good. But it is important to keep trying, anyway, so that we can feel good about ourselves in the end.

Activate Prior Knowledge

Ask the children what they liked about the selection. Ask them if the story helped them learn something new about school.

Vocabulary

Selection Vocabulary

- Review the selection vocabulary you presented in Lessons 15–18.
- Write each word on the board, point to it, and invite the children to say it with you.

coin	mother	second
father	nickel	sister
first	penny	third
jumped	pulled	whispered

- Remind the children what each of the words means, and encourage them to use each word in a sentence.

Reading Recommendations

- Reread the selection through without stopping. Pause only if children want to comment or ask questions.

Using Reading Strategies

Review the reading strategies you used in Lessons 15–18.

- Predicting
- Asking Questions

Remind the children how good readers use these strategies to learn more about a story.

Building Comprehension Skills

Remind the children how good readers use *drawing conclusions* to help them understand what happens in a story.

Reading and Responding

Responding to Literature

Discussing the Selection

Encourage the children to tell why Annabelle felt proud at the end of the story. Have them share a memory of when they felt proud about doing something. Was it at home or at school? Who did they tell about it first?

Purposes for Reading

■ Review the various purposes for reading you have covered, such as to get information or for enjoyment.

Exploring the Theme

Theme Connections

Talk About It

Have the children tell what Annabelle may have told Lucy after school. Then have them tell what they think Annabelle told their mother about her first day of school. Invite them to share which things were probably the same and which things were different.

Integrating the Curriculum

Language Arts

Independent and Collaborative Writing

Journal Writing

Have the children complete the final page of their "School Journal." Encourage them to write about the selection, specifically, what they liked or what they didn't like. If some children have difficulty thinking of a topic, have them write about what they remember from their first day of school.

Listening, Speaking, Viewing

Making Introductions

Remind the children that Mr. Blum introduced himself to Annabelle on her first day at school.

- Discuss with the children some ways of introducing themselves.

- Talk about being polite and using good manners. Have them role-play or practice introducing themselves to one another.

- You might set up situations for them to act out. For example, "It's the first day of school. You see someone sitting alone and want to introduce yourself and ask if he'd like to go to the reading corner and look at books with you."

3 **Integrating the Curriculum**

Willy the Wisher

Thinking Story 4: "Two of Everything"

Mrs. Nosho is so vague that it is often difficult for others to understand what she is talking about. When Mrs. Nosho appears in a story, the children have the opportunity to ask questions that will help clarify what she means and to suggest ways that she might say something better.

In this story, Mrs. Nosho tells Portia and Ferdie that she has two dogs, two cars, two umbrellas, and two swimming pools. However, her descriptions are so vague, it is hard for Portia and Ferdie to decide which dog, car, umbrella, or swimming pool Mrs. Nosho is talking about.

■ Tell the children that you are going to read a story about a character named Mrs. Nosho. Explain that you want them to listen closely as you read to see if they can figure out why people don't always know what Mrs. Nosho is talking about. Say that Ferdie and Portia are also in the story, and ask the children to tell you what they know about these characters.

■ Read the story to the children.

■ Through discussion, help the children to understand why people have difficulty understanding Mrs. Nosho.

Across the Curriculum

Social Studies

Classifying

In Annabelle's kindergarten class there was a *green* rug, Mr. Blum gave Annabelle a *yellow* envelope, the cafeteria was in a *pink* building, and the cafeteria lady was wearing a *red* hairnet. Have the children find as many things in the classroom of these same colors as they can. Make a chart of all the things the children find.

Sounds and Letters

Sounds, Letters, and Language

Reading the Big Book *Pickled Peppers*
"By Myself," page 8

- Display the *Pickled Peppers* **Big Book** and open it to the table of contents. Point out the poem "By Myself," and have the children identify the page number where it can be found. Have a volunteer help find the poem.

- Read the poem through.

- Have the children join in a choral reading. Signal children when to say the words *I'm a* at the beginning of each line, then you finish reading the line.

- Tell the children that you are going to make new rhymes with action words. Invite them to act out and to supply the second rhyming word of each couplet. Begin with these rhymes and then add others of your own.

I'm a dancer *dancing*
I'm a horse that's *prancing*.

I'm a bird that's *flying*
I'm a baby *crying*.

I'm a camera *clicking*
I'm a foot that's *kicking*.

Phonemic Awareness

Oral Blending

Initial Consonants

Continue the initial consonant activity from previous lesson, using words that are somewhat more difficult:

Teacher: /p/

Puppet: enny

All: penny

Continue with the following words:

b. . .rain   s. . .leep   n. . .ice   b. . .ack

Listening

Long Vowel sounds—Long *u*

- Tell the children that they are again listening for the long vowel sounds in words. Review the vowels, and remind them that a long vowel sound is when you can hear the vowel's name in the word.

- Give each child a *Uu Letter Card*. Tell children to listen for *u* to say its name in some of these words. They should hold up their card when they hear the /ū/ sound, say /ū/, and repeat the word.

- Use the following words:

unit	**use**	cry	my
menu	**few**	**nephew**	buy
hue	**cue**	go	**fuel**
tie	**pew**	**view**	**fuse**

Phonics
CD-ROM

Use the **Phonics** CD-ROM for activities that support the Phonemic Awareness Lessons.

Sounds and Letters

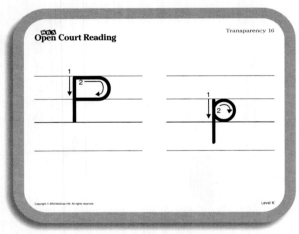

Transparency 16

Letter Recognition

Letter Names

Sing Your Way to G Game

Play the Sing Your Way to *G* game, choosing any letter from *Ss-Zz*. Try to focus on those letters that the children find most difficult.

Show Me Game

Distribute **Letter Cards** *Ii-Oo* to each child. Have the children hold up the correct letter as you give a letter name. Then encourage volunteers to lead the game, taking turns with different letters.

Secret Passletter

Choose a Secret Passletter and include it in activities throughout the day.

Letter Shapes

Exploring *Pp*

■ Using the *Pp* **Alphabet Card**, point to the capital letter *P* and the small letter *p* and tell children they will be writing these letters with you, beginning with capital *P*. Say:

> **Begin here and draw a line straight down. Then go back to the top and curve around to the right, until you touch the first line. Capital *P*.**

■ Follow the established procedure to form the capital letter on the chalkboard. Have children form the letter in the air with their fingers.

■ Have children use pencils and paper to make the letter, following the movements you demonstrated.

■ Repeat the procedure for small *p*. Say:

> **Begin here and draw a line straight down. Then go back to the top and curve around to the right, until you touch the first line. Small *p*.**

Alphabet Big Book—Pp

■ Display the *Alphabet **Big Book*** and open it to page 34. Read "Popping Popcorn," pointing to the words as you say them. Have the children "pop up" in their seats whenever you read a word with a capital *P* or a small *p*.

Alphabet Big Book, pp. 34–35

Assessment

✓ **Formal** **The Alphabet** To assess the children's abilities with the alphabet, have them complete *Skills Assessment* page 6.

Sounds and Letters

Meeting Individual Needs

Reteach

Have the children who are having trouble with the alphabet sequence complete **Reteach** page 7.

Challenge

Alphabet For a challenging activity on alphabet sequence, have children complete **Challenge** page 7.

Reading and Writing Workbook

Tell children to open the **Reading and Writing Workbook** to page 7. Show them that if they connect the dots, from letter to letter, in order from *A–N*, they will complete the picture of the bird. Tell children to color the bird after they have completed the drawing.

Reading and Writing Workbook, p.7

Reading a Pre-Decodable Book

Book 5: *At the Zoo*

High-Frequency Words

The high-frequency words introduced in this story are: *are, at, you*

Reading Recommendations

- Introduce new high-frequency words listed at the top of the page. Write each word on the chalkboard. Point to and say each word, then have the children say each word with you.

- Hold up your book. Read the title aloud, then have the children read it with you. Point to and read the author's name and explain that this is the name of the person who wrote the book. Then point to and read the illustrator's name and explain that this is the name of the person who drew the pictures in the book.

- Allow children to page through the book, commenting on what they see in the pictures and making predictions about what they think the book will tell them.

- Review the rebus pictures to ensure that the children understand each.

Responding

- Invite the children to discuss their own visits to zoos or to wild animal parks. Have volunteers pantomime the actions of zoo animals, and have the class guess the animal.

- Say the high-frequency word *are* and point to it on the chalkboard. Tell children to hold up their hands when they have found the word in their books. Have several children say the word and show the class where it is found in the book. Repeat the procedure for the words *at* and *you*.

- During Independent Work Time, encourage partners to look again at any pages that they had questions about. Have them discuss their questions and see if they are able to answer them now.

- For additional practice, you may want to use **Book 5** of the supplemental set of ***Open Court Reading Decodable Books.***

- You may want to make copies for the children of the black-and-white version of this story which is available in the ***Pre-Decodable Takehome Book.***

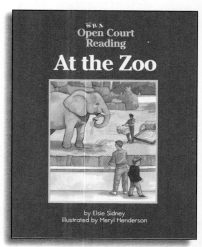

Pre-Decodable **Book 5**

Meeting Individual Needs

ESL

Teamwork Pair English-language learners with English-speaking children to read the ***Pre-Decodable Book***. Ask the English-language learners to teach their partners the names of the rebus pictures in their own language.

High-Frequency Word Wall Add the words from this book to the High-Frequency Word Wall.

Reading and Responding

Unit Wrap-up

Reading Aloud

Many books for children cover topics related to school. You may want to share one of the following books with your class.

Whole Group Discussion

Initiate a general class discussion about the unit. Have children reflect on what they learned about school in general, including:

- what students do in school and who the people are who help them.
- how other students—both real and fictional—feel about attending school.
- what they learned from looking around the school.
- what questions they still have about school
- if they are happy about being in school and if they like it.

Have the children share what they have learned about each of the above and listen to what classmates have learned.

Exploring the Theme

Theme Connections

Extending the Discussion

The discussion may be extended to include:

- an evaluation of the unit selection:
  Which selections did the children like the best?
  Which did they find most interesting, and why?
  Was there a selection that they wanted to spend more time on?

- an evaluation of the unit activities:
  Which activities did they find most enjoyable? most challenging? most informative?
  Were there any activities that they might suggest be included or excluded next time?

- an evaluation of the overall unit:
  Did the children enjoy learning about school?
  Was the topic of starting school something that was interesting to read and write about?
  Was it something they were interested in?
  Would they recommend the unit to other children just starting kindergarten?

- Did any students do any reading or writing on the topic at home with their families that they would like to share?

Supporting Reflection

Unit Celebration

Have the children share the class book with their families and members of the school staff. Invite parents into the class and have a group reading of the book. Prepare a place at the end of the book for visitors to comment. The following format is suggested:

Readers' Comments

These pages are for all readers.
Anyone can make a comment.
Please tell the authors what you liked about their book.

Ask visitors if you may take their photograph with the class. Have the children compose a sentence or two describing the book sharing. Have them help you print it in the class book.

Integrating the Curriculum

Language Arts

Independent and Collaborative Writing

Collaborative Writing

The children may enjoy doing the following writing activity.

- Have the children make color books, each page showing objects of various colors that they label with the proper color word.

Vocabulary

Vocabulary Review

Use this lesson as an opportunity to review school-related vocabulary words with the children. You might want to review the list of names of classroom objects collected in Lesson 16, or you may want to focus on words from the selections or on high-frequency words.

Across the Curriculum

Art

Make a School Collage

Purpose

To show what children know about school.

Materials

magazines and newspapers, construction paper, white paper, glue, scissors, yarn, decorative art materials

Procedure

- Have the children browse through the magazines and newspapers looking for pictures that remind them of school.
- Tell the children to cut out these pictures and then to point them in different ways until they find an arrangement they like.
- Have the children arrange their pictures on the construction paper and then glue them in place. Then have them use the decorative art materials to add interest and dimension to their collages.
- On a separate sheet of paper, have the children write or dictate one or two sentences about the subject of their collages. Then carefully attach the caption to the bottom of the collage.
- Display the finished collages around the art center.

Fine Arts   Unit I

Children can explore the unit theme *School* in images rather than words using the fine art on page 48 of the Big Book *School*. Encourage them to talk about their impressions of the artworks and how each one might relate to the unit theme *School*.

The following are questions that can initiate discussions of all types of art:

- What does this painting (sculpture, drawing, photograph, etc.) make you think about?
- How does it make you feel?
- What is interesting about it?
- Do you like it? Why or why not?

Below is some background information about each of the artworks on page 48 of the Big Book *School*.

The Artist's Son Jean, Drawing

Pierre-Auguste Renoir (1841–1919) began painting on porcelain as a young child in his birth town of Limoges, France. Best known for his work in the Impressionist school, Renoir sought to produce an immediate "impression" of a subject, rather than a highly realistic record. He often showed the dappling of sunlight reflected on people in shadow by using loose brushstrokes and color. Most of his subject matter was of leisure activities of the upper middle class in Paris.

The Artist's Son Jean, Drawing was painted in 1901 when he was no longer painting in the Impressionistic style. He gave up the loose brush strokes for a more crisp, realistic style. The child is concentrating solely on his drawing unaware of his father who is painting his portrait. Like many children he is looking closely at his picture as he works. Renoir created many intimate portraits of children.

School's Out

Allan Crite (1910–) grew up in Roxbury, Massachusetts, the city which is portrayed in *School's Out*. Crite is best known for his colorful paintings of city scenes showing African Americans during the 1930s and 1940s in Boston.

School's Out is one in a series of neighborhood paintings by Allan Crite which portrays the simple pleasures of everyday life for African Americans during the 1930s. The children are spilling out of the fenced schoolyard; some are running, others holding hands, and some are walking arm in arm with their mothers. Only females are portrayed in this painting.

Singing the Corrido

Diego Rivera (1886–1957) is best known for his enormous colorful murals that he was commissioned to paint on the walls of public buildings. It was important to him that the ordinary person could enjoy and understand his art; his simple designs on his public murals allowed this. Born in Mexico, his murals often pay homage to the people and history of his country, chiefly the peasants and industrial workers.

Singing the Corrido depicts several children who are being schooled while their mother continues her work in the factory. This painting is part of a series of murals that Diego made for the walls of the Secretariat of Education in Mexico city. His work often sought to inspire a national identity and purpose in the Mexican people.

Up-and-Down and Across Lines

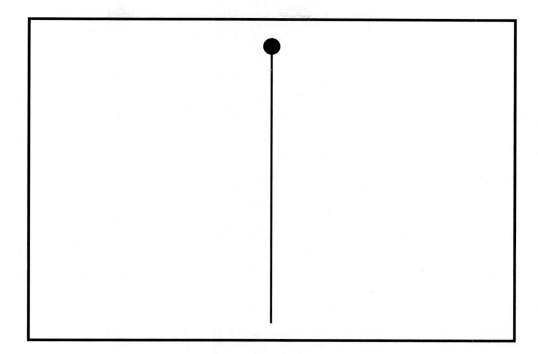

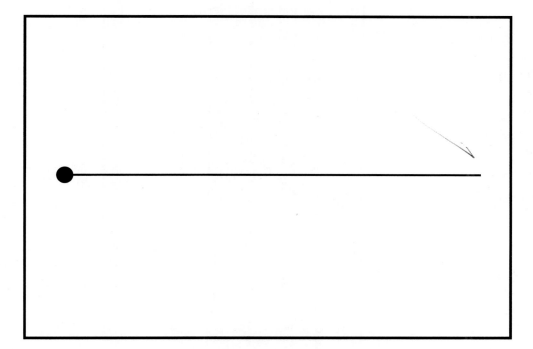

Slant Lines

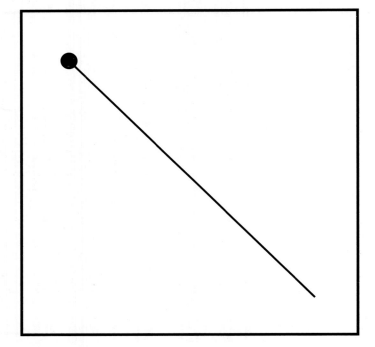

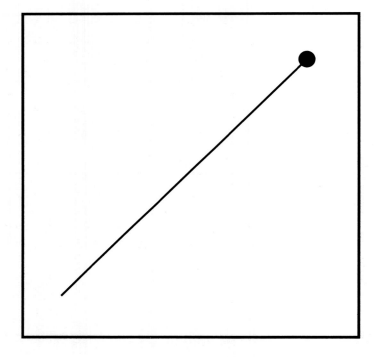

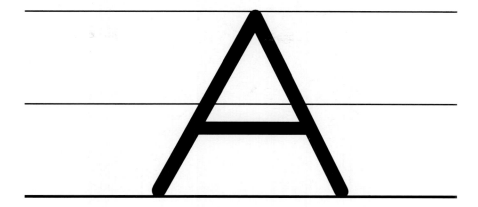

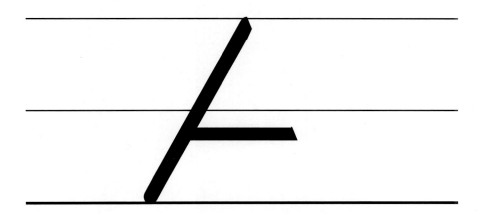

Unit 1 • School

Name _____

I would like a _____
for a pet at _____.

Curves and Circles

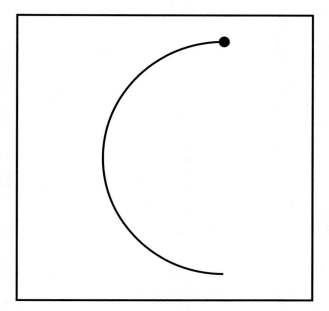 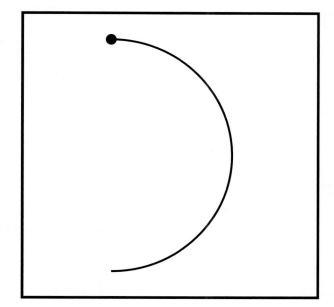

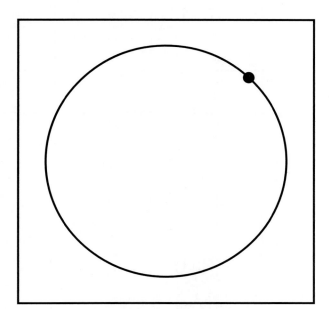

Unit 1 • School

Boomer Goes to School

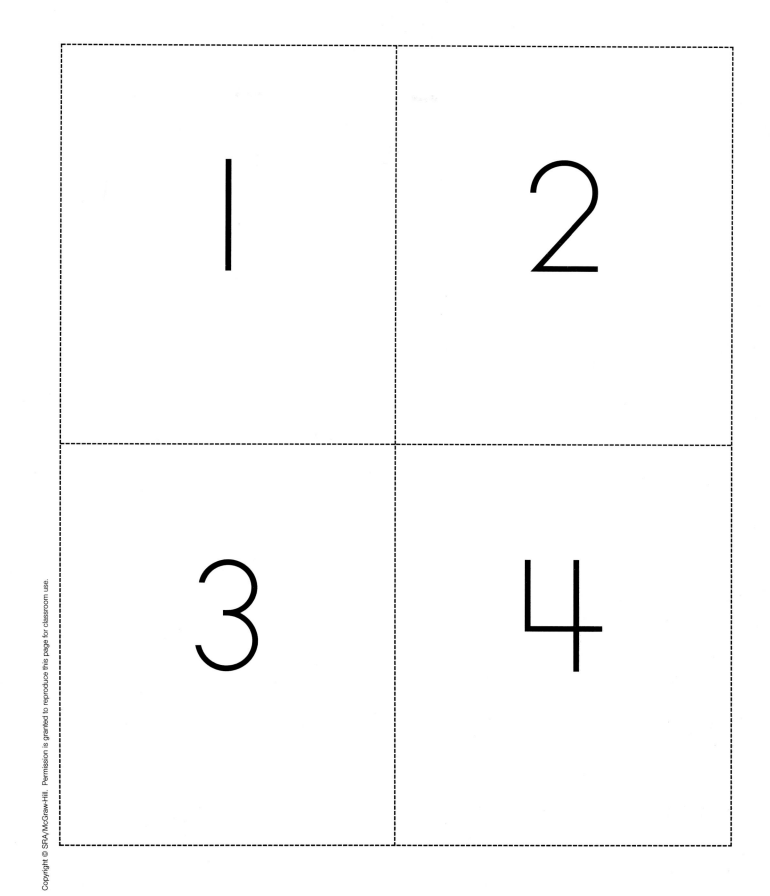

Blackline Master 7

Unit 1 • School

Name _____

My Classroom

Name_____

My Friends and I

Blackline Master 9

Unit 1 • School

Feeling Faces

Happy

Sad

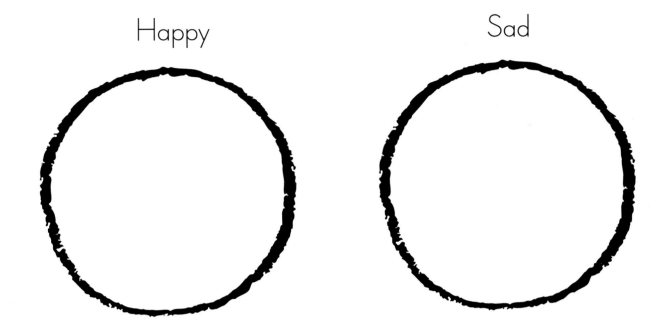

Scared

Surprised

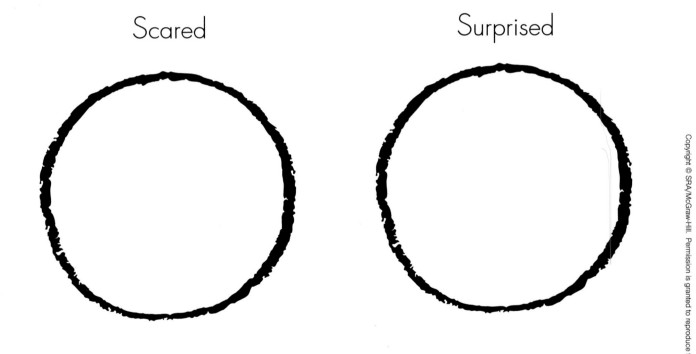

Name _____

Name _____

In school I like to _____.

Blackline Master II

Unit 1 • School

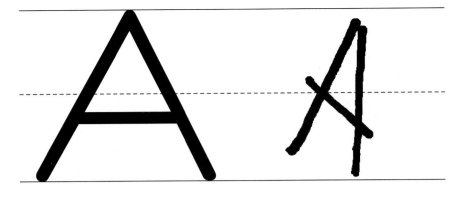

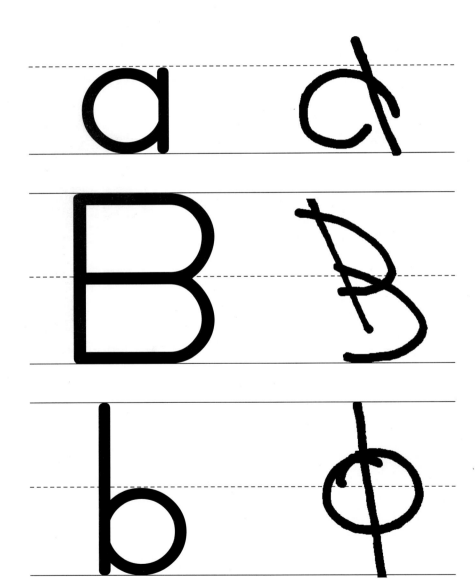

Name _____

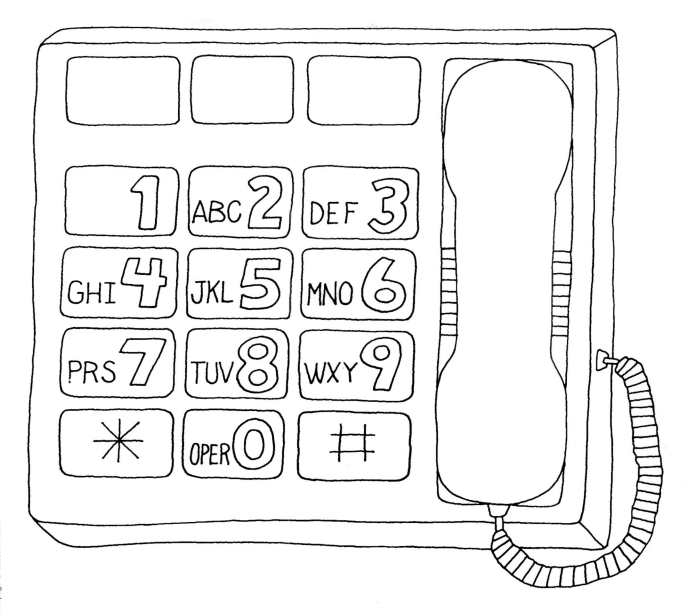

My telephone number is

___ ___ ___ - ___ ___ ___ ___.

Name_____

My address is

_____ .

Sleeping Outdoors

by Marchette Chute

illustrated by_____

Elizabeth Hauser: "Sleeping Outdoors" from RHYMES ABOUT US by Marchette Chute. Published 1974 by E.P. Dutton. Copyright 1974 by Marchette Chute. Reprinted by permission of Elizabeth Hauser.

Under the dark is a star,
Under the star is a tree,

Unit 1 • School

Blackline Master **16**

Under the tree is a blanket,

And under the blanket is me.

Blackline Master **18**

Drawing Models

Drawing Tips Guide

How to Draw Simple Figures and Objects

Remember a few basic tips, and you'll soon find that the drawing involved is both easy and fun to do:

1. Keep your drawings simple. Avoid adding a lot of decoration or animals and objects that don't relate directly to the story; such embellishments tend to distract the children from the story line.

2. Check each activity before teaching it, then practice making the drawing required.

3. As you draw, keep in mind the basic background grids. These will help you avoid making misshapen objects or figures.

4. Be sensitive to the experiences of your students. Use objects and situations in your drawings that will be familiar to them.

5. Work quickly. Don't worry about or dwell on mistakes. If the drawing doesn't turn out exactly as you had planned, laugh about it and move on.

In general, the story drawings you will create are made up of simple line drawings and stick figures. These, in turn, are made up of a few basic shapes:

- the line
- the box
- the circle
- the triangle

Focusing on these basic shapes as you draw will help you make drawings quickly and smoothly.

This guide shows a variety of examples to help you get started. You may want to begin by copying the examples. Once you feel comfortable with the drawing, however, you will no doubt want to develop a style of your own.

Drawing Models

Drawing Grids

Here are some basic background grids. These will help you keep the figures and objects you draw proportional. You may want to practice making some drawings using the grids, then picture the grids as you make a story drawing.

 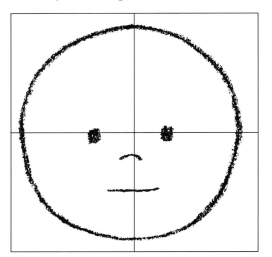

 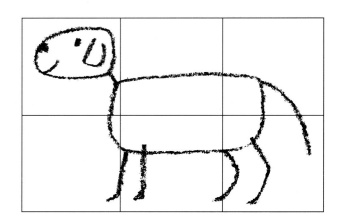

 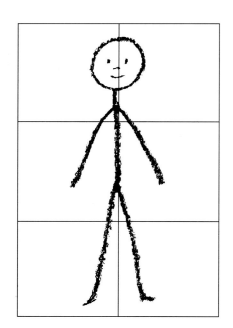

Drawing Models

Drawing Faces

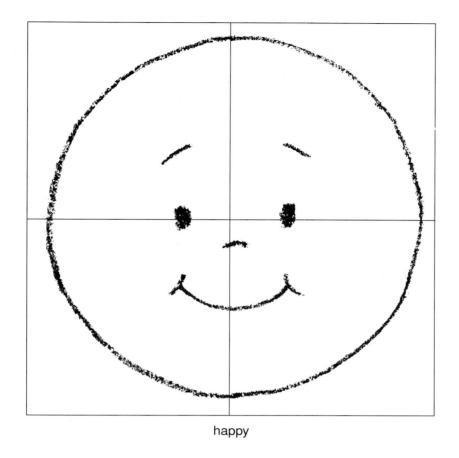

happy

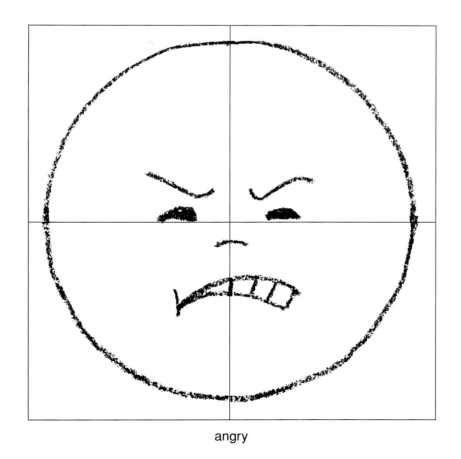

angry

Drawing Models

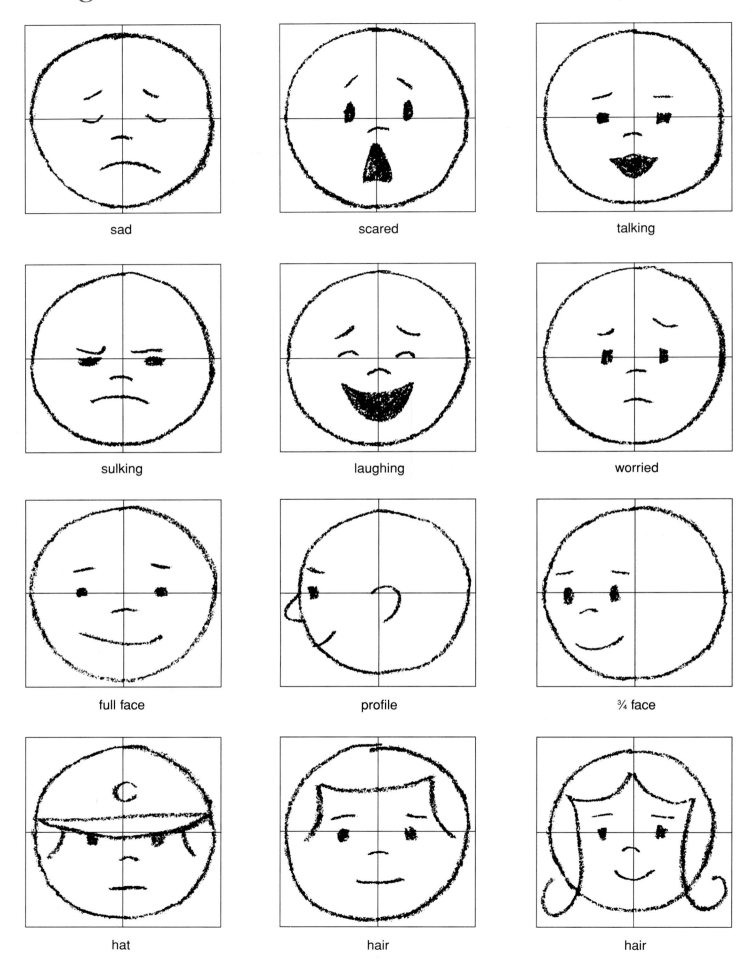

sad

scared

talking

sulking

laughing

worried

full face

profile

¾ face

hat

hair

hair

Drawing Models

Drawing Figures

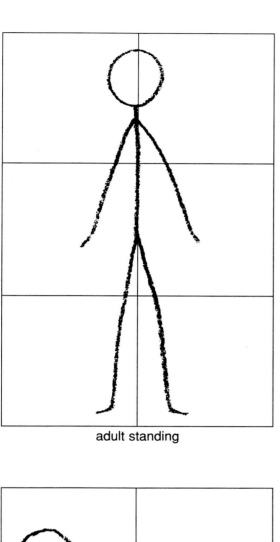

adult standing

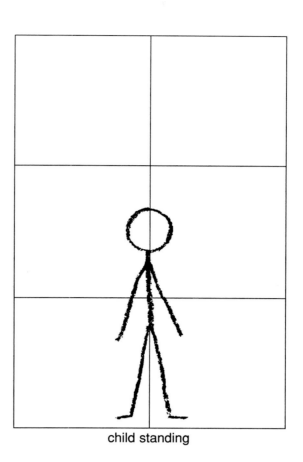

child standing

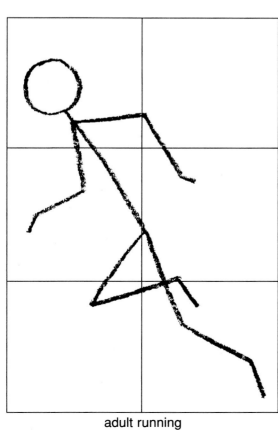

adult running

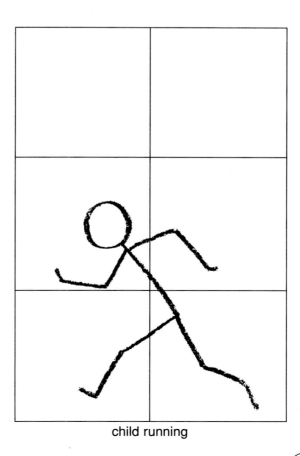

child running

Drawing Models

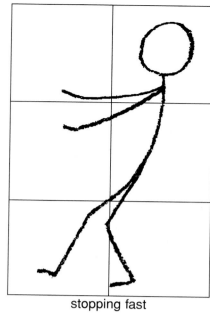

walking

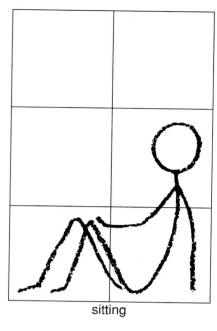

stopping fast

sitting

climbing

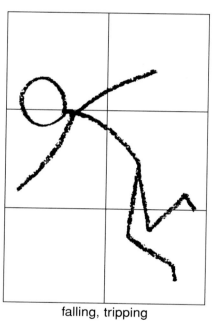

falling, tripping

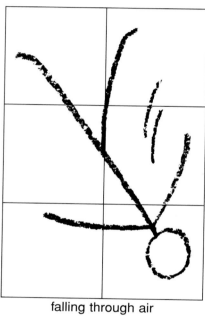

falling through air

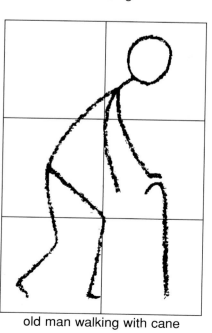

old man walking with cane

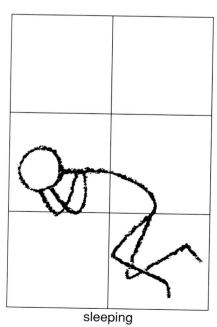

sleeping

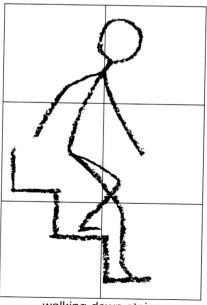

walking down stairs

Drawing Models

Drawing Objects

house

landscape

boat

bicycle

teddy bear

toy truck

skateboard

robot

Drawing Models

Drawing Animals

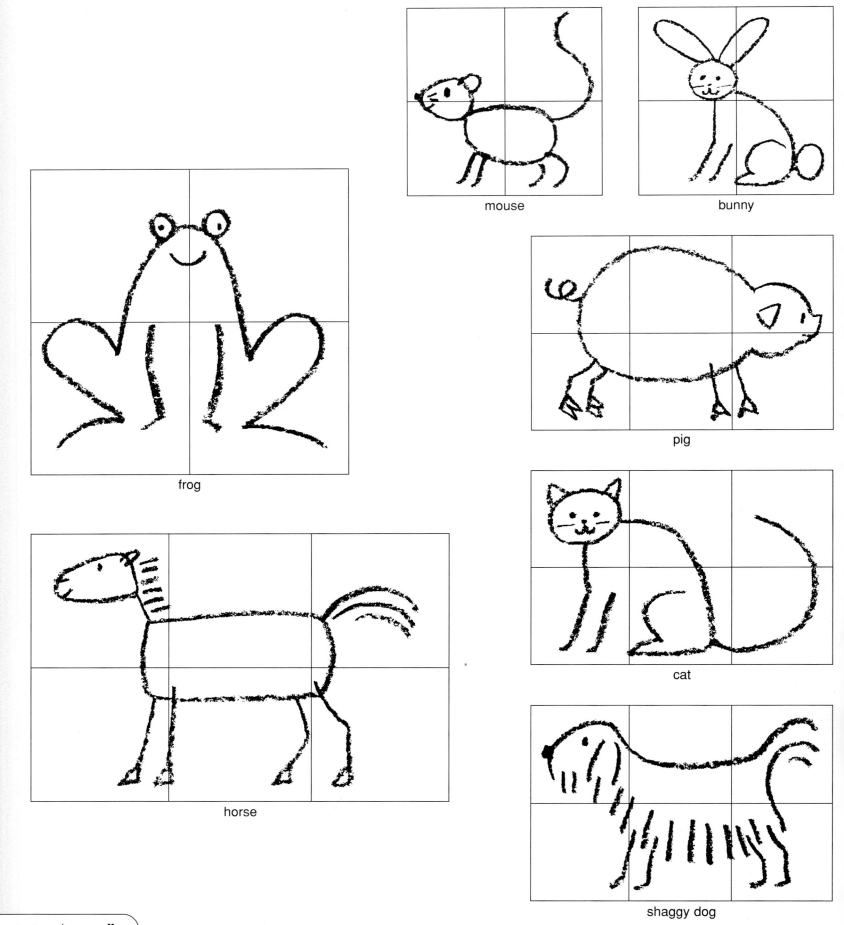

mouse

bunny

frog

pig

horse

cat

shaggy dog

Songs and Games
Alphabet Song

Purpose

To teach the names of the letters in their proper order

About the Song

There are several versions of the Alphabet Song. The children may not have heard the version used in this program before. You might explain that there are several versions of the Alphabet Song and that they will be learning a couple of them. Have them listen as you play and/or sing it.

In some versions, the alphabet letters are sung faster and with different pauses. The last two lines of the song may also differ. In this version, all letters except *W* are sung slowly. The first rhyme of the song is sacrificed, but each letter is pronounced distinctly, and the song is more instructive for the children than the traditional version.

Instruction

After listening to this version of the song two or three times, most of the children should be able to join in and sing along. The best way to teach this version of the Alphabet Song (especially if the children already know the more traditional version), is to teach it in steps: the first phrase, *A–G;* then the second phrase, *H–N;* then the next two phrases, *O–Q* and *R–T;* then two more phrases, *U–W* and *X–Z;* and finally the last two rhyming phrases.

If the Alphabet Cards are on the wall, help children make the connection between the names for the letters and their written symbols by touching each letter as you and the children sing the song. You or the children can then lead the song, touching each Alphabet Card as it is sung.

Alphabet Song

A, B, C, D,　E, F, G,　　H, I, J, K,

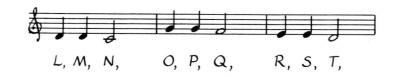

L, M, N,　　O, P, Q,　　R, S, T,

U, V, W - -　　X, Y, Z　　Now I nev-er
(dou-ble u)

will for-get,　How to say the　al-pha-bet.

musical notation by Christina T. Davidson

a b c d e f g
h i j k l m n
o p q
r s t
u v w
x y z

Songs and Games

Alphabet Rap

In addition to the traditional Alphabet Song, the children may enjoy singing this Alphabet Rap. You may want to point to the letters on the Alphabet Cards as you recite each letter.

This *A B C*
is just for me,
And *D E F*
is next you see,
G H I J
comes after that,
K L M N
I've got down pat.
O P Q R
S T U V
are all that's left,
except *W*
X Y and *Z.*

Alphabet Cheer

Another version of an alphabet song is based on cheerleading chants used at football and basketball games. After imitating a drum (Boom-boom Ch!), say each letter name loudly and emphatically. Again you might want to point to the letters on the Alphabet Cards as you say their names.

Alphabet Cheer

Boom-boom Ch!
Boom-boom Ch!
A. B. C. D.
Boom-boom Ch!
Boom-boom Ch!
E. F. G. H.
Boom-boom Ch!
Boom-boom Ch!
I. J. K. L.
Boom-boom Ch!
Boom-boom Ch!
M. N. O. P.
Boom-boom Ch!
Boom-boom Ch!
Q. R. S. T.
Boom-boom Ch!
Boom-boom Ch!
U. V.
Boom-boom Ch!
W. X. Y. Z.
Boom-boom Ch! Ch! Boom!

Another cheer-type activity to reinforce letters involves having the children find the letter and hold it up when you say, "Give me a *P.*" The group can say *P* and they can also hold up Letter Cards, or only one child could find the *P* Alphabet Card.

Songs and Games
I'm a Little Teapot

Purpose

To provide children with a song and movement activity, to increase print awareness, and to focus on the rhyming words

Instruction

Use *Pickled Peppers* to introduce the words of the song. Then introduce the music with the Listening Library Audiocassette or by singing it. Emphasize the rhyming words by reading the song again and asking whether anyone hears more words that rhyme (sound like) like *spout* and *shout*. If anyone suggests a non-rhyming word, say the two together (for example, *teapot, stout*). Say, "I don't hear the same sound, *out.*" Say that you will recite the song again and that the children should listen and stop you when you come to a rhyming word. Recite it slowly, emphasizing *stout, spout, shout,* and *out.*

I'm a Little Teapot

I'm a lit-tle tea-pot short and stout,

Here is my han-dle, here is my spout.

When I get all steamed up, hear me shout,

Tip me o-ver and pour me out.

musical notation by Christina T. Davidson

Songs and Games

Teach the children the actions:

Words	**Movements**
I'm a little teapot, short and stout,	Bend your knees and raise your hands over your head to look like a teapot.

Here is my handle,	Form a handle with one hand on your hip.

here is my spout.	Put your other arm up to form a spout.

When I get all steamed up, hear me shout, Tip me over and pour me out.	Tip over on one foot, leaning to the spout side.

Songs and Games
This Old Man

Purpose

To introduce a song that rhymes and reinforces numbers

Instruction

Read the verses of the song slowly, accentuating the rhyming words, and moving your finger from line to line.

"This Old Man" also has many words that rhyme. Point to each rhyming couplet and read it. For example, point to and say, *two;* point to and say, *shoe.*

Tell the children *shoe* also rhymes with *glue, blue, new.* Ask whether *shoe* rhymes with *true.* Continue with other words. Review the rhyming words in the couplet.

This old man, he played two,
He played knick-knack on my shoe . . .
This old man, he played three,
He played knick-knack on my knee . . .
This old man, he played four,
He played knick-knack on my door . . .
This old man, he played five,
He played knick-knack on my hive . . .
This old man, he played six,
He played knick-knack on my sticks . . .
This old man, he played seven,
He played knick-knack up in heaven . . .
This old man, he played eight,
He played knick-knack on my gate . . .
This old man, he played nine,
He played knick-knack on my vine . . .
This old man, he played ten,
He played knick-knack all over again,
With a knick-knack paddy whack,
    give the dog a bone,
This old man came rolling home.

This Old Man

musical notation by Christina T. Davidson

Vowel Song

Purpose

To reinforce the subset of letters called vowels and to introduce long vowel sounds

Instruction

Remind children that there are some special letters in the alphabet called vowels. Sometimes you can hear the names of these vowels in words. To make it easier to remember them as a group, they are colored red on the Alphabet Cards. Point to each vowel on the Alphabet Cards and say its name. Now sing the Vowel Song as a group, very slowly, so that you have time to point to each letter as it is sung. The Vowel Song is sung to the familiar tune of "B-I-N-G-O."

I can name the vowels for you

And you can name them too! Hoo!

A-E-I-O-U!

A-E-I-O-U!

A-E-I-O-U!

And you can name them too! Hoo!

Vowel Song

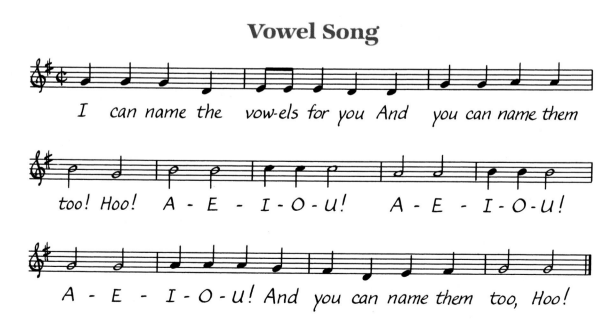

musical notation by Christina T. Davidson

Apples and Bananas

Purpose

To help the children listen for and repeat long vowel sounds

About the Song

"Apples and Bananas" is a vowel replacement song. It requires the children to consciously control vowel sounds in words while leaving the consonants unchanged.

Instruction

The song "Apples and Bananas" is a repeated couplet, as you see in the first verse.

In the second verse, some vowels are replaced with long *a:*

I like to ate, ate, ate

ayples and baynaynays.

I like to ate, ate, ate

ayples and baynaynays.

In the next verse, the same vowels are replaced with long *e:*

I like to eat, eat, eat

eeples and beeneenees.

I like to eat, eat, eat

eeples and beeneenees.

Continue in the same way with the remaining verses, replacing the vowel each time with long *i*, long *o*, and finally, long *u.*

If you sing slowly, it will be easy for the children to make these vowel replacements. As you start to sing the new verse yourself, the children will most likely announce the new verse. For example: "And now /ō/!"

Later, you may want to let volunteers lead the class. Write the letters *a, e, i, o, u* on the chalkboard and let the leader touch any letter at random to tell the children how to sing the next verse.

Apples and Bananas

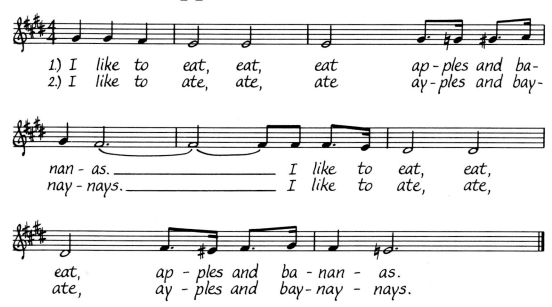

musical notation by Christina T. Davidson

Songs and Games

Bluebird, Bluebird

Purpose

To introduce a song that has repeating parts so children can see that a repeated word always contains the same letters

Background

"Bluebird, Bluebird" is a traditional African-American ring game.

Instruction

Use *Pickled Peppers* to introduce and read "Bluebird, Bluebird" to the children.

Also use "Bluebird, Bluebird" with the Pocket Chart. Assemble the Word Cards for the first and fourth sentences of the song before beginning the activity. Place the first line of the song on the chart.

Bluebird/./bluebird/./go/through/my/ window/./

Say each word as you place it on the chart. Read the second line from *Pickled Peppers*. Ask children whether there is any difference between the first line and the second. Reread if necessary. Explain that the lines must be exactly alike. With this clue, have the children place the Word Cards for the second sentence in the chart, one at a time. Do the same with the third sentence. Remind the children that when the lines are the same, they will have the same words in the same order. Reorder two words in one of the lines and ask the children whether it is still the same.

Second Verse:

Choose your partner and

Pat her on the shoulder.

Choose your partner and

Pat her on the shoulder.

Choose your partner and

Pat her on the shoulder.

Oh, Johnny what a day.

Game Directions

Form a circle. Choose one child to be the bluebird. Children in the circle join hands and hold them high to make arches for the "bluebird" to weave in and out of while moving around the circle.

For the second verse, children choose a partner to pat on the shoulder.

Bluebird, Bluebird

Blue-bird, blue-bird, go through my win-dow. Blue-bird, blue-bird, go

through my win - dow. Blue - bird, blue - bird, go

through my win - dow. Oh, John-ny what a day.

musical notation by Christina T. Davidson

Old MacDonald

Purpose

To use a familiar children's song to reinforce learning vowel and consonant sounds

Instruction

Sing the song once through with the children. Then tell the children that this time you are going to sing the song using the long vowel sounds from the Alphabet Cards instead of E-I-E-I-O. Ask the children to name the long vowel sounds on the Alphabet Cards (A-E-I-O-U). Next, review the consonant sounds you have learned in the past few lessons, for example, /b/.

Have the children think of an animal whose name begins with that sound. Then sing the song again, replacing E-I-E-I-O with the long vowels from the Alphabet Cards, and using the name of the animal with the initial /b/ sound:

Old MacDonald had a farm, A-E-I-O-U;

And on his farm he had a bird, A-E-I-O-U;

With a /b/ /b/ here and a /b/ /b/ there,

Here a /b/, there a /b/, everywhere a /b/ /b/,

Old MacDonald had a bird, A-E-I-O-U.

Continue, substituting other sounds and animals for *bird* and /b/: *cow*, /k/, *dog*, /d/, *fish*, /f/, *goat*, /g/.

Songs and Games

Old MacDonald

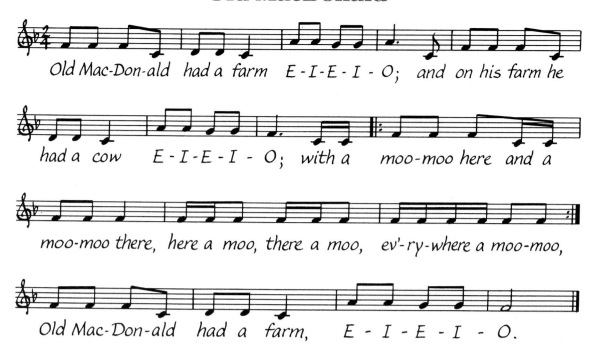

Old Mac-Don-ald had a farm E - I - E - I - O; and on his farm he

had a cow E - I - E - I - O; with a moo-moo here and a

moo-moo there, here a moo, there a moo, ev'-ry-where a moo-moo,

Old Mac-Don-ald had a farm, E - I - E - I - O.

musical notation by Christina T. Davidson

Old MacDonald had a farm, E-I-E-I-O;
And on his farm he had a pig, E-I-E-I-O;
With an oink oink here and an oink oink there,
Here an oink, there an oink, everywhere an oink oink,

Old MacDonald had a farm, E-I-E-I-O;
And on his farm he had a duck, E-I-E-I-O;
With a quack quack here and a quack quack there,
Here a quack, there a quack, everywhere a quack quack,

Old MacDonald had a farm, E-I-E-I-O;
And on his farm he had a horse, E-I-E-I-O;
With a neigh neigh here and a neigh neigh there,
Here a neigh, there a neigh, everywhere a neigh neigh,

Old MacDonald had a farm, E-I-E-I-O;
And on his farm he had some chickens, E-I-E-I-O;
With a chick chick here and a chick chick there,
Here a chick, there a chick, everywhere a chick chick,
Old MacDonald had a farm, E-I-E-I-O;

Songs and Games

Higglety, Pigglety, Pop!

Purpose

To introduce a fun song that reinforces short *a* and short *o* sounds

Instruction

"Higglety, Pigglety, Pop!" is a song both you and the children should enjoy.

- Sing the song several times, pointing to each word as you sing it. Ask children to listen for the rhyming words.

pop   **mop**
hurry   **flurry**

- Place the first two lines of the song in the Pocket Chart. Keep the Picture Cards for the first column in your lap, and place the Picture Cards for the second column within reach.

pie   **tie**
post   **toast**
pot   **knot**
pail   **tail**
pig   **wig**

Take out *pop*, put in *pie*, and say the new line. Then read the next line, pausing before *mop*. Remove *mop*, and ask a child to go to the table and find a card that will make a new rhyme.

- Ask the children whether they can make these words into short *a* words. Point to *pop* and say *pap*. Point to *dog* and say *dag*, and so on. Then sing the whole song again, substituting the short *o* words for short *a*.

Follow the same procedure in the next verse, changing all the words indicated to short *o* words. *The pog's in a hurry.*

Higglety, Pigglety, Pop!

Hig-gle-ty, pig-gle-ty, pop! The dog has eat-en the mop. The pig's in a hur-ry, The cat's in a flur-ry, Hig-gle-ty, pig-gle-ty, pop!

musical notation by Christina T. Davidson

Songs and Games

Sing a Song of Sixpence

Purpose

To use a song with repeating parts to show children that a word is always made with the same letters

Instruction

Sing the song together as a class and clap on the rhyming words at the end of the second and fourth line of each verse:

rye/pie; sing/king; money/honey; clothes/nose

Have the children find pictures of characters they think are the queen, the king, and the maid.

Explain to the children that four and twenty is just another way of saying the number twenty-four. As a group, count to twenty-four.

Look at the lines:

Four and twenty blackbirds,
Baked in a pie.

Ask the children whether they have ever had blackbird pie. Ask them to think of all the other kinds of pie they have had. Have a child name a kind of pie, and then sing the line together, substituting blackbirds with different types of fruit or pie filling:

Four and twenty apples, baked in a pie.

Four and twenty blueberries, baked in a pie, and so on.

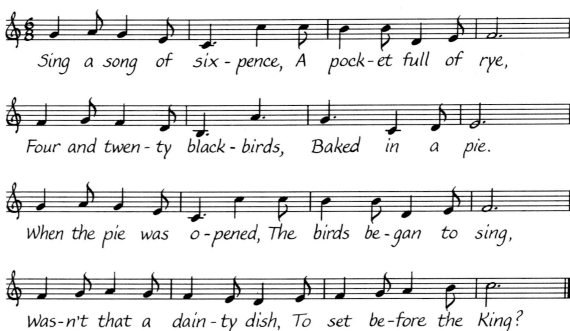

Sing a Song of Sixpence

Sing a song of six - pence, A pock-et full of rye,

Four and twen - ty black - birds, Baked in a pie.

When the pie was o - pened, The birds be - gan to sing,

Was-n't that a dain - ty dish, To set be-fore the King?

musical notation by Christina T. Davidson

The Ship Is Loaded With _____

Purpose

To provide children with a movement activity that will reinforce rhyming words and initial consonant sounds

Instruction

Have the children sit in a circle. Explain that you are loading a ship with items that sound alike. Each child will have a chance to say a rhyming word. Use a ball or anything that can be rolled from child to child. Ask for a volunteer, and have that child say, "The ship is loaded with *cheese.*" The child then rolls the ball to someone else who must repeat the line, substituting a rhyming word for *cheese,* for example, *peas, bees, keys, breeze, fleas, trees.*

At this point, you might have the child roll the ball back to the first child, who will repeat, "The ship is loaded with *cheese.*" Or, have the child roll the ball to someone else for a new rhyming word.

Try playing the game using the following words:

The ship is loaded with *cats* (*mats, rats, bats, hats*)

The ship is loaded with *logs* (*frogs, hogs, dogs, bogs*)

The ship is loaded with *cans* (*fans, bans, Dans, pans*)

Play The Ship Is Loaded With _____ game, and have the children choose words with the same initial sound. For example, if they choose /b/, the children can say:

The ship is loaded with *basketballs, begonias, baseballs, balls, blankets,* and so on.

Ordering Letters Game

Give each child a set of **Letter Cards Aa-Nn** (you may add letters as the children's knowledge of new letters increases). The cards in each set should be shuffled out of order and facing different ways.

Tell the children they should do two things with these cards. First, they should turn all of the cards so that they are showing either all capitals or all small letters. Then they should show the set to a partner to check.

Next, have the child work with a partner and match each capital letter with a small letter.

Simon Says

Purpose

To reinforce word concepts using a game format

Instruction

Tell the children that you are going to play Simon Says. For those unfamiliar with the game, explain that when Simon says to do something, they must follow the instructions. Also tell them that they should not follow any directions that do not start with the words *Simon says*. Try the following instructions:

**Simon says pat your head
(children pat their heads)**

**Simon says rub your tummy
(children rub their tummies)**

**Simon says hop on one foot
(children hop on one foot)**

**Simon says hop on your left foot
(children hop on their left foot)**

After giving several different instructions, try another one, omitting "Simon says":

Jump in place (children should stand still)

Children are "out" when they

- do something that Simon does not say to do,
- do something other than what Simon says, or
- do not do what Simon says.

When a child is "out" you can have him or her sit down, then continue the game until one child is left standing. Another alternative is to give each child a Letter Card that they have to identify if they miss an instruction. If the child correctly identifies the letter, he or she can stay in the game.

Try different and gradually more challenging instructions to reinforce language skills:

- touch their nose, turn around
- add numbers (*jump three times, clap four times, pat tummy once*)
- add prepositions and prepositional phrases designating location (*over, under, in front of, behind*)
- add conjunctions (hop *and* skip)
- use adjectives (take *big* steps)
- use adjectival strings (*take three big steps*)
- use adverbs (*clap softly*)
- add negatives (*don't clap your hands*)
- add conditionals *if, when, unless, until, while* (*rub your tummy while you pat your head . . .*)

Songs and Games

Mat Games

Purpose

To help children match sounds to letters

Instruction

Each of these games is played on a mat, using markers to move around the squares. The mat can be placed on a table or on the floor. Have the children gather around the mat, and explain to them that as they move around the squares, they will be naming letters and sounds.

Each of the game mats is basically generic and can be used not only for the games we describe here but also with games you and the children make up. You and your class might enjoy making up variations on the games described here, or you might enjoy making up entirely new games to play on the mats.

Make up new rules and difficulty levels as your class needs or wants them. Challenge the children to think of new games to play on the mats.

Difficulty Levels

The levels of difficulty described here are simply suggestions. You may feel the children need to begin with much easier tasks, or you may feel that they are not being challenged enough. Always suit the games to the activities and levels of difficulty you know your students will be most comfortable with. The games should be hard enough to challenge the children, yet easy enough for them to experience success and have fun.

Hop Along Game

The object of this game is to get one's marker from the bunny to the carrot at the end of the trail. Use a spinner or number cube to determine how many spaces a child may move the marker along the trail. If the child lands on a letter, he or she must do one of the following, depending on the level of difficulty you have chosen:

Name the letter	(Level 1)
Name the sound of the letter	(Level 2)

If the child does not name the correct letter or sound, he or she must do one of the following:

Lose a turn	(Level 1)
Go back a space until he/she is able to name the correct letter or sound	(Level 2)

If children land on a happy face, they get an extra turn. If they land on a sad face, they lose a turn.

Bus Stop, Roller Ride, Race Track, Make Tracks, The Zoo Game

All of these games are played with the same rules. Each child spins the spinner and moves the marker the correct number of spaces. Use Letter Cards for Level 1 and Alphabet-Sound Cards for the card pack on Levels 2, 3, and 4. Have children draw a card unless they land on a "lose turn" space. Depending on the level, the child will:

State the name of the letter	(Level 1)
State the sound the letter makes	(Level 2)
Name a word that begins with the sound	(Level 3)
Name the letter, the sound, and a word that begins with the sound	(Level 4)

If children do not guess correctly, they lose their next turn.

If children land on a "lose turn" space, they don't draw, and they lose their next turn.

If children land on a "free turn" space, they roll again, move, and pick a card after the second roll.

Songs and Games

Winning the Games

These games can be played quickly or you can have the children extend them. For a quick game, have the children play until the first child reaches the goal at the end of the trail. If no child has reached the goal when the cards run out, the child closest to the goal wins.

To extend the games, tell the children to shuffle the cards when the last card has been chosen and to keep playing. The number of times the cards are shuffled will determine the length of the game. Again, the child who reaches the goal or is closest to the goal when the cards run out for the last time wins the game.

Challenges

These games are designed to be played independently by the children. This means that they must determine if each answer given is correct. Encourage the children to discuss any differences of opinion they may have. If they are not able to decide if the answer is correct, tell them to raise their hands so you can help them.

Letter Formation

Purpose

To provide a systematic method for teaching children to form capital and small letters

About Letter Formation

Learning to form capital and small letters provides kinetic reinforcement as the children learn letter names. Some of the children will have prior experience with forming letters, some will not. All of them should first watch and listen as you make each letter and then form the letter with you either by tracing it in the air, on their desks, on carpet squares, on slates, or by writing it on paper or on the chalkboard.

The children should immediately proofread any letters they form on the chalkboard or on paper. They can correct their work, not by erasing, but by circling their errors and writing corrections above or beside the circles.

Instruction

Name the letter you will make and point to it on the ***Sound/Spelling Card***. Describe each stroke as you make it using the following directions. The directions are short, so you and the children should be able to describe a stroke in the same time it takes to make the stroke. Be sure that the children know the starting point for each stroke. Starting points are indicated by dots on the sample letters.

Note

The overhead projector can be a very effective device for teaching children to form letters. Children should move their pencils in synchrony with you as you form the letters on a transparency. It helps to talk the children through the making of each letter by using the following descriptions of letter strokes.

You might want to make permanent writing guidelines on the chalkboard with markers. You might also want to photocopy pages of guidelines for children to use at their desks.

 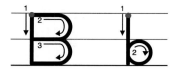 

A Starting point, slanting down left
Starting point, slanting down right
Starting point, across the middle:
capital *A*

a Starting point, around left all
the way
Starting point, straight down,
touching the circle: small *a*

B Starting point, straight down
Starting point, around right and in at
the middle, around right and in at
the bottom: capital *B*

b Starting point, straight down, back
up, around right all the way: small *b*

C Starting point, around left to
stopping place: capital *C*

C Starting point, around left to
stopping place: small *c*

D Starting point, straight down
Starting point, around right and in
at the bottom: capital *D*

d Starting point, around left all
the way
Starting point, straight down,
touching the circle: small *d*

E Starting point, straight down
Starting point, straight out
Starting point, straight out
Starting point, straight out: capital *E*

e Starting point, around left to stopping
place
Starting point, straight out: small *e*

F Starting point, straight down
Starting point, straight out
Starting point, straight out: capital *F*

f Starting point, around left and
straight down
Starting point, straight across: small *f*

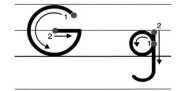 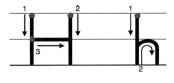 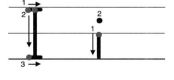

G Starting point, around left to
stopping point
Starting point, straight out: capital *G*

g Starting point, around left all
the way
Starting point, straight down,
touching the circle, around left to
stopping place: small *g*

H Starting point, straight down
Starting point, straight down
Starting point, across the middle:
capital *H*

h Starting point, straight down, back
up, around right, and straight down:
small *h*

I Starting point, across
Starting point, straight down
Starting point, across: capital *I*

i Starting point, straight down
Dot exactly above: small *i*

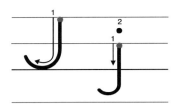
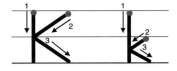
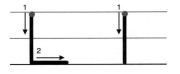

J Starting point, straight down, around left to stopping place: capital *J*

j Starting point, straight down, around left to stopping place Dot exactly above: small *j*

K Starting point, straight down Starting point, slanting down left touching the line, slanting down right: capital *K*

k Starting point, straight down Starting point, slanting down left, touching the line, slanting down right: small *k*

L Starting point, straight down, straight out: capital *L*

l Starting point, straight down: small *l*

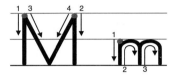
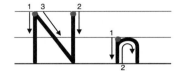

M Starting point, straight down Starting point, straight down (Mark the point.) Starting point, slanting down right to the point Starting point, slanting down left to the point: capital *M*

m Starting point, straight down, back up, around right, straight down, back up, around right, straight down: small *m*

N Starting point, straight down Starting point, straight down Starting point, slanting down right: capital *N*

n Starting point, straight down, back up, around right, straight down: small *n*

O Starting point, around left all the way: capital *O*

o Starting point, around left all the way: small *o*

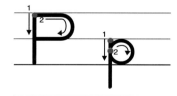
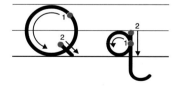

P Starting point, straight down Starting point, around right and in at the middle: capital *P*

p Starting point, straight down Starting point, around right all the way, touching the line: small *p*

Q Starting point, around left all the way Starting point, slanting down right: capital *Q*

q Starting point, around left all the way Starting point, straight down, touching the circle, curving up right to stopping place: small *q*

R Starting point, straight down Starting point, around right and in at the middle, touching the line, slanting down right: capital *R*

r Starting point, straight down, back up, curving around right to stopping place: small *r*

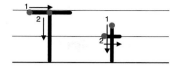

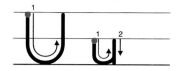

S Starting point, around left, curving right and down around right, curving left and up to stopping place: capital S

s Starting point, around left, curving right and down around right, curving left and up to stopping place: small s

T Starting point, straight across
Starting point, straight down: capital T

t Starting point, straight down
Starting point, across short: small t

U Starting point, straight down, curving around right and up, straight up: capital U

u Starting point, straight down, curving around right and up, straight up, straight back down: small u

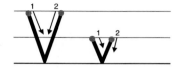

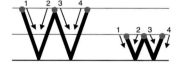

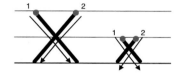

V Starting point, slanting down right
Starting point, slanting down left: capital V

v Starting point, slanting down right
Starting point, slanting down left: small v

W Starting point, slanting down right
Starting point, slanting down left
Starting point, slanting down right
Starting point, slanting down left: capital W

w Starting point, slanting down right
Starting point, slanting down left
Starting point, slanting down right
Starting point, slanting down left: small w

X Starting point, slanting down right
Starting point, slanting down left: capital X

x Starting point, slanting down right
Starting point, slanting down left: small x

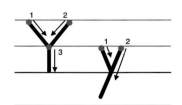

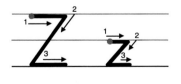

Y Starting point, slanting down right, stop
Starting point, slanting down left, stop
Starting point, straight down: capital Y

y Starting point, slanting down right
Starting point, slanting down left, connecting the lines: small y

Z Starting point, straight across, slanting down left, straight across: capital Z

z Starting point, straight across, slanting down left, straight across: small z

Continuous Stroke Models

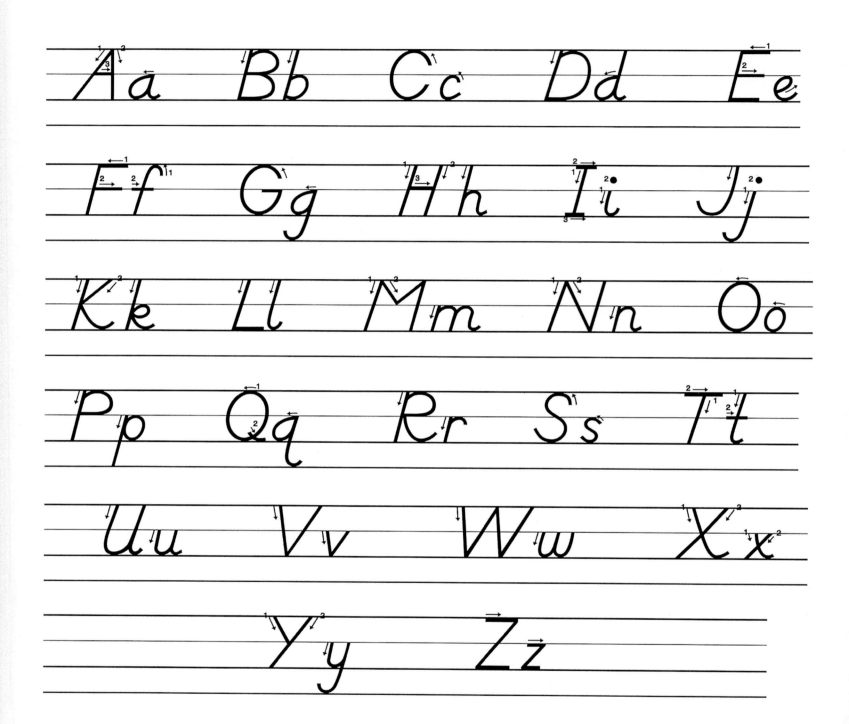

The Pocket Chart

Purpose

To provide a device that will allow children to practice word substitutions and to play with words

Instructions

The Pocket Chart will help children understand written language. Seeing a poem in *Pickled Peppers* and then seeing the same poem on the Pocket Chart will give children more exposure to print. It is easy to substitute and play with words in the Pocket Chart. Children will begin to understand the concept of words and eventually of sentences.

About the Pocket Chart

The Pocket Chart can be used to develop many concepts:

Introducing Print

In the beginning of the year, the Pocket Chart can be used as another way to introduce print to the children. Seeing the same words in *Pickled Peppers*, on the Pocket Chart, and possibly on the chalkboard or on a big sheet of paper will help children understand print.

Words

Take words out of the Pocket Chart and let children touch them. Because each word is on a separate card, children will begin to comprehend the concept of words and that some words are long and some are short.

Matching Pictures to Words

Put a word in the Pocket Chart and have the children match a picture of the word to the word. This activity should be used only after children have had many experiences with the Pocket Chart and with written words.

Sequence

Words can be arranged and read out of sequence. Children will understand that there is an order and sequence to the words in a sentence.

Rhyme

After learning a poem, you can take words or pictures out of the chart and put in other words or pictures that rhyme. Although these words or pictures will change the meaning of the poem, sometimes to nonsense, the children will hear the new rhyme.

Matching Word to Word

Using a song such as "Bluebird, Bluebird" that repeats the same line several times, have children place words on the second line to match a first line already on the Pocket Chart.

Using Sounds to Match Words to Pictures

Show a picture. Have children say the name of the picture. If, for example, they say *tree*, ask what sound the word *tree* starts with and ends with. Let children pick the word that goes with the picture based on your questions. You might ask the children to predict which letter the word starts with before showing the matching Word Card.

Substituting Words

Revise a song or poem by saying some key words with a different beginning sound. For example sing "Old MacDonald" with animals whose names begin with /b/.

Vowel Sounds

Sing a song such as "Higglety, Pigglety, Pop!" with only short *i* sounds: "Higglety, Pigglety, Pip."

Frame Sentence

Place only the beginning of a sentence on the Pocket Chart: *I hear a* _____. Then have the children finish the sentence by placing a Picture Card or a Word Card on the chart.

Prepositional Phrases

Take a phrase like *under the stars* and substitute it with other phrases such as *above the* _____. Then have the children finish the phrase by placing a Word Card or a Picture Card on the chart.

Alphabet Activities

Purpose

To provide students with activities for reinforcement of letter shapes

About Activities

In lessons that deal with letter introduction, include activities in which children can make letters during Workshop. Some activities like these are included in the lessons already, while some letter-making activities you can establish in your classroom are listed below.

Most of the children will probably need a visual model to help them get started. Use red, blue, or green markers to print the letters on sturdy cardboard or oaktag cards. Children will make yarn letters, glue letters, or other types, by tracing the model.

Yarn Letters

Give each child four 4-inch pieces, four 8-inch pieces, and four 12-inch pieces of heavy yarn (such as rug yarn) to form letters. Each different length of yarn can be a different color (for example, 4-inch—red, 8-inch—blue, and 12-inch—green). When you work with the children to form a particular letter, you can help them by using colors. For example, if children are making a capital *A*, they can use one blue piece and one red. The yarn pieces can be kept in small plastic bags for reuse each time a new letter is introduced.

Clay Letters

Have children roll modeling clay into sticks that can be broken into different lengths and curved as necessary to form letters. When they are finished, they can roll their letters back into balls of clay, which can be kept in sealed plastic bags for reuse.

Sand Letters

Provide each child with a small Styrofoam grocery tray filled halfway with sand. Have the children trace with their fingers the letters they are practicing. In later lessons, they can trace words.

Pipe Cleaner Letters

Cut 12-inch pipe cleaners into 4-inch and 8-inch pieces, leaving some 12-inch pieces. Instruct children to form letters with the different lengths of pipe cleaner.

Glue Letters

Provide each child with large printed models of the letters. Tell children to trace over the letters with glue and then sprinkle glitter, colored sand, confetti, salt, oatmeal, rice, or any other material that is not too bulky to stick to the glue. After the glue has begun to dry, have the children shake off any excess materials.

Drinking Straw Letters

Cut 8-inch drinking straws in half to make 4-inch pieces and then in fourths to make 2-inch pieces. Leave some the 8-inch length. Have children form letters using the pieces. Drinking straws are not suitable for letters that have curved lines, but work well for those with straight lines and slanted lines.

Floor Letters

Have children form letters from various classroom materials, such as jump ropes, building blocks, beads, string, and so on.

Finger-Paint Letters

Using finger paints and finger-paint paper, have children trace letters with their fingers.

Chalkboard Letters

Encourage children to use the chalkboard or chart paper to practice their letters.

All of these activities, in addition to reinforcing letter formation, will help children's visual, perceptual, and fine-motor development.

Using the Pre-Decodable Books

Minibooks play an important role in children's early literacy development by providing them with meaningful "reading" experiences before they are actually reading on their own and by expanding their awareness of the forms and uses of print. By following along as you read aloud a minibook, children learn about the left-to-right and top-to-bottom progression of print on a page, the clues that indicate the beginnings and ends of sentences, the connections between pictures and words, and important book conventions, such as front and back covers, authors' and illustrators' names, title pages, and page numbers.

The minibooks provide children with opportunities to apply their growing knowledge of letter names, shapes, and sounds, and to become familiar with individual words.

Through retelling the story in a minibook, predicting or wondering about what will happen, and asking and responding to questions about the book, children not only learn about the relationship between spoken and written language, they learn to think about what they have read.

About the Minibooks

Each minibook contains a story that engages children's interest as it provides them with opportunities to practice what they are learning in their lessons. These "Pre-Decodable" stories each contain several high-frequency words that most children already have in their spoken vocabularies and that are a basic part of all meaningful stories. Learning to identify high-frequency words quickly, accurately, and effortlessly is a critical part of children's development as fluent, independent readers. In addition, each book contains words that familiarize children with key letter patterns, or *phonograms*. Because many words can be made from a few major phonograms, becoming aware of them is an important step in learning to read. Finally, several of the stories introduce children to position words, color words, and number words. The inside back cover of each minibook contains a list of the high-frequency words and phonograms and, when appropriate, the position, color, or number words used in the book.

General Guidelines for Using Minibooks

- Before reading, introduce **new high-frequency words** listed in the box at the top of the page. Write each word on the chalkboard. Point to and say each word, and then have the children say each word with you.
- Give each child a copy of the minibook. Explain that you will read the book together.
- Hold up your book. Read the title aloud, then have the children read it with you. Point to and read the author's name and explain that this is the name of the person who wrote the book. Then point to and read the illustrator's name and explain that this is the name of the person who drew the pictures in the book.
- Allow children to page through the book, commenting on what they see in the pictures and making predictions about what they think the book will tell them.
- Help children find page 3. Hold up your copy of the book and sweep your hand under each line of text. Then read each line, pointing to each word or rebus as you say it. Encourage children to move their hands from left to right across the text as you read together.
- Continue through the book, following the same procedure.
- Reread the book, this time pointing to the picture on each page and asking children to tell what is happening in the picture.
- Invite children to discuss the book as a group.
- Provide many opportunities for children to partner read.

Supplemental Word List

The following word list can be used in a number of ways to extend the lessons. Words are listed by beginning sounds, ending sounds, and medial vowel sounds.

Beginning Sounds

Beginning /ā/
acorn
ape
apron

Beginning /a/
acrobat
alligator
apple
apple juice
astronaut

Beginning /b/
bag
bait
ball
balloon
banana
baseball
basketball
bat
beans
bed
bee
bell
bird
boat
book
bow

bowl
bowling ball
box
bread
broom
bug
bus

Beginning /k/
cake
can
cane
cap
cat
clam
coat
cook
core
cup
cut

Beginning /d/
dad
deer
dice
dime
dish
dog
doll
dollar
donkey
door
dress
drum
duck

Beginning /ē/
eagle
ear
earphones

easel
eel

Beginning /e/
eggplant
elephant
elk
envelope

Beginning /f/
falcon
fan
feet
fern
fir
fish
five
fly
food
football
fork
four
fox
Frisbee
frog

Beginning /g/
game
gate
glue
goat
goose
grass
green
guitar

Beginning /h/
ham
hand
hat

hawk
heaven
hen
hive
hog
hole
hook
horse
hot
house
hug

Beginning /ī/
ice
ice cream
icicles
iron
island
ivy

Beginning /i/
igloo
ill
inch
infant
insect

Beginning /j/
jam
jar
jeans
jellybean
jellyfish
judge
juice

Beginning /k/
kangaroo
kettle
keys

kitchen
kittens
koala

Beginning /l/
ladybug
lake
lamp
lion
lock
lockers

Beginning /m/
magnet
mailbox
man
map
mask
mat
meal
meat
milk
mittens
monkey
moon
moose
mop
mouse
mug

Beginning /n/
nails
necklace
needle
nest
newspaper
nickle
nine
noodle
nurse

Beginning /ō/
oak tree
oasis
oatmeal
oboe
ocean
overalls

Beginning /o/
octopus
olive
ostrich
otter
ox

Beginning /p/
pail
pan
panda
pants
pear
peas
pen
penny
pickle
pickled pears
pie
pig
pineapple
pink
pizza pies
plum bun
popcorn
post
pot
potatoes
pumpkins
purple

Beginning /kw/
quail
quart
queen

quill
quilt

Beginning /r/
raccoon
racer
radio
rake
rat
red
rice
road
robot
rock
rocket
rug
ruler

Beginning /s/
sack
sad
sail
Sam
sand
sandals
seal
seven
silk
six
skate
soccer ball
sock
spoon
star
stew
sticks
stir
store
storm
sun

Beginning /t/
table
tail

tap
tape
target
tear
telephone
television
ten
tie
toad
toast
toe
tomatoes
top
tree
turkey
turtle
two

Beginning /ū/
ukulele
unicorn
uniform
United States
utensil

Beginning /u/
umbrella
umpire
uncle
under
usher

Beginning /v/
van
vase
vegetables
veil
vine
violin
volcano

Beginning /w/
wagon
wallet

walrus
watch
well
wig
wing

Beginning /y/
yam
yard
yarn
yell
yellow
yo-yo
yolk

Beginning /z/
zebra
zero
zinnia
zither
zoo

Ending Sounds

Ending /ā/
away
bay
day
gray
hay
Jay
may
Monday
play
ray
say
today

Ending /b/
Bob
cab
cob
cub
cube

jab
job
mob
rob
robe
rub
scrub
tab
tub
web

Ending /d/
bad
bed
bread
did
feed
had
lid
mad
mud
red
rid
sad
seed
weed
yard

Ending /ē/
bee
Frisbee
he
key
knee
me
monkey
see
she
three
tree
turkey
we

Ending /f/
calf
cough
cuff
deaf
elf
half
laugh
off
rough
stiff
stuff
tough

Ending /g/
bag
big
dog
egg
hog
hug
jog
ladybug
leg
log
pig
rag
rug
tag
twig
wig

Ending /ī/
by
cry
die
dry
fly
high
my
pie
sigh
tie
why

Ending /k/
bike
black
clock
cook
dock
duck
elk
fork
hook
lake
like
lock
milk
pack
pink
poke
rack
rake
rock
sock
take

Ending /l/
basketball
bell
bill
eel
feel
football
oatmeal
pail
quail
rail
seal
snail
tail

Ending /m/
broom
dime
drum
game

hum
jam
room
seem
uniform
yam

Ending /n/
can
fern
green
hen
kitchen
lion
moon
ocean
queen
raccoon
spoon
sun
ten
unicorn
van
vine
violin
wagon
yarn

Ending /ō/
blow
bow
doe
flow
go
low
mow
no
radio
row
slow
so
toe
volcano

yellow
yo-yo
zero

Ending /p/
cap
cape
cup
deep
hip
hop
keep
lip
map
pup
skip
sleep
tap
tip
top
trap

Ending /r/
alligator
bar
car
core
deer
door
fur
four
guitar
jar
more
newspaper
otter
pour
roar
ruler
stir
usher

Ending /s/
bus
class
dress
goose
grass
horse
house
miss
moss
mouse
octopus
pass
toss
walrus
yes

Ending /t/
astronaut
bat
cat
coat
feet
gate
goat
hat
hot
infant
kite
knot
meat
pot
quilt
wallet
white

Ending /u/
cue
few
hue
menu
nephew
preview

rescue
review
view

Ending /v/
brave
cave
dive
dove
eve
five
gave
give
glove
have
hive
live
love
save
shave
stove

Ending /ks/
ax
box
fix
flax
fox
mix
ox
relax
six
wax

Ending /z/
breeze
buzz
daze
fizz
freeze
fuzz
haze
jazz
maze
peas

quiz
size
sneeze
squeeze
trees

Medial Sounds

Medial /ā/
date
face
fade
game
gate
gave
lake
lane
late
made
make
mate
race
rake
table
wave

Medial /a/
bat
black
can
cap
hat
jam
ham
lamp
pants
sad
van
yam

Medial /ē/
beam
bean
feet
heap

keep
mean
meat
neat
seal
seed
seen
sneeze
team
weed

Medial /e/
bed
bet
head
hen
let
men
met
nest
net
pen
pet
red
set
ten

Medial /ī/
five
hide
hive
kite
life
line
mine
nice
nine
rice
ride
right
side
sight
time
vine

Medial /i/
bib
dish
fib
fin
fish
him
kittens
lip
milk
mittens
pig
pin
pink
rip
tin
tip
wig
win

Medial /ō/
boat
bowl
coal
coat
goat
hole
home
joke
mole
nose
poem
poke
post
roll
rose
toes

Medial /o/
dot
hot
knot
lock
lot

mop
not
pot
rock
sock
top

Medial /ū/
cube
cute
feud
fuel
fuse
huge
mule

Medial /u/
bug
bun
cup
cut
duck
dust
fun
hug
must
nut
rub
rug
run
sun
tub
tug

High-Frequency Word List

a
after
all
an
and
are
as
ask
at
be
big
but
by
can
come
did
do
does
five
for
four
from
get

had
has
have
he
help
her
here
him
his
I
if
in
is
it
just
like
little
look
make
me
my
no
not

of
on
one
out
pretty
say
says
said
see
she
so
some
that
the
them
then
there
they
this
three
to
too
two

under
up
walk
was
we
what
when
where
who
will
yes
your
you

Program Appendix

The Program Appendix includes a step-by-step explanation of procedures for research-based effective practices in reading instruction that are repeatedly used throughout **SRA/Open Court Reading**. These practices may also be used in other instructional situations as well.

Table of Contents

Effective Teaching Practices

Teacher References

Program Appendix

Reading Materials and Techniques

Different reading materials and techniques are appropriate at different stages of reading development. The purpose of this section is to discuss different types of reading materials and how they may be used most effectively.

Program Appendix

Reading Big Books

Purpose

Many children come from homes where they are read to often, but a significant number of other children have not had this valuable experience. Big Books (Levels K and 1) offer all children crucial opportunities to confirm and expand their knowledge about print and reading. They are especially useful for shared reading experiences in the early grades.

The benefits of reading Big Books include engaging even nonreaders in:

- unlocking the books' messages.
- developing print awareness.
- participating in good reading behaviors.
- observing what a good reader does: remarking on the illustrations and the title, asking questions about the content and what might happen, making predictions, and clarifying words and ideas.
- promoting the insight that a given word is spelled the same way every time it occurs as high-frequency words are pointed out.
- reinforcing the correspondence between spoken and written words and spelling patterns.
- enjoying the illustrations and connecting them to the text to help students learn to explore books for enjoyment and information.
- interpreting and responding to literature and expository text before they can read themselves.

Procedure for Reading Big Books

During the first reading of the Big Books, you will model reading behaviors and comprehension strategies similar to those that will later be taught formally. During the second reading, you will address print awareness and teach comprehension skills such as categorizing and sequencing that help the reader organize information. In addition, you will teach skills such as inferencing and drawing conclusions that help the reader focus on the deeper meaning of the text. At first, teachers should expect to do all of the reading but should not prevent children from trying to read on their own or from reading words they already know.

- **Activate Prior Knowledge.** Read the title of the selection and the author's and illustrator's names. At the beginning of each Big Book, read the title of the book and discuss what the whole book is about before going on to reading the first selection.
- **Discuss Prior Knowledge.** Initiate a brief discussion of any prior knowledge the students have that might help them understand the selection.
- **Browse the Selection.** Ask children to tell what they think the story might be about just from looking at the illustrations. This conversation should be brief so that the children can move on to a prereading discussion of print awareness.

> *Big Books offer all children crucial opportunities to confirm and expand their knowledge about print and reading.*

- **Develop Print Awareness.** The focus of browsing the Big Books is to develop awareness of print. Urge children to tell what words or letters they recognize rather than what they expect the selection to be about.

  To develop print awareness, have children look through the selection page by page and comment on whatever they notice in the text. Some children may know some of the words, while others may only recognize specific letters or sounds. The key is to get the children to look at the print separately from the illustrations even before they have heard the actual text content. This process isolates print awareness so that it is not influenced by content. It also gives you a clearer idea of what your students do or do not know about print.

- **Read Aloud.** Read the selection aloud expressively. The reading enables the children simply to hear and enjoy the text as it is read through once. With this reading, you will be modeling behaviors and comprehension strategies that all children will need to develop to become successful readers—for example, asking questions, clarifying unfamiliar words, first by using the pictures and later by using context, or predicting what might happen next.

- **Reread.** Read the selection expressively again. During the second reading of the stories, you will focus on teaching comprehension skills. Also, to develop print awareness, point to each word as it is read, thus demonstrating that text proceeds from left to right and from top to bottom and helping advance the idea that words are individual spoken and written units. Invite the children to identify the rhyming words in a poem or chime in on repetitive parts of text as you point to the words. Or children can read with you on this second reading, depending on the text.

- **Discuss Print.** Return to print awareness by encouraging discussion of anything the children noticed about the words. Young children should begin to realize that you are reading separate words that are separated by spaces. Later, children will begin to see that each word is made up of a group of letters. The children should be encouraged to discuss anything related to the print. For example, you might ask children to point to a word or count the number of words on a line. Or you might connect the words to the illustrations by pointing to a word and saying it and then asking the children to find a picture of that word.

- **Responding.** Responding to a selection is a way of insuring comprehension. Invite the children to tell about the story by asking the children what they like about the poem or story or calling on a child to explain in his or her own words what the poem or story tells about. Call on others to add to the telling as needed. For nonfiction selections, this discussion might include asking children what they learned about the topic and what they thought was most interesting.

Tips for Using Big Books

- Make sure the entire group is able to see the book clearly while you are reading.
- If some students are able to read or predict words, encourage them to do so during the rereading.
- Encourage students to present and use their knowledge of print.
- Allow children to look at the Big Books whenever they wish.
- Provide small versions of the Big Books for children to browse through and try to read at their leisure.
- The reader of the Big Book should try to be part of the collaborative group of learners rather than the leader.

Purpose

An urgent task of early literacy instruction is to make written thoughts intelligible and accessible to children. First-Step Stories (Level K) are meant to provide children with a meaningful "reading" experience before they are actually reading on their own. These First-Step Stories also provide the children with the opportunity to use the reading behaviors they have seen modeled during reading aloud and supported reading with the Big Books. During class time and **Independent Work Time**, children will be able to "read" and enjoy these minibooks on their own—books they have helped to create and that are theirs to keep and share.

First-Step Stories offer children a structured and meaningful writing experience as well. Some of the First-Step Stories are text only, allowing the children to illustrate them. Others have only pictures and the children "write" the text to go with the illustrations. Some of the First-Step Stories may have incomplete text, with or without pictures. As the children complete these stories, the connection between text and pictures is highlighted. Many are related thematically to the unit themes, thus providing a reading-to-writing connection.

The First-Step Stories provide the children with a structured opportunity to read, write, illustrate, and share their own books. Whatever form these stories take, they are thoroughly introduced, read, and discussed before the children are expected to complete them on their own. These books belong to the children, and so they should be encouraged to explore them on their own, return to favorite pages, and add to the books if they so choose.

Procedure for Using the First-Step Stories

Browsing the First-Step Stories

Hand out the First-Step Stories, read the title, and have the children look through them on their own. Encourage the children to respond to the book in any way they wish. For example, the children may guess about the content based on the title. Encourage the children to talk about the pictures, as well as the incomplete text.

Reading the First-Step Stories

For the stories with text, read the selection aloud several times. Encourage the children to follow along in their own books. Hold the book facing out so that the group can see it, pointing to each word as you read. Cue the children to turn the pages at the appropriate time. On subsequent readings, encourage the children to "read" along with you. When reading the First-Step Stories aloud to the class, be sure that the children are following along with you. Have signals for turning pages, encourage the children to point at the words, etc.

For books with only illustrations, go through the selection page by page, encouraging the children to talk about what is happening on each page. This is a good place to model clarifying. For example, you might say, "When I thought about how William felt, I was able to clarify why his parents were still worried." Invite volunteers to tell a story about the pictures.

For those books with incomplete text, read the text and encourage the children to tell how they would complete the sentences.

The children should be very familiar with the First-Step Stories before they are expected to complete the books on their own. In Sounds and Letters the children work independently on their stories during Independent Work Time. As with any independent work, make sure the children understand the assignment and what they need to do.

> *First-Step Stories are meant to provide children with meaningful "reading" experience before they are actually reading on their own.*

Illustrating/Writing the First-Step Stories

The children begin working on their stories by writing their names on the lines for author and/or illustrator. (The children should be familiar with these terms.) Help the children write their names if necessary. Before the children begin working on their stories, you may wish to review the topic of the story and the children's ideas for writing or illustrating. You have already discussed these stories, so the prewriting discussion can be brief.

Planning is an important aspect of the writing process. Be sure to have discussions, which encourage the children to plan what they will write and/or draw.

Encourage the children to illustrate the stories in any way they choose. Emphasize that their pictures will make their story special. While children's drawing abilities will vary quite a bit at this age, most of the children will be able to draw something. You will want to hold brief conferences with the children as they draw, providing encouragement and feedback.

For wordless stories or those with incomplete text, have the children write about the picture or topic. Encourage the children to think about what they want to say and to try to write it. There is likely to be a wide range in the children's abilities to write words; some may be scribbling or writing random letters, while others may be beginning to use invented spelling. Remind the children to think about the sounds they hear in the word, and the sound/letter correspondences they have learned. Again, you will be circulating while the children write, providing help and encouragement, perhaps even taking down the children's dictated words.

Provide the time and materials for children to make special covers for their stories.

Sharing the First-Step Stories

Set aside time for the children to share both their work in progress and their completed stories with each other and with you. Remind the children about any class rules for sharing time. As the children show their illustrations, read their words, and seek comments, always focus on what is best about a child's work. These sharing sessions will give you valuable information about the children's progress. Later in the year, you can encourage the children to share their work with a partner.

The children will also enjoy bringing their completed First-Step Stories home to share with family members. In most cases, a Home Connection letter will be sent home with the stories. The letters offer suggestions for family members to read and share the stories with the children.

Reading the Student Anthologies

Purpose

Reading is a complex process that requires children not only to decode what they read but also to understand and respond to it. The purpose of this section is to help you identify various reading behaviors used by good readers and to encourage those behaviors in your students.

Reading Behaviors and Comprehension Strategies

There are four basic behaviors that good readers engage in during reading. These behaviors include the application of certain comprehension strategies, which are modeled while reading the Student Anthology (Levels 1–6).

Setting Reading Goals and Expectations

Good readers set reading goals and expectations before they begin reading. This behavior involves a variety of strategies that will help children prepare to read the text.

- **Activate prior knowledge.** When good readers approach a new text, they consider what they already know about the subject or what their experiences have been in reading similar material.

- **Browse the text.** To get an idea of what to expect from a text, good readers look at the title and the illustrations. They may look for potential problems, such as difficult words. When browsing a unit, have children glance quickly at each selection, looking briefly at the illustrations and the print. Have them tell what they think they might be learning about as they read the unit.

- **Decide what they expect from the text.** When reading for pleasure, good readers anticipate enjoying the story or the language. When reading to learn something, they ask themselves what they expect to find out.

Responding to Text

Good readers are active readers. They interact with text by using the following strategies:

- **Making connections.** Good readers make connections between what they read and what they already know. They pay attention to elements in the text that remind them of their own experiences.

- **Visualizing, or picturing.** Good readers visualize what is happening in the text. They form mental images as they read. They picture the setting, the characters, and the action in a story. When reading expository text, good readers picture the objects, processes or events described. Visualizing helps readers understand descriptions of complex activities or processes.

- **Asking questions.** Good readers ask questions that may prepare them for what they will learn. If their questions are not answered in the text, they may try to find answers elsewhere and thus add even more to their store of knowledge.

- **Predicting.** Good readers predict what will happen next. When reading fiction, they make predictions about what they are reading and then confirm or revise those predictions as they go.

- **Thinking about how the text makes you feel.** Well-written fiction touches readers' emotions; it sparks ideas.

Checking Understanding

One of the most important behaviors good readers exhibit is the refusal to continue reading when something fails to make sense. Good readers continually assess their understanding of the text with strategies such as:

- **Interpreting.** As they read, good readers make inferences that help them understand and appreciate what they are reading.

> *One of the most important behaviors good readers exhibit is the refusal to continue reading when something fails to make sense. Good readers continually assess their understanding of the text.*

- **Summing up.** Good readers sum up to check their understanding as they read. Sometimes they reread to fill in gaps in their understanding.

Clarifying Unfamiliar Words and Passages

Good readers pause often while reading to clarify unfamiliar words and passages. This behavior should become a natural response. Children can use a variety of clarifying strategies.

- **Apply decoding skills** to sound out unknown words.

- **Determine what is unclear** to find the source of the confusion.

- **Check a dictionary or the Glossary** to understand the meanings of words. As they read, good readers make inferences that help them understand and appreciate what they are reading.

- **Apply context clues** in text and illustrations to help them figure out the meanings of words or passages.

- **Reread the passage** to make sure the passage makes sense.

Procedures

Modeling and Thinking Aloud

Modeling and encouraging children to think aloud as they attempt to understand text can demonstrate for everyone how reading behaviors are put into practice. The most effective models will be those that come from your own reading. Using questions such as the following as well as your students' questions and comments will make both the text and the strategic reading process more meaningful to children.

- What kinds of things did you wonder about?
- What kinds of things surprised you?
- What new information did you learn?
- What was confusing until you reread or read further?

Model comprehension strategies in a natural way and choose questions and comments that fit the text you are reading, but try to present a variety of ways to respond to text.

- Pose questions that you really do wonder about.
- Identify with characters by comparing them with yourself.
- React emotionally by showing joy, sadness, amusement, or surprise.
- Show empathy with or sympathy for characters.
- Relate the text to something that has happened to you or to something you already know.
- Show interest in the text ideas.
- Question the meaning or clarity of the author's words and ideas.

Encouraging Children's Responses and Use of Strategies

Most children will typically remain silent as they try to figure out an unfamiliar word or a confusing passage. Encourage children to identify specifically what they are having difficulty with. Once the problem has been identified, ask the children to suggest a strategy for dealing with the problem. Remind children to:

- Treat problems encountered in text as interesting learning opportunities.
- Think out loud about text challenges.
- Help each other build meaning. Rather than tell what a word is, children should tell how they figured out the meanings of challenging words and passages.
- Consider reading a selection again with a partner after reading it once alone. Partner reading provides valuable practice in reading for fluency.
- Make as many connections as they can between what they are reading and what they already know.
- Visualize to clarify meanings or enjoy descriptions.
- Ask questions freely about what they are reading.
- Notice how the text makes them feel.

Reading Aloud

Purpose

Adults read a variety of materials aloud to children. These include Big Books, picture books, and novels. Research has shown that children who are read to are more likely to develop the skills they need to read successfully on their own.

Reading aloud at any age serves multiple purposes. Reading aloud:

- Provokes children's curiosity about text.
- Conveys an awareness that text has meaning.
- Demonstrates the various reasons for reading text (for example, to find out about the world around them, to learn useful new information and new skills, or simply for pleasure).
- Exposes children to the "language of literature," which is more complex than the language they ordinarily use and hear.
- Provides an opportunity to teach the problem-solving strategies that good readers employ. As the children observe you interacting with the text, expressing your own enthusiasm, and modeling your thinking aloud, they perceive these as valid responses and begin to respond to text in similar ways.
- Models adults' interest in and enjoyment of reading.

Procedures

The following set of general procedures for reading aloud is designed to help you maximize the effectiveness of Read-Aloud sessions.

- **Read-aloud sessions.** Set aside time each day to read aloud.
- **Introduce the story.** Tell the children that you are going to read a story aloud to them. Tell its title and briefly comment on the topic. To allow the children to anticipate what will happen in the story, be careful not to summarize.
- **Activate prior knowledge.** Ask whether anyone has already heard the story. If so, ask them to see if this version is the same as the one they have heard. If not, activate prior knowledge by saying, "First, let's talk a little about _____." If the story is being read in two (or more) parts, before reading the second part, ask the children to recall the first part.
- **Before reading.** Invite children to interrupt your reading if there are any words they do not understand or ideas they find puzzling. Throughout the reading, encourage them to do this.
- **Read the story expressively.** Occasionally react verbally to events or other aspects of the story. These responses might include showing surprise, asking questions, giving an opinion, expressing pleasure, or predicting events. Think-aloud suggestions are outlined in the next column.
- **Use Comprehension Strategies.** While reading aloud to the children model the use of comprehension strategies in a natural, authentic

way. Remember to try to present a variety of ways to respond to text. These include visualizing, asking questions, predicting, clarifying and summarizing.

- **Retell.** When you have finished reading the story, call on volunteers to retell it.
- **Discuss.** After reading, discuss with the children their own reactions: how the story reminded them of things that have happened to them, what they thought of the story, and what they liked best about the story.
- **Reread.** You may wish to reread the selection on subsequent occasions focusing the discussion on the unit theme.

> *Research has shown that children who are read to are more likely to develop the skills they need to read successfully on their own.*

Think-Aloud Responses

The following options for modeling thinking aloud will be useful for reading any story aloud. Choose responses that are most appropriate for the selection you are reading.

- **React emotionally** by showing joy, sadness, amusement, or surprise.
- **Ask questions** about ideas in the text. This should be done when there are points or ideas that you really do wonder about.
- **Identify with characters** by comparing them to yourself.
- **Show empathy with or sympathy for** characters.
- **Relate the text to something** that has happened to you or to something you already know.
- **Show interest** in the text ideas.
- **Question the meaning and/or clarity** of the author's words and ideas.

Questions to Help the Children Respond

At reasonable stopping points in reading, ask the children general questions in order to get them to express their own ideas and to focus their attention on the text.

- What do you already know about this?
- What seems really important here? Why do you think so?
- Was there anything that you didn't understand? What?
- What did you like best about this?
- What new ideas did you learn from this?
- What does this make you wonder about?

Reading Roundtable

Purpose

Adult readers discuss their reading, give opinions on it, and recommend books to each other. Reading Roundtable, an activity students may choose to participate in during **Independent Work Time**, provides the same opportunity for students in the classroom. Sessions can be small or large, and may be held in the classroom reading center. During Reading Roundtable, students share with their classmates reading they do on their own. They can discuss a book they have all read or one person can review a book for the others and then entertain questions from the group.

During Reading Roundtable, students can discuss and review a variety of books:

- Full-length versions of Anthology selections.
- Classroom Library selections.
- Books that children learn about when discussing authors and illustrators.
- Books related to the research or exploration of unit concepts can be shared with others who might want to read them for pleasure or for information.
- Interesting articles from magazines, newspapers, and other sources.

Procedures

Encouraging Reading

- Read aloud to your students regularly. You can read Classroom Library selections or full-length versions of Student Anthology selections.
- Provide a time each day for children to read silently. This time can be as short as ten or fifteen minutes, but it should be strictly observed. You yourself should stop what you are doing and read. Students should be allowed to choose their own reading materials during this time and to record reactions to their reading in their response journals.
- Establish a classroom library and reading center with books from the school or local library or ask for donations of books from students, parents, and community members.
- Take your students to the school library or to the public library.

Conducting a Reading Roundtable

- When several students read the same book and then discuss it during Reading Roundtable, they can use discussion starters. If the book is from a unit bibliography, they can discuss also how the book is related to the unit concepts.
- When a student reviews a book others have not read, he or she can use some of the sentence starters to tell about the book. These may include, "This book is about . . ., I chose this book because. . .,What I really like/don't like about this book is . . ." and so on.

Introducing Sounds and Letters

Purpose

In **SRA/Open Court Reading**, children learn to relate sounds to letters in Kindergarten through the use of thirty-one **Alphabet Sound Cards** (Level K). In the upper grade levels, **Sound/Spelling Cards** (Levels 1–6) are used to relate sounds and spellings. The purpose of the **Alphabet Sound Cards** is to remind the children of the sounds of the English language and their letter correspondences. These cards are a resource for the children to use to remember sound-letter associations for both reading and writing.

Each card contains the capital and small letter, and a picture that shows the sound being produced. For instance, the **Monkey** card introduces the /m/ sound and shows a monkey looking at bananas and saying /m/ /m/ /m/. The name of the picture on each card contains the target sound at the beginning of the word for the consonants, and in the middle for most of the vowels. Vowel letters are printed in red and consonants are printed in black. In addition, the picture associates a sound with an action. This action-sound association is introduced through a short, interactive poem found in the Teacher's Edition in which the pictured object or character "makes" the sound of the letter. Long vowels are represented by a tall—or "long"—picture of the letters themselves, rather than by a picture for action-sound association.

Procedures

- Display the cards 1–26 with the picture sides to the wall. Initially post the first twenty-six cards in alphabetical order so that only the alphabet letters show. The short vowel cards may be posted as they are introduced later. As you introduce the letter sound, you will turn the card to show the picture and the letter on the other side. Once the cards are posted, do not change their positions so that the children can locate the cards quickly.

- Before turning a card, point to the letter. Ask children to tell what they know about the letter. For example, they are likely to know its name and possibly its sound if the letter is one they have already worked with.

- Turn the card and show the picture. Tell the children the name of the card and explain that it will help them to remember the sound the letter makes.

- Read the poem that goes with the letter. Read it expressively, emphasizing the words with the target sound and the isolated sound when it occurs. Have the children join in to produce the sound.

- Repeat the poem a few times, encouraging all children to say the sound along with you.

- Follow the poem with the cards for the target sound. (These are listed within the lessons.)

- Name each picture and have children listen for the target sound at the beginning of the word. Ask children to repeat the words and the sound.

- For every letter sound, a listening activity follows the introduction of the cards. Lead the children in the "Listening for the Sound" activity to reinforce the letter sound.

- To link the sound and the letter, demonstrate how to form the capital and small letter by writing on the chalkboard or on an overhead transparency. The children practice forming the letter and saying the sound as they write.

Alphabet Sound Cards

The pictures and letters on the **Alphabet Sound Cards** also appear on the small sets of **Alphabet Sound Cards**. The Teacher's Edition specifically suggests that you use the **Individual Alphabet Sound Cards** for some activities. You may also use the small cards for review and for small-group reteaching and practice sessions. Have sets of the cards available for the children to use during **Independent Work Time** either alone or with partners. Add each small card to the Activity Center after you have taught the lesson in which the corresponding **Alphabet Sound Card** is introduced. Here are some suggestions for activities using the **Alphabet Sound Cards**:

1. **Saying sounds from pictures.** The leader flashes pictures as the others say the sound each picture represents.

2. **Saying sounds.** The leader flashes the letters on the cards as the others say the sound that the letters represent.

3. **Naming words from pictures.** The leader flashes pictures. The others say the sound, and then say a word beginning with that sound.

4. **Writing letters from the pictures.** Working alone, a child looks at a picture and then writes the letter for the sound that picture represents.

Tips

- Throughout the beginning lessons, help students remember that vowels are special by reminding them that vowels sometimes say their names in words. For example, the picture of the *a* on the long *a* **Alphabet Sound Card** is long because the long *a* says its name. The short *a* **Alphabet Sound Card** pictures the lamb, because the lamb makes the short *a* sound, and you can hear the sound in the word, *lamb*. In the later lessons, children will use both sets of cards to help them remember that the vowels have both a short and a long sound.

- From the very beginning, encourage children to use the **Alphabet Sound Cards** as a resource to help them with their work.

- Mastery of letter recognition is the goal children should reach so that they will be prepared to link each letter with its associated sound. If children have not yet mastered the names of the letters, it is important to work with them individually in **Independent Work Time**, or at other times during the day.

- The *Kk* card is a little tricky. A camera makes the /k/ sound when it clicks and the word *camera* begins with the /k/ sound. However, the word *camera* is not spelled with a *k*. While you need not dwell on this, be aware that some children may be confused by the fact that the *Cc* and *Kk* cards have the same picture.

- The picture on the *Qq* card depicts ducks, *quacking ducks*. Make sure that the children consistently call them *quacking ducks*, not *ducks*, and that they focus on the /kw/ sound.

The Alphabetic Principle: How the Alphabet Works

The Alphabetic Principle

Purpose

A major emphasis in the Kindergarten program is on letter recognition and attending to sounds. Children need to learn the alphabetic principle: that letters work together in a systematic way to connect spoken language to written words. This understanding is the foundation for reading. Children are not expected to master letter/sound correspondence in kindergarten, nor are they expected to blend sounds into words themselves. They are only expected to become an "expert" on their Special Letter as they learn how the alphabet works. Through this introduction to the alphabetic principle, the children will have the basic understanding required to work through the alphabet letter by letter, attaching sounds to each.

Key concepts of the Alphabetic Principle include:

- A limited number of letters combine in different ways to make many different words.
- Words are composed of sounds and letters represent those sounds.
- Anything that can be pronounced can be spelled.
- Letters and sounds can be used to identify words.
- Meaning can be obtained by using letters and sounds to figure out words.

Procedures for Kindergarten

The following steps can be used for introducing letters and sounds in Kindergarten. These steps may be adapted for students at other grades if they do not understand the alphabetic principle. The tone of these activities should be informal, fun, and fast-paced. The purpose of these activities is to familiarize the children with how the alphabet works by having them participate in group play with letters and sounds.

Introducing Letters

- Reinforce the idea that anything that can be pronounced can be spelled with the letters of the alphabet.
- Tell the children that you can spell any word. Have them give you words to spell.
- Write the words on the chalkboard and show them that the words contain the letters displayed on the **Alphabet Sound Cards**.
- Have the children help you spell the words by pointing to letters as you say them and then write them.
- Encourage the children to spell each word letter by letter.

Letter Expert Groups

- Have **Letter Cards** (Levels K and 1) available for the following set of letters: *b, d, f, h, l, m, n, p, s, t*. You will need two or three cards for each letter. (You will not need the **Alphabet Sound Cards** until later.)
- You will be the letter expert for the vowels.
- Divide the class into groups of two or three and assign each group a letter. Give each child the appropriate **Letter Card**.
- Tell the children that they are now in their Letter Expert groups and that they are going to become experts on their Special Letter's name, shape, and sound.

Children need to learn the alphabetic principle: that letters work together in a systematic way to connect spoken language to written words. This understanding is the foundation for reading.

Making Words

- Begin each lesson with a rehearsal of each group's letter name.
- Demonstrate how letters work by writing a word in large letters on the chalkboard.
- Tell the children the experts for each letter in the word should hold up their **Letter Cards** and name the letter. One member of the group should stand in front of their letter on the chalkboard.
- Continue until all letters in the word are accounted for. Remember that you are responsible for the vowels.
- Demonstrate that you can make different words by changing a letter or by changing the letter order.

Identifying Sounds in Words

- Use the **Alphabet Sound Cards** to demonstrate that every letter has at least one sound.
- Give each child the **Alphabet Sound Card** for his or her Special Letter.
- Point out the pictures on the cards. Explain that each card has a picture of something that makes the letter's sound. The picture will help them remember the sound.
- Tell each group the sound for its letter. (Remember, you are the expert for the vowels.)
- Quickly have each group rehearse its letter's name and sound.
- Write a word on the chalkboard in large letters. Say the word first sound-by-sound and then blend the word.

- For each letter/sound in the word have one child from each Letter Expert group come forward and stand in front of their appropriate letter holding their cards. Although only one member of the group may come forward with the **Letter Card** or **Alphabet Sound Card**, all the children in a Special Letter group should say the name and/or sound of their letter when it occurs in words.
- Say the word again, pointing to the **Alphabet Sound Cards**.
- Ask children who are not already standing to help you hold the vowel cards.
- Vary the activity by changing one letter sound and having an expert for that letter come forward.
- End the activity for each word by saying the sounds in the words one by one and then saying the entire word. Encourage the children to participate.

Tips

- Remind the children to use the picture on the **Alphabet Sound Card** for their Special Letter to help them remember the letter's sound. The children are expected only to "master" their own Special Letter and share the information with their classmates. They are not expected to blend and read the words by themselves. These are group activities in which you work with the children to help them gain insight into the alphabet.
- Have children note that what they learn about the letters and words applies to the words they work with in Big Book selections.
- Occasionally, have children find their special letters in a Big Book selection. Play some of the letter replacement and rearrangement games with words encountered in the Big Books.

Developing the Alphabetic Principle

Purpose

The following activities are extended to provide kindergarten students with a more thorough understanding of how sounds "work" in words. In this group of exercises the children are introduced to specific letter/sound correspondences, consonants and short vowels. The children have previously been introduced to vowels and their special characteristics. This understanding is extended by introducing children to the convention that a vowel has a short sound in addition to its long sound. With this information and a carefully structured set of activities, the children can begin to explore and understand the alphabetic principle in a straightforward and thorough manner. The children not only listen for sounds in specified positions in words, they also link sounds to their corresponding letters. The activities in this group of lessons lay the groundwork for the children to work their way through the entire alphabet, learning letter-sound associations, and to understand the purpose and the value of this learning.

Move the children quickly through these activities. Do not wait for all the children to master each letter/sound correspondence before going on. The children will have more opportunities to achieve mastery. The goal of these activities is for the children to obtain a basic understanding of the alphabetic principle.

Procedures

Introducing Consonant Letters and Sounds

- Point to the **Alphabet Sound Card** and name the letter.
- Point to the picture. Tell the children the sound of the letter and how the picture helps them to remember the sound. Repeat the sound several times.
- Tell the children you will read them a short poem or an alliterative sentence to help them remember the sound of the letter. Read the poem several times, emphasizing the words with the target sound. Have the children join in and say the sound.
- After introducing and reviewing a letter/sound correspondence, summarize the information on the **Alphabet Sound Card**.

Generating Words with the Target Sound

- Brainstorm to create a list of words that begin with the target sound. Write the words on the chalkboard or on a chart. Include any of the children's names that begin with the target sound.
- Play the *I'm Thinking of Something That Starts With* game. Begin with the target sound and add clues until the children guess the word. If the children guess a word that does not begin with the target sound, emphasize the beginning sound and ask if the word begins with the target sound.
- Silly Sentences. Make silly sentences with the children that include many words with the target sound. Encourage the children to participate by extending the sentences: *Mary mopes. Mary mopes on Monday. Mary and Michael mope on Monday in Miami.*

Listening For Initial Sound

- Give each child a **Letter Card** for the target sound, *s*.
- Point to the picture on the **Alphabet Sound Card**, and have the children give the sound, /s/.
- Tell the children to listen for the first sound in each word you say. If it is /s/ they should hold up their s cards. Establish a signal so that the children know when to respond.
- Read a list of words, some beginning with /s/, some beginning with other sounds.

Listening for Final Sound

The procedure for listening for the final sound of a word is the same as that for listening for the initial sound. The children may need to be reminded throughout the activity to pay attention to the *final* sound.

- Read a list of words, some ending with the target sound, some ending with other sounds. Avoid words that begin with the target sound.

Linking the Sound to the Letter

- **Word Pairs (initial sounds).** Write pairs of words on the chalkboard, one of each pair beginning with the target sound. Say the word beginning with the target sound and ask the children to identify it. Remind them to listen for the target sound at the beginning of the word, to think about which letter makes that sound, and find the word that begins with that letter. For example,
Target sound: /s/
Word pair: *fit sit*
Which word is *sit*?

- **Word Pairs (final sounds).** Follow the same procedure used for initial sounds, this time directing the children to think about the sound that they hear at the end of the word. Since it is often more difficult for the children to attend to the ending sound, you may need to lead them through several pairs of words. Remind the children to listen for the target sound and to think about which letter makes that sound.

- **Writing Letters.** Using either the handwriting system outlined in the Appendix of Levels K and 1 of **SRA/Open Court Reading**, or the system in use at your school, have children practice writing capital and small letters. Remind the children of the letter sound and have them repeat it.

Comparing Initial Consonant Sounds

This activity is exactly like **listening for initial sounds** except that the children must discriminate between two sounds. They are given **Letter Cards** for both sounds and must hold up the appropriate card when they hear the sound.

Comparing Final Consonant Sounds

This activity is exactly like listening for final sounds except that the children must discriminate between two sounds. They are given **Letter Cards** for both sounds and must hold up the appropriate card when they hear the sound.

Linking the Consonant Sound to the Letter

In this activity to help children link sounds and letters, the children will make words either by adding initial consonants to selected word parts or by adding a different final consonant to a consonant-vowel-consonant combination.

Introducing Short Vowel Sounds

- Remind the children that the vowels are printed in red to remind them that they are special letters. (They are not special because they are printed in red.) They are special because they have more than one sound and every word must have a vowel sound.
- Point to the long *Aa* **Alphabet Sound Card** and remind the children that this letter is called a *vowel*. Vowels sometimes say their names in words. For example, *say, day, tray.* This vowel sound is called long *a.*
- Have the children repeat the sound.
- Sometimes vowels say different sounds. Point to the picture of the lamb on the short *Aa* card and tell them that *a* also makes the sound heard in the middle of *lamb.* This is the short *a.* Read the short vowel poem to help the children remember the short *a.*
- Have all the children join in saying /a/ /a/ /a/.

Listening for Short Vowel Sounds Versus Long Vowel Sounds

- Tell the children that you will read words with long *a* and short *a.* Review the two sounds.
- Give the children a signal to indicate when they hear the vowel sound. You may want one signal for short *a,* such as scrunching down, and another for long *a,* such as stretching up tall.
- Continue with lists of words such as: *add, back, aid, tan, bake, tame.*

Linking the Vowel Sound to the Letter

- Writing Letters. Have children practice writing the letter and review the sound of the letter.
- In this activity to help children link sounds and letters, the children will make words either by adding initial consonants to selected word parts or by adding a different final consonant to a consonant-vowel-consonant combination. Change the beginning of the word or the word ending, but retain the vowel sound to make new words. For example,

at	*hat*	*mat*	*pat*
ap	*map*	*tap*	*sap*
am	*Sam*	*Pam*	*ham*

Comparing Short Vowel Sounds

This activity requires children to discriminate between short vowel sounds in the middle of words. Review the vowel sounds.

- Say a word and have the children repeat it. Establish a signal to indicate whether they hear short *a* or short *o* in the middle of the word. For example, they can hold up the appropriate **Letter Card** when they hear a sound. Sample words: *cap, cot, rat, rot, rack, rock.*
- The way in which vowel sounds—in the initial, medial, and final position—combine to make words can be observed in a large set of words that does not contain silent letters or other special spelling conventions.

Linking the Sound to the Letter

- In this activity write a word on the chalkboard and help the children say it.
- Change the word by changing the vowel. Help the children say the new word. For example, *map, mop, hot, hat, pot, pat.*
- For a variation of this activity, write the pairs of words and simply have the children say which word is the target word. For example, the children see *tap* and *top.* Ask which word is *top,* directing the children's attention to the vowel.

Tips

- Lead and model the exercises as necessary until the children begin to catch on and can participate with confidence.
- To keep the children focused on the various activities, have them tell you the task for each activity. For example, after telling the children to listen for final sounds, ask the children what they will be listening for.
- Actively involve the students by giving them opportunities to tell what they know rather than supplying the information for them. For example, Do they know the letter name? Do they know the sound? Can they think of words that begin with the sound?
- Keeping the children focused on the idea that they are learning about sounds and letters so they can read these books themselves makes the lessons more relevant for the children.

Phonemic Awareness

The basic purpose of providing structured practice in phonemic awareness is to help the children hear and understand the sounds from which words are made. Before children can be expected to understand the sound/symbol correspondence that forms the base of written English, they need to have a strong working knowledge of the sound relationships that make up the spoken language. This understanding of spoken language lays the foundation for the transition to written language.

Phonemic awareness activities provide the children with easy practice in discriminating the sounds that make up words. Phonemic awareness consists of quick, gamelike activities designed to help children understand that speech is made up of distinct, identifiable sounds. The playful nature of the activities makes them appealing and engaging, while giving the children practice and support for learning about language. Once the children begin reading and writing, this experience with manipulating sounds will help them use what they know about sounds and letters to sound out and spell unfamiliar words when they read and write.

The two main formats for teaching phonemic awareness are oral blending and segmentation. These are supported by occasional discrimination activities and general wordplay. Oral blending encourages students to combine sounds to make words. Segmentation, conversely, requires them to isolate sounds from words. Other activities support discrimination, or recognition, of particular sounds. Sometimes simple songs, rhymes, or games engage students in wordplay. In these, the children manipulate words in a variety of ways. From these playful activities, the children derive serious knowledge about language.

As the children progress through different phonemic awareness activities, they will become proficient at listening for and reproducing the sounds they hear. It is essential for their progression to phonics and reading that they are able to hear the sounds and the patterns used to make up recognizable words. The phonemic awareness activities support the phonics instruction, but the activities are oral, and do not focus on sound/spelling correspondences. Because the children are not expected to read the words they are experimenting with, any consonant and vowel sounds may be used, even if the children have not been formally taught the sound and its spellings.

Oral Blending

Purpose

In oral blending, the children are led through a progression of activities designed to help them hear how sounds are put together to make words.

Until children develop an awareness of the component parts of words, they have no tools with which to decode words or put letters together to form words. Oral blending helps children master these component parts of words, from syllables down to single sounds, or phonemes. Oral blending is not to be confused with the formal blending of specific sounds whose spellings the children will be taught through phonics instruction. Oral blending does not depend on the recognition of written words; it focuses instead on hearing the sounds.

Oral blending focuses on hearing sounds through a sequence that introduces the most easily distinguished word parts then systematically moves to sound blending that contains all the challenges of phonic decoding (except letter recognition). This sequence provides support for the least-prepared child— one who comes to first grade with no concept of words or sounds within words. At the same time,

the lively pace and playful nature of oral blending activities hold the interest of children who already have some familiarity with words and letters.

Oral blending prepares children for phonics instruction by developing an awareness of the separate sounds that make up speech. Oral blending activities then continue in concert with phonics instruction to reinforce and extend new learning. And, because these activities involve simply listening to and reproducing sounds, oral blending need not be restricted to the sounds children have been or will be taught in phonics.

The tone of the activities should be playful and informal and should move quickly. Although these activities will provide information about student progress, they are not diagnostic tools. Do not expect mastery. Those children who have not caught on will be helped more by varied experiences than by more drilling on the same activity.

Procedures

Following is a description of the progression of oral blending activities.

Syllable Blending

Syllables are easier to distinguish than individual sounds (phonemes), so children can quickly experience success in forming meaningful

words. Tell the children that you are going to say some words in two parts. Tell them to listen carefully so that they can discover what the words are. Read each word, pronouncing each part distinctly with a definite pause between syllables broken by . . . . The lists of words that follow are arranged in sequence from easy to harder. They cover different types of cues. At any point where they fit in the sequence, include multisyllable names of children in the class.

Model

TEACHER: *dino . . . saur. What's the word?*
CHILDREN: *dinosaur*

Example Words

- First part of the word cues the whole word:
  vita . . . min   vaca . . . tion
  hippopot . . . amus   ambu . . . lance
- Two distinct words easily combined:
  butter . . . fly   straw . . . berry
  surf . . . board   basket . . . ball
- Two distinct words, but first word could cue the wrong ending:
  tooth . . . ache   tooth . . . paste
  water . . . fall   water . . . melon
- First part, consonant + vowel, not enough to guess whole word:
  re . . . member   re . . . frigerator
  bi . . . cycle   bi . . . ology

- Identifying clues in second part:
  light . . . ning   sub . . . ject
  in . . . sect
- Last part, consonant + vowel sound, carries essential information:
  yester . . . day   rain . . . bow
  noi . . . sy   pota . . . to
- Changing the final part changes the word:
  start . . . ing   start . . . er   start . . . ed

Initial Consonant Sounds

Initial consonant blending prepares students for consonant replacement activities that will come later. Tell the children that you will ask them to put some sounds together to make words. Pronounce each word part distinctly and make a definite pause at the breaks indicated. When a letter is surrounded by slash marks, pronounce the letter's sound, not its name. When you see /s/, for example, you will say ssss, not ess. The words that follow are arranged from easy to harder. At any point where they fit in the sequence, include names of children in the class.

Model
TEACHER: /t/ . . . iger. What's the word?
CHILDREN: tiger

Example Words
- Separated consonant blend, with rest of word giving strong cue to word identity:
  /b/ . . . roccoli   /k/ . . . racker
  /f/ . . . lashlight   /k/ . . . reature
- Held consonant that is easy for children to hear, with rest of word giving strong cue:
  /s/ . . . innamon   /l/ . . . adybug
  /s/ . . . eventeen   /n/ . . . ewspaper
- Stop consonant that is harder for children to hear preceding vowel, with rest of word giving strong cue:
  /t/ . . . adpole   /p/ . . . iggybank
  /d/ . . . ragonfly   /b/ . . . arbecue
- Single-syllable words and words in which the second part gives a weaker cue:
  /s/ . . . ing   /l/ . . . augh   /v/ . . . ase

Final Consonant Sounds

In this phase of oral blending, the last sound in the word is separated.

Model
TEACHER: cabba . . . /j/. What's the word?
CHILDREN: cabbage

Example Words
- Words that are easily recognized even before the final consonant is pronounced:
  bubblegu . . . /m/   Columbu . . . /s/
  crocodi . . . /l/   submari . . . /n/
- Multisyllable words that need the final consonant for recognition:
  colle . . . /j/ (college)   came . . . /l/ (camel)
- Single-syllable words:
  sa . . . /d/   gra . . . /s/   snai . . . /l/

Initial Consonant Sound Replacement

This level of oral blending further develops awareness of initial consonant sounds. The activity begins with a common word, then quickly changes its initial consonant sound. Most of the words produced are nonsense words, which helps keep the focus on the sounds in the word. Note that the words are written on the chalkboard, but the children are not expected to read them. The writing is to help the children see that when the sounds change, the letters change, and vice versa.

Model
TEACHER: [Writes word on board.] This word is *magazine*. What is it?
CHILDREN: *magazine*
TEACHER: Now I'm going to change it. [Erases initial consonant.] Now it doesn't start with /m/, it's going to start with /b/. What's the new word?
CHILDREN: *bagazine*
TEACHER: That's right . . . [Writes b where m had been.] It's *bagazine*. Now I'm going to change it again. . . .

Repeat with different consonant sounds. Then do the same with other words, such as: *remember, Saturday, tomorrow, lotion, million.* Continue with single-syllable words, such as: *take, big, boot, cot, seat, look, tap, ride, late.* There are two stages in using written letters:

- The replacement letter is not written until *after* the new "word" has been identified.
- Later, the replacement letter is written *at the same time* the change in the initial phoneme is announced. For example, the teacher erases *d* and writes *m* while saying, "Now it doesn't start with /d/, it starts with /m/."

Before children can be expected to understand the sound/symbol correspondence that forms the base of written English, they need to have a strong working knowledge of the sound relationships that make up the spoken language.

You may wish to alter the procedure when the consonants used have already been introduced in phonics by writing the replacement letter and having children sound out the new word. Feel free to switch between the two procedures within a single exercise. If the children are not responding orally to written spellings that have been introduced in phonics, don't force it. Proceed by saying the word before writing the letter, and wait until another time to move on to writing before pronouncing.

One-Syllable Words

The children now begin blending individual phonemes to form words. This important step can be continued well into the year. Continued repetitions of this activity will help the children realize how they can use the sound/spellings they are learning to read and write real words.

At first, the blended words are presented in a story context that helps the children identify the words. They soon recognize that they are actually decoding meaningful words. However, the context must not be so strong that the children can guess the word without listening to the phonemic cues. Any vowel sounds and irregularly spelled words may be used, since there is no writing involved.

Model
TEACHER: *When I looked out the window, I saw a /l/ /ī/ /t/. What did I see?*
CHILDREN: *A light.*
TEACHER: *Yes, I saw a light. At first I thought it was the /m/ /o͞o/ /n/. What did I think it was?*
CHILDREN: *The moon.*
TEACHER: *But it didn't really look like the moon. Suddenly I thought, maybe it's a space /sh/ /i/ /p/. What did I think it might be?*
CHILDREN: *A space ship!*

Once the children are familiar with this phase of oral blending, they can move to blending one-syllable words without the story context.

Example Words
- CVC (consonant/vowel/consonant) words beginning with easily blended consonant sounds (/sh/, /h/, /r/, /v/, /s/, /n/, /z/, /f/, /l/, /m/):
  nip   nap
- CVC words beginning with any consonant:
  ten   bug   lip
- Add CCVC words:
  flap   step   slim
- Add CVCC words:
  most   band   went
- Add CCVCC words:
  stamp   grand   scuffs

Final Consonant Sound Replacement

Final consonant sounds are typically more difficult for children to use than initial consonants.

- Begin with multisyllable words and move to one-syllable words.
- As with initial consonants, first write the changed consonant after students have pronounced the new word.
- Then write the consonant as they pronounce it.
- Then for sound/spellings that have been introduced in phonics, write the new consonant spelling and have students identify and pronounce it.

Model
TEACHER: *[Writes word on board.] This word is* teapot. *What is it?*
CHILDREN: *teapot*
TEACHER: *Now I'm going to change it. [Erases final consonant.] Now it doesn't end with /t/, it ends with /p/. What's the word now?*
CHILDREN: *teapop*
TEACHER: *That's right . . . [Writes p where t had been.] It's teapop. Now I'm going to change it again. . . .*

Example Words
- Words that are easily recognized even before the final consonant is pronounced:
  picnic   picnit   picnis   picnil   picnid
  airplane   airplate   airplabe   airplafe

- Multisyllable words that need the final consonant for recognition:

  muffin   muffil   muffim   muffip   muffit
  amaze   amate   amake   amale   amade

- Single-syllable words:

  neat   nean   neap   neam   neaj   nead   neaf
  broom   broot   brood   broof   broop   broon

Initial Vowel Replacement

Up to now, oral blending has concentrated on consonant sounds because they are easier to hear than vowels. As you move to vowel play, remember that the focus is still on the sounds, not the spellings. Use any vowel sounds.

Model

TEACHER: [Writes word on board.] *This word is* elephant. *What is it?*

CHILDREN: *elephant*

TEACHER: *Now I'm going to change it.* [Erases initial vowel.] *Now it doesn't start with /e/, it starts with /a/. What's the word now?*

CHILDREN: *alephant*

TEACHER: *That's right . . .* [Writes *a* where *e* had been.] *It's alephant. Now I'm going to change it again. . . .*

Example Words

- Multisyllable words:

  angry   ingry   oongry   ungry   engry
  ivy   avy   oovy   evy   ovy   oivy

- One-syllable words:

  ink   ank   oonk   unk   onk   oink
  add   odd   idd   oudd   edd   udd

Segmentation

Purpose

Segmentation and oral blending complement each other: Oral blending puts sounds together to make words, while segmentation separates words into sounds. Oral blending will provide valuable support for decoding when students begin reading independently.

Procedure

Syllables

The earliest segmentation activities focus on syllables, which are easier to distinguish than individual sounds, or phonemes. Start with children's names, then use other words. As with the oral blending activities, remember to move quickly through these activities. Do not hold the class back waiting for all children to catch on. Individual progress will vary, but drilling on one activity is less helpful than going on to others. Return to the same activity often. Frequent repetition is very beneficial and allows children additional opportunities to catch on.

- Say, for example, "Let's clap out Amanda's name. A-man-da."
- Have the children clap and say the syllables along with you. Count the claps.
- Tell the children that these word parts are called *syllables*. Don't try to explain; the idea will develop with practice. Once you have provided the term, simply say, "How many syllables?" after the children clap and count.
- Mix one-syllable and multisyllable words:

  fantastic   tambourine   good
  imaginary   stand   afraid

Comparative Length of Words

Unlike most phonemic awareness activities, this one involves writing on the chalkboard or on an overhead transparency. Remember, though, that the children are not expected to read what is written. They are merely noticing that words that take longer to say generally look longer when written.

- Start with students' names. Choose two names, one short and one long, with the same first initial (for example, Joe and Jonathan).
- Write the two names on the board one above the other so that the difference is obvious.
- Tell the children that one name is Jonathan and one is Joe. Have them pronounce and clap each name. Then, have them tell which written word they think says *Joe*.
- Move your finger under each name as they clap and say it, syllable by syllable.
- Repeat with other pairs of names and words, such as: *tea/telephone, cat/caterpillar, butterfly/bug*. Be sure not to give false clues. For example, sometimes write the longer word

on top, sometimes the shorter one; sometimes ask for the shorter word, sometimes the longer; sometimes ask for the top word, sometimes the bottom; sometimes point to a word and ask the children to name it, sometimes name the word and ask the children to point to it.

Listen for Individual Sounds

Activities using a puppet help the children listen for individual sounds in words. Use any puppet you have on hand. When you introduce the puppet, tell the children that it likes to play word games. Each new activity begins with the teacher speaking to and for the puppet until the children determine the pattern. Next, students either speak for the puppet or correct the puppet. To make sure all the children are participating, alternate randomly between having the whole group or individuals respond. The activities focus on particular parts of words, according to the following sequence:

1. **Repeating last part of word.** Use words beginning with easy-to-hear consonants, such as *f, l, m, n, r, s,* and *z*. The puppet repeats only the rime, the part of the syllable after the initial consonant.

Model

TEACHER: *farm*

PUPPET: *arm*

Once the pattern is established, the children respond for the puppet.

TEACHER: *rope*

CHILDREN: *ope*

Example Words

Use words such as the following: *mine . . . ine soup . . . oup   feet . . . eet*

2. **Restoring initial phonemes.** Now the children correct the puppet. Be sure to acknowledge the correction.

Model

TEACHER: *lake*

PUPPET: *ake*

TEACHER: *No, lllake. You forgot the /l/.*

TEACHER: *real*

PUPPET: *eal*

TEACHER: *What did the puppet leave off?*

CHILDREN: */r/. It's supposed to be* real.

TEACHER: *That's right. The word is* real.

Example Words

Use words such as the following:

look . . . ook   mouse . . . ouse   sand . . . and

3. **Segmenting initial consonants.** The puppet pronounces only the initial consonant.

Model

TEACHER: *pay*

PUPPET: */p/*

Example Words

Use words such as the following:

moon . . . /m/   nose . . . /n/   bell . . . /b/

4. Restoring final consonants. The children correct the puppet. Prompt if necessary: *"What's the word? What did the puppet leave off?"*

Model

TEACHER: *run*

PUPPET: *ru*

CHILDREN: *It's run! You left off the /n/.*

TEACHER: *That's right. The word is run.*

Example Words

Use words such as the following:

meet. . . mee   cool . . . coo   boot. . . boo

5. Isolating final consonants. The puppet pronounces only the final consonant.

Model

TEACHER: *green*

PUPPET: */n/*

Example Words

Use words such as the following:

glass . . . /s/   boom . . . /m/   mice . . . /s/

6. Segmenting initial consonant blends. The sounds in blends are emphasized.

Model

TEACHER: *clap*

PUPPET: *lap*

Next have students correct the puppet.

TEACHER: *stain*

PUPPET: *tain*

CHILDREN: *It's stain! You left off the /s/.*

TEACHER: *That's right. The word is stain.*

Example Words

Use words such as the following:

blaze . . . laze   draw. . . raw   proud . . . roud

Discrimination

Purpose

Discrimination activities help children focus on particular sounds in words.

Listening for long vowel sounds is the earliest discrimination activity. Vowel sounds are necessary for decoding, but young children do not hear them easily. This is evident in children's invented spellings, where vowels are often omitted. Early in the year, the children listen for long vowel sounds, which are more easily distinguished than short vowel sounds:

- Explain to the children that vowels are special, because sometimes they say their names in words.
- Tell the children which vowel sound to listen for.
- Have them repeat the sound when they hear it in a word. For example, if the target vowel sound is long e, the children will say long e when you say *leaf* but they should not respond when you say *loaf*.
- Initially the children should listen for one long vowel sound at a time. Later they can listen for two vowel sounds. All **Example Words**, however, should contain one of the target vowels.

Procedure

Listening for short vowel sounds discrimination activities should be done once the short vowels /a/ and /i/ have been introduced. Short vowels are very useful in reading. They are generally more regular in spelling than long vowels, and they appear in many short, simple words. However, their sounds are less easily distinguished than those of long vowels. Thus, the activities focus only on /a/ and /i/. All the words provided have one or the other of these sounds. Either have the children repeat the sound of a specified vowel, or vary the activity as follows: Write an *a* on one side of the chalkboard and an *i* on the other. Ask the children to point to the *a* when they hear a word with the /a/ sound and point to the *i* when they hear a word with the /i/ sound. Use words such as the following:

bat	mat	sat	sit	spit
pit	pat	pan	pin	spin

Consonant sounds in multisyllable words. Discriminating these sounds helps children attend to consonant sounds in the middle of words.

- Say the word *rib* and have the children repeat it. Ask where they hear the /b/ in *rib*.
- Then say *ribbon* and ask the children where they hear the /b/ in *ribbon*.
- Tell the children that you will say some words and they will repeat each word.
- After they repeat each word, ask what consonant sound they hear in the middle of that word. Use words such as the following:

famous	message	picky
jogger	flavor	zipper

Phonemic Play

Purpose

Wordplay activities help the children focus on and manipulate sounds, thus supporting the idea that words are made of specific sounds that can be taken apart, put together, or changed to make new words. Through wordplay, children gain important knowledge about language.

Procedure

Producing rhymes. Many phonemic play activities focus on producing rhymes. A familiar or easily learned rhyme or song is introduced, and the children are encouraged to substitute words or sounds. An example is "*Willaby Wallaby Woo*," in which children change the rhyming words in the couplet "*Willaby Wallaby Woo/An elephant sat on you*" so that the second line ends with a student's name and the first line ends with a rhyme beginning with W (for example, "*Willaby Wallaby Wissy/An elephant sat on Missy*").

Generate alliterative words. Children can also say as many words as they can think of that begin with a given consonant sound. This is a valuable complement to discrimination activities in which the teacher produces the words and the children identify them.

Explicit, Systematic Phonics

The purpose of phonics instruction is to teach students the association between the sounds of the language and the written symbols—spellings—that have been chosen to represent those sounds.

As with all alphabetic languages, English has a limited number of symbols—twenty-six—that are combined and recombined to make the written language. These written symbols are a visual representation of the speech sounds we use to communicate. This is simply a code. The faster the children learn the code and how it works, the faster the whole world of reading opens to them.

Students are introduced to the sounds and spellings of English in a very systematic, sequential manner. This allows them to continually build on what they learned the day before. As each sound/symbol relationship is introduced, students are introduced to and practice with words containing the target sound/spelling and then reinforce their learning through the use of engaging text specifically written for this purpose.

It can be very difficult for children to hear the individual sounds, or phonemes, that make up words. When phonics instruction is explicit—students are told the sounds associated with the different written symbols—there is no guess work involved. They know that this sound /b/ is spelled *b*. Therefore, students in an ***SRA/Open Court Reading*** classroom spend time learning to discriminate individual speech sounds and then they learn the spellings of those sounds. This systematic explicit approach affords students the very best chance for early and continuing success.

Introducing the Sounds and Using the Sound/Spelling Cards

Purpose

The purpose of the **Sound/Spelling Cards** (Levels 1–6) is to remind the children of the sounds of English and their spellings. The name of the picture on each card contains the target sound at the beginning for the consonants and in the middle for most vowels. In addition, the picture associates a sound with an action. This association is introduced through an interactive story in which the pictured object or character "makes" the sound. These cards are a resource for the children to use to remember sound/spelling associations for both reading and writing.

Procedure

Posting the Cards

Initially, post the first twenty-six cards face to the wall so that only the alphabet letters on the backs show. As you introduce each card, you will turn it to show the picture and the spellings on the front of the card. If, however, most of your students already have some knowledge of the letters—this is a second or third grade classroom and students are reviewing what they learned the year before—you may want to go ahead and place the cards with the picture and the spellings facing front to provide support as they begin writing.

Make sure that the cards are positioned so that you can touch them with your hand or with a pointer when you refer to them and so that all of the children can see them easily and so that all of the children can see them easily. The cards should be placed where the children can readily see them during reading and writing.

Special Devices
- Vowel spellings are printed in red to draw attention to them. Consonants are printed in black. The blank line in a spelling indicates that a letter will take the place of the blank in a word. For example, the replacement of the blank with *t* in the spelling *a_ e*, makes the word *ate*. The blank lines may also indicate the position of a spelling in a word or a syllable. The blank in *h_* for example, means that the spelling occurs at the beginning of a word or a syllable.
- The blanks in *_ ie_* indicate that the *ie* spelling comes in the middle of a word or a syllable, while the blank in *_oy* shows that the *oy* spelling comes at the end of a word or a syllable. Uses of blanks in specific spellings are in the lessons. Please note now, however, that when you write a spelling of a sound on the chalkboard or an overhead transparency, you should include the blanks.
- The color of the background behind the spellings also has a meaning. Consonants have a white background. The colors behind vowel spellings are pronunciation clues. Short vowel spellings have a green background, which corresponds to the green box that appears before some consonant spellings. Thus, before *_ck* or *x* you will see a green box, which

indicates that a short vowel always precedes that spelling. Long vowel spellings have a yellow background; other vowel spellings, such as r-controlled vowels and diphthongs, have a blue background. The color code reinforces the idea that vowels are special and have different pronunciations.

Introducing the Sound/Spelling Cards

In first grade, each sound and spelling is introduced by using a see/hear/say/write sequence. In grades two and three the same sequence is used in the review of the cards.

1. **See:** Students see the spelling or spellings on the **Sound/Spelling Card** and the chalkboard or an overhead transparency.
2. **Hear:** Students hear the sound used in words and in isolation in the story. The sound is, of course, related to the picture (and the action) shown on the Sound/Spelling Card.
3. **Say:** Students say the sound.
4. **Write:** Students write the spelling(s) for the sound.

There are a number of important points to remember about this technique.

- The first item written on the chalkboard or an overhead transparency is the spelling of the sound being introduced. This gives the spelling a special emphasis in the mind of the child. It is the "see" part of the sequence.
- One of the causes of blending failure is the failure to teach sounds thoroughly during introduction of the **Sound/Spelling Card** and

during initial sounding and blending. To help ensure success for all children, make certain that every child is able to see the board or screen.

- After you present the sound and spelling, have several students go to the board to write the spelling. Have them say the sound as they write the spelling. After they have written the spelling of the sound, give them a chance to proofread their own work. Then give the other students the opportunity to help with proofreading by noting what is good about the spelling and then suggesting how to make it better.

Sample Lesson, Using the Letter m and the Sound /m/

- Point to the **Sound/Spelling Card** and have students tell you whether it is a vowel or a consonant. Have them tell the name of the card. If they do not know it tell them it is Monkey. Point to the *monkey* in the picture and say the word monkey, emphasizing the initial consonant sound—*mmmonkey.*
- Point to the spelling *m*. Tell students that /m/ is spelled *m*.
- If you wish make up an alliterative sentence about the Monkey or use the alliterative story that accompanies the card. (In first grade this story is printed on the page on which the card is introduced. In grades two and three, the stories are printed in the Appendix of the Teacher's Edition.) For example, *When Muzzie the monkey munches bananas, the sound she makes is /mmmmmm/.*
- If students had **SRA/Open Court Reading** in first grade, you can ask them if they learned an action such as rubbing their tummies to help them remember the sound. If your students don't have an action they associate with the cards already, make some up with your students. They will have fun and it will be another way for them to remember the sound/spelling relationships.
- Write *m* on the chalkboard or on an overhead transparency and say the sound. Write the letter again and ask the children to say the sound with you as they write the letter on slates, on paper, or with their index finger on a surface. Repeat this activity several times.

- Have the children listen for words beginning with /m/, indicating by some signal, such as thumbs-up or thumbs-down, whether they hear the /m/ sound and saying /m/ when they hear it in a word. Repeat with the sound in various positions in words. Encourage students to tell you and the class words with /m/ at the beginning and end as well as in the middle of words.
- Check students' learning by pointing to the card. Have students identify the sound, name the spelling, and discuss how the card can help them remember the sound.

Individual Sound Spelling Cards

Use the **Individual Sound Spelling Cards** for review and for small-group reteaching and practice sessions. Students can use them alone or

> *The faster the children learn the code and how it works, the faster the whole world of reading opens to them.*

with partners. Here are some suggestions for activities using the **Individual Sound Spelling Cards**:

1. **Saying sounds from pictures.** The leader flashes pictures as the others say the sound each picture represents.
2. **Saying sounds.** The leader flashes the spellings on the cards as the others say the sound that the spellings represent.
3. **Naming spellings from pictures.** The leader flashes pictures. The others name the card, say the sound, and then name as many spellings as they can.
4. **Writing spellings from the pictures.** Working alone, a child looks at a picture and then writes as many spellings for that **Individual Sound Spelling Card** as he or she can remember.
5. **Saying words from pictures.** The leader presents a series of pictures. The others form words by blending the sounds represented.

Purpose

The purpose of blending is to teach the children a strategy for figuring out unfamiliar words. Initially, children will be blending sound by sound. Ultimately, the children will sound and blend only those words that they cannot read. Eventually, the blending process will become quick and comfortable for them.

Procedure

Learning the sounds and their spellings is only the first step in learning to read and write. The second step is learning to blend the sounds into words.

Blending Techniques

Blending lines are written on the chalkboard or an overhead transparency as the children watch and participate. The lines and sentences should not be written out before class begins. It is through the sound-by-sound blending of the words and the sentences that the children learn the blending process.

Sound-by-Sound Blending

- Write the spelling of the first sound in the word. Point to the spelling, and say the sound.
- Have the children say the sound with you as you say the sound again. Write the spelling of the next sound. Point to the spelling, and say the sound. Have the children say the sound with you as you say the sound again. After you have written the vowel spelling, blend through the vowel (unless the vowel is the first letter of the word), making the blending motion—a smooth sweeping of the hand beneath the sounds, linking them from left to right, for example, *ba*. As you make the blending motion, make sure that your hand is under the letter that corresponds to the sound you are saying at the moment.
- Have the children blend through the vowel. Write the spelling of the next sound. Point to the spelling and say the sound. Have the children say the sound with you as you touch the letter and say the sound again.
- Continue as described above through the word. After pronouncing the final sound in the word, make the blending motion from left to right under the word as you blend the sounds. Then have the children blend the word. Let them be the first to pronounce the word normally.
- Ask a child to read the word again and use it in a sentence. Ask another child to extend the sentence—that is, make it longer by giving more information. Help the child by asking an appropriate question about the sentence, using, for example, *How? When? Where? or Why?* Continue blending the rest of the words.

Whole-Word Blending

Once students are comfortable with sound by sound blending, they are ready for whole-word blending.

- Write the whole word to be blended on the chalkboard or an overhead transparency.
- Ask the children to blend the sounds as you point to them.
- Then have the children say the whole word.
- Ask the children to use the word in a sentence and then to extend the sentence.
- When all of the words have been blended, point to words randomly and ask individuals to read them.

Blending Syllables

In reading the Anthologies, students will often encounter multisyllabic words. Some students are intimidated by long words, yet many multisyllabic words are easily read by reading and blending the syllables rather than the individual sounds. Following a set of rules for syllables is difficult since so many of the rules have exceptions. Students need to remember that each syllable in a word contains one vowel sound.

- Have students identify the vowel sounds in the word.
- Have students blend the first syllable sound by sound if necessary or read the first syllable.
- Handle the remaining syllables the same way.
- Have students blend the syllables together to read.

Blending Sentences

Blending sentences is the logical extension of blending words. Blending sentences helps students develop fluency, which is critical to comprehension. Encourage students to reread sentences with phrasing and natural intonation.

- Write the sentence on the chalkboard or on a transparency, underlining any high-frequency sight words—words that the children cannot decode either because they are irregular or because they contain sounds or spellings that the children have not yet learned or reviewed. If the children have not read these words before, write the words on the board or an overhead transparency and introduce them before writing the sentence. These words should not be blended but read as whole words.

Building for Success

A primary cause of children's blending failure is their failure to understand how to use the **Sound/Spelling Cards.** Students need to practice sounds and spellings when the **Sound/Spelling Cards** are introduced and during initial blending. They also need to understand that if they are not sure of how to pronounce a spelling, they can check the cards.

Early blending may be frustrating. You must lead the group almost constantly. Soon, however, leaders in the group will take over. Watch to see whether any children are having trouble during the blending. Include them in small-group instruction sessions. At that time you may want to use the vowel-first procedure described below to reteach blending lines.

Extra Help

In working with small groups during **Independent Work Time,** you may want to use some of the following suggestions to support students who need help with blending.

Vowel-First Blending

Vowel-first blending is an alternative to sound-by-sound and whole-word blending for children who need special help. Used in small-group sessions, this technique helps children who have difficulty with the other two types of blending focus on the most important part of each word, the vowels, and do only one thing at a time. These children are not expected to say a sound and blend it with another at virtually the same time. The steps to use in vowel-first blending follow:

1. Across the board or on an overhead transparency, write the vowel spelling in each of the words in the line. For a short vowel, the line may look like this:

   a   a   a

   For a long vowel, the line may look like this:

   ee   ea   ea

2. Point to the spelling as the children say the sound for the spelling.

> *Blending is the heart and soul of phonics instruction and the key strategy children must learn to open the world of written language.*

3. Begin blending around the vowels. In front of the first vowel spelling, add the spelling for the beginning sound of the word. Make the blending motion and have the children blend through the vowel, adding a blank to indicate that the word is still incomplete. Repeat this procedure for each partial word in the line until the line looks like this:

   ma__   sa__   pa__
   see__   mea__   tea__

4. Have the children blend the partial word again as you make the blending motion and then add the spelling for the ending sound.

5. Make the blending motion and have the children blend the completed word—for example, *mat* or *seed.*

6. Ask a child to repeat the word and use it in a sentence. Then have another child extend the sentence.

7. Repeat steps 4, 5, and 6 for each word in the line, which might look like this:

   mat   sad   pan
   or
   seed   meat   team

Tips

- In the early lessons, do blending with as much direction and dialogue as is necessary for success. Reduce your directions to a minimum as soon as possible. You have made good progress when you no longer have to say, "Sound—Sound—Blend," because the children automatically sound and blend as you write.

- Unless the line is used to introduce or to reinforce a spelling pattern, always ask a student to use a word in a sentence and then to extend the sentence immediately after you've developed the word. If the line is used to introduce or to reinforce a spelling pattern, however, ask the children to give sentences at the end of the line. Students will naturally extend sentences by adding phrases to the ends of the sentences. Encourage them to add phrases at the beginning or in the middle of the sentence.

- Use the vowel-first procedure in small group preteaching or reteaching sessions with students who are having a lot of trouble with blending. Remember that you must adapt the blending lines in the lessons to the vowel-first method.

- The sight words in the sentences cannot be blended. The children must approach them as sight words to be memorized. If children are having problems reading sight words, tell them the words. Cue marks written over the vowels may help students.
  - ✓ Straight line cue for long vowels
    EXAMPLES: *āpe, mē, fīne, sō, ūse*
  - ✓ Curved line cue for short vowels
    EXAMPLES: *căt, pĕt, wĭn, hŏt, tŭg*
  - ✓ Tent cue for variations of a and o
    EXAMPLES: *âll, ôff*
  - ✓ Dot cue for schwa sound with multiple-syllable words
    EXAMPLES: *saläd, planët, pencïl, wagön*

Dictation and Spelling

Purpose

The purpose of dictation is to teach the children to spell words based on the sounds and spellings. In addition, learning dictation gives students a new strategy for reflecting on the sounds they hear in words to help them with their own writing.

As the children learn that sounds and spellings are connected to form words and that words form sentences, they begin to learn the standard spellings that will enable others to read their writing. As children learn to encode correctly, they develop their visual memory for words (spelling ability) and hence increase their writing fluency. Reinforcing the association between sounds and spellings and words through dictation gives children a spelling strategy that provides support and reassurance for writing independently. Reflecting on the sounds they hear in words will help students develop writing fluency as they apply the strategy to writing unfamiliar words.

A dictation activity is a learning experience; it is not a test. The children should be encouraged to ask for as much help as they need. The proofreading techniques are an integral part of dictation. Children's errors lead to self-correction and, if need be, to reteaching. The dictation activities must not become a frustrating ordeal. The children should receive reinforcement and feedback.

There are two kinds of dictation: Sounds-in-Sequence Dictation and Whole-Word Dictation. The two types differ mainly in the amount of help they give the children in spelling the words. The instructions vary for each type.

Procedure

Sounds-in-Sequence Dictation

Sounds-in-Sequence Dictation gives the children the opportunity to spell words sound by sound, left to right, checking the spelling of each sound as they write. (Many children write words as they think they hear and say the words, not as the words are actually pronounced or written.)

- Pronounce the first word to be spelled. Use the word in a sentence and say the word again (word/sentence/word). Have students say the word.

- Tell students to think about the sounds they hear in the word. Ask, "What's the first sound in the word?"
- Have students say the sound.
- Point to the **Sound/Spelling Card**, and direct the children to check the card. Ask what the spelling is. The children should say the spelling and then write it.
- Proceed in this manner until the word is complete.
- Proofread. You can write the word on the chalkboard as a model or have a child do it. Check the work by referring to the

Dictation of words and sentences helps the children both develop a spelling strategy and integrate reading and writing. It introduces proofreading in a purposeful way.

Sound/Spelling Cards. If a word is misspelled, have the children circle the word and write it correctly, either above the word or next to it.

Whole-Word Dictation

Whole-Word Dictation gives the children the opportunity to practice this spelling strategy with less help from the teacher.

- Pronounce the word, use the word in a sentence, and then repeat the word (word/sentence/word). Have the children repeat the word. Tell the children to think about the word. Remind the children to check the **Sound/Spelling Cards** for spellings and to write the word.
- Proofread. Write or have a volunteer write the word on the chalkboard as a model. Check the word by referring to the **Sound/Spelling Cards**.

Sentence Dictation

Writing dictated sentences. Help students apply this spelling strategy to writing sentences. Dictation supports the development of fluent and independent writing. Dictation of a sentence will also help the children apply conventions of written language, such as capitalization and punctuation.

- Say the complete sentence aloud.
- Dictate one word at a time following the procedure for Sounds-in-Sequence Dictation.

Continue this procedure for the rest of the words in the sentence. Remind the children to put a period at the end. Then proofread the sentence, sound by sound, or word by word. When sentences contain sight words, the sight words should be dictated as whole words, not sound by sound. As the children learn to write more independently, the whole sentence can be dictated word by word.

Proofreading

Whenever the children write, whether at the board or on paper, they should proofread their work. Proofreading is an important technique because it allows the children to learn by self-correction and it gives them an immediate second chance for success. It is the same skill students will use as they proofread their writing. Students should proofread by circling—not by erasing—each error. After they circle an error, they should write the correction beside the circle. This type of correction allows you and the students to see the error as well as the correct form. Children also can see what needs to be changed and how they have made their own work better.

You may want to have students use a colored pencil to circle and write in the correction. This will make it easier for them to see the changes.

Procedure for Proofreading

- Have a child write the word or sentence on the board or on an overhead transparency as a model.
- Have children tell what is good.
- Have students identify anything that can be made better.
- If there is a mistake, have the student circle it and write it correctly.
- Have the rest of the class proofread their own work.

Reading Comprehension

Everything the students learn about phonemic awareness, phonics, and decoding has one primary goal—to help them understand what they are reading. Without comprehension, there is no reading.

Reading Comprehension Strategies

Purpose

The primary aim of reading is comprehension. Without comprehension, neither intellectual nor emotional responses to reading are possible—other than the response of frustration. Good readers are problem solvers. They bring their critical faculties to bear on everything they read. Experienced readers generally understand most of what they read, but just as importantly, they recognize when they do not understand and they have at their command an assortment of strategies for monitoring and furthering their understanding.

The goal of comprehension strategy instruction is to turn responsibility for using strategies over to the students as soon as possible. Research has shown that children's comprehension and learning problems are not a matter of mental capacity but rather their inability to use strategies to help them learn. Good readers use a variety of strategies to help them make sense of the text and get the most out of what they read. Trained to use a variety of comprehension strategies, children dramatically improve their learning performance. In order to do this, the teacher models strategy use and gradually incorporates different kinds of prompts and possible student think-alouds as examples of the types of thinking students might do as they read to comprehend what they are reading.

Comprehension Strategies

Descriptions of the types of strategies good readers use to comprehend text:

Setting Reading Goals

Good readers set reading goals and expectations before they begin reading. Readers who have set their own reading goals and have definite expectations about the text they are about to read are more engaged in their reading and notice more in what they read. Having determined a purpose for reading, they are better able to evaluate a text and determine whether it meets their needs. Even when the reading is assigned, the reader's engagement is enhanced when he or she has determined ahead of time what information might be gathered from the selection or how the selection might interest him or her.

Summarizing

Good readers sum up to check their understanding as they read. Sometimes they reread to fill in gaps in their understanding. Good readers use the strategy of summarizing to keep track of what they are reading and to focus their minds on important information. The process of putting the information in one's own words not only helps good readers remember what they have read, but also prompts them to evaluate how well they understand the information. Sometimes the summary reveals that one's understanding is incomplete, in which case it might be appropriate to reread the previous section to fill in the gaps. Good readers usually find that the strategy of summarizing is particularly helpful when they are reading long or complicated text.

Asking Questions

Good readers ask questions that may prepare them for what they will learn. If their questions are not answered in the text, they may try to find answers elsewhere and thus add even more to their store of knowledge. Certain kinds of questions occur naturally to a reader, such as clearing up confusion or wondering why something in the text is as it is. Intentional readers take this somewhat informal questioning one step further by formulating questions with the specific intent of checking their understanding. They literally test themselves by thinking of questions a teacher might ask and then by determining answers to those questions.

Predicting

Good readers predict what will happen next. When reading fiction, they make predictions about what they are reading and then confirm or revise those predictions as they go.

Making Connections

Good readers make connections between what they are reading and what they already know from past experience or previous reading.

Visualizing

Good readers visualize what is happening in the text. They form mental images as they read. They picture the setting, the characters, and the action in a story. Visualizing helps readers understand descriptions of complex activities or processes. Visualizing can also be helpful when reading expository text. When a complex process or an event is being described, the reader can follow the process or the event better by visualizing each step or episode. Sometimes an author or an editor helps the reader by providing illustrations, diagrams, or maps. If no visual aids have been provided, it may help the reader to create one.

Procedures

Modeling and Thinking Aloud

One of the most effective ways to help students use and understand the strategies good readers use is to make strategic thinking public. Modeling these behaviors and encouraging students to think aloud as they attempt to understand text can demonstrate for everyone in a class how these behaviors are put into practice. Suggestions for think-alouds are provided throughout the teacher's guide.

The most effective models you can offer will be those that come from your own reading experiences. What kinds of questions did you ask yourself? What kinds of things surprised you the first time you read a story? What kinds of new information did you learn? What kinds of things were confusing until you reread or read further? Drawing on these questions and on your students' questions and comments as they read will make the strategic reading process more meaningful to the students. Below are suggestions for modeling each of the comprehension strategies.

- **Modeling Setting Reading Goals.** To model setting reading goals engage students in the following:
  - **Activate prior knowledge.** As you approach a new text, consider aloud what you already know about the subject or what your experiences have been in reading similar material.
  - **Browse the text.** To get an idea of what to expect from a text, look at the title and the illustrations. Look for potential problems, such as difficult words. Have students glance quickly at each selection, looking briefly at the illustrations and the print. Have them tell what they think they might be learning about as they read the unit.
  - **Decide what to expect from the text.** Anticipate enjoying the story or the language of the text or if reading to learn something, ask what you expect to find out.
- **Modeling Summarizing.** Just as the strategy of summarizing the plot and then predicting what will happen next can enhance a student's reading of fiction, so too can the same procedure be used to the student's advantage in reading nonfiction. In expository text, it is particularly logical to stop and summarize at the end of a chapter or section before going on to the next. One way to model the valuable exercise of making predictions and at the same time expand knowledge is to summarize information learned from a piece of expository writing and then predict what the next step or category will be. Appropriate times to stop and summarize include the following:

- when a narrative text has covered a long period of time or a number of events
- when many facts have been presented
- when an especially critical scene has occurred
- when a complex process has been described
- any time there is the potential for confusion about what has happened or what has been presented in the text
- when returning to a selection.

> *Good readers use a variety of strategies to help them make sense of the text and get the most out of what they read.*

- **Modeling Asking Questions.** Learning to ask productive questions is not an easy task. Students' earliest experiences with this strategy take the form of answering teacher-generated questions. However, students should be able to move fairly quickly to asking questions like those a teacher might ask. Questions that can be answered with a simple yes or no are not typically very useful for helping them remember and understand what they have read. Many students find it helpful to ask questions beginning with *Who? What? When? Where? How?* or *Why?* As students become more accustomed to asking and answering questions, they will naturally become more adept at phrasing their questions. As their question asking becomes more sophisticated, they progress from simple questions that can be answered with explicit information in the text to questions that require making inferences based on the text.
- **Modeling Predicting.** Predicting can be appropriate at the beginning of a selection—on the basis of the titles and the illustrations—or at any point while reading a selection. At first, your modeling will take the form of speculation about what might happen next, but tell students from the start what clues in the text or illustrations helped you predict, in order to make it clear that predicting is not just guessing. When a student makes a prediction—especially a far-fetched one—ask what in the selection or in his or her own experience the prediction is based on. If the student can back up the prediction, let the prediction stand;

otherwise, suggest that the student make another prediction on the basis of what he or she already knows. Often it is appropriate to sum up before making a prediction. This will help students consider what has come before as they make their predictions about what will happen next. When reading aloud, stop whenever a student's prediction has been confirmed or contradicted. Have students tell whether the prediction was correct. If students seem comfortable with the idea of making predictions but rarely do so on their own, encourage them to discuss how to find clues in the text that will help them.

- **Modeling Making Connections.** To model making connections, share with students any thoughts or memories that come to mind as you read the selection. Perhaps a character in a story reminds you of a childhood friend, allowing you to better identify with interactions between characters. Perhaps information in an article on Native-American life in the Old West reminds you of an article that you have read on the importance of the bison to Native Americans. Sharing your connections will help students become aware of the dynamic nature of reading and show them another way of being intentional, active learners.
- **Modeling Visualizing.** Model visualizing by describing the mental images that occur to you as you read. A well-described scene is relatively easy to visualize, and if no one does so voluntarily, you may want to prompt students to express their own visualizations. If the author has not provided a description of a scene, but a picture of the scene would make the story more interesting or comprehensible, you might want to model visualizing as follows: "Let's see. The author says that the street was busy, and we know that this story is set during the colonial period. From what I already know about those times, there were no cars, and the roads were different from the roads of today. The street may have been paved with cobblestones. Horses would have been pulling carriages or wagons. I can almost hear the horses' hoofs going clip-clop over the stones." Remind students that different readers may picture the same scene quite differently, which is fine. Every reader responds to a story in her or his own way.

Reading Aloud

At the beginning of the year, students should be encouraged to read selections aloud. This practice will help you and them understand some of the challenges posed by the text and how different students approach these challenges. Make sure that you set aside time to hear each student read during the first few days of class—the days devoted to Getting Started are perfect for this—so that you can determine students' abilities and needs. **Independent Work Time** is also a good time to listen to any students who do not get to read aloud while the class is reading the selection together.

If your students have not previously engaged in the sort of strategic thinking aloud that is promoted throughout the *SRA/Open Court Reading* program, you will have to do all or most of the modeling at first, but encourage the children to participate as soon as possible.

As the year progresses, students should continue reading aloud often, especially with particularly challenging text. Model your own use of strategies not only to help students better understand how to use strategies but also to help them understand that actively using strategies is something that good, mature readers do constantly.

Most students are unaccustomed to thinking out loud. They will typically stand mute as they try to figure out an unfamiliar word or deal with a confusing passage. When this happens, students should be encouraged to identify specifically what they are having difficulty with. A student might identify a particular word, or he or she may note that the individual words are familiar but the meaning of the passage is unclear.

Active Response

Not only are good readers active in their reading when they encounter problems, but they respond constantly to whatever they read. In this way they make the text their own. As students read they should be encouraged to:

- Make as many connections as they can between what they are reading and what they already know.
- Visualize passages to help clarify their meanings or simply to picture appealing descriptions.
- Ask questions about what they are reading. The questions that go through their minds during reading will help them to examine, and thus better understand, the text. Doing so may also interest them in pursuing their own investigations. The questions may also provide a direction for students' research or exploration.
- Summarize and make predictions as a check on how well they understand what they are reading.

Tips

- Remember that the goal of all reading strategies is comprehension. If a story or article does not make sense, the reader needs to choose whatever strategies will help make sense of it. If one strategy does not work, the reader should try another.
- Always treat problems encountered in text as interesting learning opportunities rather than something to be avoided or dreaded.
- Encourage students to think out loud about text challenges.
- Encourage students to help each other build meaning from text. Rather than telling each other what a word is or what a passage means, students should tell each other how they figured out the meanings of challenging words and passages.
- Encourage students to freely share strategies they have devised on their own. You might want to write these on a large sheet of paper and tape them to the board.
- Assure students that these are not the only strategies that can be used while reading. Any strategy that they find helpful in understanding text is a good useful strategy.

- An absence of questions does not necessarily indicate that students understand what they are reading. Be especially alert to children who never seem to ask questions. Be sure to spend tutorial time with these students occasionally and encourage them to discuss specific selections in the context of difficulties they might have encountered and how they solved them as well as their thoughts about unit concepts.
- Observing students' responses to text will enable you to ascertain not only how well they understand a particular selection but also their facility in choosing and applying appropriate strategies. Take note of the following:
  ✓ Whether the strategies a student uses are effective in the particular situation.
  ✓ Whether the student chooses from a variety of appropriate strategies or uses the same few over and over.
  ✓ Whether the student can explain to classmates which strategies to use in a particular situation and why.
  ✓ Whether the student can identify alternative resources to pursue when the strategies she or he has tried are not effective.
  ✓ Whether students' application of a given strategy is becoming more effective over a period of time.

Becoming familiar and comfortable with these self-monitoring techniques gives readers the confidence to tackle material that is progressively more difficult. A good, mature reader knows that he or she will know when understanding what he or she is reading is becoming a problem and can take steps to correct the situation.

Reading Comprehension Skills

Purpose

An important purpose of writing is to communicate thoughts from one person to another. The goal of instruction in reading comprehension skills is to make students aware of the logic behind the structure of a written piece. If the reader is able to discern the logic of the structure he or she will be more able to tell if the writer's logic is in fact logical and gain an understanding both of the facts and the intent of what they are reading. By keeping the organization of a piece in mind and considering the author's purpose for writing, the reader can go beyond the actual words on the page and make inferences or draw conclusions based on what was read. These are the "between the lines" skills that strong, mature readers utilize to get a complete picture of what the writer is not only saying, but what the writer is trying to say.

Effective comprehension skills include the following:

Point of View

Point of view involves identifying who is telling the story. If a character in the story is telling the story, that one character describes the action and tells what the other characters are like. This is first-person point of view. In such a story, one character will do the talking and use the pronouns *I*, *my*, *me*. All other characters thoughts, feelings, and emotions, will be reported through this one character.

If the story is told in third-person point of view, someone outside the story who is aware of all of the character's thoughts and feelings and actions is relating them to the reader. All of the characters are referred to by their names or the pronouns *he/she*, *him/her*, *it*.

If students stay aware of who is telling a story, they will know whether they are getting the full picture or the picture of events as seen through the eyes of only one character.

Sequencing

The reader can't make any decisions about relationships or events if he or she has no idea in which order the events take place. The reader needs to pay attention to how the writer is conveying the sequence. Does he or she just simply state first this happened and then that happened? Does the writer first present the end of the story and then go back and let the reader know the sequence of events? Knowing what the sequence is and how the writer presents that sequence helps the reader follow the writer's line of thought.

Main Idea and Details

A writer shouldn't be writing if he or she doesn't have something specific to say to his or her reader. The writer may state this main idea in different ways but the reader should always be able to tell you what the writing is about.

To strengthen the main point or main idea of a piece, the writer provides details to help the reader understand. For example, the writer may use comparison and contrast to make a point, provide examples, provide facts, give opinions, give descriptions, give reasons or causes, or give definitions. The reader needs to know what kinds of details he or she is dealing with before making a judgment about the main idea.

Compare and Contrast

Using comparison and contrast is one of the most common and easiest ways a writer uses to get his or her reader to understand a subject. Comparing and contrasting unfamiliar thoughts, ideas, or things with familiar thoughts, ideas and things gives the reader something within his or her own experience base to use in understanding.

> *A good writer thinks carefully about the message he or she wants to deliver and provides a logical structure that the reader can use to help understand the message.*

Cause and Effect

What made this happen? Why did this character act the way he or she did? Knowing the causes of events helps the reader to see the whole story. Being able to use available information to help to identify the probable outcomes (effects) of events or actions will help the reader to logically anticipate the story or article.

Classify and Categorize

The relationships of actions, events, characters, outcomes, and such in a selection should be clear enough for the reader to see the relationships. Putting like things or ideas together can help the reader understand the relationships set up by the writer.

Author's Purpose

Everything that is written is written for a purpose. That purpose may be to entertain, to persuade, or to inform. Knowing why a piece is written—what purpose did the author have for writing the piece, gives the reader an idea of what to expect and perhaps some prior idea of what the author is going to say.

If a writer is writing to entertain, then the reader can generally just relax and let the writer carry him or her away.

If on the other hand, the purpose is to persuade, it will help the reader understand and keep perspective if he or she knows that the purpose is to persuade. The reader can be prepared for whatever argument the writer delivers.

Procedure

Read the Selection

First have students read the selection through using whatever strategies they need to help them to make sense of the selection. After this reading carry on a discussion about the selection that will assure you and students that they did, indeed understand what they read. Discuss any confusion they may have and make whatever clarifications are necessary.

Reread

Revisiting or rereading a selection allows the reader to attend to the specific techniques and tools that authors use to organize and present information in narratives and expository genres. Once you are sure students have a basic understanding of the piece, have students reread the selection in whole or in part concentrating on selected skills. Pick out examples of how the writer organized the piece to help the reader understand.

Limit this concentration on specific comprehension/writing skills to one or two that can be clearly identified in the piece. Trying to concentrate on too many things will just confuse students and make it harder for them to identify any of the organizational devices used by the writer. If a piece has many good examples of several different aspects, then go back to the piece several times over a span of days.

Write

Solidify this connection between how a writer writes and reading by encouraging students to incorporate these different devices into their own writing. As they attempt to use specific organizational devices in their writing, they will get a clearer understanding of how to identify them when they are reading.

Remind students often that the purpose of any skill exercise is to give them tools to use when they are reading and writing. Unless students learn to apply the skills to their own reading—in every area of reading and study—then they are not gaining a full understanding of the purpose of the exercise.

Writing

The ability to write with clarity and coherence is essential to students' success in school as well as in life. Communicating through writing is becoming more and more important in this age of computers and the information super-highway.

Purpose

Many adult writers believe that writing helps them think. For them, writing is a way of transforming knowledge into something more personal, something more useful. Most children have little experience with writing as a self-initiated, enjoyable activity that helps them think. The challenge in teaching writing is to show children how it is used by those who cherish it and use it with profit. Traditionally, students practice skills and demonstrate knowledge when they write in the classroom. In this context, students have little chance to use writing as a tool for expanding their understanding.

An environment with an emphasis on writing provides a multifaceted context for the development of higher-order thinking. Students learn to plan, which allows them to work out ideas in their heads; to set goals, which promotes interest and the ability to monitor progress; and to revise content, which engages them in the reworking and rethinking activities that elevate writing from a craft to a tool for discovery.

Reading is the ultimate source of good models for writing. Learning to read critically can dramatically expand a writer's repertoire and skills. In class discussions and in their Reading and Writing Workbook, students find and discuss exemplary writing techniques and conventions used by authors. Students are always asked to link to their own writing what they learn from writing lessons.

The Writing Process

Providing a routine or process for students to follow will help them to learn a systematic approach to writing. By following the steps of the writing process, students will learn to approach everything they write with purpose and thought. They learn that although writing takes time and thought, there are steps they can take to make their writing clear, coherent, and appealing to their audience.

Prewriting

Purpose

Prewriting is that phase of the writing process when students think through an idea they want to write about. To improve their writing, students should think about their ideas, discuss them, and plan how they want readers to respond. It is important for students to take time before writing to plan ahead so that they can proceed from one phase of the writing process to another without spending unnecessary time making decisions that should have been made earlier. Prewriting is the most time-consuming phase of the writing process, but it may be the most important.

Procedure

Noting Writing Ideas

Students can make notes of writing ideas at any time, with a special time being set aside following the discussion of each reading selection. The writing ideas students get from a discussion might be concerned with the topic of the selection they just read or with an aspect of the author's style. You should keep such a list of writing ideas also, and think aloud occasionally as you make writing idea notes.

> *Deciding what to write about is probably the one thing students find most difficult about the writing process.*

Developing Writing Ideas

When students are ready to start a new writing piece, they should:

✓ look through the Writing Ideas section of their Writing Journals for an idea.

✓ decide how to use this idea in a writing piece.

✓ think about the intended audience and how they want that audience to feel when they read the piece.

✓ talk to others about this writing idea. Write a brief statement of what they hope to accomplish in the writing piece.

Students must make many decisions during the prewriting phase of the writing process. Most students can benefit from talking with a partner or a small group of classmates about these decisions. They may want to discuss some of the following points.

Genre or format of each writing piece. Having decided to use a writing idea such as "a misunderstanding on the first day of school," the student must decide how to use it—for example, as a personal narrative, a realistic fiction story, a poem, a fantasy story, a play, a letter, or whatever.

Audience. Although students' writing pieces will be shared with classmates and with you, some may ultimately be intended for other audiences.

Writing Purpose. Each student should write a sentence that tells the purpose of the piece he or she plans to write. The purpose statement should name the intended audience and the effect the writer hopes to have on that audience. For example, a writer may want to describe her first day in school. The intended audience is kindergarten children, and she intends her story to be humorous. Her purpose statement would read, "I want to write a funny story for little children about my first day in kindergarten."

Planning Writing. Students should make notes on what to include in their writing pieces. Tell students that this list does not need to make sense to anyone but them. They should list key words or phrases to remind them of how they want to develop their ideas. For example, the writer's notes for "My First Day in School" might read:

my dream (night before)

clothes I wore

too many children no desks

last person I talked to

1st impressions of teacher

decided to go home

what my mother said

Some writers may find it helpful to brainstorm with a partner or small group to list words and phrases they might use in a piece of writing. Sometimes this list can be organized into webs of related ideas or details. This kind of prewriting activity might be particularly useful for planning a descriptive piece. For planning a comparison/contrast piece, a writer might use another kind of visual organizer, such as a Venn diagram. Students planning fiction pieces might use a story frame or plot line.

Tips

- Circulate as students make notes on writing ideas or work in small groups on prewriting activities.

- Notice which students are having difficulty coming up with writing ideas. It may help to pair these students with students who have many ideas.

- Do not worry if this phase of the process seems noisy and somewhat chaotic. Students must be allowed to let their imaginations roam in free association and to play around with words and ideas until they hit on something that seems right. They must be permitted to share ideas and help each other.

- Do not worry if, in the early sessions, the class as a whole seems to have few ideas. Through the reading and discussion of selections in the reading anthology, most students will soon have more writing ideas than they can use.

Drafting

Purpose

During the drafting phase of the writing process students shape their planning notes into main ideas and details. They devote their time and effort to getting words down on paper. Whether students are drafting on scrap paper or on computer screens, your role is to encourage each writer to "get it all down." You must also provide a suitable writing environment.

Procedure

Points to Share

Here are some points to share with students before they begin drafting:

- Drafting is putting your ideas down on paper for your own use. Drafts are "sloppy copies."
- Don't worry about spelling. When you don't know how to spell a word, guess at the first letter and leave a space. The context will help you remember the word you want to write here later, when you have time to check the spelling in a dictionary.
- Use abbreviations to help you write faster.
- Crossing out is acceptable. It's fast and won't interrupt your thoughts the way erasing will.
- When you cannot think of a word or do not know what to say at a certain point, leave a space. You can go back later and fill in the gaps.
- Write on every other line so that you will have room to make revisions.
- Write on only one side of a page so that when you revise you can see all of your draft at once.
- As you draft, keep in mind your purpose for writing this piece and your intended audience.

Modeling Drafting

Using a chalkboard, a large chart, or an overhead transparency, model drafting for students by turning your own prewriting notes into sentences and paragraphs. Think aloud as you put your ideas into words. Work as fast as you can. Stress that you are not concerned with handwriting or spelling and that you do not want to be interrupted as you work. As you model, try to do the following:

- Leave a blank space in a sentence to show that you are having difficulty thinking of the best word.
- Put parentheses around a word you intend to change.

- Use abbreviations and invented spellings.
- Cross out words and sentences, or draw arrows to indicate that they should be moved to a different place in your piece.
- Use a caret to insert new words or a new sentence in the text.

> *The purpose of drafting is to let words pour out on paper and to express ideas quickly.*

Turning Notes into Sentences

Adding Details As students begin to write from their notes, they must think about the kinds of details they want to add and write sentences about them. Depending on the kind of piece students are writing, they may want to organize certain kinds of details in a particular manner:

- A personal narrative is probably best ordered as a straightforward chronological retelling of events. Dialogue may help to tell the story.
- A process description should be told in a step-by-step order. The draft should include as much information as possible; each step must be clear. If the piece needs cutting, the student can always do it later.
- A persuasive piece appeals to feelings. It requires facts as well as expert opinions.
- An interview could be written as a series of questions and answers.
- The order of details in a descriptive piece must be easy to follow—from left to right, top to bottom, or whatever order makes sense.
- A fictional story must include details describing characters, setting, and the characters' actions. Dialogue also helps to tell the story.

Using Word Processors for Drafting

Many students enjoy drafting on the screen of a computer more than drafting on paper. Once they have mastered the keyboard, they may find it easier to think as they write. Their first attempts look less sloppy, and they are often more willing to make changes and experiment as they draft. They will certainly find it neater to use the delete key on the word processor than to correct their mistakes by crossing out. Remind students who are drafting on computers to use these features of their word processing programs:

- cut and paste—As they compose, students can move phrases, sentences, and paragraphs from one place to another by cutting and pasting.
- split-screen—If they have made prewriting notes on a computer file, students can see their notes on one part of the screen as they type their drafts on the other part of the screen. They can even copy parts of their notes and "paste" them in their drafts. This feature would be especially helpful to students who are drafting research papers. A writer could copy notes from several different files to draft the research paper.
- saving—Students should take care to save their documents as they compose on the computer. Make sure students understand how to avoid losing or erasing their draft.

Tips

Sometimes the hardest part of drafting is getting the first sentence down on paper. It may help a student who feels stuck even before she or he starts writing to begin a story in the middle or to write the word *Draft* in big letters at the top of the paper.

- If a student feels stuck during drafting, he or she may need to go back and try a different prewriting technique.
- After an initial fifteen or twenty minutes of imposed silence, some children may work better and come up with more ideas if they share as they write.
- You may find that it is difficult to get students to "loosen up" as they draft. Remember, most students have been encouraged to be neat and to erase mistakes when they write. It may help to share some of your own marked-up manuscripts with children.

Purpose

The purpose of revising is to make sure that a piece of writing expresses the writer's ideas clearly and completely. When writers revise, they work on focus, on telling enough, on clarity, and on order. They add or change information. They may experiment with new beginnings and endings. Writers revise by stepping back and reexamining their work. They reevaluate the content and ideas in their work. They ask: *Does it make sense? How can I make it clearer? What can I get rid of? Is this appropriate for my audience?* All of this helps them to become more thoughtful writers and better communicators.

Procedure

Modeling Revising

Students understand and learn best when they have good models to follow. Use the rough draft that you modeled when introducing the drafting phase and model revising it for students. The Teacher's Edition includes suggestions for introducing revising in an early lesson in unit one of each grade level. Model the process in this way:

- On an overhead transparency, show your rough draft. Be sure to include unclear and misplaced passages and incorrect word choices.

- Work quickly through your rough draft, thinking aloud as you revise. For example, "I think I should move this to the end. I need a better word here. This is good. I'll keep it as it is. I should say more about this. I'll add more details to describe this. Now this idea doesn't fit. I'll cross it out."

- Demonstrate some shortcuts for revising. Make arrows to show how you want to move words or sentences. Use an asterisk or a number to indicate an insertion. Cross out words or sentences. Tell students you will worry about neatness and correctness later.

- Elicit and discuss suggestions from students for further revisions. If you agree, make additional changes based on their suggestions. Remind students that during the revision phase of the writing process it is important to get feedback from others.

- Explain that they may revise this draft more than once, writing is a recursive process.

This brief demonstration of revising will not suffice, however, to turn your students into thoughtful revisers of their own writing. If

students need help with revising at any time throughout the year, encourage them to refer to the Writer's Handbook in the back of their anthologies. Conduct minilessons on revising whenever necessary. Most important, continue to model revising as the year progresses.

> *Revising is a difficult concept for students to understand, let alone do. Much modeling, much work in Writing Seminar, and much practice are necessary before they become good at it.*

Model asking questions like the following when revising various kinds of writing:

- About a narrative:
  - ✓ Does my first sentence get my readers attention?
  - ✓ Are events in the story told in an order that makes sense?
  - ✓ Have I included dialogue to help move the story along?
  - ✓ Does the story have a clear focus?
- About a description:
  - ✓ Have I used details that appeal to the senses?
- About a comparison/contrast piece:
  - ✓ Have I made a separate paragraph for each subject discussed?
- About an explanation:
  - ✓ Will readers understand what I am saying?
  - ✓ Are the steps of the explanation in a clear order?
  - ✓ Have I made effective use of signal words?
  - ✓ Have I included enough information?
- About fiction:
  - ✓ Have I described my characters and setting?
  - ✓ Does the plot include a problem, build to a climax, and then describe the resolution of the problem?
- About persuasive writing:
  - ✓ Have I made my position clear?
  - ✓ Does my evidence support my position?
  - ✓ Have I used opinions as well as facts, and have I said whose opinions I used?
  - ✓ Have I directed my writing to my audience?

Help students understand the value of asking questions like the following as they revise:

- About each paragraph:
  - ✓ Does each sentence belong in it?
  - ✓ Does each sentence connect smoothly with the next?
  - ✓ Does each sentence say something about the main idea?
- About each sentence:
  - ✓ Do the sentences read smoothly?
  - ✓ Have I combined sentences that were too short?
  - ✓ Have I broken sentences that were too long into two shorter sentences?
  - ✓ Have I varied the beginnings of the sentences?
- About the words:
  - ✓ Have I changed words that were repeated too often?
  - ✓ Do transition words connect ideas?

Evaluating Student Progress

Use students' writing folders to review their progress. Check first drafts against revised versions to see how each student is able to apply revision strategies. You may find that some students are reluctant to revise. You might then try the following:

- If a student doesn't see anything that needs to be changed or doesn't want to change anything, get him or her to do something to the paper—number the details in a description or the steps in a process, circle exact words, underline the best parts of the paper.

- Once a paper is marked, the student may not be so reluctant to change it. One reason many children do not like to revise is that they think they must recopy everything. This is not always necessary.

- Sometimes writers can cut and paste sections that they want to move. Or they can use carets and deletion marks to show additions and subtractions from a piece.

- Give an especially reluctant student a deadline by which she or he must revise a piece or lose the chance to publish it.

Students will hopefully be writing in other classes and on a variety of topics. Revision techniques can be used to improve writing in any curriculum area. Stress to students the importance of focusing on their intended audience as they revise.

Proofreading

Purpose

Writing that is free of grammatical, spelling, and technical mistakes is clearer and easier for readers to understand. By proofreading their pieces, students will also notice which errors they make repeatedly and will learn not to make them in the future.

After a piece of writing has been revised for content and style, students must read it carefully line by line to make sure that it contains no errors. This activity, the fourth phase of the writing process, is called proofreading and is a critical step that must occur before a piece of writing can be published. Students can begin proofreading a piece when they feel that it has been sufficiently revised.

Procedure

Using What They Have Learned

Students should be expected to proofread at a level appropriate to their grade. Young authors should not be held responsible for skills they have not yet learned. Older students will be able to check for a greater variety of errors than younger students and should be expected to take greater responsibility for their proofreading. For example, students in second grade can be expected to check for and correct omitted capital letters at the beginning of sentences, but they should not necessarily be expected to understand and correct capital letters in proper nouns or in names of organizations. Older students will have mastered many more grammatical, mechanical, usage, and spelling skills and can be expected to perform accordingly. When you spot an error related to a skill beyond a student's level, make clear to the student that you do not expect her or him to be responsible for the mistake, but do explain that the error still needs to be corrected. The following suggestions may be useful as you introduce proofreading to the children and help them develop their proofreading skills.

Proofreading Checklist

Have students use a proofreading checklist similar to the one shown here to help them remember the steps for effective proofreading. This checklist is on the Writing Folder provided with **SRA/Open Court Reading**. If your class does not have this writing folder, you might copy this checklist onto a piece of chart paper and place it in the writing center or on a bulletin board for students to refer to when they proofread.

Read each sentence.

✓ Does each sentence begin with a capital letter and end with correct punctuation?

✓ Do you notice any sentence fragments or run-on sentences?

✓ Are words missing from the sentence?

✓ Is any punctuation or capitalization missing from within the sentence?

✓ Do you notice any incorrect grammar or incorrect word usage in the sentence?

✓ Do you notice any misspelled words?

Look at the paragraphs.

✓ Are the paragraphs indented?

✓ Can very long paragraphs be broken into two paragraphs?

✓ Can very short paragraphs be combined into one paragraph?

Proofreader's Marks

Children should use standard proofreader's marks to indicate the changes they wish to make. Explain to students that these marks are a kind of code used to show which alterations to make without a long explanation. Students may also be interested to know that professional writers, editors, and proofreaders use these same marks.

You may want to review these marks one by one, illustrating on the chalkboard how to use them. For example, they may insert a word or a phrase by using a caret (^). If students wish to insert more text than will fit above the line, they may write in the margin or attach another sheet of paper. It may be a good idea, when such extensive corrections are made, for students to proofread their final copy carefully to make sure they have included all their alterations.

> *Proofreading their work helps students to communicate their ideas more effectively.*

Teacher Modeling

Model good proofreading skills for students by proofreading a piece of your own writing. You may want to be sure to include specific errors (misspelled words, incorrect capitalization, repeated words, incorrect paragraph indentation, etc.) so that you will use all the proofreader's marks as you model proofreading. Copy your draft onto an overhead transparency and proofread the piece together.

Sentence Lifting

Sentence lifting is a very effective method of showing students how to effectively proofread their own work.

- Choose several pieces of student writing and look for common errors.

- On an overhead, write several sentences. Include at least one sentence that has no errors.

- Tell students that you are going to concentrate on one type of error at a time. For example, first you will concentrate on spelling.

- Ask students to read the first sentence and point out any words they feel are spelled incorrectly. Do not erase errors. Cross them out and write the correctly spelled word above the crossed out word.

  quickly   basement
  Margie ran ~~quikly~~ through the ~~basment~~

- Next move to a different type of error. Ask students to check for capitalization and punctuation.

  quickly   basement
  Margie ran ~~quikly~~ through the ~~basment~~ ⌄

- Continue in this way, correcting errors as you go through the sample sentences.

Because students are working on their own sentences, they will be more inclined to both pay attention to what is going on and better understand the corrections that are made.

Using a Word Processor

If the children are using a word processor to write their pieces, they may wish to run a spell check on their document.

Caution them, however, that even the most sophisticated computer cannot catch every spelling error. Misuse of homophones and other words will not be caught by the computer if the misused words appear in the computer's dictionary. For example, if a student types *form* instead of *from*, the computer will not register a mistake because form is also a word.

Preparing the Final Copy

When students feel that they have thoroughly proofread their pieces, they should copy the work onto another sheet of paper, using their best handwriting, or type the work on a computer or typewriter. They should then check this copy against the proofread copy to make sure that they made all the changes correctly and did not introduce any new errors. You may need to proofread and correct students' papers one final time before publishing to make sure that they have caught all errors.

Tips

- The publishing conference is a good time to assess students' proofreading abilities. Notice their proofreading skills, including comprehension of the concept, ability to use proofreader's marks correctly, and corrections from you and other students. Also note any improvement in writing based upon proofreading corrections. For example, does a student no longer omit end punctuation because he or she noticed this error repeatedly during proofreading?

- You may also wish to circulate as children are proofreading on their own or in pairs.

  ✓ Are students able to check references when they are unsure of a spelling or usage?

  ✓ Are students criticizing each other's work constructively?

  ✓ Note students who are having difficulty. You may wish to address these difficulties during individual conferences.

Publishing

Publishing is the process of bringing private writing to the reading public.

Purpose

The purpose of writing is to communicate. Unless students are writing in a journal, they will want to present their writing to the public. Such sharing helps children to learn about themselves and others, provides an opportunity for them to take pride in their hard work, and thus motivates them to further writing.

Publishing their work helps motivate children to improve such skills as spelling, grammar, and handwriting. Publishing can be as simple as displaying papers on a bulletin board or as elaborate as creating a class newspaper. Publishing will not—indeed should not—always require large blocks of class time. Students will wish to spend more time elaborately presenting their favorite pieces and less time on other works. If students take an inordinate amount of time to publish their work, you may want to coach them on how to speed up the process.

Procedure

Publishing Conference

An individual publishing conference may be useful to students who have finished proofreading and correcting a piece of writing. In the conference, each student will discuss:

- what he or she would like to publish.
- how to prepare the piece for publication.
- what form the published work should take.

You will read through the piece, and tell the student if any corrections still need to be made. You may also make some suggestions about the best way to publish a piece if a student has trouble coming up with an idea. Make suggestions and give criticism as needed, but remember that students must retain ownership of their publishing. Leave final decisions about form and design of their work up to individual students.

Students should think about whether they want to illustrate their writing.

- Photographs might illustrate a personal narrative or biography.
- Drawings might illustrate a piece of fiction.
- A chart or graph might illustrate an article.
- Remind the children to provide captions if necessary.

Help students plan each page of their publication. They will need to decide where to place text in relation to any art they are using. Remind students to think about their intended audience when they are deciding on the form for their published piece. Will the form they have selected present their ideas effectively to the people they want to reach?

Publishing Checklist

The following checklist will help students when they are publishing their work. (Not every question applies to every form of publishing.)

✓ Have I chosen my best piece?
✓ Have I revised it to make it better?
✓ Have I proofread it carefully?
✓ Have I decided upon my illustrations?
✓ Have I recopied my piece carefully and illustrated it?
✓ Have I numbered the pages?
✓ Have I made a cover that tells the title and my name?

You may wish to copy this checklist and post it in the publishing center or in some other prominent place in the classroom.

Writing Seminar

Purpose

The purpose of Writing Seminar (Levels K–6) is for students to discuss their work in progress and to share ideas for improving it.

Writing Seminar is one of the activities in which students may choose to participate during **Independent Work Time**. Students will meet in small groups to read and discuss one another's writing. One student reads a piece in progress. Other students comment on the writing and ask questions about the ideas behind the writing. The student whose work is being critiqued writes down the comments made by his or her classmates and decides how to use these comments to make the writing better.

Procedure

Early Writing Seminar

To begin the conference, have one student writer read his or her revised draft as other students listen carefully. When the student has finished, invite other children to retell the story in their own words. If they have trouble retelling the story, the writer knows that he or she must make some ideas clearer.

Then have listeners who wish to comment raise their hands. The writer calls on each in turn. The listeners ask questions or make comments about the writing, telling, for example, what they like about it or what they might change to make it better. After several comments have been made, the writer notes any information that she or he might use. Another student then reads his or her piece.

Guidelines for Peer Conferencing

In an early session, work with students to establish guidelines for peer conferencing. You might suggest rules such as the following:

- Listen quietly while someone else is speaking.
- Think carefully before you comment on another person's work.
- Make your comments specific.
- Comment on something that you like about the piece before you comment on something that needs to be improved.
- Discuss your work quietly so as not to disturb the rest of the class.

Modeling Conference Behavior

You may need to model meaningful comments and questions. Examples of questions and sentence starters follow:

- What was your favorite part?
- I like the part where (or when)
- I like the way you describe
- What happened after . . . ?
- I'd like to know more about
- Why did _____ happen?
- What do you think is the most important part?

Teacher Conferencing

During Writing Seminar, you will want to schedule individual conferences with students to help them evaluate their writing so that they can recognize problems and find ways to solve them. Teacher conferences are useful during all phases of the writing process, but they are crucial during the revising phase. Writing conferences give you an opportunity to observe the children as they evaluate their writing, solve problems, make decisions about their work, and take responsibility for the development and completion of their work. The basic procedure for teacher conferences is as follows:

- Have the student read his or her first draft aloud. Offer a specific comment.
- Encourage the student to review feedback received on his or her draft during peer conferencing and to think aloud about possible changes.
- Ask questions that will help the student clarify her or his thinking about how to revise. (Try not to lead the student with content questions. You want to teach how to revise, not what to write.)
- Review strategies and references that the student could use to improve her or his work.
- Conclude the conference by having the student state his or her plan or goal for continuing work on the piece.

During teacher conferences, you might use the following responses to student writing.

- To open communication with the writer:
  - ✓ How is the writing going?
  - ✓ Tell me about your piece.
  - ✓ How did you get your ideas?
- To validate the writer's work and give encouragement:
  - ✓ I like the part where . . . .
  - ✓ I like the way you open your piece by . . . .
  - ✓ I like your description of . . . .
- To get the writer to think about clarity of meaning:
  - ✓ I wonder about . . . .
  - ✓ What happened after . . . .
  - ✓ Why did . . . ?
- To get the writer to think about direction and about writing strategies:
  - ✓ What do you plan to do with your piece?
  - ✓ How will you go about doing that?
  - ✓ What could I do to help you?

Concentrate on one phase of the writing process at a time. You might pay particular attention to revising content, proofreading content, or publishing. Remember to keep conferences brief and to the point. If you are calling the conference, prepare your comments in advance. Usually, a student will request a conference with you, but be sure that you confer regularly with every student if only to check that each one is continuing to write, revise, and publish. The following are some questions to ask yourself as you consider a student's first draft:

- Does the beginning capture my attention?
- Is this a good topic sentence?
- Is the ending conclusive?
- Is this information related to the topic?
- Does the sentence structure need to be varied by combining or shortening sentences?
- Is there a better word to express this idea?

As you confer with students, also recognize growth—evidence in the text that a student has applied what he or she learned in earlier conferences to another piece of writing. Some cues to look for when evaluating a student's growth as a writer include the following:

- The writer identifies problems.
- The writer thinks of solutions to a problem and understands why some solutions will work and some will not.
- The writer recognizes when and how the text needs to be reorganized.
- The writer identifies ideas in the text that need elaboration.
- The writer makes thoughtful changes and pays attention to detail.
- The writer takes advantage of peer and teacher conferences, books, and other resources to improve his or her writing.

Tips

- Completed pieces as well as works in progress can be shared during Writing Seminar. In the upper grades, as pieces become longer, a student may read only part of a piece—a favorite part, a part where she or he is having problems, one that has been revised, and so on.
- When a student requests a conference with you, focus first on the student's stated problem. Determine whether a problem really exists or whether you can simply assure the student that everything is fine. If there is no problem, you may end the conference with your reassurance. If there is a problem, continue the conference. Students who do not want to share their work may lack confidence in their writing abilities. Work with these students individually until they become acquainted with the process.

Classroom Discussion

The more students are able to discuss what they are learning, voice their confusions, and compare perceptions of what they are learning, the deeper and more meaningful their learning becomes.

Purpose

It is in discussions that students are exposed to points of view different from their own, and it is through discussion that they learn how to express their thoughts and opinions coherently. Through discussion, students add to their own knowledge that of their classmates and learn to explain themselves coherently and to ask insightful questions that help them better understand what they have read and all that they are learning through their inquiry/research and explorations. The purpose of Classroom Discussion is to provide a sequence through which discussion can proceed.

Procedure

Reflecting on the Selection

After students have finished reading a selection, provide an opportunity for them to engage in **whole-group** discussion about the selection. Students should:

- Check to see whether the questions they asked before reading have been answered. Encourage them to discuss whether any unanswered questions should still be answered and if so have them add those questions to the Concept and Question Board.

- Discuss any new questions that have arisen because of the reading. Encourage students to decide which of these questions should go on the Concept and Question Board.

- Share what they expected to learn from reading the selection and tell whether expectations were met.

- Talk about whatever has come to mind while reading the selection. This discussion should be an informal sharing of impressions of, or opinions about, the selection; it should never take on the aspects of a question-and-answer session about the selection.

- Give students ample opportunity to ask questions or to share their thoughts about the selection. Participate as an active member of the group, making your own observations about information in a selection or modeling your own appreciation of a story. Be especially aware of unusual and interesting insights suggested by students so that these insights can be recognized and discussed. To help students learn to keep the discussion student-centered, have each student choose the next speaker instead of handing the discussion back to you.

Recording Ideas

As students finish discussions about their reactions to a selection, they should be encouraged to record their thoughts, feelings, reactions, and ideas about the selection or the subject of the selection in their Writing Journals. This will not only help keep the selections fresh in students' minds, it will strengthen their writing abilities and help them learn how to write about their thoughts and feelings.

Students may find that the selection gave them ideas for their own writing, or it could have reminded them of some person or incident in their own lives. Perhaps the selection answered a question that has been on their minds or raised a question they had never thought of before. Good, mature writers—especially professional writers—learn the value of recording such thoughts and impressions quickly before they fade. Students should be encouraged to do this also.

Handing Off

Handing off (Levels 1–6) is a method of turning over to students the primary responsibility for controlling discussion. Often, students who are taking responsibility for controlling a discussion tend to have all "turns" go through the teacher. The teacher is the one to whom attention is transferred when a speaker finishes, and the teacher is the one who is expected to call on the next speaker, the result being that the teacher remains the pivotal figure in the discussion.

Having the children "hand off" the discussion to other students instead of the teacher encourages them to retain complete control of the discussion and to become more actively involved in the learning process. When a student finishes his or her comments, that student should choose (hand the discussion off to) the next speaker. In this way, students maintain a discussion without relying on the teacher to decide who speaks.

When handing off is in place, the teacher's main roles are to occasionally remind students to hand off and to monitor the discussion to ensure that everyone gets a chance to contribute. The teacher may say, for example, "Remember, not just boys (or girls)," or "Try to choose someone who has not had a chance to talk yet."

In order for handing off to work effectively, a seating arrangement that allows students to see one another is essential. A circle or a semicircle is effective. In addition, all of the students need to have copies of the materials being discussed.

Actively encourage this handing-off process by letting students know that they, not you, are in control of the discussion.

If students want to remember thoughts about, or reactions to, a selection, suggest that they record these in the Writing Journal. Encourage students to record the thoughts, feelings, or reactions that are elicited by any reading they do.

Exploring Concepts within the Selection

To provide an opportunity for collaborative learning and to focus on the concepts, have students form small groups and spend time discussing what they have learned about the concepts from this selection. Topics may include new information that they have acquired or new ideas that they have had.

Students should always base their discussions on postings from the Concept and Question Board as well as on previous discussions of the concept. The small-group discussions should be ongoing throughout the unit; during this time students should continue to compare and contrast any new information with their previous ideas, opinions, and impressions about the concepts. Does this selection help confirm their ideas? Does it contradict their thinking? Has it changed their outlook?

As students discuss the concepts in small groups, circulate around the room to make sure that each group stays focused upon the selection and the concepts. After students have had some time to discuss the information and the ideas in the selection, encourage each group to formulate some statements about the concept that apply to the selection.

Sharing Ideas about Concepts

Have a representative from each group report and explain the group's ideas to the rest of the class. Then have the class formulate one or more general statements related to the unit concepts and write these statements on the Concept and Question Board. As students progress through the unit, they will gain more and more confidence in suggesting additions to the Concept and Question Board.

Visual Aids During this part of the discussion, you may find it helpful to use visual aids to help students as they build the connections to the unit concepts. Not all units or concepts will lend themselves to this type of treatment; however, aids such as timelines, charts, graphs, or pictographs may help students see how each new selection adds to their growing knowledge of the concepts.

Encourage students to ask questions about the concepts that the selection may have raised. Have students list on the Concept and Question Board those questions that cannot be answered immediately and that they want to explore further.

Exploring Concepts across Selections

As each new selection is read, encourage students to discuss its connection with the other selections and with the unit concepts. Also encourage students to think about selections that they have read from other units and how they relate to the concepts for this unit.

Ultimately, it is this ability to make connections between past knowledge and new knowledge that allows any learner to gain insights into what is being studied. The goal of the work with concepts and the discussions is to help students to start thinking in terms of connections—how is this like what I have learned before? Does this information confirm, contradict, or add a completely different layer to that which I already know about this concept? How can the others in the class have such different ideas than I do when we just read the same selection? Why is so much written about this subject?

Learning to make connections and to delve deeper through self-generated questions gives students the tools they need to become effective, efficient, lifelong learners.

Tips

- Discussions offer a prime opportunity for you to introduce, or seed, new ideas about the concepts. New ideas can come from a variety of sources: students may draw on their own experiences or on the books or videos they are studying; you may introduce new ideas into the discussion; or you may, at times, invite experts to speak to the class.

- If students do not mention an important idea that is necessary to the understanding of some larger issue, you may "drop" that idea into the conversation and, indeed, repeat it several times to make sure that it does get picked up. This seeding may be subtle ("I think that might be important here") or quite direct ("This is a big idea, one that we will definitely need to understand and one that we will return to regularly").

Discussion is an integral part of learning.

- In order to facilitate this process for each unit, you must be aware of the unit concepts and be able to recognize and reinforce them when they arise spontaneously in discussions. If central unit concepts do not arise naturally, then, and only then, will you seed these ideas by direct

modeling. The more you turn discussions over to students, the more involved they will become, and the more responsibility they will take for their own learning. Make it your goal to become a participant in, rather than the leader of, class discussions.

- Help students to see that they are responsible for carrying on the discussion. After a question is asked always wait instead of jumping in with a comment or an explanation. Although this wait time may be uncomfortable at first, students will come to understand that the discussion is their responsibility and that you will not jump in every time there is a hesitation.

- As the year progresses, students will become more and more adept at conducting and participating in meaningful discussions about what they have read. These discussions will greatly enhance students' understanding of the concepts that they are exploring.

Discussion Starters

- I didn't know that . . . .
- Does anyone know . . . .
- I figured out that . . . .
- I liked the part where . . . .
- I'm still confused about . . . .
- This made me think . . . .
- I agree with _____ because . . . .
- I disagree with _____ because . . . .
- The reason I think . . . .

Inquiry/Research and Exploration

Research and Exploration form the heart of the **SRA/Open Court Reading** program. In order to encourage students to understand how reading can enhance their lives and help them to become mature, educated adults, they are asked in each unit to use what they are learning in the unit as the basis for further exploration and research. The unit information is simply the base for their explorations.

There are two types of units in the **SRA/Open Court Reading** program—units based on universal topics of interest such as Friendship, Perseverance, and Courage and research units that provide students a very solid base of information upon which they can base their own inquiry and research. Units delving into such areas as fossils, astronomy, and medicine invite students to become true researchers by choosing definite areas of interest—problems or questions to research in small cooperative groups and then present to their classmates. In this way, students gain much more knowledge of the subject than they would have simply by reading the selections in the unit.

The selections in the units are organized so that each selection will add more information or a different perspective to students' growing bodies of knowledge.

Exploring through Reflective Activities

Purpose

The units in **SRA/Open Court Reading** that deal with universal topics will be explored through reflective activities. These units—such as Courage, Friendship, and Risks and Consequences—are organized to help students expand their perspectives in familiar areas. As they explore and discuss the unit concepts related to each topic, students are involved in activities that extend their experiences and offer opportunities for reflection. Such activities include writing, drama, art, interviews, debates, and panel discussions. Throughout each unit, students may be involved in a single ongoing exploratory activity, or they may participate in a number of different activities. They may choose to produce a final written project or a visual aid to share with the rest of the class the new knowledge that they have gained from their reflective activities. During **Independent Work Time** students will work individually or in collaborative groups on their exploration and/or projects.

The reflective activities will be activities of students' own choosing that allow them to explore the unit concepts more fully. They are free, of course, to make other choices or to devise activities of their own.

Procedure

Choosing an Area to Explore

Students may work on the reflective activities alone, in pairs, or in small groups. They have the option of writing about or presenting their findings to the whole group upon completion. Before choosing a reflective activity, students should decide what concept-related question or problem they wish to explore. Generally, it is better for students to generate questions or problems after they have engaged in some discussion but before they have had a chance to consult source materials. This approach is more likely to bring forth ideas that students actually wonder about or wish to understand. Students may also look at the questions posted on the Concept and Question Board or introduce fresh ideas inspired by material they have just finished reading. Students who are working in pairs or in small groups should confer with one another before making a decision about what to explore. Some of the students may need your assistance in deciding upon, or narrowing down, a question or a problem so that it can be explored more easily. A good way to model this process for students is to make webs for a few of your own ideas on the chalkboard and to narrow these ideas down to a workable question or problem.

Organizing the Group

After a question or a problem has been chosen, the children may choose an activity that will help them to explore that problem or question. The students' next responsibility is to decide who is going to explore which facet of the question or the problem (when they are conducting a literature search, for example) or who is going to perform which task related to the particular reflective activity (when they are writing and performing an original playlet or puppet show, for example). Lastly, students need to decide how, or if, they want to present their findings. For instance, after conducting a literature search, some students may want to read and discuss passages from a book with a plot or theme that relates to a unit concept. Other students may prefer acting out and discussing scenes from the book.

Deciding How to Explore

The following suggestions may help you and your students choose ways in which to pursue their explorations. You may want to post this list in the classroom so that groups have access to it as they decide what they want to explore and how they want to proceed.

Exploration Activities

- Conduct a literature search to pursue a question or a problem. Discussion or writing may follow.
- Write and produce an original playlet or puppet show based on situations related to the concepts.
- Play a role-playing game to work out a problem related to the concepts.
- Stage a panel discussion with audience participation on a question or problem.
- Hold a debate on an issue related to the concept.
- Write an advice column dealing with problems related to the concepts.
- Write a personal-experience story related to the concepts.
- Invite experts to class. Formulate questions to ask.
- Conduct an interview with someone on a subject related to the concepts.
- Produce and carry out a survey on an issue or question related to the concept.
- Produce a picture or photo essay about the concept.

EXAMPLE: In the Heritage unit in grade 5 of **SRA/Open Court Reading,** students read "In Two Worlds: A Yup'ik Eskimo Family." This selection is about how three generations of Eskimos living in Alaska near the Arctic strive to adopt the best of modern ways without abandoning their traditional values. During the class discussion, some students may note that Alice and Billy Rivers want their children to learn both the new and the old ways of living. As the discussion continues, many students may conclude from the story that the older generations hope that future generations will continue to value their roots and their cultural traditions. Students then relate this story to their own heritage. Some students may share information about their customs or traditions.

Students choose some reflective activities that will help them learn more about family heritage and that will answer some of their questions about the unit concepts. Some students may be interested in interviewing family members or close family friends about their cultural traditions and heritages. These students review what they know about interviewing. They proceed by:

- Contacting in advance the person(s) they want to interview.
- Preparing a list of questions to ask.
- Preparing a list of subjects to discuss, deciding how to record the interview (by audiotape, videotape, or taking notes).
- Deciding whether to photograph the person and, if so, getting permission to do so in advance—collecting the equipment necessary for conducting the interview.

After they conduct the interviews, students decide how they wish to present the information that they have collected.

> *Exploring through reflective activities allows students to gain a wider perspective on a concept by relating it to their own experiences. Students quickly become aware that it is their responsibility to learn and to help their peers learn more about the unit concepts.*

EXAMPLE: Another group of students in the same fifth-grade class may be more interested in planning a photo essay about one family or about a neighborhood with many families belonging to a particular culture. These students may decide to reexamine "In Two Worlds" to notice how the text and the photographs complement each other and what information is conveyed in each photograph. They may also decide to examine some photo essays listed in the unit bibliography. These students will need to make some advance preparations as well. They proceed by:

- Determining which neighborhood and which family or families to photograph.
- Contacting in advance the persons to be interviewed and photographed.
- Touring the neighborhood in advance of the photo shoot.
- Making a list of questions to ask the family or families about their heritage or about their neighborhood.

- Thinking about what information to include in their essay so that they can determine what photographs to take.
- Collecting the equipment necessary for conducting interviews and photographing subjects.

After students collect the information and take photographs, they may write and organize the photo essay and present it to the class. The teacher should remind students of the phases of the writing process and encourage them to proofread and revise their work until they are completely pleased with it. Students can continue discussing family heritage and raising any new questions that they wish to explore. The teacher should remind them that as they read further, they may think of a variety of ways to explore the unit concepts. The teacher should then ask students to post on the Concept and Question Board any new questions they have about family heritage. Students should sign or initial their questions so that they can identify classmates with similar interests and exchange ideas with them. The teacher should encourage students to feel free to write an answer or a note on someone else's question or to consult the board for ideas for their own explorations. From time to time, the teacher should post his or her own questions on the Concept and Question Board.

Tips

- The bibliographies located at the end of each unit in the student anthology and the Classroom Library contain books related to the unit concepts. Remind students that these are good sources of information and that they should consult them regularly— especially when they are exploring concept-related ideas and questions.
- Some students work better within a specified time frame. Whenever they are beginning a new activity, discuss with the children a reasonable period of time within which they will be expected to complete their explorations. Post the completion date somewhere in the classroom so that students can refer to it and pace themselves accordingly. At first, you may have to help them determine a suitable deadline, but eventually they should be able to make this judgment on their own.

Exploring through Research

Purpose

Students come to school with a wealth of fascinating questions. Educators need to capitalize on this excitement for learning and natural curiosity. A classroom in which only correct answers are accepted and students are not allowed to make errors and consider alternative possibilities to questions can quickly deaden this natural curiosity and enthusiasm. The purpose of the research aspect of this program is to capitalize on students' questions and natural curiosity by using a proven structure. This structure helps students to not get lost or bogged down but at the same time to preserve the open-ended character of real research, which can lead to unexpected findings and to questions that were not originally considered.

There is a conventional approach to school research papers that can be found, with minor variations, in countless textbooks. It consists of a series of steps such as the following: select a topic, narrow the topic, collect materials, take notes, outline, and write. By following these steps a student may produce a presentable paper, but the procedure does not constitute research in a meaningful sense and indeed gives students a distorted notion of what research is about. We see students in universities and even in graduate schools still following this procedure when they do library research papers or literature reviews; we see their dismay when their professors regard such work as mere cutting and pasting and ask them where their original contribution is.

Even elementary school students can produce works of genuine research—research that seeks answers to real questions or solutions to real problems. This skill in collecting and analyzing information is a valuable tool in the adult world in which adults, as consumers, are constantly analyzing new information and making informed decisions on the basis of this information. Preparing students for the analytic demands of adult life and teaching them how to find answers to their questions are goals of education.

Procedure

In order to make the Research productive, the following important principles are embodied in this approach:

1. Research is focused on problems, not topics.
2. Conjectures—opinions based on less than complete evidence or proof—guide the research; the research does not simply produce conjectures.
3. New information is gathered to test and revise conjectures.
4. Discussion, ongoing feedback, and constructive criticism are important in all phases of the research but especially in the revising of problems and conjectures.
5. The cycle of true research is essentially endless, although presentations of findings are made from time to time; new findings give rise to new problems and conjectures and thus to new cycles of research.

Following a Process

While working with the research units, students are encouraged to follow a set pattern or cycle in order to keep their research activities focused and on track. Students may go through these steps many times before they come to the end of their research. Certainly for adult researchers, this cycle of question, conjecture, research, and reevaluate can go on for years and in some cases lifetimes.

This cycle includes:

1. **Decide on a problem or question to research.** Students should identify a question or problem that they truly wonder about or wish to understand and then form research groups with other students who have the same interests.
   - My problem or question is _____

2. **Formulate an idea or conjecture about the research problem.** Students should think about and discuss with classmates possible answers to their research problems or questions and meet with their research groups to discuss and record their ideas or conjectures.
   - My idea/conjecture/theory about this question or problem is _____

3. **Identify needs and make plans.** Students should identify knowledge needs related to their conjectures and meet with their research groups to determine which resources to consult and to make individual job assignments. Students should also meet periodically with the teacher, other classmates, and research groups to present preliminary findings and make revisions to their problems and conjectures on the basis of these findings.
   - I need to find out _____
   - To do this, I will need these resources _____
   - My role in the group is _____
   - This is what I have learned so far _____
   - This is what happened when we presented our findings _____

4. **Reevaluate the problem or question based on what we have learned so far and the feedback we have received.**
   - My revised problem or question is _____

5. **Revise the idea or conjecture.**
   - My new conjecture about this problem is _____

6. **Identify new needs and make new plans.**
   - Based on what I found out, I still need to know _____
   - To do this, I will need these resources _____
   - This is what I have learned _____
   - This is what happened when we presented our new findings _____

Procedure for Choosing a Problem to Research

1. Discuss with students the nature of the unit. Explain to students that the unit they are reading is a research unit and that they will produce and publish in some way the results of their explorations. They are free to decide what problems or questions they wish to explore, whom they want to work with, and how they want to present their finished products. They may publish a piece of writing, produce a poster, write and perform a play, or use any other means to present the results of their explorations and research. They may work with partners or in small groups.

2. Discuss with students the schedule you have planned for research projects: how long the project is expected to take, how much time will be available for research, when the first presentation will be due. This schedule will partly determine the nature of the problems that students should be encouraged to work on and the depth of the inquiry students will be encouraged to pursue.

3. Have students talk about things they wonder about that are related to the unit subject. For example, in the grade 3 unit, Money, students might wonder where money in the money machine comes from or how prices are determined. Conduct a free-floating discussion of questions about the unit subject.

4. Brainstorm possible questions for students to think about. It is essential that the children's own ideas and questions be the starting point of all inquiry. *Helpful hint:* For the first research unit, you might wish to generate a list of your own ideas, having students add to this list and having them choose from it.

5. Using their wonderings, model for the children the difference between a research topic and a research problem or question by providing several examples. For example, have them consider the difference between the topic California and the problem, *Why do so many people move to California?* Explain to them that if they choose to research the topic California, everything they look up under the subject heading or index entry California will be related in some way to their topic. Therefore, it will be quite difficult to choose which information to record. This excess of information also creates problems in organizing their research. Clearly, then, this topic is too broad and general. Choosing a specific question or problem, one that particularly interests them, helps them narrow their exploration and advance their understanding. Some possible ideas for questions can be found in the unit introduction. Ideas can also be generated as you and your students create a web of their questions or problems related to the unit subject. For example, questions related to the subject California might include the following:

- Why do so many people move to California?
- How have the different groups of people living in California affected the state?

6. A good research problem or question not only requires students to consult a variety of sources but is engaging and adds to the groups' knowledge of the concepts. Furthermore, good problems generate more questions. Help students understand that the question, *Why do so many people move to California?* is an easy one to research. Many sources will contribute to an answer to the question, and all information located can be easily evaluated in terms of usefulness in answering the question. Helpful hint: Students' initial responses may indeed be topics instead of problems or questions. If so, the following questions might be helpful:
   - What aspect of the topic really interests you?
   - Can you turn that idea into a question?

7. Remember that this initial problem or question serves only as a guide for research. As students begin collecting information and collaborating with classmates, their ideas will change, and they can revise their research problem or question. Frequently, students do not sufficiently revise their problems until after they have had time to consider their conjectures and collect information.

8. As students begin formulating their research problems, have them elaborate on their reasons for wanting to research their stated problems. They should go beyond simple expressions of interest or liking and indicate what is puzzling, important, or potentially informative, and so forth, about the problems they have chosen.

9. At this stage, students' ideas will be of a very vague and limited sort. The important thing is to start them thinking about what really interests them and what value it has to them and the class.

10. Have students present their proposed problems or questions, along with reasons for their choices, and have an open discussion of how promising proposed problems are. As students present their proposed problems, ask them what new things do they think they will be learning from their exploration and how that will add to the group's growing knowledge of the concepts. This constant emphasis on group knowledge building will help set a clear purpose for students' research.

Even elementary school students can produce works of genuine research—research that seeks answers to real questions or solutions to real problems.

11. Form research groups. To make it easier for students to form groups, they may record their problems on the chalkboard or on self-sticking notes. Final groups should be constituted in the way you find best for your class—by self-selection, by assignment on the basis of common interests, or by some combination of methods. Students can then meet during **Independent Work Time** to agree on a precise statement of their research problem, the nature of their expected research contributions, and lists of related questions that may help later in assigning individual roles. They should also record any scheduling information that can be added to the planning calendar.

Using Technology

The **Research CD-ROM** (Levels 1–6), an interactive software program supports student research by helping them organize and conduct their research. In addition, SRA's Home Page on the World Wide Web directs students to resources they can use in their research. Also, a Student Bulletin Board supports communication and collaboration with students across the country. Just click on www.SRA-4kids.com/student.

Students using *SRA/Open Court Reading* have the opportunity and the wherewithal to expand their research groups nationwide and find out what other *SRA/Open Court Reading* students are doing with their unit explorations.

Tips

- If students are careful about the problems or questions they choose to research, they should have few problems in following through with the research. If the problem is too broad or too narrow, they will have problems.
- Have students take sufficient time in assessing their needs—both knowledge needs and physical needs in relation to their research. Careful preplanning can help the research progress smoothly with great results.
- Encourage students to reevaluate their needs often so they are not wasting time finding things they already have or ignoring needs that they haven't noticed.
- Interim presentations of material are every bit as important, if not more so, than final presentations. It is during interim presentations that students have the opportunity to rethink and reevaluate their work and change direction or decide to carry on with their planned research.

Independent Work Time

Every teacher and every student needs time during the day to organize, take stock of work that is done, make plans for work that needs doing, and finish up incomplete projects. In addition, time is needed for individualization and for peer conferencing.

Purpose

Independent Work Time is the period of time each day in which students work independently or collaboratively to practice and review material taught in the lessons.

A variety of activities may occur during this time. Students may work on a specific daily assignment, complete an ongoing project, work on unit exploration activities, focus on writing, or choose from among a wide range of possibilities. With lots of guidance and encouragement, students gradually learn to make decisions about their use of time and materials and to collaborate with their peers.

A goal of **Independent Work Time** is to get students to work independently. This is essential since **Independent Work Time** is also the time during which the teacher can work with individuals or groups of children to reinforce learning, to provide extra help for those having difficulties, to extend learning, or to assess the progress of the class or of individuals.

Procedure

Initially, for many students, you will need to structure **Independent Work Time** carefully. Eventually, students will automatically go to the appropriate areas, take up ongoing projects, and get the materials they will need. **Independent Work Time** will evolve slowly from a very structured period to a time when children make choices and move freely from one activity to the next.

Adhere firmly to **Independent Work Time** guidelines. By the time the children have completed the first few weeks of school, they should feel confident during **Independent Work Time**. If not, continue to structure the time and limit options. For young children, early periods of **Independent Work Time** may run no more than five to eight minutes. The time can gradually increase to fifteen minutes or longer as the children gain independence. Older students may be able to work longer and independently from the very beginning of the school year.

Introducing Independent Work Time

Introduce **Independent Work Time** to the children by telling them that every day there will be a time when they are expected to work on activities on their own or in small groups. For young children in the beginning, you will assign the **Independent Work Time** activities to help

the children learn to work on their own. Point out the shelf or area of the classroom where **Independent Work Time** materials are stored. Tell the children that when they finish working with the materials for one activity, they are to choose something else from the **Independent Work Time** shelf. New activity materials will be added to the shelf from time to time. Make sure that the children know that they may always look at books during **Independent Work Time**. If children have writing journals, you may want to make these available at the **Independent Work Time** shelf as well.

Tell older students that they will have an opportunity each day to work on their unit explorations, their writing and other projects. Students will be working independently and collaboratively during this time.

Guidelines

- Make sure each child knows what he or she needs to do during **Independent Work Time**.

- Demonstrate for the whole group any activity assigned for **Independent Work Time**; for example, teaching the children a new game, introducing new materials or projects, or explaining different areas.

- For young children, it is essential to introduce and demonstrate different activities and games before the children do them on their own. With games, you may want to have several children play while the others watch. Make sure that all the children know exactly what is expected of them.

- In the beginning, plan to circulate among the children providing encouragement and help as necessary.

- Once students are engaged in appropriate activities and can work independently, meet with those children who need your particular attention. This may include individual students or small groups.

- Let the children know that they need to ask questions and clarify assignments during **Independent Work Time** introduction, so that you are free to work with small groups.

- Be sure that students know what they are to do when they have finished an activity and where to put their finished work.

Establish and discuss rules for **Independent Work Time** with the children. Keep them simple and straightforward. You may want to write the finalized rules on the chalkboard or on a poster. You may want to review these rules each day at

the beginning of **Independent Work Time** for the first few lessons or so. You may also wish to revisit and revise the rules from time to time. Suggested rules include:

- ✓ Be polite.
- ✓ Share.
- ✓ Whisper.
- ✓ Take only the materials you need.
- ✓ Return materials.

Setting Up Your Classroom for Independent Work Time

Carefully setting up your classroom to accommodate different **Independent Work Time** activities will help assure that the **Independent Work Time** period progresses smoothly and effectively. While setting up your classroom, keep the primary **Independent Work Time** activities in mind. During **Independent Work Time** the children will be doing independent and collaborative activities. In kindergarten and first grade, these activities may include letter recognition and phonemic awareness activities and writing or illustrating stories or projects. In addition, they will be working on individual or small group projects.

Many classrooms have centers that the children visit on a regular or rotating basis. Center time can be easily and efficiently incorporated into the **Independent Work Time** concept. For example, the activities suggested during **Independent Work Time** can be incorporated into reading and writing centers. Other typical classroom centers include an art center, math center, science table, play area, etc.

The following are suggestions for space and materials for use during **Independent Work Time**:

1. **Literacy or Reading Center** supplied with books and magazines. The materials in the Literacy Center should be dynamic—changing with students' abilities and reflecting unit themes they are reading. You may wish to add books suggested in unit bibliographies and books from the literature collections available with each unit.

2. **Writing Center** stocked with various types and sizes of lined and unlined paper, pencils, erasers, markers, crayons, small slates, and chalk. The area should also have various **Letter Cards**, other handwriting models, and worksheets for those students who want to practice letter formation or handwriting.

Students should know that this is where they come for writing supplies. In addition to the supplies described above, the Writing Center can also have supplies to encourage the children to create and write on their own:

✓ magazines and catalogs to cut up for pictures; stickers, paint, glue, glitter, etc. to decorate books and book covers; precut and stapled blank books for the children to write in. (Some can be plain and some cut in special shapes.)

✓ cardboard, tag board, construction paper, etc., for making book covers. (Provide some samples.)

✓ tape, scissors, yarn, hole punches for binding books.

✓ picture dictionaries, dictionaries, thesaurus, word lists, and other materials that may encourage independence.

3. **Listening Center** supplied with tape recorder, optional headphones, and tapes of stories, poems, and songs for the children to listen to and react to. You might also want to provide blank tapes and encourage the children to retell and record their favorite stories or make up and tell stories for their classmates to listen to on tape. You may also want to make available the audiocassettes that are available with the program.

4. **Independent Work Time Activity Center** supplied with daily Alphabet Flash Cards, individual Alphabet-Sound Card sets (Kindergarten), **Individual Sound/Spelling Cards** and **High-Frequency Word Flash Cards** (Grades 1-3), and other materials that enhance what the children are learning. Other commonly used classroom materials that enhance literacy can be included (for example, plastic letters, puzzles, workbooks).

   Since students will be working on their inquiry/research projects during **Independent Work Time**, make sure there are adequate supplies to help them with their research. These might include dictionaries, encyclopedias, magazines, newspapers, and computers—preferably with internet capability.

5. **Game Corner** with the games introduced during **Independent Work Time**, along with any other educational games you normally use.

   Students thrive in an environment that provides structure, repetition, and routine. Within a sound structure, the children will gain confidence and independence. This setting also provides opportunities for flexibility and individual choice that allow the children to develop their strengths, abilities, and talents to the fullest.

Suggestions for English as a Second Language Learners

Independent Work Time affords students who are English as a Second Language Learners a wealth of opportunities for gaining proficiency in English. It also encourages them to share their special backgrounds with their peers. Since you will be working with all students individually and in small groups regardless of their reading ability, those students who need special help with language will not feel self-conscious about working with you. In addition, working in small groups made up of students with the same interests rather than the same abilities will provide them with the opportunity to learn about language from their peers during the regular course of **Independent Work Time** activities.

Some suggestions for meeting the special needs of children with diverse backgrounds follow:

- Preread a selection with English as a Second Language Learners to help them to identify words and ideas they wish to talk about. This will prepare them for discussions with the whole group.
- Preteach vocabulary and develop selection concepts that may be a challenge for students.
- Negotiate the meaning of selections by asking questions, checking for comprehension, and speaking with English as a Second Language Learners as much as possible.

> *Independent Work Time is the period of time each day in which students work independently or collaboratively to practice and review material taught in the lessons.*

- Draw English as a Second Language Learners into small group discussions to give them a sense that their ideas are valid and worth attention.
- Pair English as a Second Language Learners with native English speakers to share their experiences and provide new knowledge to other children.
- Have English as a Second Language Learners draw or dictate to you or another student a description of a new idea they may have during **Independent Work Time** activities.

Tips

- **Establish clear, easily articulated guidelines** for the children to follow during **Independent Work Time**. Make sure the children know what is expected of them. Have children tell you what they will be doing during **Independent Work Time**, including how to play games and complete Activity Sheets.
- **Encourage responsibility and independence** by reminding the children to follow the rules set up for **Independent Work Time**—showing respect for each other and the materials that are provided.
- **Encourage cooperation and collaboration** by providing the children with opportunities to engage in age-appropriate group activities. Games are an ideal group endeavor for young children, as are simple plays and art projects.
- **Encourage respect for individual differences** and talents by providing a wide range of activities and projects. There should be some activity to showcase every child's unique abilities.
- **Establish areas and times for** the children to display and present their work to you and each other.
- **Encourage group projects** that help develop each student's ability to work cooperatively.
- **Look for special talents and abilities** in each student and provide opportunities for students to display these special talents.
- **Encourage children to try new things.** Provide opportunities for the children to expand their horizons. For example, have children work with a new partner or a small group to try out a new activity. Or have a grab bag of activities day in which children pick a card delineating their assignment for the day.

Assessment

Assessment can be one of your most effective teaching tools if it is used with the purpose of informing instruction and highlighting areas that need special attention.

Purpose

Assessment is a tool the teacher uses to monitor students' progress and to detect students' strengths and weaknesses. Evaluation of student learning is addressed in two ways: Informal Assessment and Formal Assessment. Informal, observational assessment, or a quick check of students' written work is presented in the *Teacher's Edition* in the form of assessment suggestions. Formal Assessment consists of performance assessment (both reading and writing) and objective tests (multiple choice and open response).

Procedure

Informal Assessment

Observation

Observing students as they go about their regular classwork is probably the single most effective way to learn in depth your students' strengths and areas of need. The more students become accustomed to you jotting down informal notes about their work, the more it will become just another part of classroom life that they accept and take little note of. This gives you the opportunity to assess their progress constantly without the interference and possible drawback of formal testing situations.

In order to make informal assessment of student progress a part of your every day classroom routine, you might want to start by preparing the materials you will need on hand.

- Enter students' names in the Teacher's Observation Log.
- Before each day's lesson begins, decide which students you will observe.
- Keep the Teacher's Observation Log available so that you can easily record your observations.
- Decide what aspect of the children's learning you wish to monitor.
- During each lesson, observe this aspect in the performances of several children.
- Record your observations.
- It may take four to five days to make sure you have observed and recorded the performance of each student. If you need more information about performance in a particular area for some of your students, you may want to observe them more than once.

Written Work

Students are writing one thing or another all day long. Each of these pieces of writing can provide you with valuable information about your students. Two very helpful resources that students will work in daily are the *Reading and Writing Workbook* (Levels K–6) and the *Inquiry Journal* (Levels 2–6).

- The *Reading and Writing Workbook* includes skills practice lessons that act as practice and reinforcement for the skills lessons taught during the reading of the lesson or in conjunction with the lesson. These skill pages give you a clear picture of students understanding of the skills taught. Use them as a daily assessment of student progress in the particular skills taught through the program. In the Reading and Writing Workbook, students practice each of the skills taught in the program.

- The *Inquiry Journal* can give you invaluable information on how students are progressing in many different areas. In the *Inquiry Journal*, students

  ✓ Record what they know about the concepts and what they learn. You will be able to monitor their growing ability to make connections and use their prior knowledge to help them understand new concepts.

  ✓ Keep a record of their research. What resources they need, what they have used, where they have looked, and what they have found. You can keep track of students' growing ability to find the resources and knowledge base they need to answer the questions they pose.

  ✓ Keep track of their work with their collaborative groups. This will give you a good idea of students' growing ability to work with peers for a common goal—the acquisition of new knowledge.

  ✓ Practice study and research skills that will help them in all of their schooling. You can easily keep track of how well they are learning to use such things as library resources, reference books, visual organizers, and much, much more.

Dictation

In grades 1–3, students use dictation to practice the sound/spelling associations they are learning and/or reviewing. Collect the dictation papers and look through them to see how the children are doing with writing and with proofreading their words. Record notes on the papers and keep them in the student portfolios.

Portfolios

Portfolios are more than just a collection bin or gathering place for student projects and records. They add balance to an assessment program by providing unique benefits to teachers, students, and families.

- Portfolios help build self-confidence and increase self-esteem as students come to appreciate the value of their work. More importantly, portfolios allow students to reflect on what they know and what they need to learn. At the end of the school year, each student will be able to go through their portfolios and write about their progress.

- Portfolios provide the teacher with an authentic record of what students can do. Just as important, portfolios give students a concrete example of their own progress and development. Thus, portfolios become a valuable source of information for making instructional decisions.

- Portfolios allow families to judge student performance directly. Portfolios are an ideal starting point for discussions about a student's achievements and future goals during teacher/family conferences.

You will find that there are many opportunities to add to students' portfolios.

Reading

- During partner reading, during **Independent Work Time**, or at other times of the day, invite students, one at a time, to sit with you and read a story from an appropriate Decodable (grades 1–3) or from the Anthology.

- As each student reads to you, follow along and make note of any recurring problems the student has while reading. Note students' ability to decode unknown words as well as any attempt—successful or not—to use strategies to clarify or otherwise make sense of what he or she is reading. From time to time, check students' fluency by timing their reading and noting how well they are able to sustain the oral reading without faltering.

- If the student has trouble reading a particular Decodable story, encourage the student to read the story a few times on her or his own before reading it aloud to you. If the Decodable has two stories, use the alternate story to reassess the student a day or two later.

- If after practicing with a particular Decodable and reading it on his or her own a few times, a student is still experiencing difficulty, try the following:
  - Drop back two Decodables. (Continue to drop back until the student is able to read a story with no trouble.) If the student can read that book without problems, move up one book.
  - Continue the process until the student is able to read the current Decodable.

Standardized Tests

Throughout their school careers, the students will be expected to show their achievement through the use of standardized tests. A standardized test is simply a test of specific tasks and procedures that can be compared across geographical areas. These are the national and state achievement tests that many students take yearly. These are generally the tests that are used for accountability purposes.

Standardized tests are generally a combination of easily scored items such as multiple choice, true or false, fill-the-in-blank, or very short completion tasks. In order to be sure that you are testing the students' knowledge of what is being taught, you need to be sure that the students are familiar with the type of test you are giving and know how to produce the answers. Many students have had difficulty with such tests simply because they did not understand the test format and, although thoroughly familiar with subject content, they could not exhibit their knowledge because of confusion with the test itself.

Each of the Formal Assessment Components in **SRA/Open Court Reading** discussed below, contain standardized-test-format questions as well as performance assessment items. As students progress through the grades, they will become very familiar with these different test formats assuring that they will be able to easily adjust to whatever test format they are required to use.

Preparing for Formal Assessment

Written Tests

- Have the children clear their desks.
- Make sure the children can hear and see clearly.
- Explain the instructions and complete one or two examples with students before each test to make sure they understand what to do.

> *Observing students as they go about their regular classwork is probably the single most effective way to learn in depth your students' strengths and areas of need.*

- Give students ample time to finish each test.

Selection Tests Students using **SRA/Open Court Reading** in grades 1–6 are given the opportunity after reading and discussing each selection to exhibit what they have learned and practice their test-taking skills by completing the comprehension assessment found in the Comprehension and Writing Assessment Book.

Each of these tests contains multiple choice items that are primarily concerned with simple recall and literal comprehension. In addition, students are asked to complete short-answer items that require them to make connections to other stories in the unit and give a written account of what they read. The combination of multiple choice and written response gives you the best view of what students understand and how well they are able to connect their new knowledge to what they already know.

End-of-Unit Tests (levels 1–6) At the conclusion of each unit, students are given a fairly extensive test that requires them to transfer what they have learned to new selections on the same concept as the selection in the student anthology. In addition to simply reading the new selections and answering questions, students must explain how the new piece adds to the pieces they read in the unit and what new learning they have gleaned from the piece.

In addition, students are asked to write short pieces on specific subjects related to the unit concepts. Through this writing, they must exhibit their growing ability to organize their writing and produce finished pieces that are not only coherent but also structurally and technically correct. Spelling, punctuation, sentence structure, and such are formally assessed through these writing pieces. Scoring rubrics are provided to help guide you through students' writing.

Tips

- When observing students, do not pull them aside; rather, observe students as part of the regular lesson, either with the whole class or in small groups.

- Encourage students to express any confusion they may be experiencing. The questions students ask can give you valuable insight into their progress and development.

- The more comfortable students become with standardized-test formats—usually multiple choice—the more confident you and they will be in the fact that the test is testing their knowledge of a subject rather than their test-taking skills.

- Make sure students know that the ultimate purpose of assessment is to keep track of their progress and to help them continue to do better.

Audiovisual and Technology Resource Directory

This directory is provided for the convenience of ordering the Technology Resources listed on the Technology pages in each Unit Overview.

AIMS Multimedia

9710 DeSoto Avenue
Chatsworth, CA 91311-4409
800-367-2467

AIT (Agency for Instructional Technology)

1800 No. Stonelake Drive
Bloomington, IN 47404
800-457-4509
www.ait.net

BFA Educational Media

468 Park Avenue South
New York, NY 10016
800-221-1274

Brøderbund Software

500 Redwood Blvd.
P.O. Box 6125
Novato, CA 94948-6125
800-521-6263
Fax: 415-382-4671

Churchill Films

6465 North Avondale Avenue
Chicago, IL 60631-1996
800-CLEARVU (253-2788)
Fax: 800-444-9855

Coronet/MTI

108 Wilmot Road
Deerfield, IL 60015
800-777-8100

Great Plains National (GPN)

P.O. Box 80669
Lincoln, NE 68501-0669
800-228-4630

National Geographic Educational Services

Washington, DC 20036
800-368-2728

Orange Cherry New Media

P.O. Box 505
Pound Ridge, NY 10576
914-764-4104
Fax: 914-764-0104
Email: nmsh@cloud9.net

Pied Piper/AIMS Multimedia

9710 DeSoto Avenue
Chatsworth, CA 91311-4409
800-367-2467

SRA/McGraw-Hill

220 East Danieldale Road
De Soto, TX 75115-9960
888-SRA-4543
www.sra-4kids.com

Open Court Reading
Glossary of Reading Terms

This glossary includes linguistic, grammatical, comprehension, and literary terms that may be helpful in understanding reading instruction.

acronym a word formed from the initial letter of words in a phrase, **scuba (self-contained underwater breathing apparatus)**.

acrostic a kind of puzzle in which lines of a poem are arranged so that words or phrases are formed when certain letters from each line are used in a sequence.

adjective a word or group of words that modifies a noun.

adventure story a narrative that features the unknown or unexpected with elements of excitement, danger, and risk.

adverb a word or group of words that modifies a verb, adjective, or other adverb.

affective domain the psychological field of emotional activity.

affix a word part, either a prefix or a suffix, that changes the meaning or function of a word root or stem.

affricate a speech sound that starts as a stop but ends as a fricative, the /ch/ in **catch**.

agreement the correspondence of syntactically related words; subjects and predicates are in agreement when both are singular or plural.

alliteration the repetition of the initial sounds in neighboring words or stressed syllables.

alphabet the complete set of letters representing speech sounds used in writing a language.

alphabet book a book for helping young children learn the alphabet by pairing letters with pictures whose sounds they represent.

alphabetic principle the principle that there is an association between sounds and the letters that represent them in alphabetic writing systems.

alveolar a consonant speech sound made when the tongue and the ridge of the upper and lower jaw stop to constrict the air flow, as /t/.

anagram a word or phrase whose letters form other words or phrases when rearranged, for example, **add** and **dad**.

analogy a likeness or similarity.

analytic phonics also deductive phonics, a whole-to-part approach to phonics in which a student is taught a number of sight words and then phonetic generalizations that can be applied to other words.

antonym a word that is opposite in meaning to another word.

appositive a word that restates or modifies a preceding noun. For example, **my daughter, Charlotte**.

aspirate an unvoiced speech sound produced by a puff of air, as /h/ in **heart**.

aspirated stop a stop consonant sound released with a puff of air, as /k/, /p/, and /t/.

auditory discrimination the ability to hear phonetic likenesses and differences in phonemes and words.

author's purpose the motive or reason for which an author writes, includes to entertain, inform, persuade and explain how.

automaticity fluent processing of information, requiring little effort or attention.

auxiliary verb a verb that precedes another verb to express time, mood, or voice, includes verbs such as **has**, **is**, **will**.

ballad a narrative poem, composed of short verses to be sung or recited, usually containing elements of drama and often tragic in tone.

base word a word to which affixes may be added to create related words.

blank verse unrhymed verse, especially unrhymed iambic pentameter.

blend the joining of the sounds of two or more letters with little change in those sounds, for example /spr/ in **spring**, also **consonant blend** or **consonant cluster**.

blending to combine the sounds represented by letters to sound out or pronounce a word, contrast with **oral blending**.

breve the symbol placed above a vowel to indicate that it is a short vowel.

browse to skim through or look over in search of something of interest.

canon in literature, the body of major works that a culture considers important at a given time.

case a grammatical category that indicates the syntactic/semantic role of a noun phrase in a sentence.

cause-effect relationship a stated or implied association between an outcome and the conditions that brought it about, also the comprehension skill associated with recognizing this type of relationship as an organizing principle in text.

chapter book a book long enough to be divided into chapters, but not long or complex enough to be considered a novel.

characterization the way in which an author presents a character in a story, including describing words, actions, thoughts, and impressions of that character.

choral reading oral group reading to develop oral fluency by modeling.

cinquain a stanza of five lines, specifically one that has successive lines of two, four, six, eight, and two syllables.

cipher a system for writing in code.

clarifying a comprehension strategy in which the reader rereads text, uses a dictionary, uses decoding skills, or uses context clues to comprehend something that is unclear.

clause a group of words with a subject and a predicate used to form a part of or a whole sentence, a dependent clause modifies an independent clause, which can stand alone as a complete sentence.

collaborative learning learning by working together in small groups.

command a sentence that asks for action and usually ends with a period.

common noun in contrast to **proper noun**, a noun that denotes a class rather than a unique or specific thing.

comprehension the understanding of what is written or said.

comprehension skill a skill that aids in understanding text, including identifying **author's purpose**, **comprehending cause and effect relationships**, **comparing and contrasting** items and events, **drawing conclusions**, distinguishing **fact from opinion**, identifying **main ideas**, making **inferences**, distinguishing **reality from fantasy**, and understanding **sequence**.

comprehension strategy a sequence of steps for understanding text, includes asking questions, clarifying, making connections, predicting, summarizing, and visualizing.

conjugation the complete set of all possible inflected forms of a verb.

conjunction a part of speech used to connect words, phrases, clauses, or sentences, including the words **and, but, or**.

consonant a speech sound, and the alphabet letter that represents that sound, made by partial or complete closure of part of the vocal tract, which obstructs air flow and causes audible friction.

context clue information from the immediate text that helps identify a word.

contraction a short version of a written or spoken expression in which letters are omitted, for example, **can't**.

convention an accepted practice in spoken or written language, usually referring to spelling, mechanics, or grammar rules.

cooperative learning a classroom organization that allows students to work together to achieve their individual goals.

creative writing prose and poetic forms of writing that express the writer's thoughts and feelings imaginatively.

cuing system any of the various sources of information that help to identify an unrecognizable word in reading, including phonetic, semantic, and syntactical information.

Glossary of Reading Terms (continued)

cumulative tale a story, such as The Gingerbread Man, in which details are repeated until the climax.

dangling modifier usually a participle that because of its placement in a sentence modifies the wrong object.

decodable text text materials controlled to include a majority of words whose sound/spelling relationships are known by the reader.

decode to analyze spoken or graphic symbols for meaning.

diacritical mark a mark, such as a breve or macron, added to a letter or graphic character, to indicate a specific pronunciation.

dialect a regional variety of a particular language with phonological, grammatical, and lexical patterns that distinguish it from other varieties.

dialogue a piece of writing written as conversation, usually punctuated by quotation marks.

digraph two letters that represent one speech sound, for example /sh/ or /ch/.

diphthong a vowel sound produced when the tongue glides from one vowel sound toward another in the same syllable, for example /oi/ or /ou/.

direct object the person or thing that receives the action of a verb in a sentence, for example, the word **cake** in this sentence: **Madeline baked a cake**.

drafting the process of writing ideas in rough form to record them.

drama a story in the form of a play, written to be performed.

edit in the writing process, to revise or correct a manuscript.

emergent literacy the development of the association of meaning and print that continues until a child reaches the stage of conventional reading and writing.

emergent reading a child's early interaction with books and print before the ability to decode text.

encode to change a message into symbols, for example, to change speech into writing.

epic a long narrative poem, usually about a hero.

exclamatory sentence a sentence that shows strong emotion and ends with an exclamation mark.

expository writing or **exposition** a composition in writing that explains an event or process.

fable a short tale that teaches a moral.

fantasy a highly imaginative story about characters, places, and events that do not exist.

fiction imaginative narrative designed to entertain rather than to explain, persuade, or describe.

figure of speech the expressive, nonliteral use of language usually through metaphor, simile, or personification.

fluency freedom from word-identification problems that hinder comprehension in reading.

folktale a narrative form of genre such as an epic, myth, or fable that is well-known through repeated storytellings.

foreshadowing giving clues to upcoming events in a story.

free verse verse with irregular metrical pattern.

freewriting writing that is not limited in form, style, content, or purpose, designed to encourage students to write.

genre a classification of literary works, including tragedy, comedy, novel, essay, short story, mystery, realistic fiction, poetry.

grammar the study of the classes of words, their inflections, and their functions and relations in sentences; includes phonological, morphological, syntactic, and semantic descriptions of a language.

grapheme a written or printed representation of a phoneme, such as **c** for /k/.

guided reading reading instruction in which the teacher provides the structure and purpose for reading and responding to the material read.

handing off a method of turning over to the students the primary responsibility for controlling discussion.

indirect object in a sentence, the person or thing to or for whom an action is done, for example, the word **dog** in this sentence: **Madeline gave the dog a treat**.

inference a conclusion based on facts, data, or evidence.

infinitive the base form of a verb, usually with the infinitive marker, for example, **to go**.

inflectional ending an ending that expresses a plural or possessive form of a noun, the tense of a verb, or the comparative or superlative form of an adjective or adverb.

interrogative word a word that marks a clause or sentence as a question, including **interrogative pronouns who**, **what**, **which**, **where**.

intervention a strategy or program designed to supplement or substitute instruction, especially for those students who fall behind.

invented spelling the result of an attempt to spell a word based on the writer's knowledge of the spelling system and how it works, often with overemphasis on sound/symbol relationships.

irony a figure of speech in which the literal meaning of the words is the opposite of their intended meaning.

journal a written record of daily events or responses.

juvenile book a book written for children or adolescents.

legend a traditional tale handed down from generation to generation.

leitmotif a repeated expression, event, or idea used to unify a work of art such as writing.

letter one of a set of graphic symbols that forms an alphabet and is used alone or in combination to represent a phoneme, also **grapheme**.

linguistics the study of the nature and structure of language and communication.

literary elements the elements of a story such as **setting**, **plot**, and **characterization** that create the structure of a narrative.

macron a diacritical mark placed above a vowel to indicate a long vowel sound.

main idea the central thought or chief topic of a passage.

mechanics the conventions of capitalization and punctuation.

metacognition awareness and knowledge of one's mental processes or thinking about what one is thinking about.

metaphor a figure of speech in which a comparison is implied but not stated, for example, **She is a jewel**.

miscue a deviation from text during oral reading in an attempt to make sense of the text.

modeling an instructional technique in which the teacher serves as an example of behavior.

mood the literary element that conveys the emotional atmosphere of a story.

morpheme a meaningful linguistic unit that cannot be divided into smaller units, for example, **word**; **a bound morpheme** is a morpheme that cannot stand alone as an independent word, for example, the prefix **re-**; a **free morpheme** can stand alone, for example, **dog**.

myth a story designed to explain the mysteries of life.

narrative writing or **narration** a composition in writing that tells a story or gives an account of an event.

nonfiction prose designed to explain, argue, or describe rather than to entertain with a factual emphasis, includes biography and autobiography.

noun a part of speech that denotes persons, places, things, qualities, or acts.

novel an extended fictional prose narration.

onomatopoeia the use of a word whose sound suggests its meaning, for example, **purr**.

oral blending the ability to fuse discrete phonemes into recognizable words; oral blending puts sounds together to make a word, **see also segmentation**.

orthography correct or standardized spelling according to established usage in a language.

oxymoron a figure of speech in which contrasting or contradictory words are brought together for emphasis.

paragraph a subdivision of a written composition that consists of one or more sentences, deals with one point, or gives the words of one speaker, usually beginning with an indented line.

participle a verb form used as an adjective, for example, **the skating party**.

personification a figure of speech in which animals, ideas, or things take on human characteristics.

persuasive writing a composition intended to persuade the reader to adopt the writer's point of view.

phoneme the smallest sound unit of speech, for example, the /k/ in **book**.

phonemic awareness the ability to recognize that spoken words are made up of discrete sounds and that those sounds can be manipulated.

phonetic spelling the respelling of entry words in a dictionary according to a pronunciation key.

phonetics the study of speech sounds.

phonics a way of teaching reading that addresses sound/symbol relationships, especially in beginning instruction.

phonogram a letter or symbol that represents a phonetic sound.

plot the literary element that provides the structure of the action of a story, which may include rising action, climax, and falling action leading to a resolution or denouement.

plural a grammatical form of a word that refers to more than one in number; an **irregular plural** is one that does not follow normal patterns for inflectional endings.

poetic license the liberty taken by writers to ignore conventions.

poetry a metrical form of composition in which language is chosen and arranged to create a powerful response through meaning, sound, or rhythm.

possessive showing ownership either through the use of an adjective, an adjectival pronoun, or the possessive form of a noun.

predicate the part of the sentence that expresses something about the subject and includes the verb phrase; a **complete predicate** includes the principal verb in a sentence and all its modifiers or subordinate parts.

predicting a comprehension strategy in which the reader attempts to figure out what will happen and then confirms predictions as the text is read.

prefix an affix attached before a base word that changes the meaning of the word.

preposition a part of speech in the class of function words, such as **of**, **on**, **at**, that precede noun phrases to create prepositional phrases.

prewriting the planning stage of the writing process in which the writer formulates ideas, gathers information, and considers ways to organize them.

print awareness in emergent literacy, a child's growing recognition of conventions and characteristics of written language, including reading from left to right and top to bottom in English, and that words are separated by spaces.

pronoun a part of speech used as a substitute for a noun or noun phrase.

proofreading the act of reading with the intent to correct, clarify, or improve text.

pseudonym an assumed name used by an author, a pen name or nom de plume.

publishing the process of preparing written material for presentation.

punctuation graphic marks such as comma, period, quotation marks, and brackets used to clarify meaning and give speech characteristics to written language.

question an interrogative sentence that asks a question and ends with a question mark.

realistic fiction a story that attempts to portray characters and events as they actually are.

rebus the use of a picture or symbol to suggest a word or syllable.

revise in the writing process, to change or correct a manuscript to make its message more clear.

rhyme identical or very similar recurring final sounds in words, often at the ends of lines of poetry.

rime a vowel and any following consonants of a syllable.

segmentation the ability to break words into individual sounds; **see also oral blending**.

semantic mapping a graphic display of a group of words that are meaningfully related to support vocabulary instruction.

semantics the study of meaning in language, including the meanings of words, phrases, sentences, and texts.

sentence a grammatical unit that expresses a statement, question, or command; a **simple sentence** is a sentence with one subject and one predicate; a **compound sentence** is a sentence with two or more independent clauses usually separated by a comma and conjunction, but no dependent clause; a **complex sentence** is a sentence with one independent and one or more dependent clauses.

sentence combining a teaching technique in which complex sentence chunks and paragraphs are built from basic sentences.

sentence lifting the process of using sentences from children's writing to illustrate what is wrong or right to develop children's editing and proofreading skills.

sequence the order of elements or events.

setting the literary element that includes the time, place, and physical and psychological background in which a story takes place.

sight word a word that is taught to be read as a whole word, usually words that are phonetically irregular.

simile a figure of speech in which a comparison of two things that are unlike is directly stated usually with the words **like** or **as**, for example, **She is like a jewel**.

spelling the process of representing language by means of a writing system.

statement a sentence that tells something and ends with a period.

study skills a general term for the techniques and strategies that help readers comprehend text with the intent to remember, includes following directions, organizing, locating, and using graphic aids.

style the characteristics of a work that reflect the author's particular way of writing.

subject the main topic of a sentence to which a predicate refers, including the principal noun; a **complete subject** includes the principal noun in a sentence and all its modifiers..

suffix an affix attached at the end of a base word that changes the meaning of the word.

summarizing a comprehension strategy in which the reader constructs a brief statement that contains the essential ideas of a passage.

syllable a minimal unit of sequential speech sounds comprised of a vowel sound or a vowel-sound combination.

symbolism the use of one thing to represent something else in order to represent an idea in a concrete way.

synonym a word that means the same as another word.

syntax the grammatical pattern or structure of word order in sentences, clauses, and phrases.

tense the way in which verbs indicate past, present, and future time of action.

text structure the various patterns of ideas that are built into the organization of a written work.

theme a major idea or proposition that provides an organizing concept through which by study, students gain depth of understanding.

topic sentence a sentence intended to express the main idea of a paragraph or passage.

tragedy a literary work, often a play, in which the main character suffers conflicts and which presents a serious theme and has an unfortunate ending.

usage the way in which a native language or dialect is used by the members of the community.

verb a word that expresses an action or state that occurs in a predicate of a sentence; an **irregular verb** is a verb that does not follow normal patterns of inflectional endings that reflect past, present, or future verb tense.

visualizing a comprehension strategy in which the reader constructs a mental picture of a character, setting, or process.

vowel a voiced speech sound and the alphabet letter that represents that sound, made without stoppage or friction of the air flow as it passes through the vocal tract.

vowel digraph a spelling pattern in which two or more letters represent a single vowel sound.

word calling proficiency in decoding with little or no attention to word meaning.

writing also **composition** the process or result of organizing ideas in writing to form a clear message, includes persuasive, expository, narrative, and descriptive forms.

writing process the many aspects of the complex act of producing a piece of writing, including prewriting, drafting, revising, proofreading, and publishing.

Scope and Sequence

Reading

Level	K-A	K-B	K-C	K-D	K-E	1-A	1-B	1-C	1-1	1-2	2-1	2-2	3-1	3-2	4	5	6
Print/Book Awareness (Recognize and understand the conventions of print and books)																	
Capitalization			✔		✔	✔	✔	✔	✔								
Constancy of Words																	
End Punctuation			✔			✔	✔	✔	✔								
Follow Left-to-right, Top-to-bottom																	
Letter Recognition and Formation	✔				✔	✔	✔	✔	✔	✔							
Page Numbering																	
Picture/Text Relationship			✔	✔													
Quotation Marks																	
Relationship Between Spoken and Printed Language																	
Sentence Recognition																	
Table of Contents																	
Word Length																	
Word Boundaries																	
Phonemic Awareness (Recognize discrete sounds in words)																	
Oral Blending: Words/Word Parts				✔				✔									
Oral Blending: Initial Consonants/Blends					✔		✔										
Oral Blending: Final Consonants			✔			✔	✔										
Oral Blending: Initial Vowels																	
Oral Blending: Syllables								✔		✔							
Oral Blending: Vowel Replacement																	
Segmentation: Initial Consonants/Blends																	
Segmentation: Final Consonants																	
Segmentation: Initial Vowels						✔	✔										
Segmentation: Words/Word Parts																	
Rhyming						✔											
How the Alphabet Works																	
Letter Knowledge						✔											
Letter Order	✔					✔	✔										
Sounds in Words						✔	✔	✔	✔	✔							
Letter Sounds					✔	✔	✔										
Phonics (Associate sounds and spellings to read words)																	
Blending Sounds into Words								✔									
Consonant Clusters									✔	✔							
Consonant Digraphs								✔				✔					
Consonant Sounds and Spellings						✔											
Phonograms							✔										
Syllables										✔							
Vowel Diphthongs								✔	✔	✔							
Vowels: Long Sounds and Spellings					✔			✔	✔	✔							
Vowels: *r*-controlled								✔	✔								
Vowels: Short Sounds and Spellings						✔	✔	✔	✔	✔							

Skills, strategies, and other teaching opportunities

✔ Formal or informal testing opportunities

Reading (continued)

Level	K-A	K-B	K-C	K-D	K-E	1-A	1-B	1-C	1-1	1-2	2-1	2-2	3-1	3-2	4	5	6
Comprehension Strategies (Self-monitoring techniques)																	
Asking Questions/Answering Questions																	
Clarifying																	
Predicting/Confirming Predictions																	
Making Connections																	
Summarizing																	
Visualizing																	
Comprehension Skills (Deciphering the meaning of text)																	
Author's Point of View												✔	✔	✔	✔	✔	✔
Author's Purpose												✔	✔	✔	✔	✔	✔
Cause/Effect				✔					✔			✔	✔	✔	✔	✔	✔
Classify/Categorize				✔			✔					✔	✔	✔	✔	✔	✔
Compare and Contrast			✔			✔					✔		✔	✔	✔	✔	✔
Draw Conclusions			✔				✔				✔		✔	✔	✔	✔	✔
Fact/Opinion												✔	✔	✔	✔	✔	✔
Main Idea and Details											✔	✔	✔	✔	✔	✔	✔
Making Inferences											✔	✔			✔	✔	✔
Reality/Fantasy											✔						
Sequencing								✔							✔	✔	✔
Vocabulary																	
Antonyms				✔	✔						✔	✔			✔	✔	
Comparatives/Superlatives									✔		✔				✔	✔	
Compound Words								✔			✔	✔			✔	✔	✔
Connecting Words																	
Context Clues											✔	✔	✔	✔	✔	✔	✔
Contractions																	
High-Frequency Words	✔				✔			✔			✔						
Homophones/Homonyms												✔	✔	✔	✔	✔	✔
Idioms																	
Inflectional Endings							✔	✔					✔		✔	✔	
Irregular Plurals								✔		✔	✔		✔		✔	✔	✔
Multiple Meaning Words															✔	✔	✔
Multisyllabic Words																	
Position Words				✔		✔											
Prefixes											✔	✔		✔	✔	✔	✔
Question Words																	
Root Words															✔	✔	✔
Selection Vocabulary	✔	✔	✔	✔	✔	✔	✔	✔	✔	✔	✔	✔	✔	✔	✔	✔	✔
Suffixes								✔	✔	✔		✔		✔	✔	✔	✔
Synonyms		✔					✔						✔		✔	✔	✔
Time and Order Words (Creating Sequence)				✔				✔				✔					
Utility Words (Body Parts, Colors, Common Classroom Objects, Days of the Week, Time of Day, Weather Words)			✔						✔	✔							
Word Families															✔	✔	✔

Scope and Sequence

Writing/Composition

Level	K-A	K-B	K-C	K-D	K-E	1-A	1-B	1-C	1-1	1-2	2-1	2-2	3-1	3-2	4	5	6
Approaches																	
Collaborative Writing																	
Group Writing																	
Process																	
Brainstorming																	
Drafting																	
Proofreading																	
Publishing																	
Revising																	
Forms																	
Biography/Autobiography															✔	✔	✔
Describe a Process										✔				✔	✔	✔	✔
Descriptive Writing																	
Expository															✔	✔	✔
Folklore (Folktales, Fairytales, Talltales, Legends, Myths)															✔	✔	✔
Historical Fiction															✔	✔	✔
Informational Text															✔	✔	✔
Journal Writing																	
Letter Writing																	
Narrative																	
Personal Narrative																	
Persuasive Writing															✔	✔	✔
Play/Dramatization																	
Poetry																	

Skills, strategies, and other teaching opportunities

✔ Formal or informal testing opportunities

Writing/Composition (continued)

Level	K-A	K-B	K-C	K-D	K-E	1-A	1-B	1-C	1-1	1-2	2-1	2-2	3-1	3-2	4	5	6
Writer's Craft																	
Characterization			✔					✔	✔			✔		✔	✔	✔	✔
Descriptive Writing												✔	✔	✔	✔	✔	✔
Dialogue																	
Effective Beginnings											✔	✔		✔	✔	✔	✔
Effective Endings																	
Event Sequence																	
Figurative Language								✔			✔			✔	✔	✔	✔
Identifying Thoughts and Feelings																	
Mood and Tone																	
Plot (Problem/Solutions)				✔					✔		✔			✔	✔	✔	✔
Point of View																	
Rhyme	✔					✔					✔						
Setting			✔						✔		✔		✔		✔	✔	✔
Suspense and Surprise																	
Topic Sentences											✔	✔	✔	✔	✔	✔	✔
Using Comparisons																	
Purposes																	
Determining Purposes for Writing																	

Scope and Sequence

Integrated Language Arts

Level	K-A	K-B	K-C	K-D	K-E	1-A	1-B	1-C	1-1	1-2	2-1	2-2	3-1	3-2	4	5	6
Grammar																	
Parts of Speech																	
Adjectives			✔							✔	✔	✔			✔		✔
Adverbs															✔		✔
Conjunctions										✔					✔	✔	✔
Nouns					✔			✔		✔	✔		✔	✔	✔	✔	✔
Prepositions						✔									✔		
Pronouns								✔		✔	✔		✔	✔	✔	✔	✔
Verbs		✔								✔		✔			✔	✔	✔
Sentences																	
Parts (Subjects/Predicates)										✔			✔	✔	✔	✔	✔
Structure (Simple, Compound, Complex)							✔					✔			✔	✔	✔
Types (Declarative, Interrogative, Exclamatory, Imperative)					✔		✔					✔		✔	✔	✔	✔
Verb Tenses										✔			✔	✔	✔	✔	✔
Verbs (Action, Helping, Linking, Regular/Irregular)											✔				✔		
Usage																	
Adjectives			✔										✔	✔	✔	✔	✔
Adverbs													✔	✔	✔	✔	✔
Nouns					✔			✔					✔	✔	✔	✔	✔
Pronouns								✔					✔	✔	✔	✔	✔
Verbs		✔				✔		✔					✔	✔	✔	✔	✔
Mechanics																	
Capitalization (Sentence, Proper Nouns, Titles, Direct Address, Pronoun *I*)			✔		✔			✔							✔	✔	✔
Punctuation (End punctuation, comma use, quotation marks, apostrophe, colon, semicolon, hyphen, parentheses)			✔					✔	✔		✔				✔	✔	✔
Spelling																	
Contractions										✔		✔	✔				
Inflectional Endings										✔		✔	✔	✔		✔	
Irregular Plurals										✔		✔			✔	✔	
Long Vowel Patterns										✔	✔					✔	✔
Multisyllabic Words																	
Phonograms																	
r-controlled Vowel Spellings							✔				✔						
Short Vowel Spellings																	
Sound/Letter Relationships						✔	✔	✔	✔	✔							
Special Spelling Patterns (*-ough, -augh, -all, -al, -alk, -ion, -sion, -tion*)																	
Listening/Speaking/Viewing																	
Listening/Speaking																	
Analyze and evaluate intent and content of Speaker's Message																	
Answer Questions																	
Compare Language and Oral Traditions																	

Skills, strategies, and other teaching opportunities

✔ Formal or informal testing opportunities

Integrated Language Arts (continued)

Level	K-A	K-B	K-C	K-D	K-E	1-A	1-B	1-C	1-1	1-2	2-1	2-2	3-1	3-2	4	5	6
Listening/Speaking (continued)																	
Determine Purposes for Listening																	
Follow Directions																	
Learn about Different Cultures through Discussion																	
Listen for Poetic Language (Rhythm/Rhyme)																	
Participate in Group Discussions																	
Respond to Speaker																	
Speaking																	
Compare Language and Oral Traditions																	
Conduct Interviews/Surveys																	
Describe Ideas and Feelings																	
Give Directions																	
Learn about Different Cultures through Discussion																	
Participate in Group Discussions																	
Present Oral Reports																	
Read Fluently with Expression, Phrasing and Intonation																	
Read Orally																	
Share Information																	
Summarize/Retell Stories																	
Use Appropriate Vocabulary for Audience																	
Viewing																	
Appreciate/Interpret Artists' Techniques																	
Compare Visual and Written Material on the Same Subject																	
Gather Information from Visual Images																	
View Critically																	
View Culturally Rich Materials																	
Inquiry & Research/Study Skills																	
Charts, Graphs, and Diagrams/Visual Aids											✔		✔	✔	✔	✔	✔
Compile Notes																	
Follow Directions																	
Formulate Questions for Inquiry and Research																	
Give Reports																	
Make Outlines																	
Maps and Globes												✔	✔	✔	✔	✔	✔
Note Taking											✔		✔	✔	✔	✔	✔
Parts of a Book											✔		✔				
Summarize and Organize Information																	
Time Lines												✔	✔	✔	✔	✔	✔
Use Appropriate Resources (Media Source, Reference Books, Experts, Internet)										✔		✔	✔		✔	✔	✔
Using a Dictionary/Glossary													✔		✔	✔	✔
Using a Media Center/Library									✔	✔				✔	✔	✔	✔
Using an Encyclopedia									✔						✔	✔	✔
Using Newspapers and Magazines																	
Using Visual Aids																	

Kindergarten Index

Kindergarten Index (continued)

D

E

Kindergarten Index (continued)

I

Kindergarten Index (continued)

Kindergarten Index (continued)

Kindergarten Index (continued)

V

Verbs
    action,
        Book A: T64, T156, T205, T239, T251, T254, T296
        Book C: T264
        Book D: T135, T341
        Book E: T140, T150
    tense,
        Book B: T276
        Book E: T74, T112, T150

Visualizing, *see* Comprehension

Voake, Charlotte, Book B: T106

Vocabulary development
    concept vocabulary,
        Book A: T28, T50, T74, T82, T102, T174, T190, T208, T239, T251, T265, T296, T306, T314, T328, T332, T344
        Book B: T76, T152, T159, T210, T235, T340
        Book C: T153
        Book D: T158
        Book E: T121
    developing meaning through context clues,
        Book B: T201, T297, T345
        Book E: T200, T244
    developing meaning through discussion,
        Book A: T44, T112, T130, T208
        Book C: T26, T56, T72, T88, T104, T124, T138, T181, T252, T268, T288, T304, T318, T330
        Book D: T50, T64, T80, T96, T114, T129, T182, T202, T218, T246, T260, T280, T308, T328, T348
        Book E: T48, T88, T106, T150, T190, T206, T218, T230, T270, T282, T296, T310
    multiple meaning words,
        Book A: T94
        Book C: T226
        Book D: T232
    position words,
        Book A: T184, T187, T198, T233, T256
        Book B: T38
        Book D: T74, T192, T265
        Book E: T170
    school vocabulary (numbers, shapes, colors, calendar),
        Book A: T90, T117, T227, T326, T328, T344
        Book B: T60
        Book C: T206, T209
        Book E: T62

    through reference sources
        glossaries, Book D: T172
    see also Antonyms, High-Frequency words, Rhyming, Synonyms, Verbs

Vowels,
    Book A: T172, T258, T311
    Book C: T195, T249, T329
    Book D: T355
    a,
        Book A: T92–T93
        Book C: T54–T55, T196–T197, T207–T208
    e,
        Book A: T172–T173
        Book C: T315–T317, T328–T329
    i,
        Book A: T234–T235
        Book D: T93–T95, T112–T113
    o,
        Book A: T346–T347
        Book C: T136–T137, T147–T148
        Book D: T257–T259
    u,
        Book B: T88–T89
        Book E: T44–T47, T60–T61
    long,
        Book B: T118, T336
        Book C: T284, T301, T315
    long a,
        Book A: T292
        Book C: T70, T196, T207–T208
    long e,
        Book A: T310
        Book C: T315, T328
    long i,
        Book A: T329
        Book D: T93–T95, T112
    long o,
        Book A: T345
        Book C: T136, T148
        Book D: T257–T259
    long u,
        Book A: T357
        Book E: T44, T46, T60
    short, Book C: T265, T327
    short a, Book C: T69–T70, T196, T207–T208
    short e, Book C: T316, T328
    short i, Book D: T94–T95, T112–T113
    short o,
        Book C: T136–T137, T147, T148
        Book D: T258–T259
    short u, Book E: T45–T46, T60

Kindergarten Index (continued)

Program Appendix

Notes

Use this page to record lessons or elements that work well
or need to be adjusted for future reference.

Lessons that work well.

_____
_____
_____
_____
_____
_____
_____
_____
_____
_____
_____
_____

Lessons that need adjustments.

_____
_____
_____
_____
_____
_____
_____
_____
_____
_____
_____

Notes

Use this page to record lessons or elements that work well
or need to be adjusted for future reference.

Lessons that work well.

Lessons that need adjustments.

Notes

Use this page to record lessons or elements that work well
or need to be adjusted for future reference.

Lessons that work well.

_____
_____
_____
_____
_____
_____
_____
_____
_____
_____
_____
_____
_____
_____
_____
_____

Lessons that need adjustments.

_____
_____
_____
_____
_____
_____
_____
_____
_____
_____
_____
_____
_____
_____

Notes

Use this page to record lessons or elements that work well
or need to be adjusted for future reference.

Lessons that work well.

_____

_____

_____

_____

_____

_____

_____

_____

_____

_____

_____

_____

Lessons that need adjustments.

_____

_____

_____

_____

_____

_____

_____

_____

_____

_____

Notes

Use this page to record lessons or elements that work well
or need to be adjusted for future reference.

Lessons that work well.

_____

_____

_____

_____

_____

_____

_____

_____

_____

_____

_____

_____

_____

_____

_____

Lessons that need adjustments.

_____

_____

_____

_____

_____

_____

_____

_____

_____

_____

_____

_____

_____

Notes

Use this page to record lessons or elements that work well
or need to be adjusted for future reference.

Lessons that work well.

_____
_____
_____
_____
_____
_____
_____
_____
_____
_____
_____
_____
_____

Lessons that need adjustments.

_____
_____
_____
_____
_____
_____
_____
_____
_____
_____
_____
_____
_____

SRA Open Court Reading

Program Evaluation

As part of SRA's interest in updating and improving our curricula, we ask that you take a few moments to complete this questionnaire and return it to us.

You can tear this page out, fold and seal it with the address showing, or you may feel free to add additional comments, using another piece of paper and your own envelope.

We look forward to your comments and suggestions.

Sincerely,
SRA/McGraw-Hill

Your name _____ **Grade Level Reviewed** _____

Your title _____ **Date** _____

School _____

Address _____

City _____ **State** _____ **Zip** _____

1. How long have you been teaching *Open Court Reading?* _____

2. What do you consider to be *Open Court Reading's* strongest features? _____

3. What do you consider to be *Open Court Reading's* weakest features? _____

4. Do the lessons provide appropriate information for teaching each literature selection? _____

5. Is the phonics lesson material clear and helpful? _____

6. Is the instruction for comprehension skills and strategies clear and helpful? _____

7. Are the language arts skills materials clear and helpful? _____

8. Are the unit themes and activities appropriate and useful? _____

9. Are you satisfied with the achievement of your class using *Open Court Reading?* _____

10. What specific changes, if any, would you like to see in the next edition of *Open Court Reading?* _____

11. Is the pacing of each lesson appropriate? _____

12. How would you compare *Open Court Reading* with other reading programs you have taught? _____

Additional comments

_____

BUSINESS REPLY MAIL
FIRST-CLASS MAIL   PERMIT NO 4168   COLUMBUS OH

POSTAGE WILL BE PAID BY ADDRESSEE

SRA MCGRAW HILL
8787 ORION PL
COLUMBUS OH   43240 - 9915